① 1-1 China
② 1-2 giant panda
③ 1-3 red-crowned crane
④ 1-4 Yangtze River dolphin
⑤ 1-5 Zhuang nationality
⑥ 1-6 Uyghur nationality
⑦ 1-7 Miao nationality
⑧ 2-1 writings on tortoise shell
⑨ 2-2 Qin Shihuang
⑩ 2-3 terra cotta
⑪ 2-4 the Grand Canal
⑫ 5-1 Confucius
⑬ 5-2 Mencius
⑭ 5-3 Laozi

① 9-1 Yixing teapot
② 10-1 plum blossom
③ 10-2 peony
④ 10-3 chrysanthemum
⑤ 10-4 orchid
⑥ 10-5 chinese rose
⑦ 10-6 azalea
⑧ 10-7 camellia
⑨ 10-8 lotus
⑩ 10-9 the sweet-scented osmanthus
⑪ 10-10 narcissus
⑫ 10-11 bamboo

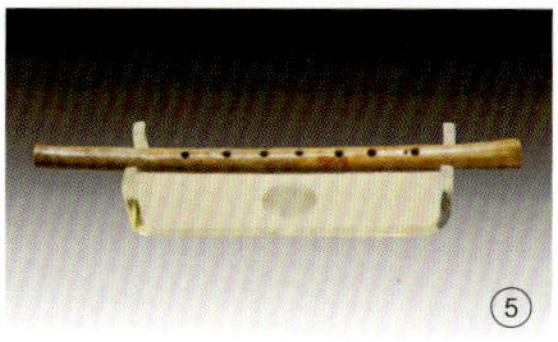

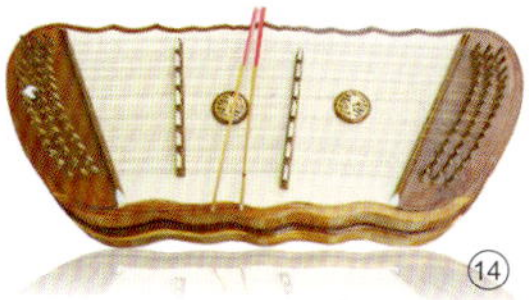

① 11-1 bride in red silk veil
② 11-2 sedan chair
③ 12-1 walking on stilts
④ 12-2 waist-drum dance
⑤ 17-2 bone flute
⑥ 17-1 Zeng Houyi bells
⑦ 17-3 liuqin
⑧ 17-4 qing
⑨ 17-5 erhu
⑩ 17-6 guqin
⑪ 17-7 konghou
⑫ 17-8 pipa
⑬ 17-9 xun
⑭ 17-10 yangqin

① 19-1 papercutting of Chinese character
② 19-2 Chinese knot
③ 19-3 Su embroidery
④ 19-4 Xiang embroidery
⑤ 19-5 Shu embroidery
⑥ 19-6 Yue embroidery
⑦ 21-1 Yueyang Tower
⑧ 21-2 the Yellow Crane Tower
⑨ 21-3 the Tengwang Pavilion
⑩ 21-4 the Penglai Pavilion

中国文化概览

（第二版）

A Bird's-Eye View of Chinese Culture

英汉对照

龙毛忠　贾爱兵　颜静兰　◎主编

华东理工大学出版社
·上海·

图书在版编目(CIP)数据

中国文化概览:英汉对照 / 龙毛忠,贾爱兵,颜静兰主编. —2版. —上海:华东理工大学出版社,2016.8(2022.3重印)

ISBN 978-7-5628-4740-3

Ⅰ.①中… Ⅱ.①龙…②贾…③颜… Ⅲ.①中华文化-英、汉 Ⅳ.①K203

中国版本图书馆CIP数据核字(2016)第168525号

项目统筹 / 舒欣如
责任编辑 / 舒欣如
出版发行 / 华东理工大学出版社有限公司
地址:上海市梅陇路130号,200237
电话:021-64250306
网址:www.ecustpress.cn
邮箱:zongbianban@ecustpress.cn
印　　刷 / 苏州古得堡数码印刷有限公司
开　　本 / 710mm×1000mm　1/16
印　　张 / 19
字　　数 / 511千字
版　　次 / 2016年8月第2版
印　　次 / 2022年3月第4次
定　　价 / 35.00元

本书编委会

主　编　龙毛忠　贾爱兵　颜静兰

编　委　胡　平　贾静静　赵　蕾

Preface

前　言

随着中国改革开放的日益深化，介绍外国文化的书籍、影片、电视节目等不断涌入，充斥着我们的文化阵地，有关外国的人文学科也在各大专院校陆续开设。这种现状导致很多年轻学生对西方的文明极其钦羡向往，而对自己祖国的文化或一无所知，或不知如何用外语对外介绍，如此便形成了不均衡的交流态势。

我们认为任何交流都应是双向的。我们的学生在对目的语国家的文化予以关注的同时(这是学好外语的必要条件)，也应该为自己国家悠久的历史、灿烂的文化、优良的文学感到自豪，担起向世界介绍我们国家的历史、政治、经济、文化、教育等情况以及风土人情、风俗习惯等一般人文知识的职责(这是学习外语的主要目的之一)。中国文学是世界文学宝库中的一朵奇葩，汉语语言瑰丽多彩；中国的风俗习惯多姿多彩，源远流长；中国的音乐悠扬动听，美妙绝伦；中国传统工艺异彩纷呈，美轮美奂；中国智慧更是令人叹为观止；中国的宗教哲学博大精深，其影响力不仅深入中华民族的骨髓，而且在全世界也产生了积极作用(连美国前总统里根都曾经在 1987 年国情咨文中引用过老子的名言："治大国若烹小鲜。")。

通过实施教学，使学生对中国文化有一定了解，接触到中国文化的方方面面，由衷地产生对祖国及其文化的自豪和热爱，拓展文化视野，丰富文化内涵，学会使用英语流利地介绍中国文化，这样就可以避免在与外国人交流时出现这样的现象：谈起英美滔滔不绝，眉飞色舞，如数家珍，而提到自己国家的文化时却嗫嗫嚅嚅，抓耳挠腮，词不达意。要让中国文化传播得更远，让更多的人了解它，我们炎黄子孙责无旁贷。

为此，我们选编了《中国文化概览(英汉对照)》，在书中简要介绍了诸多人们感兴趣的中国文化元素，以供英语学习者、有心对外介绍中国灿烂文化的人士、志在成为中西文化交流大使的外国留学生以及外交领域的有识之士使用。承蒙读者厚爱，此书自 2009 年面世以来，到 2015 年已重印 6 次，深受大家的肯定。本次改版在保留原版实用性、知识性和趣味性的基础上，根据师生教学和读者使用中发现的问题以及提出的意见和建议，对全书的架构和部分章节内容做了调整。同时，每个章节补充了**思考题和测验题**，并均附有**参考答案**，这样不仅有利于教学，而且方便读者自用。希望《中国文化概览(英汉对照)(第二版)》能继续受到读者的关注和支持,为大家带来更愉悦的阅读体验。

本书的编写与出版得到了华东理工大学教务处教材立项经费的资助和华东理工大学出版社的大力支持,在此编者表示诚挚的感谢!在编写本书的过程中,我们参考借鉴了不少作者的著作和观点,在此谨表由衷的谢意。囿于编者的学识和水平,书中定有可商榷之处,恳请专家和读者指正。

龙毛忠

2016 年 6 月

于华理苑

Contents

目 录

Chapter 1

A General Outline of China

中国概况

China, whose full name is the People's Republic of China, has a vast land with boundless natural resources, a long history, spectacular landscapes, colorful cultural heritage and varied national customs. The Chinese nation created a glorious civilization in the early stage of mankind's history. The compass, gunpowder, the art of paper-making and movable type printing invented by the ancient Chinese have contributed tremendously to the progress of mankind in the world. The Great Wall, the Grand Canal and other projects built by the Chinese people are regarded as engineering feats on the globe.

1. Location and Territory

1) Location

China is located in eastern Asia, on the west coast of the Pacific Ocean. The total land area of China is 9,600,000 * square kilometers, slightly smaller than that of Europe, and it is the largest country in Asia and the third largest country in the world next only to Russia and Canada.

2) Territory

From east to west, the territory of China extends from the confluence of the Heilong River and Wusuli River to the Pamirs, which covers a distance of about 5,200 kilometers; from north to south, China stretches from the center of the Heilong River north of the town of Mohe to the Zengmu Reef at the southernmost tip of the Nansha Islands, covering a distance of about 5,500 kilometers.

China shares a boundary of some 22,800 kilometers, bordered by North Korea to the east; Mongolia to the north; Russia to the northeast; Kazakhstan, Kyrgyzstan and Tajikistan to the northwest; Afghanistan, Pakistan, India, Nepal and Bhutan to the west and southwest; and Myanmar, Laos and Vietnam to the south. Across the seas to the east and southeast are the South Korea, Japan, the Philippines, Brunei, Malaysia and Indonesia.

3) Territorial Waters and Island

The Chinese mainland is flanked to the east and south by the Bohai Sea as China's

---

* 注：本书所涉及数字为作者写作时数据，与当前数据或有出入，仅供读者作为语言学习参考使用。

continental sea, Yellow Sea, East China Sea and South China Sea as marginal seas of the Pacific Ocean. The coastline of China's mainland is about 18,000 kilometers, with a flat topography and many excellent ice-free docks and harbors.

China's territorial waters are 4.73 million square kilometers. There are many islands lying offshore of China, the largest of which are Taiwan Island with an area of about 36,000 square kilometers, and Hainan Island with an area of 34,000 square kilometers. There are a lot of archipelagoes such as the Zhoushan Islands and the islands in the East and South China Seas. There are a number of peninsulas along the coast; the largest ones are the Shandong Peninsula, Liaodong Peninsula and Leizhou Peninsula.

2. Topography

The topography of China is characterized by high west part and low east part, gradually descending in elevation from the west towards the east to form three steps. The highest step is the Qinghai-Tibet Plateau with the elevation being generally more than 4,500 meters above sea level, hence known as "the roof of the world". To the east of the Qinghai-Tibetan Plateau is the second step with much lower elevations, ranging between 1,000 meters and 2,000 meters and alternating with huge basins. The third step stretches from the line in the west composed of the Greater Hinggan Mountains, Taihang Mountain, Wu Mountain and the eastern rim of the Yunnan-Guizhou Plateau to the coast in the east, and embraces alternating hills and plains, and there are large areas of low mountains and hills at elevations of less than 500 meters above sea level with only a few peaks being at 2,000 meters, and the elevation of plains is all less than 200 meters.

The plains are the important industrial and agricultural bases and economic centers of China. They are distributed in the north to south direction, including Northeast Plain, North China Plain, Middle to Lower Yangtze Plain and Pearl River Delta Plain. According to the types of topography, mountains in China account for 33.3% of the national land area, plateaus 26.0%, basins 18.8%, hills 9.9% and plains 12.0%.

Most rivers in China flow west to east into the Pacific Ocean except a few in the Southwest that flow to the South. The Yangtze River, 6,300 kilometers long, is the largest river in China, which originates from the Tanggula Mountain on the Qinghai-Tibet Plateau and flows to the East China Sea. It is the third longest river after the Nile and the Amazon. The Yellow River is 5,500 kilometers long, the second longest river in China, flowing to the Bohai Sea. Both rivers are the birthplaces of ancient Chinese civilization with a wealth of historical sites and relics.

3. Climate

China is a country with diverse climates. From the south to the north, the country is divided into tropical, subtropical, temperate and frigid climate zones. The climate in China varies greatly. For instance, Hainan Island in the south has long, hot summers and no winters, while the winter temperature drops to below 30℃ in Heilongjiang, Jilin and Liaoning provinces in the northeastern part of China.

Most of China lies in the North Temperate Zone, characterized by a warm climate and distinctive seasons, a climate well suited for habitation. Most parts of China are subject to strong monsoon climate. From September to April the following year, the dry and cold winter monsoons blow from Siberia and the Mongolian Plateau, resulting in cold and dry winters and great differences between the temperatures of north and south China. From April to September, warm and humid summer monsoons blow from the seas in the east and south, resulting in overall high temperatures and plentiful rainfall, and little temperature difference between north and south China.

Precipitation gradually declines from the southeastern to the northwestern inland area, and the average annual precipitation varies greatly from place to place and from season to season. The average annual precipitation in China is 648 mm, or 19% less than the world average 800 mm on land. The annual precipitation in the southeastern coastal areas and parts of the southwestern areas is more than 2,000 mm, but that in the northwestern China is usually less than 200 mm, and 50 mm in the Tarim and Turpan basins in Xinjiang and Chaidamu Basin in Qinghai, etc., even less than 25 mm at centers of those basins.

4. Natural Resources

1) Cultivated Land, Forest and Grassland

China's cultivated lands, forests and grasslands are among the world's largest in terms of sheer area. However, due to China's large population, the per-capita areas of cultivated land, forest and grassland are small, especially in the case of cultivated land — only one third of the world's average.

In China, 130.04 million hectares of land are cultivated, mainly on the Northeast Plain, the North China Plain, the Middle-Lower Yangtze Plain, the Pearl River Delta and the Sichuan Basin. The fertile black soil of the Northeast Plain, the largest plain in China with an area of more than 350,000 square kilometers, abounds in wheat, corn, sorghum, soybeans, flax and sugar beet. The deep brown topsoil of the North China Plain is planted with wheat, corn, millet and cotton. The Middle-Lower Yangtze Plain's flat terrain and many lakes and rivers make it particularly suitable for paddy rice and freshwater fish; therefore, it is called "a land of fish and rice." This area also produces large quantities of tea and silkworms. The purplish soil of the warm and humid Sichuan Basin is green with crops in all four seasons, including paddy rice, rapeseed and sugarcane. The Pearl River Delta abounds with paddy rice, harvested

2 – 3 times every year.

Forests cover about 175 million hectares of China. The Greater Hinggan Mountains, the Lesser Hinggan Mountains and Changbai Mountain Ranges in the northeast are China's largest natural forest areas. Major tree species found here include conifers, such as Korean pine, larch and Korean larch, and coniferous-broadleaf trees such as white birch, oak, willow, elm and Northeast China ash. Major tree species in the southwest include the dragon spruce, fir and Yunnan pine, as well as teak, red sandalwood, camphor, nanmu and so on. Xishuangbanna, often called a kingdom of plants, in the south of Yunnan Province, is a rare tropical broadleaf forest area in China, playing host to more than 5,000 plant species.

Grasslands in China cover an area of 400 million hectares, stretching more than 3,000 kilometers from the northeast to the southwest. They are the centers of animal husbandry. The Inner Mongolian Prairie is China's largest natural pastureland, and home to the famous Sanhe horses, Sanhe cattle and Mongolian sheep. The important natural pasturelands in north and south of the Tianshan Mountains in Xinjiang are ideal for stockbreeding, where the famous Ili horses and Xinjiang fine-wool sheep are raised.

2) Mineral Resources

China has deposits of almost all the minerals known in the world. Minerals of 151 different kinds have been verified, which lead the world in the reserves of tungsten, antimony, rare earth, molybdenum, vanadium and titanium. Other deposits which are among the largest in the world are coal, iron, lead-zinc, copper, silver, mercury, tin, nickel, phosphorus and asbestos.

China's basic coal reserves total 334.2 billion tons, mainly distributed in north, northwest, northeast and southwest China with Xinjiang Uygur Autonomous Region, Shanxi Province and the Inner Mongolia Autonomous Region heading the field. China's 21.24 billion tons of the basic iron ore reserves are distributed mainly in northeast, north and southwest China such as Liaoning Province, eastern Hebei and western Sichuan provinces. Tungsten reserves are concentrated in southeastern Hunan, southern Jiangxi, and northern Guangdong, western Fujian and eastern Guangxi, though they are found in 19 provinces and autonomous regions across China.

China also abounds in petroleum, natural gas, oil shale, phosphorus and sulfur. Petroleum reserves are mainly found in northwest, northeast and north China, as well as in the continental shelves of east China.

3) Water Resources

Freshwater in China mainly comes from rivers and lakes. China's territory includes numerous lakes, most of which are found on the Middle-Lower Yangtze Plain and the Qinghai-Tibet Plateau. Freshwater lakes such as Poyang Lake, Dongting

Lake, Taihu Lake, and Hongze Lake mostly lie in the former area, while in the latter are saltwater lakes, such as Qinghai Lake, Nam Co Lake and Siling Co Lake. Poyang Lake in the north of Jiangxi Province, with an area of 3,583 square kilometers, is the largest of its kind. Qinghai Lake, in northeast Qinghai Province and with an area of 4,583 square kilometers, is the largest one of its kind.

China's rivers can be categorized as exterior and interior systems. The catchment area of the exterior rivers that empty into the oceans accounts for 64% of the country's total land area. The Yangtze, Yellow, Heilong, Pearl, Liaohe, Haihe and Huaihe rivers flow east, and empty into the Pacific Ocean. The Yarlung Zangbo River in Tibet, which flows first east and then south into the Indian Ocean, boasts the Yarlung Zangbo Grand Canyon, the largest canyon in the world, 504.6 kilometers long and 6,009 meters deep. The Ertix River flows north from the Xinjiang Uygur Autonomous Region to the Arctic Ocean. The catchment area of the interior rivers that flow into inland lakes or disappear into deserts or salt marshes makes up about 36% of China's total land area. Its length of 2,179 kilometers makes the Tarim River in southern Xinjiang China's longest interior river.

The Yangtze River, 6,300 kilometers long, is the largest river in China, and the third largest in the world, next only to the Nile in Africa and the Amazon in South America. Passing through high mountains and deep valleys, the upper section of the Yangtze River is abundant in water resources. Known as the "golden waterway," the Yangtze is a transportation artery linking west and east, its navigation benefiting from excellent natural channels. The middle and lower Yangtze River areas have a warm and humid climate, plentiful rainfall and fertile soil, making them important agricultural regions. The Yellow River is the second largest river in China with a length of 5,500 kilometers. The Yellow River valley was one of the birthplaces of ancient Chinese civilization. It has lush pasturelands along its banks, flourishing agriculture and abundant mineral deposits.

The Heilong River is a large river in north China with a total length of 4,350 kilometers, of which 3,420 kilometers are in China. The Pearl River, 2,210 kilometers long, is a large river in south China. In addition to those bestowed by nature, China has a famous man-made river — the Grand Canal, running from Beijing in the north to Hangzhou in Zhejiang Province in the south. Work first began on the Grand Canal as early as in the 5th century B.C. It links five major rivers: the Haihe River, Yellow River, Huaihe River, Yangtze River and Qiantang River. With a total length of 1,801 kilometers, the Grand Canal is the longest as well as the oldest man-made waterway in the world.

5. Wildlife

China is one of the countries with the greatest diversity of wildlife in the world.

There are more than 6,266 species of vertebrates, 10% of the world's total. Among them, 2,404 are terrestrial and 3,862 fishes. There are more than 100 wild animal species unique to China including such well-known rare animals as the giant panda, golden-haired monkey, South China tiger, brown-eared pheasant, red-crowned crane, crested ibis, Yangtze River dolphin, takin, Chinese Alligator and so on.

China lies in two of the world's major zoogeographic regions, the Palaearctic and the Oriental. The Qinghai-Tibet Plateau, Xinjiang and Inner Mongolia autonomous regions, northeastern China, and all areas north of the Yellow River are in the Palaearctic region. Central, southern, and southwest China lie in the Oriental region. In the Palaearctic zone, many important mammals are found such as the river fox, horse, camel, tapir, mouse hare, hamster, and jerboa. Among the species found in the Oriental region are the civet cat, Chinese pangolin, bamboo rat, tree shrew, gibbon and various other species of monkeys and apes. Some overlap exists between the two regions because of natural dispersal and migration, and deer or antelope, bears, wolves, pigs, and rodents are found in all of the diverse climatic and geological environments. The famous giant panda is found only in a few mountain ranges in Sichuan, Shaanxi, and Gansu provinces.

A giant panda (see picture 1 - 1) weighs on average 135 kg and lives on tender bamboo leaves and bamboo shoots. Because it is extremely rare — just over 1,500 are left at present — it has become the symbol of the world's protected wild animals. The red-crowned crane (see picture 1 - 2), which could be as tall as 1.2 m, is covered with white feathers, with a distinctive patch of exposed red skin crowning its head and is regarded as a symbol of longevity in East Asia. The Yangtze River dolphin (see picture 1 - 3) is one of only two species of freshwater whales in the world. In 1980, a male Yangtze River dolphin was caught for the first time in the Yangtze River, which aroused great interest among dolphin researchers worldwide.

6. Population

The population of China, which is the largest in the world, is over 1.3 billion with 56 ethnic groups.

The Chinese population is unevenly distributed and the population density exceeds 100 persons per square kilometers in most parts of the country east of the line drawn between Harbin and Kunming, and it is more than 400 persons per square kilometers in some areas. Population density is below 50 persons per square kilometers in the vast region west of the line, and in many areas it is less than one person per square kilometers. The eastern part of China is densely populated, while the western part is sparsely populated.

The population of the Han nationality is the largest, accounting for over 91% of the national total. The Zhuang nationality (see picture 1 - 4) population is over 16 million, and coming next are the populations of the Manchu, Hui, Uygur (see picture 1-5), Miao (see picture 1 - 6), Yi, Tujia, Mongol, Tibetan, Buyi, Dong, Yao, Korean, Bai, Hani, Kazak, Li and Dai nationalities. The population of each of these ethnic groups exceeds one million. That of the smallest ethnic minorities comes to only a few thousands.

The Han population is distributed over vast regions, but most of it is concentrated in eastern China. The areas in which ethnic minority peoples dwell in compact communities are, for the most part, located in Southwest, Northwest and Northeast China that make up more than half of Chinese territory. The populations of many ethnic groups are relatively concentrated in some areas, though many of their members are scattered all over the country. Such a distribution pattern is conducive to economic and cultural exchanges among the nationalities. This has given rise to a relationship of mutual interdependence and an unbreakable link of friendship among the nationalities in China.

The Han people have their own spoken and written language, known as the Chinese language, which is commonly used throughout China. The Hui and Manchu ethnic groups also use the Han (Chinese) language. The other 53 ethnic groups use their own spoken languages and 23 ethnic groups have their own written languages.

Word Bank

the Pamirs	帕米尔高原
China's continental sea	中国的内海
archipelagoes	群岛
peninsulas	半岛
topography	地形,地形学
precipitation	降水量
sorghum	高粱
flax	亚麻
sugar beet	甜菜
conifers	针叶树
larch	落叶松
Olga Bay larch	长白落叶松
white birch	白桦
Northeast China ash	水曲柳
dragon spruce	云杉
teak	柚木
red sandalwood	紫檀
camphor tree	樟树
nanmu	楠木
tungsten	钨
antimony	锑
rare earth	稀土
molybdenum	钼
vanadium	钒
titanium	钛
lead-zinc	铅锌
phosphorus	磷
asbestos	石棉
sulfur	硫黄
terrestrial vertebrates	陆栖脊椎动物

red ibis	朱鹮，朱鹭	civet cat	麝香猫，香猫
takin	羚牛	pangolin	穿山甲
Palaearctic	古北区的	tree shrew	树鼩
tapir	貘	gibbon	长臂猿
hamster	仓鼠	red-crowned crane	丹顶鹤
jerboa	跳鼠		

参考译文

中华人民共和国，简称中国，幅员辽阔，历史悠久，资源丰富，景色优美，文化遗产星光璀璨，民族习俗多姿多彩。中华民族在人类社会早期便创造了光辉灿烂的文明。指南针、火药、造纸术和活字印刷术的发明对世界人类进步产生了深远影响；万里长城、京杭大运河等浩瀚工程也被誉为世界工程史上的丰功伟绩。

1. 地理位置与领土

1）地理位置

中国位于亚洲大陆东部、太平洋西岸。陆地面积约960万平方千米，相当于整个欧洲大陆，是亚洲面积最大的国家，也是世界上领土面积仅次于俄罗斯和加拿大的第三大国家。（见图1-1）

2）领土

中国领土东起黑龙江与乌苏里江汇合处，西到帕米尔高原，东西相距约5 200千米。北起漠河以北的黑龙江江心，南到南沙群岛南端的曾母暗沙，南北相距约5 500千米。

中国陆地边界长达2.28万千米，东邻朝鲜民主主义人民共和国，北邻蒙古，东北邻俄罗斯，西北邻哈萨克斯坦、吉尔吉斯斯坦、塔吉克斯坦，西部和西南部与阿富汗、巴基斯坦、印度、尼泊尔、不丹等国家接壤，南部与缅甸、老挝和越南相连。东部和东南部同韩国、日本、菲律宾、文莱、马来西亚和印度尼西亚隔海相望。

3）海域和岛屿

中国陆地东部与南部濒临渤海、黄海、东海和南海。渤海为中国的内海，黄海、东海和南海是太平洋的边缘海。中国陆地海岸线全长约1.8万千米。海岸地势平坦，多优良港湾，且多为终年不冻港。

中国海域面积为473万平方千米。在中国海域上，分布着众多岛屿。其中最大的为台湾岛，面积3.6万平方千米；其次是海南岛，面积3.4万平方千米。东海与南海上群岛众多，舟山群岛便是其中一个。环海岸线上半岛星罗棋布，其中最大的是山东半岛、辽东半岛和雷州半岛。

2. 地形

中国地势西高东低，海拔由西而东逐级下降，形成三个阶梯。最高一级阶梯是青藏高原，平均海拔超过4 500米，号称“世界屋脊”。青藏高原向东是较低的第二级阶梯，平均海拔1 000米至2 000米，盆地在此纵横交错。第三阶梯西接大兴安岭、太行山、巫山和雪峰山，东环云贵高原，向东直达海岸。群山交织，多为低海拔山峰，地势下降到海拔500米，仅有少数山峰海拔可至

2 000米，平原海拔均在200米以下。

平原地区是中国重要的工农业生产基地和经济中心。自北向南分布着东北平原、华北平原、长江中下游平原以及珠江三角洲。根据地形分类来看，中国山脉面积约占国土面积的33.3%，高原占26.0%，盆地占18.8%，丘陵占9.9%，平原占12.0%。

中国的河流除西南部有几条向南流以外，多数是由西向东流入太平洋。长江是中国第一大河，全长6 300千米，发源于青藏高原的唐古拉山，向东汇入东海，仅次于非洲的尼罗河和南美洲的亚马孙河，为世界第三大河。黄河是中国第二大河，全长5 500千米，向东汇入渤海。长江与黄河都是中国古代文明的发祥地，两河流域文物古迹众多。

3. 气候

中国气候类型多样。从南到北分为热带、亚热带、温带和寒带，气候差异明显。例如，南方的海南岛夏季漫长炎热，没有冬季；而东北地区的黑龙江、吉林与辽宁三省冬季的气温则降至零下30摄氏度。

中国的大部分地区位于北温带，气候温和，四季分明，适宜人类居住与生存。大陆性季风气候是中国气候的主要特点。每年9月至次年4月，干寒的冬季风从西伯利亚和蒙古高原吹来，寒冷干燥，南北温差甚大。每年的4月至9月，暖湿的夏季风从东部和南部海洋吹来，普遍高温多雨，南北温差甚小。

内陆降水量从东南向西北逐渐减少，各地年平均降水量因季节不同差异很大。全国年平均降水量为648毫米，较全球陆地年平均降水量800毫米少19%。东南沿海和部分西南地区年降水量可达2 000毫米以上，西北内陆则不到200毫米，而新疆塔里木和吐鲁番盆地以及青海柴达木盆地等地区年降水量仅有50毫米，这些盆地的中心区域年降水量甚至不足25毫米。

4. 自然资源

1）耕地、森林、草原

中国耕地、森林、草原面积的绝对数量均居世界前列，但由于人口众多，人均数量却很少。尤其是耕地，仅为世界人均数量的三分之一。

中国现有耕地13 004万公顷。东北平原、华北平原、长江中下游平原、珠江三角洲和四川盆地是耕地分布最为集中的地区。面积35万多平方千米的东北平原是中国第一大平原，大部分是黑色沃土，盛产小麦、玉米、高粱、大豆、亚麻和甜菜。华北平原土层松厚，土质肥沃，盛产小麦、玉米、小米和棉花等。长江中下游平原地势低平，河流和湖泊星罗棋布，是中国主要的水稻、淡水鱼产区，素称“鱼米之乡”，并且盛产茶叶和桑蚕。四川盆地多为紫色土壤，气候暖湿，农作物可四季生长，盛产水稻、油菜和甘蔗。珠江三角洲盛产水稻，每年可收获二至三次。

中国森林面积约为17 500万公顷。东北地区的大兴安岭、小兴安岭和长白山区，是中国最大的天然林区，遍布着望不到边的红松、落叶松、黄花松等针叶林及白桦、橡树、柳树、榆树、水曲柳等阔叶林。其次为西南天然林区，该区主要树种有云杉、冷杉、云南松，还有柚木、紫檀、樟树、楠木等；云南省南部的西双版纳是中国少有的热带阔叶林区，森林植物5 000余种，有“植物王国”之称。

中国的草原面积约40 000万公顷。在从东北到西南绵延3 000多千米的草原带上，分布着多个畜牧业基地。内蒙古草原为中国最大的天然牧场，出产著名的三河马、三河牛和蒙古绵羊。新疆天山南北也是中国重要的天然草场和牲畜良种基地，出产著名的伊犁马和新疆细毛羊。

2）矿产资源

目前，世界上已知的矿产在中国都能找到。中国已经探明储量的矿产有151种，其中钨、锑、稀土、钼、钒和钛的储量居世界之最。其他储量居前列的还有煤炭、铁、铅、锌、铜、银、水银、锡、镍、磷和石棉。

中国煤炭基础储量为 3 342 亿吨，主要分布在华北、西北、东北、西南地区，尤以新疆、山西、内蒙古最为丰富。铁矿石的基础储量为 212.4 亿吨，主要分布在东北、华北和西南地区，如辽宁省、河北省东部和四川省西部地区。稀有金属钨尽管在全国 19 个省和自治区都有探明，但主要储量集中在湖南东南部、江西南部、广东北部、福建西部和广西东部。

中国石油、天然气、油页岩磷和硫黄储量丰富。石油储量集中在西南、东北、华北地区和中国东部大陆架。

3）水资源

淡水资源主要来自河流和湖泊。中国境内湖泊众多，长江中下游地区和青藏高原是湖泊最多的两个地区。前者为淡水湖最集中的地区，主要有鄱阳湖、洞庭湖、太湖、洪泽湖等，其中江西省北部的鄱阳湖最大，面积为 3 583 平方千米。后者主要分布着咸水湖，有青海湖、纳木错湖、色林湖等，其中以青海省东北部的青海湖最大，面积为 4 583 平方千米。

河流分为外流河和内流河。注入海洋的外流河，流域面积约占全国陆地总面积的 64%。长江、黄河、黑龙江、珠江、辽河、海河、淮河等向东流入太平洋；西藏的雅鲁藏布江向东流出国境再向南注入印度洋，河流的上方是长 504.6 千米、深 6 009 米的世界第一大峡谷——雅鲁藏布江大峡谷；新疆的额尔齐斯河则向北流出国境注入北冰洋。流入内陆湖或消失于沙漠、盐滩之中的内流河，流域面积约占全国陆地总面积的 36%。新疆南部的塔里木河是中国最长的内流河，全长 2 179千米。

长江是中国第一大河，全长 6 300 千米，仅次于非洲的尼罗河和南美洲的亚马孙河，为世界第三大河。其上游穿行于高山深谷之间，蕴藏着丰富的水力资源。长江也是中国东西水上运输的大动脉，天然河道优越，有“黄金水道”之称。长江中下游地区气候温暖湿润、雨量充沛、土地肥沃，是中国重要的农业区。

黄河为中国第二长河，全长 5 500 千米。黄河流域牧场丰美、农业发达、矿藏富饶，是中国古代文明的发祥地之一。

黑龙江是中国北部的大河，全长 4 350 千米，其中有 3 420 千米流经中国境内；珠江为中国南部的大河，全长 2 214 千米。除天然河流外，中国还有一条著名的人工河，那就是贯穿南北的大运河。它始凿于公元前五世纪，北起北京，南抵浙江杭州，连通海河、黄河、淮河、长江、钱塘江五大水系，全长 1 801 千米，是世界上开凿最早、最长的人工河。

5. 野生动物

中国是世界上野生动物种类最多的国家之一，仅脊椎动物就有 6 266 多种，约占世界脊椎动物种类的 10%，其中陆栖脊椎动物 2 404 种，鱼类 3 862 种。大熊猫、金丝猴、华南虎、褐马鸡、丹顶鹤、朱鹭、白鳍豚、羚牛和扬子鳄等百余种中国特产的珍稀野生动物闻名于世。

中国位于世界两大主要动物地理学区域，古北区和东洋区。青藏高原、新疆和内蒙古自治区、东北地区以及整个黄河以北地区都属于古北区。华中、华南和西南地区属于东洋区。在古北区生存的哺乳动物有狐狸、马、骆驼、貘、鼠兔、仓鼠和跳鼠等。东洋区发现的物种包括麝猫、穿山甲、竹鼠、树鼩、长臂猿以及其他各类猿猴物种等。由于自然分布和迁徙等原因，一个物种会同时生存在两个区域。鹿、羚羊、熊、狼、猪和啮齿类动物生活在不同气候和地理环境中，著名的大熊猫仅在四川、陕西和甘肃的少数山区可见。

大熊猫（见图 1－2）体重可达 135 千克，靠吃嫩竹和竹笋为生。目前只剩下 1 500 余只，由于极其珍贵,已成为世界受保护野生动物的标志。丹顶鹤(见图 1 - 3),体长可达 1.2 米,身上覆盖着白色羽毛,头顶上长着一小块丹红色的裸露皮肤,在东亚地区被视为“长寿”的象征。白鳍豚(见图 1 - 4)是世界上仅有的两种淡水鲸类之一。1980 年首次在长江流域捕获一头雄性白鳍豚,引起了世界豚类研究界的极大兴趣。

6. 人口

中国是世界上人口最多的国家,全国总人口超过 13 亿,由 56 个不同的民族构成。

中国人口分布很不均匀,以哈尔滨和昆明两点画线为界,以东大部分地区人口密度超过 100 人/平方千米,个别地区超过 400 人/平方千米;以西很多地区不足 1 人/平方千米。中国东部人口稠密,西部地广人稀。

汉族人口最多,占全国总人口的 91% 以上。壮族(见图 1 - 5)人口超过 1 600 万。满族、回族、维吾尔族(见图 1 - 6)、苗族(见图 1 - 7)、彝族、土家族、蒙古族、藏族、布依族、侗族、瑶族、朝鲜族、哈尼族、哈萨克族、黎族和傣族人口总数都超过 100 万。人口最少的少数民族只有几千人。

汉族分布广泛,但主要集中在中国东部。少数民族聚集地大多位于西南地区、西北地区和东北地区,占中国国土总面积的二分之一。尽管各个少数民族分布在全国各地,但大部分少数民族居住地相对集中。这种分布模式有益于民族间的经济文化交流,形成了各民族间的相互依存和密切联系。

汉族的语言和文字是中国通用的语言和文字,回族和满族也使用汉语。其余 53 个民族都使用本民族的语言,23 个民族有自己的文字。

Exercises

Section A　Thought-provoking questions

1. What are the characteristics of the topography of China?
2. Generally speaking, how many climate zones are there in China?
3. What can be included in natural resources of China?
4. Can you name at least 15 ethnic minority groups in China?

Section B　Fill in the blanks by choosing the appropriate words from the grid

lunched	developmental	provincial	carried	dietetic
conservation	Local	ecological	food	protection

CWCA (China Wildlife Conservation Association), founded in December 1983, in Beijing, is a nonprofit national organization under the framework of China Science Association. As the largest __1__ conservation organization in China, CWCA became one of the nongovernmental organizations of International Union for Conservation of Nature and Natural Resources, IUCN. So far, CWCA has 31 __2__ and 622 regional branches through out China with over 200 thousand members who love wildlife and work on wildlife __3__, scientific research, wildlife breeding and domestication, natural conservation and so on. The mission of the CWCA is to promote sustainable development of China's wildlife.

There still exists a bad habit of eating wildlife in China, which leads to disturbance on ecological balance. At the end of 1999, CWCA __4__ a survey on status of eating wildlife. According to the obtained result, CWCA suggested that the public not eat wildlife and set a new __5__ fashion. Many cooks try to be the Green Cuisine Ambassador, refusing to cook wildlife any more. So far, CWCA successfully collected signature from over 300,000 cooks and the sum is expected to increase to one million by the end of 2008. More and more people are joining in our efforts and activities, and it is believed to be of great help to protect the wildlife in China.

※ **Heaven is eternal, the Earth everlasting. How come they to be so? It is because they do not foster their own lives. That is why they live so long.**

From Laozi: *Dao De Jing*

(天地长久,天地所以能长且久者,以其不自生,故能长生。)

——老子·《道德经》

※ **Never embark on a vain cause nor commit yourself to any undeserving project.**

From Guan Zhong: *Guanzi*

(不作无补之功,不为无益之事。)

——管仲·《管子》

Chapter 2

A Brief History of China

中国历史简介

China is a country with a long and rich history and ancient civilization. The History of China can date back to as early as 4000 B.C. Chinese civilization began with the legendary sage-emperors Huang Di and Yan Di in the area of the Yellow River Basin. After centuries, the two tribes gradually merged into one by the time of the Xia Dynasty. Chinese people, therefore, usually regard themselves as "the descendants of Yan and Huang", or call themselves "Hua Xia People" or "Hua People". It was these people who established a state in the region of the Yellow River Basin, which was believed to be the center of the world, so the state was named the "Middle Kingdom".

Chinese generally tell the history from the Xia Dynasty, which began in the 21st century B.C. and was followed by various dynasties until 1912 when Dr. Sun Yat-sen was proclaimed the provisional president of the Republic of China.

1. The Xia Dynasty (2070 B.C.–1600 B.C.)

Xia is the first prehistoric dynasty in Chinese history. It is said that when the legendary ruler Yu died, his son was chosen to be the leader, thus created the Xia Dynasty and established the system of hereditary dynastic rule. There were 14 generations with 17 rulers in Xia Dynasty before it was taken place of by the Shang Dynasty. Scientific excavations by archaeologists uncovered urban sites, bronze implements, and tombs that provided the evidence of the existence of Xia civilization.

The Xia were agrarian people, and by the time of Yao, Shun and Yu, farming and stockbreeding were considerably developed. People were familiar with the phenomena of seasonal changes and arranged their farm activities according to the alterations of the seasons.

2. The Shang Dynasty (1600 B.C.–1046 B.C.)

The Shang Dynasty consisted of 17 generations and 31 kings, and it controlled the central part of China, extending over much of modern Henan, Hubei, Shandong, Anhui, Shanxi, and Hebei provinces. Its civilization was based on agriculture, hunting and animal husbandry. The Shang was often at war with neighboring peoples and they had to move their capital for seven times.

The Shang enjoyed the most advanced bronze civilization in the world. The excavated bronze weapons, bronze fittings for chariots and harnesses and ceremonial bronze vessels with inscriptions dating back to the Shang period show the highly skillful technique in bronze making.

The development of a writing system can be witnessed on the oracles like tortoise shells or animal bones, and these writings were the beginning of the written Chinese language. (see picture 2-1)

The Shang king's rule was based on both religious and military power. The king made animal sacrifices and communicated with his ancestors by interpreting the cracks on heated cattle bones or tortoise shells that had been prepared by professional diviners. Kings were buried with ritual vessels, weapons, jades, and human sacrifice. Sometimes, when a ruler died, more than one hundred slaves were forced to join him in the grave. Some of them would be decapitated first, and some of them were just cruelly thrown into the tomb alive.

3. The Zhou Dynasty (1046 B.C.-256 B.C.)

The Zhou Dynasty reigned for more than 800 years with 37 kings, the longest period of all Chinese dynasties. The Zhou Dynasty falls into several sub-periods: the Western Zhou, the Eastern Zhou which is further divided into the Spring and Autumn Period (770 B.C.-476 B.C) and the Warring States Period (475 B.C.-256 B.C.)

The Kings Wen and Wu, the founders of the Zhou Dynasty, were regarded as the ideal monarchs by the Confucians for they reined with morality, humanity and righteousness. The Zhou Dynasty was a turning point in Chinese history for it evolved into the feudal system, and witnessed the territorial expansion, economic prosperity and cultural flourishing.

The Zhou Dynasty was characterized by great intellectual achievements in terms of the rise of Confucianism, Daoism and the development of Chinese philosophy. Confucius, the founder of Confucianism, and Laozi, the founder of Daoism together with other philosophers and theorists such as Mencius, Mozi, Zhuangzi, Han Feizi, Xunzi etc., made unprecedentedly huge impact on Chinese culture.

The Spring and Autumn and Warring States periods are famous for the cultural prosperity with "Hundred Schools of Thought". During this era, many poets voiced their opinions of criticism and emotions, many of which were preserved in the *Book of Poetry*, the first important work of literature in Chinese history.

The concept of the ruler as the "Son of Heaven" originated during the Zhou period and the concept of the "mandate of heaven" gained the popularity. It was believed that the emperor ruled by divine right and his dethronement would prove that he had lost the mandate, and heaven expresses disapproval of an evil rulers through natural disasters such as earthquakes, floods and plagues and through rebellions.

4. The Qin Dynasty (221 B.C.-206 B.C.)

Qin Shihuang (see picture 2-2), the first Emperor of China, established the first centralized, unified, multi-ethnic feudal state in Chinese history — the Qin Dynasty after a few hundred years of disunity. Although the rule of the two Qin emperors lasted only about two decades, it marks the beginning of a more than two thousand years long history of a centralized state with an emperor being the head of a state and a comparatively uniformed culture.

Qin Shihuang made many changes and reforms to unify China and help his administrative tasks. He standardized the written script so as to create a consistent way to help people communicate across the country. Weights, measures and currencies were also standardized, and the system of prefectures and counties were solidly established. The sovereigns of the next 2,000 years actually followed the feudal governmental structure established by the Qin.

Qin Shihuang is an epoch-making historic emperor in China's history. He was praised as a unifier and centralizer, but was attacked and criticized as a cruel tyrant. Under his rule, many constructive public projects were undertaken. Roads and irrigation canals were built throughout the country, and in order to fend off barbarian invasion, the fortification walls were built to make a 5,000-kilometer-long great wall. On the other hand, he executed 400 of his opponents and burned the books written before the Qin Dynasty to wipe out ideas which conflicted with the Emperor. The public works and taxes were too great a burden to the population. He forced huge labors to build his tombs, and hundreds upon thousands of the terra cotta armies and horses (see picture 2 - 3) were found at the burial site, which meant to protect the tomb for the Qin.

5. The Han Dynasty(206 B.C. - 220 A.D.)

In 206 B.C. Liu Bang succeeded in founding a new empire, the Han Dynasty, with its capital at Chang'an. The reign of the Han lasted 406 years with 24 generations, and it is regarded as one of the greatest dynasties in Chinese History. The ethnic majority of Chinese still call themselves as the "Han people". The Han dynasty fell into three periods: Western Han (206 B.C.- 8 A.D.), Wang Mang's Xin Dynasty (8 - 22), and Eastern Han (25 - 220).

The new empire basically remained much of the Qin administrative structure but retreated some from centralized rule by establishing vassal principalities in some areas for political purpose. Under the Han Emperors, the empire expanded into southern China, northern Vietnam and parts of Korea, westward as far as the rim of the Tarim Basin, and forged trade route called "the silk road" through Central Asia to Antioch, Baghdad, and Alexandria.

Confucian ideals of government were adopted as the canon of the Han Empire, and Confucian scholars gained conspicuous status as the core of the civil service. An imperial examination system was also initiated to select officials. China's most famous historian Sima Qian was in the Han period, whose *Historical Records* provides an elaborated chronicle of the politics, economy, culture and history of 3,000 years from the time of the legendary Xia emperor to the Western Han Dynasty.

In the Han dynasty, science and technology made remarkable achievements. Paper, the compass, and the seismograph were invented, and steel was manufactured and advances in medicine, astronomy, and cartography were also noteworthy in history.

6. Three Kingdoms (220 – 280), Jin (265 – 420), Southern and Northern Dynasty (420 – 589)

The collapse of the Han dynasty was followed by a long period of disunity and civil war. The first period was the Three Kingdoms: Wei in northern China, Shu to the west, and Wu in the east. Continuous wars among the three states developed various wise political and military thoughts and produced talented persons such as Zhuge Liang, Cao Cao, who demonstrated their special ability not only in military and political affairs but also in literature.

Jin historically fell into two periods: the Western Jin (265 – 317) with Luoyang as its capital city, and Eastern Jin (317 – 420) as Jiankang (present Nanjing) as its capital city. Jin Dynasty did not last long with a lot of confrontations and conflicts, and people surrounding the capital suffered due to the fighting and began a migration out from the center of the empire to the more peaceful frontier regions.

After Jin was destroyed, there appeared the Dynasties of the North and South, which lasted 160 years. It was an age of civil war and political disunity. The northern dynasties consisted of the Northern Wei, the Eastern Wei, the Western Wei, the Northern Qi and the Northern Zhou. The southern dynasties consisted of the Song, the Qi, the Liang and the Chen four generations.

The Dynasties of the North and South was an era of the quick and wide spread of Buddhism, the flourishing in poetry, music, calligraphy, painting with the remarkable representatives like the great calligrapher Wang Xizhi and outstanding painter Gu Kaizhi. It also enjoyed the considerable advancements in technology, for example, Zu Chongzhi (429 – 501) made unique contribution to mathematics, who introduced the approximation 355/113 to π which is correct to 7 decimal places.

7. The Sui Dynasty (581 – 618)

China was reunified by the Sui dynasty founded by emperor Sui Wendi, Yang Jiang, with the capital at Chang'an. The dynasty was short-lived, lasting for 38 years with only three emperors.

However, in this time period, the social economy underwent rapid recovery and development. Governmental power was centralized and the "Three Departments and Six Ministries" system officially instituted. Great efforts were devoted to the improvement of the national defense and the expansion of the Great Wall. The land equalization system was exercised in order to enhance agricultural productivity and reduce the gap between the rich and poor social groups. The Sui dynasty witnessed various reforms and achievements such as the construction of the engineering feats like the Grand Canal (see picture 2 - 4) from Beijing to Hangzhou and Zhaozhou Bridge. Confucianism began to regain popularity, and Buddhism was further spread and encouraged throughout the empire to reunite the people of different regions.

However, due to the crushing burden of taxes and forced labor imposed on people, the disastrous military warfare against Koguryo, and Yang Di's extravagance and corruption, peasant uprisings broke out and soon swept the whole country, which finally brought about the downfall of the dynasty.

8. The Tang Dynasty (618 – 907)

The Tang Dynasty was established by Li Yuan in 618 with its capital at Chang'an, lasting 290 years with 21 emperors. The Tang dynasty is considered to be a high point in Chinese civilization in history. The boundaries of China were extended to Siberia in the North, Korea peninsula in the east, Vietnam in the South, and west in Aral Sea in mid-Asia.

The Tang Dynasty witnessed a period of political, economic and cultural boom in China. At that time, China was so powerful and prosperous that it ranked among the most advanced countries in the world. It established friendly ties with Japan and many countries in West Asia, Europe and even Africa, which secured peace and safety on overland trade routes reaching as far as Syria and Rome, with its capital Chang'an as center of economical and cultural exchange between various countries.

During the Tang period, Buddhism flourished and gradually became localized as an important part of Chinese traditional culture. A Buddhist monk called Xuan Zang traveled from Chang'an through Gansu, Xinjiang and central Asia to India for the furtherance of Buddhist classics. The imperial examination system was perfected under Tang rule to discover and attract the best talents without social connections to serve as government officials.

The Tang period was also the golden age of literature and art, which produced the most brilliant poetry of the country. Among the hundreds of poets of the Tang Dynasty, the best known are Li Bai, Du Fu and Bai Juyi.

In the mid-8th century, the "An Lushan and Shi Siming Rebellion" brought about political disturbance and considerably weakened the power and authority of the court. Misrule, court intrigues, rebellions and peasant uprisings weakened the empire, finally put the ever powerful and mighty Tang Dynasty to an end in 907. The next half-century saw the fragmentation of China into five northern dynasties and ten southern kingdoms.

9. The Song Dynasty (960 – 1279)

The Song period was divided into two phases: Northern Song (960 – 1127) and Southern Song (1127 – 1279). With a thriving economy, radiant education and culture, the Song Dynasty was considered to be another period of prime time in Chinese history after the glorious Tang Dynasty.

The Northern Song was founded in 960 by Zhao Kuangyin in Bianliang (in current Kaifeng of Henan Province). In 1127, the Northern Song Dynasty was destroyed by the Jin Dynasty. Zhao Gou fled to Nanjing Yingtianfu (in current Shangqiu of Henan Province) and established the Southern Song Dynasty there. Later, the capital city was moved to Lin'an (in current Hangzhou). The Song Dynasty lasted 320 years with 18 emperors altogether.

The Song Dynasty had dramatic increase of population, which in some degree fomented and fueled an economic revolution in China. During this period, agriculture, handicraft industry, shipbuilding industry and commerce flourished, and science and technology made impressive advancements. The Song dynasty was notable for the development of cities for administrative purposes and for the development of trade, industry, and maritime commerce as well. There was a thrivingness in calligraphy, painting, sculpture and weaving art. Achievements in porcelain manufacture surpassed all previous dynasties, and the Song porcelain was transported through sea route to overseas countries. Gunpowder widely used for military purposes, the compass employed for navigation, and the movable type printing by Bi Sheng are huge contributions to the world civilization.

Song poetry was a newly emergent literary form extremely popular at that time with famous poets such as Liu Yong, Su Shi, Xin Qiji, Li Qingzhao. Shen Kuo, who excelled in many fields of study and statecraft, wrote *Dream Pool Essays* which covers different fields like astronomy, physics, chemistry, geology, meteorology, medical and so on, astounding the people of the world.

10. The Yuan Dynasty (1271 – 1368)

The Yuan Dynasty was established by Kublai Khan, the grandson of Genghis Khan—the Mongols leader, lasting 163 years with 11 emperors. The Yuan Dynasty gradually adopted Chinese political and cultural models. However, during the 1340s and 1350s, internal political cohesion disintegrated as growing factionalism at court, rampant corruption, and a succession of natural calamities led to rebellion and, finally, the dynasty collapsed.

Due to the renewed national unification, the economy was boosted which promoted science and culture, improved the ties between various nationalities and increased contacts and communications with foreign nations. The first records of travel by the Venetian Marco Polo accounted his trip to China, which aroused both great interest and awe of the world.

The religious culture of the Yuan Dynasty received an all-round development. The Mongolians' own religion, Buddhism as well as the traditional Chinese religion of Daoism simultaneously acquired their positions in the Yuan society. There was a remarkable cultural flowering; especially a new kind of literature form Yuan Drama was prosperous during that period. The Yuan drama was one of the outstanding Chinese literary heritages. The most influential works are Wang Shifu's *Romance of the Western Chamber*, Guan Hanqing's *Dou E Yuan*.

11. The Ming Dynasty(1368 – 1644)

The Ming Dynasty was founded by a peasant uprising leader Zhu Yuanzhang at 1368. He drove the Mongol emperor away from the capital (now Beijing), and restored Han nationality rule in China. The Ming Dynasty lasted 277 years with 16 emperors with its capital first at Nanjing and later from 1421 year at Beijing. In 1644 the Ming Dynasty was overthrown by the peasant armies under Li Zicheng.

During the Ming Dynasty, the development of agriculture and handicraft production brought an expansion to the commodity economy. From the middle of Ming times onward, capitalism began to burgeon in some handicraft industries along the coastal regions. There were enormous projects of construction including the restoration of the Grand Canal and the Great Wall and the establishment of the Forbidden City in Beijing. Overseas contacts also greatly increased with the growth of ship building industry and navigation technology. Zheng He, a famous navigator, traveled to the West in seven epic voyages from 1405 to 1433, visiting over 30 countries throughout South Pacific, Indian Ocean, Persian Gulf and distant Africa.

There was a great amount of literary achievements in the Ming Dynasty. The travel literature author Xu Xiake's *Travel Diaries* is of high scientific and literary value. The classic fictional novel *The Romance of the Three Kingdoms*, *Water Margin*, *Pilgrimage to the West*, and *The Golden Lotus* (*Jin Ping Mei*) were very well received and noticed. One of the most famous plays in Chinese history, *the Peony Pavilion*, written by the Ming playwright Tang Xianzu is still on show.

12. The Qing Dynasty(1636 – 1911)

In 1616, after reunifying all the Nuzhen tribes, Nurhachu set up "Latter Jin" and proclaimed himself emperor. In 1636, Huang Taiji, son of Nurhachu changed the regime title into "Qing", thus established the Qing Dynasty. In 1644, the Manchus seized the control of Beijing, and in October of the same year, the capital was moved to Beijing. The Qing Dynasty lasted 276 years with 11 emperors.

The Qing Dynasty reached its peak during the reigns of emperors Kang Xi, Yong Zheng and Qian Long, which is known as the *Kang Qian Sheng Shi*. Its territory was extensive; economy and commerce developed; literature and arts flowered and culture of various forms thrived. However, due to the isolation policy and corruption, the late years of the Qing Dynasty began to decline with intensified social conflicts and continuous uprisings. In 1840, when the Opium War broke out, the Qing court was confronted with crisis at home and abroad. In the end, the revolution of 1911 led by Sun Yat-sen broke out and overthrew the Qing Dynasty.

Before Daoguang age, the Qing enjoyed great culture achievements with the eminent theoreticians and thinkers like Wang Fuzhi, Gu Yanwu, and the important history critics Huang Zongxi etc. The Qing promoted the collection of knowledge and writing of China, and the most famous collection that tried to summarize all existent writings that had ever been published was *The Imperial Collection of Four*, the largest collection of books in Chinese history and also probably the most ambitious editorial enterprise in the history of the world. The most conspicuous accomplishments in the Qing were the creations of novels like Cao Xueqin's *A Dream of Red Mansions*, Wu Jingzi's *The Scholars*. Other literary forms were also very well received, such as the short story collection *Strange Tales of the Make-Do studio* by Pu Songling, the theatre plays *The Hall of Everlasting Life* by Hong Sheng and *The Peach Blossom Fan* by Kong Shangren.

13. The Opium Wars (1840 - 1842, 1856 - 1860)

The Opium Wars or Sino-British Opium War, lasting from 1840 to 1842 and 1856 to 1860 respectively, was a turning point for China to be reduced into a semi-colonial and semi-feudalist country.

The First Opium War started in 1840 when British smuggled opium from British India into China and the Qing government exerted its efforts to enforce the drug laws. In March 1839, the Emperor appointed Lin Zexu as the governor of Canton with the goal of reducing and eliminating the Opium trade. He enforced the imperial demand that there be a permanent halt to drug shipments into China, and then imposed a trade embargo on the British. He arrested about 1,700 opium dealers, and destroyed about 2.6 million pounds of opium by dissolving it with water, salt and lime and dumping it into the ocean, burning it in public. British government started war of invasion by first seizing Hong Kong and then sent a large British Indian army to take Canton, occupied Dinghai, Zhenghai, Ningbo and Shanghai, and sailed up the Yangtze River and reached Jiangning (Nanjing) on August 5, 1842. The Qing authorities sued for peace, which concluded with the Treaty of Nanjing. In the treaty, China was forced to pay an indemnity to Britain, and agreed to open five ports, Guangzhou, Fuzhou, Xiamen, Ningbo and Shanghai, for trade, and ceded Hong Kong to Queen Victoria.

The Second Opium War broke out in 1856 when the Qing court rejected the unreasonable demands from Britain, France, Russia and the USA, who formed an alliance and conspired the invasion. Taking the advantage of Arrow Incident, the British attacked Guangzhou. The alliance cruised north to capture the Taku Forts and soon reached Tianjin. The Qing government succumbed again with humiliating Treaty of Tianjin, which opened more ports to Western trade. In Feburary 1860, a larger Anglo-French force (11,000 British, 6,700 French) with 173 ships sailed from Hong Kong, and soon captured the port cities of Yantai and Dalian. After taking Tianjin, the Anglo-French forces entered Beijing on October 13 and began looting and burning the Old Summer Palace (Yuanmingyuan). On October 24 and 25, the Qing Court surrendered to the alliance, and the Treaty of Tianjin was finally ratified and the Treaty of Peking was signed, bringing the Second Opium War to an end. The Chinese had to pay 8 million taels to Britain and France. Britain acquired Kowloon, and Tianjin was opened as a trade port. The opium trade was legalized and Christians were granted full civil rights.

The Qing Dynasty succumbed to the west invaders in both wars, and humiliatingly signed the unequal treaties, which brought about tragic consequences for the development of China. Many Chinese were infuriated and fought bravely in various forms resulting in the Taiping Uprising (1850 - 1864), the Boxer Movement (1899 - 1901), and finally the downfall of the Qing Dynasty in 1911.

14. Republic of China (1912 - 1949)

Guided by the Three Principles of the People, "nationalism, democracy, and people's livelihood", Dr. Sun Yat-sen (1866 - 1925) led people to overthrow the Qing Dynasty through the renowned 1911 Revolution and gave birth to the Republic of China, ending the feudal monarchic rule in China which lasted for more than 2,000 years.

In 1919 the May 4th Movement broke out which was an anti-imperialism and feudalism movement. This brought about a drastic change in society that fueled the birth of the Communist Party of China which was founded in 1921. From July 1937 to August 1945 were the periods of Chinese people fighting bravely against the Japanese aggressors. The War of Resistance against Japan was a turning point in modern Chinese history, for it ended the divided situation since the Opium War of 1840 and greatly enhanced the Chinese people's national spirit to get united and protect their state sovereignty.

15. Emergence of New China (1949)

On October 1, 1949, the People's Republic of China was officially established with the famous declaration of Chairman Mao Zedong on the Tian'anmen Square "the Chinese people have ever since stood up". Beijing is the capital of new China and Chinese people entered a new modern age.

Word Bank

bronze implement	青铜器
excavations	发掘，出土文物
archaeologists	考古学家
diviner	占卜者，占卦的人
the terra cotta armies and horses	兵马俑
the Confucians	儒家
dethronement	废除
barbarian invasion	外夷入侵
Antioch	安提阿(古叙利亚首都，现土耳其南部城市)
Alexandria	亚历山大城，埃及北部的城市，位于尼罗河三角洲西端的地中海沿岸
seismograph	地震仪，测震仪
the vassal principalities	诸侯国
calligrapher	书法家
Aral Sea	咸海，旧译阿拉海
Kublai Khan	忽必烈
Genghis Khan	成吉思汗
Nurhachu	努尔哈赤
the Opium War	鸦片战争
Arrow Incident	"亚罗号事件"，是英国政府蓄意挑起侵华战争的借口，导致第二次鸦片战争爆发
Taku Forts	大沽炮台
Taels	银两，过去在中国使用的一种货币单位
Kowloon	九龙
the Taiping Uprising	太平军起义
the Boxer Movement	义和团运动
state sovereignty	国家主权

参考译文

中国是个历史悠久的文明古国，其历史可以追溯到公元前4000年。中国文明始于传说中以黄帝和炎帝为首的两个部落，经过几个世纪，到夏朝两个部落逐渐融为一体。因而，中国人往往称自己为"炎黄子孙"，或者"华夏民族"或"华人"。他们在黄河流域定居建国，并认为是在世界中部，故称为"中国"。

中国历史一般从夏朝开始讲述，自公元前21世纪始，历经无数朝代，直到1912年孙中山宣誓就任中华民国临时大总统。

1. 夏朝(公元前2070年—公元前1600年)

夏朝是中国历史上第一个王朝。传说大禹死后，其子被推为王，建立了夏朝，开了王位世袭制的先河。夏共历14代17王。考古学家发掘的遗址、青铜器和墓葬为夏朝文明提供了证明。

夏朝的经济活动以农业为主，在尧、舜、禹时代，农业和畜牧业发展很快，人们已掌握季节变化，并且根据四季安排农活。统治者用一些烦琐的礼节来巩固他们的统治地位。

2. 商朝（公元前1600年—公元前1046年）

商朝共历17代31王，疆土范围控制在中国中部，包括今天的河南、湖北、山东、安徽、山西、河北等地。商朝文明建立在农业、狩猎和畜牧业之上。商朝战乱不断，都城也多次迁徙。

商朝的青铜器制造业有很大的发展，其青铜器文化誉满天下。出土的商朝青铜兵器、车马器和刻有铭文的礼器充分展现了那一时期精湛的青铜制造技术。

商朝人刻写在龟甲或兽骨上的文字被称为“甲骨文”，中国有文字可考的历史从商朝开始。（见图2-1）

商朝统治者宗教和军事并用。他们常用牲畜祭祀，通过用龟甲、兽骨上的裂纹来占卜吉凶。死后陪葬品有礼器、兵器、玉和活人。有时会有上百名奴隶被迫为死去的统治者陪葬，有的死前被砍头，有的则被残忍地活活扔进坟墓陪葬。

3. 周朝（公元前1046年—公元前256年）

周朝是中国历史上最长的朝代，共历时800多年传37王。周朝分为西周和东周，东周又分为春秋和战国两个时期。

周文王和周武王是周朝的奠基人，他们以德、仁、义治理国家，故被儒家尊为理想的统治者。周朝从奴隶制转向封建制，是中国历史的一个转折点。周朝期间，疆土扩大，经济繁荣，文化兴旺。

周朝时期，儒家和道家思想兴起，中国哲学思想得以发展。儒家思想的创始人孔子和道教创始人老子以及其他的哲学家和思想家，如：孟子、墨子、庄子、韩非子、荀子等，对中国文化的影响极其深远。

春秋和战国时代以“诸子百家”的思想文化繁荣而著称。在这一时期，诗人们用诗歌来表达他们的观点和情感，许多诗歌被收存在《诗经》中。《诗经》是中国历史上第一部重要的文学作品。

源于周代的“天子”理念和“天命”思想当时较为普遍。人们认为皇帝的统治权力是神授的，如被废除或推翻是因为统治者有违天命。“上天”通过地震、洪水、瘟疫等自然灾害或者通过被统治者的造反来表达对恶君的不满。

4. 秦朝（公元前221年—公元前206年）

秦始皇（见图2-2）建立了中国历史上第一个中央集权和多民族统一的封建王朝，成为统一中国后的第一位皇帝。虽然秦朝历史短暂，但是标志着2 000多年文化相对统一、以皇帝为统治者的中央集权政权历史的开始。

秦始皇推行一系列巩固统一、加强中央集权的政策措施。他统一文字，方便人们沟通。他还统一了度量和货币单位，实施牢固的郡县制。在此后的2 000年里，封建君主们基本按照秦朝时奠定的封建政权结构进行统治。

秦始皇是中国历史上一个划时代的皇帝。他统一中国，建立中央集权，为世人称道。但是，他因苛刑暴政而被唾骂批判。在他统治期间，实施了一系列公共项目，如全国修路、挖渠灌田、修筑万里长城以抵御外夷的入侵。另一方面，他残杀了400个政敌，焚书坑儒；百姓劳役赋税繁重，大量劳力被强征去修建陵墓。在他的陵墓处发现了大量用来陪葬的陶制兵马俑（见图2-3）。

5. 汉朝（公元前206年—公元220年）

公元前206年，刘邦灭秦，称帝，国号汉，建都长安。汉代共历24帝406年，是中国历史上强大的封建王朝之一。中国大部分人仍然自称为“汉人”。汉朝可以分为西汉(公元前 206 年—公元 8 年)、王莽新政(8 年—22 年)和东汉(25 年—220 年)三个时期。

汉朝基本沿用了秦朝大部分的政权管理制度,但是出于政治目的,建立了一些诸侯国。汉朝疆土扩至中国南疆、越南北部和朝鲜半岛部分地区,西至塔里木盆地,并且打通了称为“丝绸之路”的商道。该商道穿越中亚,抵达安提阿(古叙利亚首都,现土耳其南部城市)、巴格达和埃及的亚历山大城。

儒家的治国思想在汉朝占主导地位,儒家学者在朝廷上地位显著,而朝廷官员选拔则通过新建立的考试制度来实行。汉代著名史学家司马迁所著的《史记》详细地记录了从夏朝到西汉这 3 000 年间的政治、经济、文化和历史变迁。

汉朝科技发展辉煌,发明了纸、指南针和地动仪。冶炼技术得以发展,医学、天文学和绘图在历史上都有重要地位。

6. 三国(220 年—280 年)、晋(265 年—420 年)、南北朝(420 年—589 年)

汉朝崩溃后中国出现长时间的分裂和割据纷争。三国形成于公元 220 年,北魏、西蜀、东吴三足鼎立。不断的战争造就了一批优秀的军事人才和杰出精英,如诸葛亮、曹操等,他们不仅在政治和军事方面展现出过人的才能,而且在文学上也有突出的才华。

晋分为两个时期:西晋(265 年—317 年),建都洛阳;东晋(317 年—420 年),建都建康(现南京)。晋朝虽然时间不长,但是战争冲突不断,人民饱受战乱之苦,纷纷外迁。

自公元 420 年东晋灭亡之后,中国历史上形成南北对峙的南北朝时期,历经 169 年。南北朝时期内战纷乱,政权更迭。北朝历经北魏、东魏、西魏、北齐、北周五个朝代;南朝历经宋、齐、梁、陈四个朝代。

南北朝时期佛教迅速传播发展,诗歌、音乐、书法、绘画繁荣兴旺,杰出代表人物有书法家王羲之、画家顾恺之等。这个时期的科技也大有进步,祖冲之(429 年—501 年)在数学上成就巨大,他是世界上第一个把圆周率的准确数值算到小数点后 7 位数字的人。

7. 隋朝(581 年—618 年)

隋文帝杨坚建立隋朝,重新统一全国,建都长安。隋朝持续时间较短,共历 3 帝 38 年。

隋朝虽短,但是社会经济恢复和发展迅速。隋朝实行中央集权,建立三省六部制。甲兵强锐,扩建长城,实行均田制来提高农业生产力,缩小贫富差距。隋朝改革发展成就较大,修成京杭大运河(见图 2-4),建造赵州桥。儒家思想重被重用,佛教继续得到传播和鼓励,以此来团结各族人民。

不幸的是,沉重的徭役和兵役、对高句丽发动的灾难性战争、隋炀帝的奢靡腐败等使农民爆发起义,隋政权因此土崩瓦解。

8. 唐朝(618 年—907 年)

公元 618 年,李渊称帝,国号唐,建都长安,共历 21 帝 290 年。唐朝是历史上中国文明最兴盛的时期,疆土北至西伯利亚,东至朝鲜半岛,南至现今的越南,西达中亚咸海。

唐朝时期政治、经济、文化等各方面都繁荣发展,居于当时世界领先地位。唐朝与日本和西亚许多国家以及欧洲甚至非洲国家建立了友好的外交关系,保障了远达叙利亚和罗马的陆上商路安全。首都长安成为世界各国经济文化交流的中心。

唐朝期间,佛教兴旺并且逐渐本土化,成为中国传统文化的一个重要部分。一位名叫玄奘的和尚从长安出发,穿过甘肃、新疆和中亚地区来到印度学习佛教经典。科举考试制度进一步完善，挖掘、吸纳没有社会背景的优秀人才到朝廷做官。

唐朝也是文学艺术发展的黄金时期，诗歌艺术灿烂辉煌，产生了像李白、杜甫、白居易这样的伟大诗人。

公元 8 世纪中叶的“安史之乱”使唐朝政治混乱，朝廷权力和威信大大削弱。暴政、朝廷阴谋、叛乱和农民起义使唐朝日渐衰弱，最终使强大辉煌的唐朝在公元 907 年结束了统治。在其后半个世纪里，中国进入“五代十国”时期。

9. 宋朝(960 年—1279 年)

宋朝可分为北宋(960 年—1127 年)与南宋(1127 年—1279 年)，合称两宋。宋朝是继唐朝后中国历史上经济与文化教育繁荣的又一黄金时期。

公元 960 年赵匡胤称帝，国号宋，建都汴梁(今河南开封)，史称北宋。公元 1127 年金兵攻入开封，北宋亡。赵构逃到南京应天府(现河南商丘)称帝，后迁都至临安(今杭州)，史称南宋。宋朝共历 18 帝 320 年。

宋朝时期，中国人口数量急剧增加，一定程度上推动了中国经济的革命性发展。在这一时期，农业、手工业、造船业和商业繁荣，科技有了显著的发展。宋代城市发展令人瞩目，这不仅是为了方便行政管理，而且是为了商业、工业和海上贸易的更好发展。书法、绘画、雕塑和编织在宋代均有繁荣发展。宋瓷成就超越以往，所产瓷器通过海上商贸远销海外各国。火药用于战争、指南针用于航海、毕昇发明活字印刷术，这些都是宋朝对世界文明的巨大贡献。

宋词作为一种新的文学形式在当时非常流行，出现了柳永、苏轼、辛弃疾、李清照等著名词人。沈括是宋代学术和政治方面都非常杰出的优秀人才，他的《梦溪笔谈》涵盖诸多领域，令全世界惊叹不已。

10. 元朝 (1271 年—1368 年)

元朝由蒙古族领袖成吉思汗的孙子忽必烈建立，共历 11 帝 163 年。元朝逐步采纳汉式政治文化模式。1340 年到 1350 年期间，蒙古政治势力联盟瓦解，朝廷派系活动剧增，腐败奢靡，加之一连串自然灾害，最终导致了农民起义，由此推翻了元朝。

由于元朝统一了国家，经济得到发展，促进了科学文化进步，改善了各民族间的关系，增加了与不同国家的接触交往。第一本记录威尼斯旅行家马可·波罗中国之旅的书籍引起了世人的兴趣和惊叹。

元代多种宗教文化发展兴盛。蒙古人信奉的宗教、佛教和中国传统的道教同时得到发展。文化昌盛，特别是元剧灿烂辉煌，最有影响力的是王实甫的《西厢记》和关汉卿的《窦娥冤》。

11. 明朝 (1368 年—1644 年)

公元 1368 年，农民起义领袖朱元璋称帝，国号明。他把蒙古皇帝赶出首都大都(现北京)，恢复汉人政权。明朝共历 16 帝 277 年。初建都南京，1421 年迁都至北京。1644 年明朝政权被农民起义领袖李自成推翻。

明朝时期，农业和手工业产品的发展带动了商品经济的发展。明朝中叶，资本主义在一些沿海地区的手工产业中萌芽。明朝进行了一些包括修建大运河和长城以及建造紫禁城在内的浩大工程。同时，海外联系日益增加，造船业发达，航海技术进步。著名航海家郑和在 1405 年到 1433 年期间七下西洋，穿越南太平洋、印度洋、波斯湾，远及非洲，造访了 30 多个国家。

明朝文学成就显著，徐霞客的《徐霞客游记》具有很高的科学和文学价值。古典小说《三国演义》《水浒传》《西游记》《金瓶梅》广受欢迎和关注。著名戏剧《牡丹亭》由汤显祖创作，流传至今。

12. 清朝（1636 年—1911 年）

公元 1616 年，努尔哈赤统一女真部落，建立后金政权，自封为汗。1636 年，努尔哈赤之子皇太极改国号为清，建立清朝。1644 年，清军占领北京，同年十月迁都北京。清朝共历 11 帝 276 年。

清朝在康熙、雍正和乾隆统治期间达到顶峰，称为“康乾盛世”。那时，疆土广阔，商业经济发达，文学艺术繁荣，各种文化兴盛。但是，由于闭关自守政策和腐败，社会矛盾加剧，起义不断，清朝后期逐渐走向衰亡。1840 年鸦片战争爆发后，清政府面临国内外危机。最终孙中山领导的辛亥革命推翻了清朝统治。

清朝在道光以前的文化成就巨大，出现了杰出的思想家王夫之、顾炎武及史学家黄宗羲等。当时清朝重视知识和作品的收集，出现了中国历史上乃至世界上堪称规模最大的官修大型丛书《四库全书》，力图囊括古代所有书籍。清朝的小说创作成就最大，有曹雪芹的《红楼梦》、吴敬梓的《儒林外史》等。其他形式的文学作品也成就非凡，短篇小说集有蒲松龄的《聊斋志异》，戏剧作品有洪昇的《长生殿》和孔尚任的《桃花扇》。

13. 鸦片战争(1840 年—1842 年，1856 年—1860 年)

鸦片战争是中国由封建社会变为半殖民地半封建社会的转折点。

第一次鸦片战争始于 1840 年，当时英国从英属印度走私大量鸦片到中国，清政府则严禁鸦片进入中国。1839 年 3 月，清朝钦差大臣林则徐到达广州，目的是减少、最终消除鸦片贸易。他厉行朝廷永久禁止鸦片进入中国的命令，逮捕了 1 700 个不法烟商，通过在鸦片中注水、盐和石灰以及把鸦片抛入大海或当众焚烧等方法销毁了鸦片约 260 万磅。英国侵略中国的战争从占领香港开始，然后英政府派兵占领广州，攻陷定海、镇海、宁波和上海，沿长江西进，于 1842 年 8 月 5 日到达江宁(南京)。清政府被迫签订了《南京条约》，赔款给英国，开放广州、福州、厦门、宁波和上海五个通商口岸城市，并把香港割让给了英国。

1856 年，当清政府拒绝英、法、俄、美的无理要求后，第二次鸦片战争在联军的阴谋下爆发。英国利用中国走私船“亚罗号”事件攻占广州。后英、法、俄、美四国联军攻下大沽炮台，溯河而上到达天津。清政府再一次向外国侵略者屈服，签订了可耻的《天津条约》，开放更多的通商口岸。1860 年 2 月，英法联军(英军人数为 11 000，法军人数为 6 700)携 173 艘舰船驶离香港，很快占领了大连和烟台这两座港口城市。英、法联军攻陷天津后，10 月 13 日攻占北京，占领圆明园。在肆意抢劫破坏之后，又放火焚烧了圆明园。10 月 24 日、25 日，清朝廷向英、法投降，交换《天津条约》批准书，并签订《北京条约》，第二次鸦片战争至此结束。《北京条约》的规定包括：对英、法赔款增加到 800 万两白银，把九龙割让给英国，开天津为商埠，鸦片贸易合法化，天主教徒获得公民权等。

清政府在两次鸦片战争中都向西方侵略者屈服，签订了可耻的不平等条约，对中国发展产生了极为严重的后果。中国人民义愤填膺，英勇奋战，引发了太平军起义(1850 年—1864 年)和义和团运动(1899 年—1901 年)等，最终清朝于 1911 年走向灭亡。

14. 中华民国(1912 年—1949 年)

1911 年，在民族、民权、民主的“三民主义”思想指引下，孙中山通过辛亥革命，领导人民推翻了清朝政府。中华民国诞生，结束了中国长达 2 000 多年的封建统治。

1919 年，反帝国主义和反封建的五四运动爆发，社会变革剧烈，中国共产党于 1921 年成立。1937 年 7 月到 1945 年 8 月，中国人民与日本侵略者进行了英勇的斗争。抗日战争是中国现代史的又一个转折点，它结束了1840年鸦片战争以来的纷争局面，中国人民的民族精神得到发扬，大家团结一致，同仇敌忾，共同捍卫国家的主权。

15. 新中国诞生(1949年)

1949年10月1日，毛泽东主席在天安门城楼上宣布“中国人民站起来了”，中华人民共和国正式成立。北京是新中国的首都，中国人民进入了一个新的时代。

Exercises

Section A　Thought-provoking questions

1. Why do Chinese usually call themselves “the descendants of Yan and Huang” or “Hua Xia People”?
2. What is the significance and contribution of the Qin Dynasty?
3. What can we learn from the Opium Wars?
4. What is the purpose for us to get well acquainted with Chinese history?

Section B

1. Translate the following terms into Chinese

(1) the system of hereditary dynastic rule
(2) Hundred Schools of Thought
(3) bronze fittings for chariots and harnesses
(4) the mandate of heaven
(5) Three Departments and Six Ministries System
(6) The land equalization system
(7) the An Lushan & Shi Siming Rebellion
(8) the Three Principles of the People: nationalism, democracy, and people's livelihood
(9) the 1911 Revolution
(10) the Republic of China

2. Translate the following works into Chinese

(1) *The Book of Poetry*
(2) *Historical Records*
(3) *Dream Pool Essays*
(4) *Romance of the Western Chamber*
(5) *Travel Diaries*
(6) *The Romance of the Three Kingdoms*
(7) *Water Margin*
(8) *Pilgrimage to the West*
(9) *The Golden Lotus*

(10) *The Peony Pavilion*

(11) *A Dream of Red Mansion*

(11) *The Scholars*

(13) *Strange Tales of the Make-Do studio*

(14) *The Hall of Everlasting Life*

(15) *The Peach Blossom Fan*

※ **You cannot rule men nor serve heaven unless you have laid up a store. This "laying up a store" means quickly absorbing. And "quickly absorbing" means doubling one's garnered "power". Double your garnered power and it acquires a strength that nothing can overcome.**

From Laozi: *Dao De Jing*

(治人事天,莫若啬。夫唯啬,是谓早服;早服谓之重积德;重积德则无不克。)

——老子·《道德经》

※ **Do not worship the ancient ways nor be entrenched in your opinions. Adjust yourself as the times and prevailing custom change.**

From Guang Zhong: *Guangzi*

(不慕古,不留今,与时变,与俗化。)

——管仲·《管子》

Chapter 3

Ancient Chinese Philosophy and Religion

中国古代哲学和宗教

Chinese tradition, culture, religion and historical development are greatly influenced by the philosophy of Confucianism, Daoism, two great indigenous philosophical traditions of China, and Buddhism. They guide Chinese in both governing and people's behaviors, and have formed an important part of Chinese traditional values. Chinese philosophy is closely connected with the religion in China. A sound knowledge of Chinese philosophy and the development of Chinese religion will help us to be well acquainted with all the aspects of Chinese culture.

1. Confucianism

Confucianism has influenced the Chinese for thousands of years and is deeply rooted in Chinese culture. Confucianism is an integration of intellectual, political, and religious tradition with the focus on the individual morality and ethics in daily life and the proper exercise of political power.

1) Confucius Thought

Confucius (551 B.C.-479 B.C.) (see picture 3-1), founder of Confucianism, was not only a great philosopher and thinker but also a distinguished statesman and educator in Chinese history. Confucius laid down a pattern of thinking followed by all the Chinese people in the world. It is believed that no matter what religion, no matter what form of government, the Chinese culture, civilizations and the way of thinking can in some way be shown to have Confucian elements or influences.

The landmark of Confucianism is *The Analects*, which was written by his disciples after his death. It consists of sayings and answers to the questions raised by his students, usually serving as an introduction to Chinese philosophy and Confucianism. *The Analects* illustrates the life of Confucius, his mission as a teacher and the main principles and concepts of his philosophy. The core of Confucius' philosophy are the concepts of *ren* (benevolence), *li* (ritual), and other concepts like *xiao* (filial piety) and *zhong* (loyalty) are also important elements of Confucius thought.

Ren is the fundamental virtue of Confucianism. Confucius defines it as "*ai ren*," that is, to love others. The Chinese character *ren* consists of "a person (人)" on the left and "*two* (二)" on the right indicating the relationship between people. *Ren* contains benevolence, sympathy, charity, humanity and kindness. Confucius often used the idea of *ren* to exhort the rulers to be benevolent to the people. He emphasizes that one should never do to others what one would not like to do. In Confucianism, *ren* is the summation of human virtues, a quality that every human should strive to achieve, and an endless aspiration for ethical perfection. Confucianism strongly advocates reforming government which should be based on the virtue of *ren* and should work for the benefit of the people, and cultivating virtue especially in government officials.

Li refers to the rules of human conduct and moral norms such as politeness, courtesy, propriety, proper etiquette and good manners ranging from speech and behavior to the performance of rituals which are usually codified and treated as an all-embracing system of social norms. *Li* is intended to regulate men's passions, cultivate their character, and form good habits. Confucius said: "A man who is not benevolent, what can he have to do with ritual?" In Confucius's thought, *li* cannot be separated from *ren* and a man without *ren* is impossible to well exercise *li*.

Xiao refers to the filial piety, which was regarded as one of the greatest of virtues in Chinese tradition, denoting the respect and obedience that the children should show to their parents. Confucius holds that *xiao* should start from the love and respect of the parents, and then extend it to the specific duties and veneration to all the elderly and the veteran people of the society. The concept of filial piety has contributed greatly to the stable construction of the family and society and has continued to exert considerable influence on present day Chinese culture.

Confucius also holds that ***zhong*** (loyalty) is a great virtue, which emphasizes the obligations and duties to the superior, to friends, family, and spouse. He asserts that cultivation of the self was a central point in a person's life, and every one should try to become a noble person, exerting virtue to the society, having loyalty to the friends and filial piety to the elderly.

2) Mencius' Thought

Mencius (372 B.C.-289 B.C.) (see picture 3-2), entitled "second sage" in China, was one of the most important philosophers in the Confucian school. His idea that human nature is innately good is one of the basic tenets of Confucianism.

According to Mencius' thought, there are four innate "sprouts" (*duan*) of the four cardinal virtues—"Compassion is the sprout of benevolence; being aware of shame is the sprout of rightness; paying deference to others is the sprout of ritual propriety; knowledge of good and evil is the sprout of wisdom."

In order to preserve and extend human's good nature, Mencius believes that man should cultivate the goodness inherent in our nature and serve humanity. The importance of internal concentration or reflection in cultivating an ethical sense is also emphasized and advocated.

3) Four Books and Five Classics

The authoritative books of Confucianism are called "Four Books and Five Classics", which refer to *The Great Learning*, *The Doctrine of the Mean*, *The Analects and The Mencius* (Four Books), *Classic of Changes*, *Classic of Poetry*, *Classic of Rites*, *Classic of History and Spring* and *Autumn Annals* (Five Classics).

These works cover widely in the fields of history, literature, philosophy, education, ethics, arts and so on. They have long been considered classic and compulsory textbooks especially in the imperial examination. They are believed to include the basic theories and teachings of self-cultivation and the way to govern the state.

The teachings of Confucius were never intended to be a religion or exercised as a religion, but its impact upon Chinese intellectual, social history and people's conduct is immeasurable and still influential.

2. Daoism

Daoism (or Taoism), like Confucianism, has made huge contributions to the Chinese philosophical thought. Daoism is based on the theory of Laozi (see picture 3-3) and Zhuang Zi as its basic doctrine. Daoism believes that behind all the material things and all the changes in the world lies one fundamental, universal principle: the Way or ***Dao***. This principle gives rise to all existence and governs everything, every change and every aspect of life. Daoism is of a conception of the universe and a conception of life, which is both naturalistic and mystical.

Laozi or Lao Tzu (570 B.C. - 490 B. C.) is the founder of Daoism and the author of *Dao De Jing* (or *Tao Te Ching*). He observed nature with great interest and scrutiny, and he believed that all things are in a constant change between opposites such as being and non-being, have and non-have, success and failure, activity and tranquility. In *Dao De Jing*, the philosophical elaborations range from the essentials of human nature to the practice of government, with the focus on the relationship between human behavior and the way or *Dao* and *De* which are two important conceptions of Daoism.

1) *Dao*

Dao means a road, the way or the method, the law, the principle people must follow. *Dao* is unchanging and permeates everything and it is everywhere in the world.

Laozi believes "*Dao nourishes everything*". *Dao* is the essence and ultimate end of all things, and it is the process of reality itself, the way things come together while they are still transforming. *Dao* is a kind of constant, universal principle that underlies all phenomena.

Dao has no fixed form and sound, and it has always existed and has no beginning of itself. People and everything in the universe should follow *Dao*, and through *Dao* everything can be achieved without effort and exertion, without rules and regulations, and without interference with nature.

2) *De*

De means virtue or quality, and it is the whole of the spontaneity or naturalness of the world derived from *Dao*.

De is the intrinsic quality of everything in the universe. It is *De* that makes a man become a real man, so *De* is the ingrain quality of human being, the summation of man's gift and talent.

Laozi held, "*Dao* produces a thing; *De* maintains it." Zhuang Zi believed "That which things get in order to live is called *De*."

The relation between *De* and *Dao* is just like that between the water in river. *De* is what an individual thing receives from *Dao*, the materialization of *Dao*.

3) *Wuwei*

Wuwei is another important tenet of Daoism. *Wuwei* means "*non-doing*", but it does not mean "doing nothing", yet it does mean "to do or act naturally", "the effortless action".

This Daoist philosophical thought involves knowing when to act and when not to act. It is the natural action just as planets revolve around the sun; they "do" this revolving, but without "doing" it; or as trees grow, they "do", but without "doing". There is no need for man interfering with the flow of reality, but it is action that should be spontaneous and effortless.

Zhuangzi turns to analogies and fables to illustrate the idea of *wuwei*, one of which is the story of a butcher called Ding who learned what it means to *wuwei* through the perfection of his craft.

On the whole, the concept of *wuwei* is a state of mind for man to gain spiritual peace and tranquility, and it is the principle towards life for man to act naturally or to do the natural things.

4) *Dao De Jing*

Dao De Jing (*Book of the Way and its Power*) is the doctrine of Daoism consisting of both prose and poetry with 81 chapters and about 5,000 words. The book is divided into two parts: the *Daojing* (Chapters 1 – 37) and the *Dejing* (Chapters 38 – 81). It begins by explaining that "the *Dao* that can be told of or illustrated is not the same as the *Dao* that cannot be told of or explained," which immediately highlights the gist point of the book, which is the significance of *Dao*.

Dao De Jing is fundamental to both the Daoist school of Chinese philosophy and Chinese religion, and it considerably influenced other schools, such as Legalism, Neo-Confucianism and Chinese Buddhism. Many Chinese artists have taken the advantage of the book as a source of inspiration for artistic creation.

With hundreds of translations into foreign languages, the influence of the *Dao De Jing* has spread extensively in Asia and even in Europe and America.

5) *Zhuangzi*

Another important classics of Daoism is *Zhuangzi* or the *Book of Master Zhuang* or *Nan Hua Jing* because Zhuang Zi was conferred with the title "Perfect Man of Nanhua" by Emperor Xuanzong of Tang Dynasty.

Zhuangzi consists of *Inner Chapters* (7 chapters), *Outer Chapters* (15 chapters), and *Miscellaneous Chapters* (11 chapters). Scholars and experts generally hold that the *Inner chapters* were written by Zhuang Zi himself and the other chapters are elaborations and explanations of Zhuang Zi's ideas partially written by Zhuang Zi's disciples or supplemented by people of later ages.

Some fables and analogies used by Zhuang Zi to illustrate his ideas have become household idioms, such as "Zhuang Zhou and the butterfly", "learn the Handan walk", "the happiness of fish", "three at dawn and four at dusk", "Butcher Ding".

Daoism as religion flourished in the Wei and Jin dynasties. The Tang Dynasty esteemed Daoism and the emperors regarded Laozi as the ancestor of the Royal Li family by revering Laozi as "Tai Shang Xuan Yuan Emperor" (Super-sovereign). Emperors in Song Dynasty, most notably Huizong, were very active in promoting Daoism. However, Daoism began to decline gradually in Qing Dynasty because the rulers gave preference to Lamaism.

Daoism has been influential in all aspects of Chinese culture, for example, Chinese alchemy, astrology, fengshui culture, witchcraft, some martial arts and styles of qigong, traditional medicine, even cuisine are closely related with Daoism.

3. Buddhism

Chinese Buddhism with a history of about 2,000 years has been playing an important role in forming the outlook of the Chinese people in terms of philosophy, politics, aesthetics, literature, and so on.

1) Development of Buddhism

Buddhism was first introduced to China from India in the early part of the Eastern Han Dynasty and it flourished after the 4th century. Chinese Buddhism integrated the ideas of Confucianism, Daoism and other indigenous philosophical systems, and what was initially a foreign religion came to be a significant part of Chinese civilization with its unique characteristics.

Buddhism in many ways is in conflict with Chinese cultural tradition. For example, Chinese people usually consider the continuation of the generation line to be of tremendous importance, but Buddhism advocates celibacy. Confucianism holds that the human body is the sacred inheritance from one's parents and so it should be protected from being impaired or injured, but Buddhism adheres to asceticism and self-sacrifice.

With the development of Daoism in China, Buddhism was gradually accepted by people because they share the naturalistic and nihilistic philosophical thought. In the Tang Dynasty, Buddhism thrived with the support of the emperors. Xuan Zang began his pilgrimage journey to India. After studying in India for 20 years, Xuan Zang returned with volumes of precious Buddhist scriptures, and he, together with other monks and scholars, dedicated all the time and energy to translating the scriptures into Chinese. Xuan Zang made unique contributions to Chinese Buddhism and greatly enriched Chinese culture.

The two main branches of Buddhism are Theravada and Mahayana, which include Tibetan and Zen Buddhism. Mahayana has been active in Japan, Korea, Nepal, Mongolia, and China, which teaches social concern and universal salvation. Theravada has been the predominant religion of continental Southeast Asia such as Thailand, Myanmar, Cambodia, Laos and Sri Lanka. It is also practiced by some ethnic groups of southwest China. Theravada promotes the concept of self-cultivation and gaining insight from the aspirant's experience, critical investigation, and reasoning instead of by blind faith.

2) The Four Noble Truths

Buddhism held that the world permeates bitterness and suffering and everything is unstable. The Four Noble Truths is one of the basic teachings:

(1) The condition of all existence is suffering;

(2) Suffering is caused by sin;

(3) Sin can be exterminated;

(4) Suffering can be alleviated by the right path of understanding, meditation and endeavour. The Buddhist ideas of transmigration and retribution are also widely accepted.

3) The Concept of Emptiness

The concept of "Emptiness" is another key concept in Buddhism (The Sanskrit word is *Sunya*). Emptiness is not nothing, but it is the condition of existence of everything. It permeates all phenomena, making their evolution possible.

Emptiness is an abstract idea representing impermanence, instability, transience and relativity in the nature of all existence. According to Buddhism, nothing is permanent and everything is dependent on causes and conditions. Whenever the causes and conditions that produce or sustain a phenomenon are removed, that phenomenon will cease to exist.

Furthermore,In the *Avatamsaka Sutra* we can read this gatha: "All things are birthless. All things have no extinction. You are also like that. If you know how to look at things this way, you can see and touch all Buddhas at any time."

4) Buddha, Amitabha and Guan Yin Bodhisattva

According to *the Lotus Sutra*, everyone has the Buddhata, and the Buddha is full of compassion, and that is why Shakyamuni Buddha always tries to help.

Amitabha is the Sanskrit word, and literally it means boundless light and boundless life. According to Buddhism, people recite or call upon his name by the time of dying will be born in the Land of Ultimate Bliss with the reception by Amitabha.

Bodhisattva, who is called Guan Shi Yin or Guan Yin Bodhisattva, is very popular in China. Originally represented as a male, the images are now generally those of a female figure. It is believed that she has the greatest compassion and mercy and rescues all beings by hearing their voices of suffering and cries for help. Guan Yin can transform into many different shapes in order to cross over to the beings.

5) Eight Precepts, Eight Sufferings, the Winds of the Eight Directions and Eight Right Ways

The Buddhist Eight Precepts, Eight Sufferings, the Winds of the Eight Directions, Eight Right Ways are very important in the practice of Buddhism.

The Buddhist *Eight Precepts* are:

(1) No killing;
(2) No stealing;
(3) No sexual misconduct;
(4) No lying;
(5) No alcoholic drink;
(6) No cosmetic, no personal adornments;
(7) No sleeping on fine beds;
(8) No eating after noon.

According to Buddhism, there are *Eight Sufferings* for human to be tortured while living. They are:

(1) Suffering of birth;
(2) Suffering of old age;
(3) Suffering of sickness;
(4) Suffering of death;
(5) Suffering of being apart from the loved ones;
(6) Suffering of being together with the despised ones;
(7) Suffering of not getting what one wants;
(8) Suffering of the flourishing of the five skandhas.

Most people are usually moved by *the Winds of the Eight Directions*. They are:

(1) Praise;

(2) Ridicule;

(3) Suffering;

(4) Happiness;

(5) Benefit;

(6) Destruction;

(7) Gain;

(8) Loss.

There are *Eight Right Ways* leading to Nirvana:

(1) Right view;

(2) Right thought;

(3) Right speech;

(4) Right action;

(5) Right livelihood;

(6) Right effort;

(7) Right remembrance;

(8) Right concentration.

Buddhism has been playing the mainstream role in Chinese religious life and it has exerted tremendous influence on Chinese culture together with its process of localization. It provides a new approach to the development of Chinese philosophy, and the translation of Buddhist scriptures has added something unique to the classic Chinese literature, commencing the field of translation study. The Buddhist influence on the Chinese painting, architecture and even dancing is also of considerable value.

Word Bank

Confucianism	儒教,儒家	*Classic of Changes*	《周易》
Daoism, Taoism	道教	*Classic of Poetry*	《诗经》
The Analects	《论语》	*Classic of Rites*	《礼记》
benevolence	仁爱,慈善	*Classic of History*	《尚书》
filial piety	孝,孝顺	*Spring* and *Autumn Annals*	《春秋》
rituals	礼节,仪式	*Dao De Jing*, *Tao Te Ching*	《道德经》
Four Books and Five Classics	四书五经	*Perfect Man of Nanhua*	南华真人
The Great Learning	《大学》	household idioms	家喻户晓的成语
The Doctrine of the Mean	《中庸》	Zhuang Zhou and the butterfly	庄周梦蝶

learn the Handan walk	邯郸学步
three at dawn and four at dusk	朝三暮四
Butcher Ding	庖丁
Lamaism	喇嘛教
alchemy	炼丹术
astrology	占星术
fengshui culture	风水文化
witchcraft	巫术
martial arts	武术
celibacy	独身,禁欲
asceticism	禁欲主义,苦行
Theravada	小乘佛教
Mahayana	大乘佛教
transmigration	轮回
retribution	报应
Sanskrit	梵语
gatha	偈言,偈语,偈颂(佛经中的唱颂词)
Avatamsaka Sutra	《华严经》
the Lotus Sutra	《法华经》
Shakyamuni Buddha	释迦牟尼佛
Amitabha	〈梵〉[佛]阿弥陀佛
Bodhisattva	菩萨,观世音菩萨
Eight Precepts	八戒
Land of Ultimate Bliss	极乐世界

参考译文

中国的传统文化和历史发展都深受中国本土传统哲学儒家思想和道家思想以及外来的、后又融入本土的佛家思想的影响。中国的统治和人们的行为准则都受其指导,成为中国传统价值观的重要部分。中国的哲学思想与中国的宗教也有着密不可分的联系。对中国哲学和宗教发展的了解有助于深入了解中国文化的方方面面。

1. 儒家

儒家思想影响中国几千年,在中国文化中根深蒂固。儒家思想是一种思想、政治和宗教传统的结合,其重点在于人们日常生活中的个人道德规范和政治权利的恰当行使。

1) 孔子思想

孔子(公元前551年—公元前479年)(见图5-1)是中国伟大的思想家、哲学家和儒家学派创始人,他还是中国历史上杰出的政治家和教育家。他的学说和哲学思想影响了全世界的华人。不管他们信仰哪种宗教,不管哪个朝代,中国文化和中国人的思维中都能体现儒家思想的影响。

儒家思想的重要标志《论语》,由孔子的弟子及再传弟子编纂而成,记录孔子及其弟子的言行,往往作为了解中国哲学思想和儒家学说的入门。《论语》记录了孔子的生活,诠释了其教育使命和哲学理念的基本思想。孔子哲学思想的核心理念是"仁""礼""孝""忠"等。

"仁"是儒家的基本道德观。孔子认为"仁"就是爱别人。中国字"仁"就是"人"加上"二",表明了人与人之间的关系。"仁"涵盖了仁爱、同情、慈善、人性和善良。孔子常常用"仁"来告诫统治者对人民要行善。他认为:"己所不欲勿施于人。"在儒家思想中,"仁"是人性的集合,是每个人都应该努力具备的品质,是不断追求道德完美的渴望。儒家强烈提倡仁政,为人民谋利,官员要有德行。

"礼"指的是人们的行为准则和道德规范,如:礼貌、谦恭、得体、恰当和良好的礼节,包括从说话、举止行为到仪式中的表现。这些"礼"的要求往往是规定的,人们把它作为社会和生活的准则来对待。"礼"意在调控情绪、修养性格、形成良好习惯。孔子说:"人而不仁,如礼何?""礼"在孔子的思想体系中是同"仁"分不开的,一个不仁的人也不可能是一个很好施礼的人。

"孝"指的是对父母的尊敬和顺从,是中国传统美德中最重要的部分之一。孔子认为"孝"源自对父母的爱和尊敬,而后延伸及对社会上老年人的尊重和责任。"孝"的理念对家庭和社会的稳定作用很大,至今在中国社会文化中有着较大的影响。

孔子认为"忠"也是一大美德,它是对上级、朋友、家庭和配偶的一种责任和义务。他声称"修己"是人生的重要任务,每个人应该努力成为一个君子,对社会道德,对朋友忠诚,对长者孝顺。儒家思想对中国思想、社会历史和人们操行的影响不可估量,至今仍有很大影响。

2) 孟子思想

被加封为"亚圣"的孟子(公元前372年—公元前289年)(见图5-2)是儒家学派中最重要的哲学家之一。他的"性善说"是儒家的重要思想基础之一。

根据孟子的学说,人性之所以是善的,是因为人生来就具有"善端":"恻隐之心,仁之端也;羞恶之心,义之端也;辞让之心,礼之端也;是非之心,智之端也。"(《孟子·公孙丑 上》)

为了维持并延伸人的"善性",孟子认为人要修身养性,为人造福。他也很注重内省的道德修养。

3) 四书五经

儒家思想的权威书籍是"四书五经"。"四书"指的是《大学》《中庸》《论语》《孟子》这四本著作;"五经"指的是《周易》《诗经》《礼记》《尚书》和《春秋》。

四书五经内容涉及面广,包括史学、文学、哲学、教育、伦理、艺术等各个方面,一直被奉为经典和必读书籍,尤其在科举考试中。人们认为其中有修身之学,有治国之道。

儒家思想从未被作为一种宗教来信奉,但它对中国的思想、文化、社会历史和人们的操行产生了不可估量的影响,至今在中国和亚洲仍影响很大。

2. 道家

与儒家思想一样,道家思想对中国哲学思想做出了巨大贡献。道家把老子和庄子的理论作为其思想学说,核心理念是"道","道生万物"。"道"是世上所有物质和变化的法则,统治世上一切的变化和生命。道家思想是宇宙论与生命论的学说,具有自然主义和神秘主义特点。

老子(公元前570年—公元前490年)(见图3-3)是道教的创始人,也是《道德经》的作者。他饶有兴趣又非常仔细地观察大自然。他认为天地万物都相反相成,如:兴旺与衰亡、有为与无为、成功与失败、喧嚣与宁静。《道德经》一书中的思想讨论涉及人性本质、统治理念等,重点强调人的行为"道"与"德"的关系。

1) 道

"道"的意思是道路、途径或方法、规律、人们必须遵守的法则。"道"是一成不变的,渗透万物,世上随处可见。

老子指出:"道生万物","道"是万物的精髓和终极,是使万物得以相生、相续、转化发展的实现性原理。"道"是一种永恒的、涵盖所有现象的宇宙准则。

"道"无形状,无声无息,无始无终,永恒不灭。人与天地万物皆应循"道"而为。循"道"行事,可轻松自在、无章无法、不扰自然而获成就。

2) 德

"德"的意思是美德或品质,是万物顺应"道"而形成的自性或本然。

"德"是万物各自的一种内在的品质。"德"使人之所以成为人,所以"德"是人的本质,是人的天赋才能的总汇。

老子认为:"道生之,德畜之。"庄子认为:"物得以生谓之德"。

"道"与"德"的关系犹如水在河中的关系。"德"是从"道"中而来的个体事物,是"道"的体现。

3) 无为

"无为"是道家思想的另一个重要原则。"无为"并非无所作为,而是指顺应自然、不妄为。

这一道家思想包含应知道何时去"为",何时不去"为"。"为"与"不为"须顺自然,犹如行星环绕太阳转,它们转但并非自觉转,或者像树的成长,是自然而然并非刻意。人不必干预自然去作为,而应顺其自然去作为。

庄子用类比法或寓言来阐明无为思想,如"庖丁解牛"的故事告诉人们,技艺精湛可达到无为境界。

总之,"无为"是一种怡然自得、平和虚静的心态,是一种能顺其自然的生活原则。

4)《道德经》

《道德经》是道家的经典,用散文和诗歌形式撰写。共 81 章,5 000 字左右。该书分为两部分:道经(第 1—37 章)和德经(第 38—81 章)。开首就指出:"道可道,非常道。"突出了本书的重点是"道"的意义。

《道德经》是中国哲学和宗教——道教学派的基础,也深刻地影响了别的学派,如法家、新儒学派和中国的佛教。许多中国艺术家从该书中获得创作灵感。

《道德经》被翻译成多种外国文字,其影响遍及亚洲、欧洲乃至美洲。

5)《庄子》

另外一部道家的重要经典书籍是《庄子》,又称为《南华经》,因为唐朝玄宗皇帝封庄子为"南华真人"。

《庄子》一书分为《内篇》(7 章)、《外篇》(15 章)和《杂篇》(11 章)。学者和专家一般认为《内篇》为庄子本人所写,而其他阐释庄子思想的篇章由庄子的门徒撰写或由后人增补。

庄子运用类比和寓言法来阐释道理的例子已成为家喻户晓的成语,如"庄周梦蝶""邯郸学步""安知鱼乐""朝三暮四""庖丁解牛"。

道教作为宗教兴盛于魏晋。唐代崇奉道教,尊祖老子,封老子为"太上玄元皇帝"。道教在宋朝仍被推崇,尤其得到宋徽宗的器重。到了清朝由于朝廷转向喇嘛教,道教逐渐衰落。

道教在中国文化各方面都有很大的影响,如中国的炼丹术、占星术、风水文化、巫术、武术,甚至气功、医药和饮食都和道教关系密切。

3. 佛教

中国的佛教已有 2 000 年的历史,对中国人世界观的形成起到很大的作用,在哲学、政治、美学和文学等方面影响颇大。

1) 佛教的发展

佛教在东汉早期传入中国,公元 4 世纪后开始兴盛。中国的汉传佛教融合了儒教、道教和其他本土哲学的思想理念,使一个外来的宗教成为具有中国特色的、中华文明中重要的一部分。

佛教在不少方面与中国传统文化有冲突。譬如:中国人一般认为传宗接代是件大事,而佛教却提倡独身禁欲;儒教认为"身体发肤,受之父母,不敢毁伤",而佛教坚持克己与节制的苦行生活。

随着道教在中国的发展,佛教也慢慢为人所接受,因为两者皆有自然主义和虚无主义的哲学思想。从唐代开始,由于得到皇家支撑,佛教发展兴盛。玄奘开始了去印度的朝圣旅行。在印度学习了 20 年后,他带回许多经卷,并与其他和尚和学者一起倾注大量时间和精力翻译经书。玄奘对中国佛教贡献独特,大大地丰富了中国文化。

佛教主要分支是小乘佛教和大乘佛教。大乘佛教流传于日本、朝鲜、尼泊尔、蒙古和中国，教导人们关心社会和普度众生。小乘佛教集中在东南亚地区，如：泰国、缅甸、柬埔寨、老挝、斯里兰卡等国家和中国西南地区的一些少数民族。小乘佛教注重个人修行和悟道，悟道则源于个人的体验、观察和分析，不是盲目的信仰。

2）“四真谛”

佛教认为世间充满了痛苦，一切事物都是无常的。“四真谛”是基本教义之一，即——

“苦”：活着就是痛苦；

“集”：苦的原因是罪孽或业；

“灭”：苦、集是可以消除的；

“道”：消业要有正确的理解和修行途径。

佛教的轮回和报应理念也广为接受。

3）“空”

“空”（梵语为 *Sunya*）是佛教的另一重要理念。“空”并非一切皆无，而是万物生存的条件。它渗透一切现象，使进化成为可能。

“空”是一种抽象的理念，代表无常、不定、稍纵即逝和大自然生物的相对性。佛教认为没有一成不变的东西，万物皆有因果，没有因果事物即不存在。

另外，在《华严经》中我们可以读到这样的偈颂：“一切法无生，亦复无有灭，若能如是解，斯人见如来。”

4）佛、“阿弥陀佛”和观世音菩萨

根据《法华经》，每个人都具有佛性，佛由慈悲所成，所以释迦牟尼佛愿意尽力帮助大众。

“阿弥陀佛”梵文的意思是“无量光”“无量寿”。根据佛教，临终前吟诵或呼叫“阿弥陀佛”的名字，阿弥陀佛会在极乐世界迎接。

观世音菩萨或观音菩萨在中国流传甚广，其原为男像，现在一般均以女像出现。人们认为她大慈大悲，听到呼唤和受难声就会去救苦救难。观音菩萨可以随机应变出种种化身，前往拯救众生的苦难。

5）八戒、八苦、八风、八正道

佛家中“八戒、八苦、八风、八正道”的理念很重要。

“八戒”是：一戒杀生，二戒偷盗，三戒淫佚，四戒妄语，五戒饮酒，六戒着香华，七戒坐卧丽床，八戒非时食。

人在世上有“八苦”，即：生苦、老苦、病苦、死苦、爱别离苦、怨憎苦、求不得苦、五阴炽盛苦（五阴即是五蕴，五阴集聚成身，如火炽燃，前七苦皆由此而生。）

人容易受“八风”影响，即：誉、讥、苦、乐、利、毁、得、失。

有“八正道”可以达到佛教最高理想境地的涅槃，即：正见（正确的见解）、正志（正确的思维）、正语（不妄语）、正业（正确的行为）、正命（正当生活）、正精进（毫不懈怠地修行）、正念（念念不忘四谛真理）、正定（专心致志地修习）。

佛教在中国人的宗教生活中起着主流作用，随着其本地化进程，对中国文化影响巨大。它为中国哲学的发展提供了一个新的途径，而佛经的翻译为中国古典文学添上了独特的一笔，并且开创了翻译研究领域。佛教对中国绘画、建筑乃至舞蹈的影响都具有很大的价值。

Exercises

Section A Thought-provoking questions

1. What exerts the most important influence on Chinese tradition and culture in terms of philosophy and religion? Why?
2. What is the core of Confucius' philosophy? What is the relationship between *ren* and *li* in Confucius concepts?
3. What is *Dao* and *De*? What is the relationship between *Dao* and *De*?
4. In what way is Buddhism in conflict with Chinese cultural tradition? Please explain with examples.
5. In what way will the knowledge of Chinese philosophy and religion help us to have a better understanding of Chinese culture?

Section B Fill in the blanks with appropriate words or phrases

1. *Four Books and Five Classics* are regarded as the authoritative books of Confucianism. *Four Books* include ________, ________, ________, and ________; *Five Classics* include ________, ________, ________, ________, and ________.
2. Daoism is based on the theory of ________ and ________ as its basic doctrine.
3. The two main branches of Buddhism are Theravada and Mahayana, which includes ________ Buddhism and ________ Buddhism.
4. The Buddhist Eight Precepts is very important which includes: ________, ________, ________, ________, ________, no cosmetic, personal adornments, no sleeping on fine beds and no eating after noon.
5. Eight Sufferings for human to be tortured while living are: suffering of birth, suffering of ________, suffering of ________, suffering of ________, suffering of ________, suffering of ________, suffering of not getting what one wants, suffering of the flourishing of the Five Skandhas.

※ **To understand others is to have knowledge; to understand oneself is to be illuminated. To conquer others needs strength; to conquer oneself is harder still to be content with what one has is to be rich.**

From Laozi: *Dao De Jing*

(知人者智，自知者明。胜人者有力，自胜者强。知足者富。)

——老子·《道德经》

※ **Man is not endowed with knowledge when he is born. Who then can avoid? Where man is confused but refuses to consult with a teacher, his perplexities will never be removed.**

From Han Yu: *The Way of Teaching*

(人非生而知之者，孰能无惑？惑而不从师，其为惑也，终不解矣。)

——韩愈·《师说》

Chapter 4

Ancient Chinese Education

中国古代教育

1. Brief Introduction

1) Beginning of Ancient Education

The historical importance of education in Chinese culture is derived from the teachings of Confucius and philosophers of the middle and late Zhou eras. Education in China has been an equalizing force from ancient times. It has become the means by which individuals from even the humblest backgrounds can rise to great heights. At the same time, it is also a powerful mechanism for implementing the ethical and social norms of Chinese society.

In the Spring and Autumn Period, private schools prevailed and many scholars of different schools of thought spread their teaching in this way. Confucius, the great educator, devoted all his life to the private school system and instructed most students. It is said that over 3,000 disciples followed him and 72 of them made outstanding achievements. Besides that, other schools such as Taoism were also taught widely and this led afterwards to "a hundred schools of thought" in the Warring States Period.

2) Development of Ancient Education

In 136 B.C. during the reign of Emperor Wudi (156 B.C.- 87 B.C.), the government introduced a system which was named "Taixue" or Great Academy. Usually the students were provided with a free diet and mainly studied the classical Confucian books. Students who were admitted to the "Taixue" were destined for careers in the civil service after they passed the internal exams and were competitively selected for various positions. Initially only fifty-five students were admitted to the Great Academy. By 8 B.C., the Academy had an enrollment of three thousand students. During the Han Dynasty provincial schools were established and the Confucian tradition of education was spread across China. In the Han Dynasty there had been no system for testing a person's ability, and the most prevalent method was merely through observation. Officials would see who was intelligent and recommend individuals to their superior. The curriculum at the Great Academy was based on the Confucian "Five Classics" and classes were taught by professors of the "Five Classics" who were known as Boshi. The basis of Chinese education did not change throughout the imperial history till the reign of the last Qing emperors.

In the Sui Dynasty, Imperial Examination as the main form of education began to be put into practice. It lasted more than 1,300 years until the last examination during the Qing Dynasty. It enjoyed a long and dominant position in the history of ancient Chinese education.

The Tang Dynasty adopted the personnel selection system and gradually refined it. The main subjects of the examinations were writing and study of classical books, which were the most popular, as well as mathematics, law, calligraphy, etc. Most of prime ministers during that feudal period were titled "Jinshi", and were good at writing. The candidates almost always came from two sources. These were students of official schools and also intelligent people undergoing the exams in their local county, who were entitled "Juren" when they achieved the necessary qualifications to take the central government examinations held each spring.

The form and content of the exams varied from one another. The one testing knowledge of the classical books followed the method of filling in blanks. Usually one page of a book was chosen and several lines would be omitted. The candidates were required to fill the missing lines. Alternatively, they might be required to explain some of the lines in the book. Therefore the need to be able to recite the work was important. While the tests for "Jinshi" were not so easy, they required a talent for literature.

Candidates who passed the highest imperial examination would have a promising future as court officials. The dragon had always been regarded as the symbol of mighty power and especially that of the rights exercised by the emperor; consequently the success of examination candidates was proudly called "stepping into the dragon's door". The most successful scholar was then granted the title of "Zhuangyuan".

In the Song Dynasty subjects raised by government had been much less than that in the Tang Dynasty, but the examination for "Jinshi" was still fashionable. Most of the prime ministers of high rank also had to pass the exam in a subject which then was regarded as an exclusive subject of prime ministers. Meanwhile, regardless of form and content, the system underwent great innovation.

Firstly, the extension of matriculation was broadened. In the former dynasties like the Tang Dynasty, each year the "Jinshi" were no more than twenty to thirty in number but in the Song Dynasty, there were as many as hundreds of people passing the exams and even those who failed the exams many times could apply for tolerance of the emperor and so serve as officials with less important positions.

Secondly, the frequency of exams was limited to a fixed once every three years. The local tests came first in autumn and in the following spring the qualifying candidates would trudge to the capital for the higher imperial examination.

Thirdly, so far as content was concerned, while the earlier examinations laid much stress on the ancient classical texts, the great reformer Wang Anshi (1021 - 1086) advocated an innovation which was much more practical. He changed the blank-filling of verses into composition about the verse, giving free reign to the ability of the candidates. However, this was opposed by other grandees and did not last for long.

Finally, to prevent the practice of favoritism, examinees' names were closely covered on their papers which were then exchanged among different local examiners. This did indeed greatly reduce the incidence of cheating.

In the Song Dynasty, few governmental schools were erected, but it was the vogue for scholars to set up numerous private educational organizations — "*Shuyuan*". The function of this kind of school was to cultivate talented people, to encourage a devotion to learning, as well as to spread culture. The four most reputed "*Shuyuan*" were named Bailudong Institute of Jiangxi, Songyang Institute and Yingtian Institute of Henan, and Yuelu Institute of Hunan. Scholars were invited to give lectures and students were provided with dormitories, desks and food while basically studying on their own. Subsequently, most of these institutes became places where students prepared for exams.

With the coming of the Ming Dynasty, the imperial examination system reached its period of full bloom. Great attention was given to the administrative procedures and the tests became more rigorous. The Ming government managed to found schools, and strengthened their function to be the only road by which people could take the exams. The provincial and metropolitan examiners tested only "eight-legged" (eight-part) essays. Candidates were required to write in a fixed style with a fixed word count — it had to be eight paragraphs, while imitating the tone of the classics. But this method neglected other forms and contents. Thus it was harmful as it stifled both creativity and imagination.

3) Decline of Ancient Education

Since the Qing Dynasty was dominated by the Manchu ethnic group, they gave their people priority over the Han people. Manchu people attending the imperial examination were not tested but required only to undertake some translation, yet the Han people were still formed a majority of the examinees. As the tight hold on affairs held by the Qing Dynasty became more and more unpopular, the education system also needed fresh ideas and input as it was a disservice to the country. A trend appeared towards the way in which the positions of court officials could be purchased and this sometimes even gave rise to unlawful pass to the degraded system.

It is interesting to note that Fan Jin, one of the characters depicted in the novel of *The Scholars* by Wu Jingzi, is quite a typical victim of the declining system. The hero Fan Jin took pains time and time again to achieve a pass in the provincial examination. Never once to give up, he was in his fifties when his efforts were finally rewarded. When he got the news that he had finally ranked on the list of successful candidates, he was in a delirium with great joy!

In contrast to western education, particularly in regard to the model of higher education in Medieval and Renaissance universities where students were encouraged to engage in disputation, traditional Chinese education consisted primarily of rote learning and memorization of the Classics. Candidates for the Imperial Examinations were required to memorize a vast amount of classical materials and were never required to demonstrate the ability to either theorize or challenge a particular premise. The purpose of the scholar class after all was: the creation of bureaucratic generalists familiar with an accepted ethical outlook and body of knowledge, not with the growth of knowledge or with academic specialization.

2. Imperial Examination System

1) The Imperial Examination System

The imperial examination system (also called Keju examination system) is commonly regarded as having started around the year 606 and was officially ended in 1905, for about 1,300 years. During this time, the exams became the central focus of a state-orchestrated system of high-stakes employment tests and test-driven education. Through these exams, Chinese emperors identified individuals who would initially serve as scholars in the imperial secretariat known as the Hanlin Academy. From these positions, the scholars might be promoted to serve as district magistrates, prefectural governors, provincial governors, national departmental ministers or even prime ministers or grand councilors. These exams were used to select individuals for high-level, high-power positions; along with all the prestige, legal privileges and advantages, power and financial rewards for the candidate and the entire extended family, and ancestry that came with such positions.

In its most common and stable form, the exams, which included Confucianism, poetry, official documents and national politics, consisted of three progressive levels: local district exam, provincial exam, and palace exam. First, a candidate took the local district exams known as the Tongshi. These exams were given once every two years. Next level was the provincial exams called Xiangshi, which was given once every three years at the provincial capital. The third set of exams took place in the national capital and was given the spring after the provincial exams. The third level consisted of two steps: The "joint" exams called Huishi, to be followed by the palace exams, Dianshi. One can take these exams as many times as desired. The system was open to all males. However, in the early years during the Sui and Tang dynasties, to be eligible to take the exams, each examinee was required to identify an official who had agreed to serve as his mentor. This requirement was removed starting from the Song

Dynasty.

Both the earliest district exams and the final palace exams were one-day long. The provincial exams and the joint exams in between, however, were very harsh experiences. Each of these 2 sets of exams was nine days and nine nights long.

2) Baguwen (Eight-Part Essay)

During the Ming and Qing dynasties, candidates sitting at imperial examinations were required to write essays in accordance with baguwen, a rigid eight-part form.

The eight-part essay was the form adopted for the explication of the Confucian classics, which formed the basis for the imperial examination system. Thus, the eight-part essay and imitations of the classical literary language of the earlier eras of Chinese cultural greatness became the major written genres of the time. There were no further breakthroughs in literary writing, except for a style of artistically heightened descriptions of everyday life experiences, called xiaopinwen (familiar essays), which emerged in the 15th and 16th centuries.

3. Confucius

1) Educator as well as Philosopher

One of the most famous people in ancient China was a wise philosopher named Confucius. He was born Kong Qiu, styled Zhong Ni. Confucius was an educator as well as philosopher. He made many wise phrases and theories about law, life, and government. It's these thoughts and theories that teach other people lessons about moral principles and rules of life. He traveled about and instructed the small body of disciples that had gathered around him. He lectured to them on the ancient classics. His fame as a man of learning and character and his reverence for Chinese ideals and customs soon spread through the principality of Lu. His theories and principles were spread throughout China by his disciples, and soon many people learned from his wise sayings.

Confucius had, however, no opportunity to put his theories to a public test until, at the age of 51, he was appointed magistrate of Chung-tu, and the next year minister of crime of the state of Lu. His administration was successful; reforms were introduced; justice was fairly dispensed; crime was almost eliminated. So powerful did Lu become that the ruler of a neighboring state maneuvered to secure the minister's dismissal. Confucius left his office in 496 B.C., traveling about and teaching, vainly hoping that some other prince would allow him to undertake measures of reform. In 484 B.C., after a fruitless search for an ideal ruler, he returned for the last time to Lu. He died in Lu in 479 B.C.

Yet, when the philosopher died, people honored all of Confucius' work by building temples in every city in China to honor Confucius. Confucius' teachings and philosophy have been influencing China for nearly 2,500 years. It is called Confucianism.

2) Confucius and Education

A hallmark of Confucius' thought is his emphasis on education and study. He disparages those who have faith in natural understanding or intuition and argues that the only real understanding of a subject comes from long and careful study. Study, for Confucius, means finding a good teacher and imitating his words and deeds. A good teacher is someone older who is familiar with the ways of the past and the practices of the ancients. While he sometimes warns against excessive reflection and meditation, Confucius' position appears to be a middle course between studying and reflecting on what one has learned. "He who learns but does not think is lost. He who thinks but does not learn is in great danger (*Analects of Confucius*)." Confucius, himself, is credited by the tradition with having taught altogether 3,000 students, though only 72 are said to have truly mastered the arts he cherished most. Confucius is willing to teach anyone, whatever their social standing, as long as they are eager and tireless. He taught his students morality, proper speech, government, and the refined arts. While he also emphasizes the "Six Arts" — ritual, music, archery, chariot-riding, calligraphy, and computation — it is clear that he regards morality the most important subject. Confucius' pedagogical methods are striking. He never discourses at length on a subject. Instead he poses questions, cites passages from the classics, or uses apt analogies, and waits for his students to arrive at the right answers. "I only instruct the eager and enlighten the fervent. If I hold up one corner and a student cannot come back to me with the other three, I do not go on with the lesson (*Analects of Confucius*)."

Confucius' goal is to create gentlemen who carry themselves with grace, speak correctly, and demonstrate integrity in all things. His strong dislike of the sycophantic "petty men" whose clever talk and pretentious manner win them an audience, is reflected in numerous *Analects of Confucius* passages. Confucius finds himself in an age in which values are out of joint. Actions and behavior no longer correspond to the labels originally attached to them. "Rulers do not rule and subjects do not serve (*Analects of Confucius*)," he observes. This means that words and titles no longer mean what they once did. Moral education is important to Confucius because it is the means by which one can rectify this situation and restore meaning to language and values to society. He believes that the most important lessons for obtaining such a moral education are to be found in the canonical *Book of Songs*, because many of its poems are both beautiful and good. Thus Confucius places the text first in his curriculum and frequently quotes and explains its lines of verse. For this reason, the *Analects of Confucius* is also an important source for understanding the role which Confucius' poetry and art play in the moral education of as well as in the reformation of society.

Word Bank

equalize	(使某事物在大小、数量等)相等
enrollment	入学,入伍,入会,登记,注册
curriculum	课程
matriculation	被录取入学
vogue	风行,流行
rigorous	严厉的,严格的
disservice	危害,损害
delirium	精神错乱
disputation	争论,辩论
memorization	记忆力
standardize	使标准化
theorize	使理论化
explicate	详细解说和分析
dispense	施与某物,分配某物
principality	侯国
manoeuvere (AmE) maneuvre	熟练巧妙地引导某人
hallmark	特点,特征
disparage	贬低,轻视
reflection	沉思,考虑
meditation	沉思,冥想
pedagogical	教学法的
discourses	长篇大论
pose	引起,提出
fervent	热情的,热忱的,激情的
sycophantic	阿谀奉承的
pretentious	自命不凡的,自负的
out of joint	紊乱的
rectify	纠正
internalize	使……内化为
conceivable	可以想到的
repletion	饱足,充足
yardstick	比较衡量的标准

参考译文

1. 中国古代教育简介

1) 中国古代教育开端

中国古代教育在中国文化中起着举足轻重的作用。中国古代教育最早可以追溯到周朝中、后期诸子百家的教育思想。古代中国的教育给人们提供了一个平等的发展机会,任何人即便出身贫寒都有可能步入仕途。与此同时,它也起着调节社会秩序、规范社会伦理道德的作用。

春秋时期,私人学堂(私塾)盛行,不同的学派通过学堂传播他们的思想主张。教育家孔子通过私塾,据说培养了3 000多名学生,其中72名取得了非凡成就。其他学派,如道家,也纷纷宣传自己的主张,出现了百家争鸣的局面。

2) 中国古代教育发展

汉武帝(公元前156年—公元前87年)时代,兴"太学"或称"大学"。学子们免交伙食,主要研读经书。通过考试的学生,金榜题名之后,前途无量,仕途亨通。起初,太学仅招收55人,到公元前8年,已经招收3 000人。汉朝开始建立地方学校,学校遍及全国,儒家教育思想广为传播。

汉朝尚没有严格意义上的考试制度，只是通过观察，来选贤任能。有才识的人由各级官员层层推荐。学校传授的课程为"四书五经"。由熟谙"四书五经"的学者(或称"博士")传授。这种传统一直延续到晚清。

隋朝开始了科举考试，并一直延续到清朝，约 1 300 年，在古代中国教育中占主导地位。

唐朝继承、完善了科举取士的制度。考试内容包括写作、经书、数学、法律和书法等。那时候的许多宰相是"进士"出身，都能写一手好文章。这些考生要么出自官府学校，要么通过了地方严格的筛选、成为有资格参加政府每年春天举行的考试的"举人"。

科举考试的形式和内容不尽相同。题目有填空或默写。通常从经书上选取某页内容，然后空上几行，要求应试者填上。或者，也可能要求考生解释诗句。因此，熟读经书至关重要。考"进士"并非易事，那要求很高的文学天赋。

通过科举考试的人前程无量，仕途通达。"龙"是权力的象征，因此，人们把考科举称为"跳龙门"。考得最好的就是"状元"。

宋朝的教育历经很大的变革。宋朝的科举考试中官府主持的科目比唐朝时的少，但考"进士"依然很流行，并且身居高位的大臣都必须通过相关科目的考试。考试体制在形式和内容上都有很大变革。

变革之一是招生规模扩大。唐朝每年的"进士"不到 20 或 30 人，但在宋朝每年却有数百人通过考试。甚至对于那些多次考试但屡考不中的人，皇帝也会给他们提供一些次要的岗位。

第二个变革是考试的频率确定为每 3 年一次。地方考试定在秋季，通过地方考试的人次年春天到都城参加考试。

第三个变革是考试内容。以前的考试强调经书，改革家王安石 (1021 年—1086 年) 强调考试要切合实际。他把填诗、默诗变成作诗、作文。但这种主张受到了贵族阶层的批评，没有持续多久。

最后，为了体现公平竞争，应试者的姓名被封住，试卷在不同地区交换阅卷，减少了舞弊现象。

宋朝官府的学校不多，但书院(即早期的私人学校或组织)却很盛行。书院的目的就在于培养人才，传播文化，弘扬学术。宋朝四大书院是江西省的"白鹿洞书院"、河南省的"嵩阳书院"和"应天书院"、湖南省的"岳麓书院"。书院邀请知名学者讲学，并为学生提供膳食。这样，书院就成了学生们备考的地方。

明朝的科举考试达到了巅峰。考试程序、过程更加严格。明朝政府建立学校，加强学校的功能，让其成为考生参加科举考试的必由之路。考试内容是八股文：固定的文体、固定的字数、固定的八个部分。这种方法忽视了别的形式和内容，限制了人们的创造性和想象力，是十分有害的。

3) 中国古代教育衰退

清朝是满族统治，汉人地位低。满族人参加科举考试只需要做些翻译，参加科举考试的大部分是汉人。清政府的高压统治引起了当时人们的不满情绪，旧的教育制度需要注入新的思想和观念。买官卖官的倾向日益蔓延，破坏了考试的公平竞争。

吴敬梓的小说《儒林外史》所描写的主人公就是这种腐朽考试制度的牺牲品。范进屡考不中，考到五十多岁才得到回报。当他得知最后通过了省试，欣喜若狂，结果却精神错乱，疯疯癫癫。

与西方教育尤其是中世纪和文艺复兴时期的高等教育模式相比，中、西方教育模式迥然不同。西方教育重辩论，中国教育重背诵("四书五经")。科举考试需要背诵大量的经典著作，目的是培养一批封建官僚统治者，而不在于促进知识的更新和学术的进步。

2. 科举制

1) 科举制的实施

一般认为科举制大约开始于 606 年，结束于 1905 年，持续近 1 300 年。在此期间，科举考试变成了一种由国家精心安排、备受人注目的用人选拔制度。通过科举考试，皇帝能选拔一批翰林院学者、人才，然后择优者出任地方或中央的各级官员，如地方治安官、县官、大臣、皇帝顾问等。他们不仅享有特权、荣耀和地位，而且常常是"一人得道，鸡犬升天"。

科举考试的形式和内容都很僵化，一成不变，包括儒家思想、古代诗歌、官方文献和国家政治等。它分三个层次：地方考、省考和宫廷考。考生首先参加地方考即"童试"，每两年一次；然后是省考即"乡试"，每三年一次；最后是宫廷考，包括会试和殿试。只要考生愿意，他们可以参加多次考试。只有男性才能参加科举考试。在隋唐早期，每一个应试的考生必须有一位官员作为顾问提供指导。这个要求在宋朝就废止了。

最初的地方考试和最后的宫廷考试都是一整天。然而，省考和会试非常漫长，两种考试都需 9 天 9 夜。

2) 八股文

在明清时期，参加科举的考生必须考"八股文"。

"八股文"有严格的格式要求，考试内容为儒家经典。因此，"八股文"就构成了那个时代语言文学尤其是文学创作的一个主要特征，并且一直没有什么突破，直到 15 和 16 世纪着重描写日常生活的小品文的出现。

3. 孔子

1) 教育家和哲学家

中国古代最著名的人物之一就是孔子，名丘，字仲尼。孔子既是教育家又是哲学家。他发表了很多关于法律、生活和政治的论断，他的思想理论规范影响着人们的伦理、道德、法律和生活等方方面面。他周游列国，广收门徒，传播他的学说主张，他博学多识、君子品格的声誉迅速传遍鲁国。他的学术理论被他的门徒传遍中国。

但是，直到 51 岁，孔子才得以把他的理论付诸实践。那年他被任命为中都的一个地方官，第二年成为主管鲁国法律治安的官员。他推行改革，公平执政，成绩显赫，犯罪率明显下降。他的改革非常成功，但又危及邻国，邻国的君主施计让他被免职。公元前 496 年，他放弃仕途，四处讲学，期待着有朝一日，能继续推行他的改革理想。公元前 484 年，在寻求理想君主的希望破灭后，孔子回到鲁国，于公元前 479 年患病不愈而卒。

孔子去世后，为了纪念他的丰功伟绩，人们到处修建孔庙。他的哲学与教育思想影响了中国近 2 500 年。他的学说主张被称为"儒家思想"。

2) 孔子与教育

孔子思想的特征之一是他十分强调教育与学习。他蔑视那些自以为是天才的人，主张真正了解事物要靠长期认真的学习。对孔子而言，学习意味着找一位好老师，然后学习他的言和行。老师就是通晓事理、经验丰富的长者。在思与学的关系上，他反对只思考不学习，也反对只学习不思考。他认为："学而不思则罔，思而不学则殆。"据说孔子一生共有 3 000 弟子，但其中只有 72 人真正领会孔子的教诲。孔子教学生，不考虑学生的社会地位，只要他们有热情、不倦怠，孔子都愿意教。孔子教授学生礼仪、道德、言行、政治和艺术等。尽管孔子强调"礼、乐、射、御、书、数"等"六艺"，但他认为道德是最为重要的。孔子很讲究教学方法。他不擅长长篇大论地探讨一个问题，而是提出问题，或引经据典，或巧妙使用类比，启发学生自己得出结论。他认为“不愤不启，不悱不发。举一隅不以三隅反，则不复也。”(《论语·述而》)

孔子培养的是言谈举止高雅得体、诚实可信的君子。他不喜欢自命不凡、阿谀奉承的“小人”，这一点在《论语》中的很多部分有所体现。孔子处在一个百家争鸣的时代，社会价值、行为准则有待规范。所以，他提出：“其身正，不令而行；其身不正，虽令不从。”(《论语·子路》)对孔子来说，道德教育最为重要，因为它可以改变风气、规范社会。他认为道德教育的好教材是《诗经》。在教学中，孔子把《诗经》放在首位，并常常引用其中的诗句。因此，《论语》也是人们理解孔子的诗歌和艺术在道德教育和社会改革方面所起作用的重要途径。

Exercises

Section A Thought-provoking questions

1. Has education in China been an equalizing force from ancient times?
2. What did the imperial exams include? How many levels did they consist of and what were they?
3. As an educator and philosopher, how did Confucius influence Chinese people?
4. What are “Six Arts”?
5. What did Confucius regard as the most important subject?

Section B Decide whether the following statements are true or false

1. All of the historical education in Chinese culture is derived from the teachings of Confucius.
2. There is a definite connection between Confucius and the official Chinese educational system.
3. In contrast to western education, traditional Chinese education encouraged students to engage in disputation.
4. We can infer that the scholars could be promoted to serve as officials by the imperial examinations.
5. The imperial exam system was opened to both men and women.
6. Confucius' thoughts and theories teach other people lessons about moral, principles and rules of life.
7. Confucius' teachings and philosophy have a great impact on China.
8. Confucius stresses the importance of study, and the attitude to study.
9. Confucius' pedagogical methods are striking because he discourses at length on a subject.
10. Confucius finds himself in an ideal age.

Chapter 5

Chinese Names

中国姓名

1. Name Culture

Name, as a sign or cultural symbol that indicates the blood tie within a certain social structure, has very complex and rich implications and, as system culture, possesses comprehensive cultural characteristics. Due to the difference in race, language, faith, etc., the name system in different countries and races will undoubtedly be greatly varied, Chinese name system being, in particular, worth mentioning.

As we all know, every person has his or her name since he or she was born and one may bring his name into the social activities. However in ancient Chinese society, the names have a far deeper meaning.

In the long history of China, the culture of Chinese name has been an important part of Chinese life. In the fields of politics, culture and social activities, the name is crucial. As early as one million years ago, Chinese began to be the residents on the ancient land and the relevant materials have already proved it. The history of the family name dates back to the matriarchal clan society, which is 5,000 to 6,000 years ago. The feature of matriarchal clan society means that in the clan the women are the leaders of important issues. And marriages are allowed only among different clans.

1) *Xing*, *Shi* and *Ming*

In ancient China, one person usually had several names, and naming involved *xing*, *shi*, *ming*, and *zi*. Today, people use *xingshi* to refer to a person's surname, *mingzi* to refer to one's given name. *Xing* and *shi*, *ming* and *zi* are not used separately. In ancient times, however, each of these four words meant a different thing. Study of ancient Chinese documents shows that *xing* originally referred to the names of different matriarchal tribes. It also had something to do with the place where people lived. Therefore, family names, which are used to judge the different places and clans, emerged.

For example, according to historical record, Shennong Yandi's mother lived by the Jiang River, so her *xing* was Jiang; Xuanyuan Huangdi's mother lived by the Ji River, so her surname was Ji. The other source was the totems ancient tribes worshipped. For instance, the names of some animals that ancient tribes worshipped, such as *long* (dragon), *xiong* (bear) and *feng* (phoenix) were adopted as names for certain tribes and therefore became *xing*. People within a tribe shared a common *xing*. The purpose of adopting *xing* was to clarify one's race and ancestry and to determine whether it was appropriate for one person to marry another.

Xing and *shi* were closely related, and *shi* had the following sources: *zhuhou* had the names of their territories as their *shi*, for instance, Chen *shi*, Song *shi*. Normally, *zhuhou*'s sons were called Gongzi, Gongzi's sons were called Gongsun, Gongsun's sons took their grandfather's *zi* as their *shi*. Officials had the names of their titles as their *shi*, for instance, Sima *Shi*, Sikong *Shi*; common people only had names, without *shi*. Even influential common people did not have *shi*; they could only add their profession before their names such as Butcher Ding, Mason Shi, Doctor He, etc. Later some professions became common surnames.

Xingshi was related to one's clan name or family name, and *ming* and *zi* were one's given names. *Xingshi* was shared while *ming* and *zi* were for individuals. People got their *xingshi* (surnames) the moment they were born, while they got their *ming* and *zi* (given names) later.

2) Evolution of Names

According to the research of Gu Yanwu of Qing Dynasty, there are about 22 oldest family names in China. Maybe there are more, but a lot of them disappeared in history. About 4,000 to 5,000 years ago, China entered the patrilineal clan society. During this time the society went from a clan society to a class society. One of the main features of this period is the emergence of the conflict among the clans by different ancestors. The clans that won in the conflict were considered superior to the clans that lost. So the new structure of class society appeared. In addition, a lot of social members who had feats gained new territory and awards. And they were allowed to go to their new territory with their families, affiliates and the captives they got hold of in the conflicts. These people also gained a new symbol related with their territory — clan name.

After the unification of China by Qin, there was a combination of family name with clan name. The condition changed several times during the 2,000 years of feudal society. The dynasties changed and every time there was new territory, new family or clan names emerged. Names became the symbols of class and a special culture was formed around the names. The culture was handed down through the inherent. And the center of the culture is the consciousness of recognizing the ancestors.

3) Significance of Names

In old China, one's surname was revered because the individual bearing it was but a small link in the long history of an illustrious clan. One would never change his name, especially his surname. If a person did so, he or she had probably committed a grave and heinous crime and wanted to sever ties with the past through a name change. Such a person would most likely move away from home to start life anew.

People with the same surname shared a commonality and considered themselves relatives regardless of the number of generations removed, the geographical distance or lack of consanguinity. Since the commonality was derived from a common ancestor at some point in time, it was considered an insult when a person with the same surname disclaimed family or other close relationships. For the same reason, old Chinese custom prohibited marriages of couples with the same surname.

2. Number of Names

It is often claimed that there are approximately 500 surnames in China. This belief seems to derive from a well-known book entitled *One Hundred Family Surnames*, written by an unknown author in what we know as Hangzhou today at the beginning years of the Song Dynasty. This book was widely used as a vocabulary text for students in old China, and it lists 484 surnames, of which 408 consist of one character and 76 of two characters. This list, however, is by no means exhaustive. At present, according to the latest statistics, there, historically speaking, used to be 11,969 surnames and there are around 200 Chinese surnames commonly used today, only 100 of which are most commonly-seen single-character surnames. Names are derived from many sources, such as the names of ancient states or townships, official titles, given names, posthumous names, and specific localities or trades.

According to the latest statistics issued by the Ministry of Public Security of China in 2007, the most common surnames in China, in descending order, are Wang (taking up approximately of 7.25% of the total Han people), Li (7.19%) and Zhang (6.38%). The population of these three surnames is over 270 million. The next seven surnames, of which the population is separately over 20 million, are Liu, Chen, Yang, Huang, Zhao, Wu and Zhou. Xu, Sun, Ma, Zhu, Hu, Guo, He, Gao, Lin, Luo, Zheng, and Liang are the 12 surnames of which the population is separately over 10 million.

3. Naming

1) Given Names

A Chinese may have many given names throughout his life. One month after birth, an infant is given a "milk name". This name is used by family members, relatives and close friends. The name is usually selected either by the family elder or by a literate friend. Names for boys reflect the parents' wishes for his good health, longevity, prosperity, expected talents, virtues, diligence, filial piety, patriotism or intelligence. Girls are named after exotic flowers, pretty birds, musical instruments or jewels. Girls might also be named for feminine attributes such as beauty, grace, thrift and purity. In some rural families, however, girls are not given names but are simply referred to as the "oldest girl", "second girl", "third girl" and so forth.

Frequently, all the boys in one family would be given names that shared the same first character, or adjective. This is sometimes done with the girls in the family as well. Since the two characters of the given name go together, they should be spelled together as a single word or occasionally hyphenated when the name is anglicized.

Another method for selecting a given name is based on the child's horoscope and its relationship to the "Five Elements". A fortune teller, after studying the month, day and hour of the birth, determines whether the infant has a full complement of the Five Elements of metal, wood, water, fire and earth. If any element is lacking in the child, a character with the radical or root of the missing element is used in the name to correct the deficiency and make the child "complete". For example, if the child was lacking water, he might be given the name Hai, Yang, Jiang, He, Hu, Bo, etc., meaning "sea, ocean, river, lake, wave, etc." because those characters are based on the radical of water.

In comparison, meanings in given names are always chosen to reflect elements of the era. In the old days, characters meaning "wealth", "fortune", and "happiness" were very common in names. Characters with the meanings of "gifted", "handsome", and "clever" were often chosen by parents as well wishes for their children to be beautiful, capable, and intelligent. During 1950s and 1960s, many boys were given the name with the meaning of "building the country", "celebrating the nation", "fighting the American imperialist", and "surpassing the British". The reform and opening policies have also provided more choices of characters, such as "bo" meaning "strive", "si" meaning "thoughtful", and "yuhang" meaning "aeronautics". Parents would like to have their children to learn more knowledge, to be more thoughtful, and to have great aspirations. Some people also like to use translated Western names such David, Richard, Lisa and Linda.

There are no "juniors" in Chinese names. A son is never named after his father, nor do parents name their children after relatives. Each child is considered an entirely unique individual. When a child gets enrolled in school, he or she is given a "school name" or "book name". This name is used by his or her teachers and schoolmates and alluded to his or her intelligence, diligence or scholarship.

In old China, it was considered improper for a married woman to reveal or use her given or maiden name. For example, if her maiden surname was Li and she was married to a man whose surname was Wang, she called herself Wang-Li Shi, which meant Mrs. Wang nee Li. However, since the founding of the People's Republic of China, women have been granted equal rights as citizens with men. They can keep their former maiden name after marriage.

2) Nicknames and Other Names

Nicknames are common. These names are often based on a physical defect, a peculiarity in personality in the individual's life. Some nicknames may be given with good will and used by others without hostility, manifesting the friendly relationships between the addressee and the addresser. But some others may be derogatory or even hostile, aiming at jeering at or ridiculing or hurting the feelings of the addressee. Therefore, it is essential that cautions be taken to those who have the habit of giving and addressing others nicknames just in case that diverse effect may be caused.

Writers, artists and actors used to have "special names" that were equivalent to pen names or stage names. In Chinese history, a scholar who passed the old imperial examination and became a government official was given an "official name". Some important such as emperors and some privileged people were given a "posthumous name" after they died, and a deceased emperor was usually granted a "temple name".

Generally speaking, Chinese names usually consist of three characters, which differ from those in the western countries and the spelling of which is also different from that of the English-speaking world, with the first character being the surname and the following two characters, taken together, constituting the given name. The first character of the given name is, in most cases, an adjective modifying the second character, a noun. Now more and more people have single-character given name, such as Jiang Jiang, Shen Yu, Zhang Xin, the first being the surname and the latter the given name.

3) The Spelling of Chinese Names

Anglicization of Chinese names used to have created much confusion, because a name might be spelled in many ways depending on the dialect spoken and how the translator interpreted the sound of the name. Moreover, although Chinese write their surname first and then the two characters of the given name, as in a directory or name file, many Westerners assume that the last character is the surname. In time, through common Western usage, some Chinese have even replaced their surname with the anglicized given name.

Some Chinese living abroad have also changed their surnames and given names to conform to names used in their adopted countries. In the United States, for example, the surname He has been changed to Holt, Luo has become Loew, Xie has become Shea and Zhong has become June.

Currently, overseas Chinese people, still have the tradition to recognize the ancestor in Mainland China. In recent years the culture of Chinese name has become a huge history treasure of China as it can help people to learn Chinese history in a different way. A series of the core features of ancient Chinese society such as the autocracy system, family social system and the rules of act are all shown through the name culture, which is the reason why it is constantly noted in the field of academia. Nowadays, since more and more foreigners are interested in Chinese culture and taking pains to learn Chinese, many of them feel quite proud to have a Chinese name exactly according to the Chinese way, which indicates the charm of the Chinese culture and the fun learning Chinese can bring to people.

Word Bank

matriarchal	母系的
clan	部落，氏族
surname	姓
given name	名
totem	图腾
patrilineal	父系的
affiliate	附属人员
heinous	十恶不赦的
consanguinity	血缘，血亲
single-character surname	单姓
official title	封号
posthumous name	谥号
special name	别号
temple name	庙号
single-character given name	单名
Anglicization	英语化

参考译文

1. 姓名文化

姓名作为一种文化符号往往标志着社会结构中的一种血缘关系，它所包含的内涵是非常复杂丰富的，作为一种制度文化，它具有综合性的文化特征。由于民族、语言、宗教信仰等因素的不同，各个国家和民族的姓名制度是多种多样的。中国的姓名制度尤其值得一提。

众所周知，每个人从呱呱坠地时起，就有了自己的姓名，然后带着它参与社会活动，使之起到代表自我而与他人相区别的最实际的作用。但是，在古代中国社会里，姓名的意义远远不止如此。

在漫长的历史中，中国人的姓名文化曾是中华民族生活中的重要部分之一，在政治、文化及社会活动诸领域中，都发挥着极其重要的作用。考古资料已经证明，中国人早在100多万年之前就在自己古老的国土上生活栖息了。“姓”的历史从距今五、六千年的母系氏族社会时开始。母系社会的特征，是妇女在氏族内部事务管理中，居于主导地位，同时实行不同氏族间相互通婚、氏族内部禁婚的制度。

1) 姓、氏、名

在古时，一个人可有好几个名字，命名通常包括姓、氏、名、字。而今人们用“姓氏”来指姓，“名字”来指名，姓、氏、名、字不分开使用。在古时，这四个字互不相同。古代文献的研究表明姓最初是用来指称不同母系的部落称号，也与人们的居住地有关。为了区别人们的居住地和所属氏族，家族的姓就出现了。

比如，据史料记载，神农氏炎帝的母亲居于姜水，因此就姓了姜；轩辕氏黄帝的母亲居于姬水，因此便姓了姬。姓氏的另一个来源是古代部落崇拜的图腾，例如，有些古代部落用崇拜的动物的名字，如龙、熊、凤等来命名自己的部落，这些动物的名字就成了部落的姓。同一个部落的人都享有同一个姓，目的在于清楚断定每个人的所属、祖宗是谁、能否通婚。

姓和氏紧密相关，氏有以下几个来源：诸侯通常以受封的国名为氏，比如陈氏、宋氏等。诸侯之子称公子，公子之子称公孙，公孙之子则以其祖父的字为氏。此外，官员以官职为氏，比如司马氏、司空氏。普通人只有名而无姓氏，即使是很有影响的普通人，也只能在名之前冠以职业，而无姓氏。比如庖丁、匠石、医和等。后来，有些职业名便成了普通姓氏名。

姓氏是氏族或家族的称号，名字才是个人的称号。姓氏是公共的，名字才是自己的。姓氏是与生俱来的，名字则是后起的。

2）姓氏的演变

根据清代学者顾炎武的考证，中国最古老的姓共有 22 个，但很可能还有更多的姓随着整个氏族的消失而淹没在历史的波涛中了。大约在距今 4 000—5 000 年以前，中国人在经过母系氏族社会后，进入父系氏族社会阶段，开始由氏族社会向阶级社会的转变。这个过渡时期的基本特点之一，就是不同祖先的氏族之间的相互影响和相互斗争趋于频繁，由此导致氏族间领导和臣服格局的出现，阶级社会的雏形开始出现。与之相伴产生的是许多有功绩的社会成员得到了占有新领地的封赏，并且被允许带领他们的家人、部属以及在战争中获得的俘虏一起前往，共同开辟新的生活区域。这些派分出去的人还得到了一种与地域有联系的新的标识——氏。

到公元前 3 世纪，秦统一中国后，最初来源于母系氏族社会的“姓”与来源于父系氏族社会的“氏”开始一体化。此后，在中国长达 2 000 多年的封建社会中，朝代更迭数十次，而每一次更迭都产生新的封地，新的封地又产生新的姓氏。因此，姓氏成为阶级地位的标志，并以姓名为中心形成了独特的文化，这种文化通过子孙繁衍而传承。而强烈的数典认祖、追宗寻根意识便是这个整体的核心所在。

3）姓名的意义

在古代中国，一个人的姓因其出身而受到人们尊敬，特别是出身名门望族。他决不会改变自己的姓名，尤其是自己的姓。如改了的话，那或许是他犯了严重的不可饶恕的罪行，或是他想通过改变姓名来断绝与过去的联系，很可能他会离家出走以便开始一种新的生活。

共用一个姓的人拥有一个共同点，他们常认为天下同姓是一家，而不管其辈分的久远、处所的不同以及血缘关系的缺乏。而由于这个共同点的产生基于他们拥有一个共同的祖先，所以如果有人否认与家庭的关系或相近的关系，那么他就会被认为大不敬；同样的原因，中国旧习俗禁止同姓人结婚。

2. 姓氏知多少

人们经常说在中国大概有 500 个姓氏，这也许源自《百家姓》。这本由宋代初年今杭州的一位不知姓名的作者编撰的书在过去被用作学生的认字书，收集了当时常见的 484 个姓氏，其中 408 个单姓，76 个复姓。当然，它并非列举了所有的姓氏。当前，根据最新统计数字，中国历史上共有姓氏 11 969 个，可是现在常用的姓氏不过 200 个左右，其中最常用的单姓只有 100 个。中国的姓氏是从多处派生来的，如古代国家的名称或城镇的名称、官衔名称、起的名字、谥号以及具体的处所或不同的行业。

根据中国公安部 2007 年对全国户籍人口的一项统计分析显示：王姓是我国第一大姓，占全国人口总数的 7.25%；第二大姓是李姓，占全国人口总数的 7.19%；第三位是张姓，占全国总人口的6.38%。这三大姓人口总数超过2.7亿。姓氏人口总数在2 000万以上的姓还有7个，依次为：刘、陈、杨、黄、赵、吴、周。徐、孙、马、朱、胡、郭、何、高、林、罗、郑和梁这12个姓氏人口数均在1 000万到2 000万之间。

3. 命名

1) 起名

中国人一生会有好多名字。满月过后，人们就会给婴儿取个乳名，这个乳名只有家庭成员、亲朋好友能用。名字由家里的长辈或有文化的朋友来取。男孩的名字反映了父母的愿望，希望他健康、长寿、宝贵、有才、有德、勤勉、孝顺、爱国、聪明。女孩的名字一般与奇异的花儿、可爱的鸟儿、动听的乐器、发光的珠宝等有关。女孩名字有时根据女性特有的特点，例如美丽、文静、节俭、纯洁。然而，在一些农村家庭女孩一般不给取名字，而只是简单地依次叫大妹、二妹、三妹等。

通常，在一个家庭里所有男孩名字的第一个汉字都是相同的，有时女孩也一样。由于这两个汉字构成了一个人的名字，因此它们应该被拼在一起作为一个单词，或者当名字以英语的方式拼写时用连字符把它们连在一起。

另一个取名的方式是基于孩子的星宿及其与“五行”的关系。算命先生在研究了婴儿的出生月、日、时后来决定其是否具有完整的五行星宿：金、木、水、火、土。如果缺少任何一行，那么就要为孩子用一个与所缺行相关的汉字来弥补孩子的缺陷，使孩子完整。例如，如果其缺水，就可以取一个与水相关的名字，如“海、洋、江、河、湖、波”等。

相比较而言，名字与时代紧密相关。旧时以“富、发、福”取名的多，因为它们有发财祈福之意；以“杰、俊、才”为名的，是父母希望自己的孩子能美丽、贤能、聪慧。20世纪50年代和60年代，男孩子多取名“建国、国庆、抗美、超英”；改革开放后，取名字的范围更广，叫“博、思、宇、航”的多，是父母希望孩子拥有现代化的知识，有思想有远大的志向。借用外国人名字的也不少，男孩叫“大卫、查理”，女孩叫“丽莎、琳达”等。

中国人的名字里没有与父亲或家中长辈相同的名字，也不与亲戚同名。人们认为每个孩子就是一个完全不同的个体。孩子上学后，会有一个老师和同学使用的“学名”或“书名”。这个名字暗指他的才智、勤勉或学识。

旧时女人结婚后，还用自己出嫁前的闺名就不合适了。因此，如果婚前她娘家姓李，现在嫁给了一个姓王的男子，那么她就被称作王李氏，意思是娘家姓李的王夫人。但新中国成立以后，妇女被赋予了与男子同样的公民权，婚后能继续使用自己的名字。

2) 绰号以及其他名字

绰号也很普遍。这些名字一般是源于某人身体的缺陷或怪异的性格。有些绰号是善意的，可以表明被叫者和叫人者之间的亲密关系。但有些恐怕带有贬义甚至敌意，目的是在嘲笑或讽刺或伤害他人。所以，无论是给人起绰号还是叫人绰号都须谨慎，以免带来负面的效果。

作家、艺术家、演员都有别名，相当于笔名或艺名。在古代，书生通过了皇家科举考试后，进入官场，会被封一个官名；帝王或其他有特殊社会地位的人死后追加谥号，死去的皇帝通常被给予庙号。

总的来说，中国人的姓名一般包括三个汉字，第一个汉字是姓，第二个和第三个字合在一起构成一个人的名，这与西方国家不同，且拼写方式也与英语不同。通常名的第一个汉字是形容词，而第二个则是名词，所以第一个常用来修饰第二个。现在，越来越多的人取单名，比如，姜江、沈虞、张欣，前一个字是姓，后一个字是名。

3）中文姓名的拼写

中国人名英文化会引起很大麻烦。首先，根据方言和译员发音的不同，拼写方式也会不同。其次，中国人姓在先名在后，而许多西方人总认为最后一个汉字是姓。有些经常使用英语的人甚至用其英文名字代替了他们的姓。

有些旅居国外的中国人也改变了他们的姓和名字来适应其所在国的命名方式。例如在美国，"何"被转变成"Holt"，"罗"变成"Loew"，"谢"成了"Shea"，"钟"成了"June"。

时至今日，居住在国外的华人华侨仍然有到中国寻根问祖的传统。近年来，中国姓名文化已成为人们从一个新的角度来学习中华民族悠久历史的巨大库藏。中国古代社会的一系列本质特征，如专制制度、家族型社会结构、以忠君孝亲为核心的道德伦理观念与行为准则等，无不通过姓名文化得到充分展示，这也是它越来越受到学术界高度重视的原因。现在，越来越多的外国人对中国文化产生了浓厚的兴趣，并且下苦功夫学习汉语。他们中不少人还为有个中文名字而感到自豪。这些足以证明中国文化的魅力及学习汉语可以给人们带来的乐趣。

Exercises

Section A Thought-provoking questions

1. Do you know any of the superstitions, taboos, and stories relevant to naming in China?
2. Can you figure out what surnames the following indicate：
彭城流芳，颍川流芳，太原流芳，汝南流芳，京兆流芳，南阳流芳，范阳流芳，博陵流芳，陇西流芳，荥阳流芳
3. Do you have any idea how Chinese ancient literary men gave themselves or were given hao (literary name)?
4. To what kind of society can you trace the origin of the following surnames：
姜（Yan Di，炎帝），姬（Yellow Emperor，黄帝），嬴（Shao Hao，少昊），姚（Yu Shun，虞舜），姒（Xia Yu，夏禹）

Section B Match the following courtesy name

1.	Confucius	Mengde（梦得）	6.	Su Shi	Letian（乐天）
2.	Liu Yuxi	Zhongni（仲尼）	7.	Zhuge Liang	Mengruan（梦阮）
3.	Sun Wu	Li Taibai（李太白）	8.	Cao Xueqin	Kongming（孔明）
4.	Li Bai	Changqing（长卿）	9.	Cao Cao	Yishan（义山）
5.	Bai Juyi	Zizhan（子瞻）	10.	Li Shangyin（李商隐）	Mengde（孟德）

※ **The humble is the basis of honor. The low is the foundation of Tao.**

From Laozi: *Dao De Jing*

(贵以贱为本，高以下为基。)

——老子·《道德经》

※ **The weak and the tender overcomes the hard and the strong.**

From Laozi: *Dao De Jing*

(柔弱胜刚强。)

——老子·《道德经》

Chapter 6

Chinese Language and Characters

中国语言文字

1. Language

The official language of the People's Republic of China (PRC for short) is Chinese, which is based on the northern dialect. It is usually referred to in the west as "Mandarin", but the Chinese call it *Putonghua*. *Putonghna* is variously referred to as the "Han language" (*hanyu*), the "national language" (*guoyu*) or simply "Chinese".

The Chinese language is among the most beautiful languages in the world. The Chinese characters have been used for the longest time, over the widest area and by the largest number of people in the world. It is the epitome of the wisdom and creativity of the Chinese people and the carrier and manifestation for the specific patterns and features of Chinese thinking, and for the rich cultural heritance. To understand the Chinese, one should set about understanding their language.

1) The Origin of Chinese Characters

The origin of the Chinese antique script is very long and there are not enough documentary resources about its history. There have been various stories about the origin of the Chinese script. In China, the invention of writing has been attributed to: (1) Fuxi, who is supposed the creator of *Bagua*, from which the Chinese characters evolved; (2) Shennong, who initiated the recording by tying the knots; and (3) Cang Jie, who is said to have four eyes and see the footprints of birds and beasts, which inspired him to create written characters. Anyhow, the invention of a language is a great achievement which can neither be done by a deity, nor can it be made by a single person in his life time. Its appearance and growth into maturity have to undergo a fairly long period of trial and experiment by the masses of the people to meet the needs of social life and activities of production.

In ancient China, characters began as simple drawings of natural objects — trees, river water, mountains and hills, horses and oxen, human beings themselves, etc. The earliest character-like drawings are thus "pictographic" in quality. Compared with other scripts in the world, Chinese characters appeared much earlier with the first evidence of the characters around 5,000 or more years old. More than 50 kinds of carved symbols appeared around the *Banpo* Site and other nearby places. They were structured and arranged in a certain order, having simple strokes and regular shapes, such as the the vertical stroke, horizontal stroke, the bevel stroke, and the angular stroke, and they have the same characteristics as today's simple characters — scholars deem them to be the original Chinese characters. From the grey pottery in the *Dawenkou* Cultural Ruins were found some carved pictographic signs. In fact, these signs became the later pictograms.

2) The Evolution of Chinese Characters

The evolution of Chinese characters underwent several stages. The Chinese characters were systemized during the Shang Dynasty during which Chinese civilization reached and developed to a relatively high level with the appearance of *Jiaguwen* (Oracle Bone Script). Oracles are ancient characters carved onto tortoise shells and beast bones and are the earliest form of Chinese characters.

The Oracles are systematic characters which form the foundations for the development of modern Chinese characters. Later, the Chinese characters took various different forms. *Jinwen* (Bronze Script, inscriptions on ancient bronze objects), *Xiaozhuan* (Lesser Seal Script), *Lishu* (Clerkly Script), *Kaishu* (Standard Script) and they have been used fairly unchanged to present day.

The Chinese characters have been gradually standardized. *Xiaozhuan* set down the number of strokes of each character; *Lishu* shaped the new forms of the Chinese characters; *Kaishu* helped establish the new form and basic strokes — horizontal, vertical, left-falling, dot, right-falling, rising and turning stroke. For more than 1,000 years, *Kaishu* remained the standard form of Chinese characters.

The most important change in Chinese writing since the standardization in the Qin Dynasty occurred in the middle of the 20th century. In 1949, the People's Republic of China (PRC) introduced simplified characters (*jiantizi*) to replace the traditional *Kaishu* characters. In addition to Mainland China, Singapore also adopted this script. However, other Chinese-speaking places such as Taiwan, Hong Kong, and various Chinese communities in Southeast Asia and the Americas rejected this new system and continued to use the traditional script.

3) Characteristics of Chinese Characters

The Chinese Han characters are neat in appearance and, no matter how many strokes they have, they all occupy the same spacing in printing. With respect to this trait, therefore, Chinese Han characters are figuratively referred to as "square script".

The Chinese characters are a meaning-oriented character system based on pictograms and consisting of pictographic-phonetic characters. The total number of characters is around 56,000, the majority of which are archaic and only 3,000 are used frequently. They are used to construct an infinite number of sentences and meanings.

In the course of the historical development, the coinage of the Chinese characters has undergone tremendous changes. At first pictograms dominated, and later were dominantly replaced by pictographic-phonetic characters. The system of the Chinese characters incorporate sounds, forms as well as meanings. Simply put, the Chinese words have the following special characteristics:

(1) The Chinese words are ideographs that are not connected directly with pronunciation. In the respect of the forms, the Chinese words in their square forms can reflect directly and comprehensively their meanings and their pronunciations. For instance, the word "忍" (endure) is composed of "心" (heart, mind) and "刃" (knife with an edge). "人" (man) indicates a person with his feet standing on land. The meaning is evident upon a glance at it. They are all vivid and perceivable images.

(2) Chinese is a tonal language that belongs to the Sino-Tibetan family, whereas English is an intonation language that belongs to the Indo-European family. In the light of pronunciation, the Chinese words are syllabic. One Chinese word requires only one single syllabic pattern. It depends on its sound and its tone to convey its meaning jointly. That also explains why Chinese has so many homophones. Tones provide wider range for the use of the words in the Chinese language. A very typical example is the word "ma", which may mean differently such as mother, numb, horse, and curse by the 4 different tones.

(3) In terms of connotations, the Chinese words are imaginable and perceivable. Since the Chinese words are combinations of forms and meanings, they have the property of imaginableness and comprehensibility. For instance, the Chinese women in the old days had a low social status and were looked upon as the sources of disasters and evils. So such words that have "女" as radical bear, more or less, a derogatory sense, as "奸"(treacherous), "婪"(avaricious), "娼"(bitch), "妓"(prostitute), "妖" (demon) etc. Even some words with neutral meaning show male-chauvinism, such as, "安"(safe), implying a woman staying at home and not going out, and "妥" (appropriate) implying a woman under the control of man. Of Chinese words, a character has in itself an actual meaning. And phrases, sentences and articles composed of meaningful characters can make their contents even richer and more effective.

(4) Succinctness and brevity is another feature of the Chinese language and the Chinese words. According to statistics, of all the United Nations documents printed in different languages, the Chinese version is the thinnest copy. So, with regard to frugality in time and paper, the advantage of Chinese words is far superior to the Western words.

4) The Formation of Chinese Characters

As is well known, written Chinese is not an alphabetic language, but a script of ideograms. Their formation follows three principles:

(1) Hieroglyphics or the drawing of pictographs

As explained before, this was the earliest method by which Chinese characters were designed and from which the other methods were subsequently developed. For instance, the sun was written as ⊙, the moon as , water as , the cow as  and so on. These picture-words underwent a gradual evolution over the centuries until the pictographs changed into "square characters", some simplified by losing certain strokes and others made more complicated but, as a whole, from irregular drawings they became stylized forms.

(2) Associative compounds

The principle of forming characters by drawing pictures is easy to understand, but pictographs cannot express abstract ideas. So the ancients invented the "associative compounds", i.e., characters formed by combining two or more elements, each with a meaning of its own, to express new ideas. Thus, the sun and the moon written together became the character 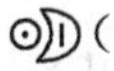(ming), which means "bright"; the sun placed over a line representing the horizon formed the ideogram (dan) which means "sunrise" or "morning".

(3) Pictophonetics

Though pictographs and associative compounds indicate the meanings of characters by their forms, yet neither of the two categories gives any hint as to pronunciation. The pictophonetic method was developed to create new characters by combining one element indicating meaning and the other sound. For instance, "爸 (ba)" the Chinese character for "papa" is formed by the element "巴 (ba)" which represents the sound and the element "父 (fu)" which represents the meaning (father). Likewise the character "芭 (ba)" is formed by "巴 (the sound)" and "艹", indicating a plant. In this way, more and more characters were made until such pictophonetics constitute today about 90% of all Chinese characters.

2. Grammar and Tones

Chinese grammar is much simpler than that of European languages. There are no article (a, an, the), no tenses and no plurals. The basic point is that, like English, Chinese word order is subject-verb-object. In other words, a basic English sentence like "I (subject) love (verb) you (object)" is constructed in exactly the same way in Chinese. The catch is mastering the tones.

Chinese is a language with a large number of words with the same pronunciation but a different meaning; what distinguishes these "homophones" is their "tonal" quality — the raising and lowering of pitch on certain syllables. Chinese has four tones — high, rising, falling — rising and falling, plus a fifth "neutral" tone which can be all but ignored. The pronunciation of the Chinese words to indicate four kinds of life style for getting weight is "tang". When pronounced with the four tones respectively, it means having a lot of soup or broth, favoring sugar or sweet food, sleeping or lying excessively and eating food while it is boiling hot, and they will sure make a person put on extra weight. The variation of tones not only affects the meaning, but also the grammatical functions.

3. Pinyin

The Chinese in 1958 adopted a system of writing their language using the Roman alphabet. It's known as pinyin. Since 1979 all translated texts of Chinese diplomatic documents, as well as Chinese magazines published in foreign languages, have used the pinyin system for spelling names and places, pinyin replaces the old Wade-Giles system of Romanizing Chinese script. Thus, under pinyin, "Mao Tse-tung" becomes Mao Zedong, "Chou En-lai" turns into Zhou Enlai, and "Peking" is now read Beijing. The name of the country remains as it has been written most often into "China" in English and German, and "Chine" in French — in pinyin it's "Zhongguo". The same is true of some other names which still remain as they are, such as "Peking University", "Qiang Kai-shek" (Jiang Jieshi), "Kuomintang"(Guomindang), for they are already widely accepted worldwide.

4. The Future of Chinese

As it is said that in the light of examining the cultural traits of a nation it is imperative to acquire a perspective through a window of its language and script. Language and script function as a threshold leading human beings from ignorance to civilization. The language and script of every nation are not molded at random, but hinge on the features and patterns of thinking of that nation, carry its rich cultural contents. Thus the Chinese language truly and fully presents the way of life and the thinking pattern of the Chinese.

The creation and application of the Chinese characters has not only propelled the development of Chinese culture, but also greatly influenced world culture. For instance, the creation of the Chinese characters profoundly influenced the writing systems of neighboring countries. The characters of Japan, Vietnam and Korea were all created on the same basis as the Chinese characters.

A language is the cultural sign deeply rooted in the soul and flesh and blood of a nation, providing a true record of the nation's progress and enabling the extension of the culture to the future on the very basis of its history. To us Chinese, any abandonment and ignorance of our own mother tongue is an unpardonable crime that will surely bring shame on us.

Word Bank

pictographic	象形文字的
stroke	笔画
vertical stroke	竖
horizontal stroke	横
bevel stroke	斜
angular stroke	叉
ideograph	象形文字,表意文字
homophone	同音字
connotation	含义
derogatory	贬损的
succinctness	简洁
brevity	简短
hieroglyphic	象形文字
associative compound	会意词
pictophonetics	形声字
four tones	四声,声调
high tone	阴平
rising tone	阳平
falling-rising tone	上声
falling tone	去声
the Wade-Giles system	威妥玛式拼音法

参考译文

1. 汉语

中华人民共和国的官方语言是汉语。汉语在西方被称作"官话",但中国人将其称为"普通话",普通话也叫汉语、中文。

汉语是世界上最美的语言之一,是世界上使用时间最久、空间最广、人数最多的文字之一,它是中国人民智慧和创造力的集中体现,是中国人民思维形式与思维特征的载体和表现形式,有着丰富的文化传承。想要了解中国人,就必须着手了解汉语语言。

1) 汉字的起源

中国汉字的存在已经有相当长的历史。有关汉字的起源,自古以来众说纷纭。有的说汉字是伏羲氏发明的;还有的说是神农氏创造的;第三种说法是仓颉用自己的四只眼睛看着鸟兽的足迹想出来的。无论如何,文字创造是一件伟大的功绩。汉语文字的产生既不是神造,也不可能是某个个人的行为。它的出现和成形经历了一个相当长的过程,经过很多人的使用、完善,以满足社会生产活动的需要。

中国汉字起源于先民对周围自然景物如树木、河水、山川、马牛、人等的简单描摹。这些早期的描摹实际上就是象形文字的萌芽。与世界上其他文字相比,中国汉字起源较早。大约在距今5 000多年的半坡遗址等地方,已经出现刻画符号,共达50多种,符号笔画简单,形状规则,竖、横、斜、叉均有,有一定的规律性,具备了简单文字的特征,学者们认为这可能是汉字的萌芽。在距今5 000年前的大汶口文化遗址中还发现灰陶器上刻有一些象形符号,这些符号实际上就演变为后来的象形文字。

2) 汉字的演变

汉字经历了种种演变。汉字成为系统的文字大约是在商朝。考古证实,在商朝早期,中国文明已发展到相当高的水平，其主要特征之一就是甲骨文的出现。甲骨文是刻在龟甲和兽骨上的古老文字，是汉字最早的形式。

甲骨文是一种成熟而系统的文字，为后世的汉字发展奠定了基础。此后，汉字又经历了金文（铜铭文）、小篆、隶书、楷书等形式，并一直沿用至今。

汉字的演变过程是汉字字形、字体逐步规范化、稳定化的过程。小篆使每个字的笔画数固定下来；隶书构成了新的笔形系统，字形渐成扁方形；楷书诞生以后，汉字的字形、字体就稳定下来，确定了“横、竖、撇、点、捺、挑、折”的基本笔画。1 000 多年来，楷书一直是汉字的标准字。

自秦朝规范汉字以来，汉字的重大改革发生在 20 世纪中叶。中华人民共和国 1949 年成立后即着手简化汉字以取代传统楷书。除了中国大陆地区外，新加坡也采用了简体汉字。不过其他说汉语的地区例如中国台湾、中国香港以及东南亚和美洲的华人地区没有采用简体汉字，仍然继续使用传统的汉字书写体。

3) 汉字的特点

中国的汉字，形状整齐，无论一个字笔画是多是少，占的地方都一样大。因此，针对汉字的这个特点，人们形象地称汉字为“方块字”。

汉字是以象形字为基础、以形声字为主体的表意文字体系，总数约有 56 000 个，其中大部分为古汉字，最常用的有 3 000 个左右。这些常用汉字可以组成无穷多的词组，进而组成各种各样的句子。

从历史发展来看，汉字造字过程经历诸多变化。从最初以象形字为主，到后来发展为以形声字为主的音、形、义结合的文字系统。简单说来，汉字具有以下几个特点：

(1) 汉字是表意文字，它不和语音发生直接联系。从字形来说，汉字以它的方块形式直接反映它的意义和发音方式。如“忍”字是“心”上一把“刃”，“人”指示的是两脚立地的形象。从字形可以一眼看出字的含义，生动且易于表意。

(2) 从字音来看，汉字是音节字。汉语是声调语言，属于汉藏语系（而英语是语调语言，属于印欧语系）。作为音节字的汉字，其音节结构简单，一字只有一个音节。词的信息由靠音节的声音结构和声调来承担。这就说明了汉语中同音字特别多的原因。不同的音调能传达不同的意思，一个典型的例子就是“ma”，赋予其不同的音调就有不同的意思，它可以是“妈”，或“麻”，或“马”，或“骂”。

(3) 从字义来看，汉字是具象可感的。汉字是形意合一的，所以都是具象的，带有明显的可解性。例如，中国古代妇女地位低下，女人常被看成祸水，因而许多与“女”有关的字都带有贬义，如“奸、婪、娼、妓、妖”等。即使一些中性词，也带有对女性的歧视，如“安”表示女人在家不出门，“妥”表示女人在男人的手爪之下，即控制之下等。单个汉字本身就有实际的意义。由本身就有意义的字组成的词、句、文章，内容则更加丰富。

(4) 中国文字还有一个特点是简洁。据统计，用各种文字来记录的联合国的文件，只有中文的文件是最薄的。单从节约时间、节约纸张来讲，中国汉字的优点也是西方文字所不及的。

4) 汉字的组成

众所周知，汉语不是拼音语言，而是表意文字。汉字的组成方式有以下三种：

(1) 象形字：如前所述，图画符号是汉字最早形成的方式，在此基础上逐渐产生了其他的造字方法。例如，太阳就写成，月亮是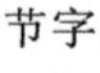，水是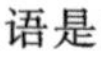，而牛就画成的模样。多少个世纪过去了，这些图画字经过不断的演变进化，直到变成“方块字”，有些字减少了笔画变成简体字，而有些字变得更加繁复，但总的说来，汉字从不规则的图画符号变成了规范的字形。

(2) 会意字:以象形图画的方式造出的词意思容易明白,但是象形文字不能表述抽象意思。因此古人就创造了“会意词”,即由两个或两个以上的字合并在一起,并把它们的字义合起来,就组成一个新字。这样,把太阳和月亮写在一起就成为,意为明亮,在太阳的下面画一条横线,就可表达“日出”或“早晨”的概念。

(3) 形声字:象形字和会意字可由其形来断定其义,然而却不能依其形来决定其读音。因此人们用形声组词法把表义的和表读音的两个字结合在一起组成新字。例如,汉语中表示父亲的字是“爸”,它是由表发音的“巴”和表父亲意义的“父”组成。同理,芭蕉的“芭”字也是由表音的“巴”加上表示植物意思的“艹”组成。很多字都是以此种方法构成,现在形声字已占汉字的90%左右。

2. 语法和声调

汉语语法比欧洲语言的语法简单得多。汉语里没有冠词,没有时态,没有复数形式。但基本的一点同英语一样,汉语语序也是主—谓—宾。换言之,像“I (主) love (谓) you (宾)”这样的英语句子,其结构与汉语完全相同,关键在于声调的掌控。

汉语是由大量同音不同义的字组成的语言;区别这些同音词的标志是声调,也就是某些音节上音高的升降。普通话有四个基本声调,阴平、阳平、上声、去声,还有第五种轻声。比如说,可能让人长胖的四种方式的拼音都是“tang”,但是如果按照这四个音调来读就成了“汤”“糖”“躺”“烫”。汉语声调变化不仅具有语义功能,更有语法形态上的功能。

3. 汉语拼音

1958年,中国开始采用罗马字母来书写汉字,即拼音。

从1979年起,所有中国的外交文献译文以及外语出版的中国杂志,都采用拼音来拼人名、地名,拼音取代了威妥玛式罗马拼音法。因此,“Mao Tse-tung”改为Mao Zedong,“Chou En-lai”改为Zhou Enlai,“Peking”就拼成Beijing了。“中国”的国名仍旧保持原来的形式,英语、德语中是China,法语中是Chine,汉语拼音则是Zhongguo。由于有些名字已经在世界范围内被广泛接受,因此仍然沿用原来的拼法,比如说“北京大学”“蒋介石”“国民党”等。

4. 汉语的未来

正如人们所说,考察一个民族的文化特征,必须透过语言文字这个窗口。语言文字是人类脱离愚昧、跨入文明的门槛。而且,每个民族的语言文字都不是随便形成的。它取自于民族内部的思维特征和思维模式,承载着民族本身丰富的文化内涵。

汉字的创造和应用不仅推进了中华文明的发展,而且对世界文明的发展产生了深远的影响。例如,汉字产生以后,对周边国家产生了深刻影响。日本、越南、朝鲜半岛等国家和地区的文字都是在汉字的基础上创造的。

语言是根植于民族灵魂与血液中的文化符号,真实记录了一个民族的文化进程,成为接续历史与未来的血脉。丢弃了母语、冷落了母语,我们以及我们的后人都将会愧对列祖列宗,成为千古罪人。

Exercises

Section A Thought-provoking questions

1. What does it mean by the six categories of Chinese characters?
2. Do you know how the Shang bone oracles were found?

Section B Fill in the blanks

A. *Jiaguwen*	B. calligraphy	C. less
D. others	E. *Lishu*	F. modern
G. efficient	H. resemble	I. turtle
J. pictographic		

Jiaguwen, or Oracle Bone Script is the earliest form of Chinese writing, likely used from the Middle to the Late Shang dynasty and was etched onto __1__ shells and animal bones, which were then used for divination in the royal Shang court, hence the name "oracle bones". The shape of these characters are often described as "pictographic", in that they __2__ stylized drawings of objects they represent.

Dazhuan, or Greater Seal Script. This stage of Chinese writing flourished from the Late Shang to the Western Zhou dynasties. Unlike __3__, which was carved on bones, *Dazhuan* mainly appeared on cast bronze vessels. In fact, *Jiaguwen* and *Dazhuan* overlapped in time, and they might have been the same script but as they were inscribed on different surface types their visual styles differ due to the quality of the surfaces.

Xiaozhuan, or Lesser Seal Script. This elegant script is the direct parent of the modern, unsimplified Chinese script. Whereas *Dazhuan* characters still resemble *Jiaguwen* and hence somewhat "__4__", *Xiaozhuan* characters are more linear, but have not attained the "angular" look of later Chinese scripts. This script has survived the passage of time and continues to be used in the present age in __5__ and seals.

Lishu, or Clerkly Script. As its name implies, this script was used by government bureaucrats. While it probably appeared at approximately 500 B.C., *Lishu* became widely used in the Qin and Han dynasties when the bureaucrats needed a fast and __6__ script to handle state matters. The marked difference between this script and the *Xiaozhuan* is that *Lishu* characters have __7__ strokes and a more flowing style, therefore easily adaptable to brushes and pens. *Lishu* is still occasionally used in the modern age.

The shape of *Lishu* characters are identical to __8__ Chinese characters. Furthermore, characters were standardized to remove regional variations, and these standard characters are for the most part the same characters written in the present. Therefore, it can be said that Chinese writing reached its maturity at this time (until the 20th century).

Evolution of Chinese writing after *Lishu* is a trend of increasing cursive scripts. These scripts are the ones used in calligraphy.

Kaishu, or Standard Script, is essentially the traditional script used today. It is very similar to __9__, but slightly more cursive and contains serif-like (hook or anchor-like) elements at the corners and end of strokes. *Kaishu* appeared toward the end of the Han dynasty.

Xingshu, or Running Script, can be considered a cursive version of *Kaishu*. Often several strokes are merged into one, especially sequential dots or two strokes perpendicular to each other. It also appeared shortly after the Han dynasty.

Caoshu, or Grass Script, is the most cursive Chinese script. It appeared during the Qin dynasty. The shape of its characters often do not resemble the corresponding *Lishu* or *Kaishu* character, because in that some strokes are merged into one and __10__ are simply left out.

※ **He who grudges expense pays much more in the end. He who has hoarded most will suffers the heaviest loss.**

From Laozi: *Dao De Jing*

(甚爱必大费,多藏必厚亡。)

——老子·《道德经》

※ **Water is the softest thing in the world; but when attacking things hard and resistant, nothing is superior to it.**

From Laozi: *Dao De Jing*

(天下莫柔弱于水,而攻坚强者莫之能胜。)

——老子·《道德经》

Chapter 7

Chinese Idioms and Fables

中国成语和寓言故事

Being an important part of the Chinese language and culture, Chinese idioms and fables are precious gems of Chinese wisdom. As a matter of fact, almost every Chinese idiom has a story behind it. Each idiom alludes to a particular narrative preserved and savored by the Chinese as an encapsulation of unique and significant comments upon life and society.

Fables are lively description of social phenomenon and vivid representation of history. Each fable contains a brief story with an underlying moral. Sometimes the implied common sense moral is evident, while other times it is not so. Some of these stories involve deities, while some involve only mortals or commoners. The merits of these stories lie not so much in their literary worth as in the common folk wisdom they convey. Often, they are short, have a simple plot, and can be told in just a few minutes. Today, many of these folktales have survived as idioms, widely used and understood in the Chinese language. Whether in written or spoken text, the use of idioms can help make the utterance more vivid.

Fifteen source narratives have been selected and rewritten for presentation in this chapter. The significance of these folktales is the display of Chinese values. Some of the common themes are: the triumph of justice over injustice; the supremacy of wisdom over sheer physical strength; examples of cleverness or resourcefulness — to mention just a few. These are all important traditional Chinese values which are passed from one generation to the next through the telling of fables.

1. The Fox Borrows the Tiger's Terror

One day a tiger was hunting around in a forest. An unlucky fox was caught by the tiger.

For the fox, the inescapable fate was very clear — death. Despite the danger, the fox thought hard to find a way out. Promptly, the fox declared to the tiger, "How dare you kill me!"

On hearing the words the tiger was surprised and asked for the reason. The fox raised his voice a bit higher and declared arrogantly: "To tell you the truth, it's I who was accredited by God to the forest as the king of all the animals! If you kill me, it will be against the God's will, you know?" Seeing that the tiger became suspicious, the fox added: "Let's have a test. Let's go through the forest. Follow me and you will see how the animals are frightened of me."

The tiger agreed. So the fox walked ahead of the tiger proudly through the forest. As you can imagine, the animals, seeing the tiger behind, were all terribly frightened and ran away. Then the fox said proudly, "There is no doubt that what I said is true, isn't it?"

The tiger had nothing to say but to acknowledge the result. So the tiger nodded and said, "You are right. You are the king."

2. The Donkey of Guizhou

Thousands of years ago, there was no donkey in Guizhou Province. So someone officious shipped one there. But finding no use for it, he set it loose at the foot of the mountain.

One day, a tiger was walking around to find something to eat, when he saw the strange animal. The huge new comer frightened him quite a bit. He hid himself in the bushes and studied the donkey watchfully. It seemed all right. So the tiger came near to the donkey to have a close look. "Hawhee..." a loud noise burst out, which sent the tiger running away as fast as he could. He could not have any time to think before he settled himself home. The humiliation stung in him. He must come back to that strange thing to see it clearly though he was still haunted by the terrible noise.

The donkey was enraged when the tiger got too close. So the donkey brought his unique skill to bear on the offender — to kick with his hooves. After several bouts, it became very clear that what the donkey had was so much. The tiger jumped upon the donkey in time, cut its throat, and ate it up.

People always tell the story to speak of one's limited tricks.

3. A Foolish Man Buys Shoes

In the past there lived a foolish man in a small kingdom called Zheng. One day he wanted to buy himself a pair of new shoes. He measured his feet with a ruler first and wrote down his size. But he was in such a hurry to set out that he left the measurement at home.

When he arrived at a shoe shop, he felt in the pocket only to find that it was not there. So he said apologetically, "I have left the measurement at home and don't know the size. I'll fetch it in one minute." With these words he hurried off as fast as his legs could carry him.

He ran back home, found it and then went to the shop again. But still it took him quite a while and the shop was already closed then. He had gone to all this trouble for nothing and did not get his shoes.

Then someone asked him, "Did you buy the shoes for yourself or someone else?"

"For myself, of course." he answered. "Then why don't you try the shoes on by yourself?"

"No. Only the measurement is reliable, not my feet. I'd rather trust my measurement than trust my feet."

4. No More Tricks, Mr. Nan Guo!

In the Warring States period of China, there was a state called Qi, the king of which was very fond of listening to the music played on the *yu*. He convened a band of 300 players from his state. Everyday the band was called in to play the *yu* for his Majesty at teatime. The king seemed to be very satisfied with the band and the harmonies performed.

As a matter of fact, one of the players, Nan Guo, knew nothing about the instrument. But he boasted about his skill of playing the *yu*: "Your Majesty, I'm a repute musician. Everybody is deeply touched when they listen to my music. Even the birds, the animals and the plants would dance to my music. I'd very much like to present my performance to you." The king was very pleased to hear that and he recruited him as a member of the band. Nan Guo did manage to pass himself off and went on well with his tricks that each time he tried to seat himself behind and pretended to be playing the *yu* together with the others. Everything seemed good for him. He had never been exposed.

Finally, his days were gone when the prince ascended the throne. As the latter would enjoy solo rather than harmony, the players were called each in to play alone before the king. This time, as we have guessed, Nan Guo was embarrassed to find there was no place for him any more. He could do nothing but wrap up his luggage.

5. Bringing the Painted Dragons to Life by Putting Pupils in Their Eyes

During the Northern and Southern Dynasties, once lived a famous painter named Zhang Sengyao who was highly praised for his fine art by the emperor Liang Wudi.

Once the emperor asked Zhang to do a wall painting of four dragons for the Temple of Andong in Jinling (present city of Nangjing in Jiangsu Province). Zhang Sengyao accepted and completed the paintings in only three days. The painting was beautiful and the dragons were vividly lifelike, as though they were actual dragons!

When Zhang Sengyao was finished, many visitors came in praise of the paintings. However, when people looked closely, they discovered that the otherwise complete dragons were all missing the pupils of their eyes. Everyone repeatedly asked Zhang Sengyao to paint in the pupils, to which he replied, "To give the dragons pupils would not be difficult, but if I did so, these dragons would break out of the wall and fly away." But people didn't believe him.

Finally, he gave up explaining, and agreed to paint in the dragons' eyes. That day, many people gathered in front of the painted wall. Zhang Sengyao stood in front of the crowd and raised his brush. Deftly, he painted in the eyes of two dragons, and a strange thing occurred. Just as he finished the eyes of the second dragon, the sky suddenly was covered with thick, black clouds, a violent wind kicked up from all directions, thunder roared, and lightning flashed. In the flash of a lightning bolt, people could see that the two dragons were shaking the wall apart and rising into the air. Displaying teeth and brandishing claws, they mounted the clouds and mist and rose towards the heavens.

After a moment had passed, the skies cleared and people stood dumbfounded and speechless. Looking at the wall, only the two dragons which were not given eyes remained.

6. The Frog in the Shallow Well

Have you not heard of the frog that lived in a shallow well? It said to a turtle that lived in the East Sea, "I am so happy! When I go out, I jump about on the railing beside the mouth of the well. When I come home, I rest in the holes on the broken wall of the well. If I jump into the water, it comes up to my armpits and holds up my cheeks. If I walk in the mud, it covers up my feet. I look around at the wriggly worms, crabs and tadpoles, and none of them can compare with me. Moreover, I am the lord of this trough of water and I stand up tall in this shallow well. My happiness is full. My dear sir, why don't you come often and look around my place?"

Before the turtle from the East Sea could get its left foot in the well, its right knee got stuck. It hesitated and retreated. The turtle told the frog about the East Sea.

"Even a distance of a thousand *li* cannot give you an idea of the sea's width; even a height of a thousand *zhang* cannot give you an idea of its depth. In the time of King Yu of the Xia Dynasty, there were floods nine years out of ten, but the waters in the sea did not increase. In the time of King Tang of the Shang Dynasty there were droughts seven years out of eight, but the waters in the sea did not decrease. The sea does not change along with the passage of time and its level does not rise or fall according to the amount of rain that falls. The greatest happiness is to live in the East Sea."

After listening to these words, the frog of the shallow well was shocked into realization of his own insignificance and became very ill at ease.

7. His Spear against His Shield

A man of the state of Chu had a spear and a shield for sale. He was loud in praises of his shield.

"My shield is so strong that nothing can pierce it through."

He also sang praises of his spear.

"My spear is so strong that it can pierce through anything."

"What would happen," he was asked, "if your spear is used to pierce your shield?"

It is impossible for an impenetrable shield to coexist with a spear that finds nothing impenetrable.

8. Aping a Beauty

Xi Shi was a famous beauty of the state of Yue in the Spring and Autumn Period. Once she had a pain in her bosom, so she had a frown on her face when she went out. An ugly girl who lived nearby saw her and thought she looked very beautiful. Therefore when she went home, she also put her hands on her bosom and had a frown on her face.

When the rich men in the neighborhood saw her, they shut their doors tightly and did not go out. When the poor men saw her, they took thier wives and children away and gave her a wide berth.

She only knew Xi Shi's frown looked beautiful but she did not know the reason for its beauty.

9. Marking the Boat for a Dropped Sword

A man from the State of Chu was crossing a river in a boat. His sword fell into the water. Immediately he made a mark on the boat.

"This is where my sword fell off," he said.

When the boat reached the bank, he went into the water to look for his sword at the place where he had marked the boat.

The boat had moved but the sword had not. Is this not a very foolish way to look for a sword?

10. Blessing or Blame

Long ago, near the frontier lived an old man. One day he found his horse missing. It was said that the horse was seen running outside the border of the country. The neighbors came to comfort him for the unfortunate loss. But the old man was unexpectedly calm and said, "It doesn't matter; it may not be a bad event, on the contrary, I think it can be a good thing."

One night the old man heard some noise of horses and got up to see what was going on. To his surprise, he saw a beautiful horse together with his own horse. It was clear that his horse had brought a companion home. Hearing the news, the neighbors all came to say congratulation on his good luck. At the greetings, however, the old man was very calm and thoughtful. He said, "It is true that I got a new horse for nothing, but it is hard to say whether it is good or bad. It may be an unlucky thing."

What he said was testified right. The son of the old man was very fond of the horse brought home, and one day, when he was riding the horse, he fell down from the horseback and his left leg was badly injured. Since then he was never able to walk freely. "Nothing serious," the old man said, "perhaps it is a good thing."

A year later, many of the youth there were recruited to fight in a war and most of them died. The son of the old man was absolved from the obligation for his disability, so he escaped death.

11. An Illusory Snake in a Goblet

In Jin Dynasty there was a man named Yue Guang who was fond of drinking alcohol. One day, he invited a friend to his house to drink together. Suddenly, his friend saw the reflection of a snake swimming in the goblet.

He got so much frightened that he took ill on bed after getting home. Neither any doctor nor any medicine could cure his illness. Yue Guang came to see him and asked about the cause of his disease. When he got to know the cause, he pulled his friend from the bed immediately and took him to his house.

Yue Guang made his friend sit where he used to, pouring a goblet of alcohol for him, and asked him, "Is there any snake reflection in the goblet?" There was still a "snake reflection" in the goblet! Yue casually took away the bow hanging on the wall. This time, the "snake reflection" disappeared. "So it was the bow reflection that was in the goblet!" His friend at once got well from his illness.

12. A Walk Learner in Handan

During the Warring States Period, Handan, the capital of the State of Zhao, was famous for people's walking style. They walked in vigorous elegant strides. People in other places admired them very much. They thought the Handanners' way of walking was the best under the heaven. A young lad in the town of Shouling, the state of Yan, heard about that and went a long way there to learn the strides.

Arriving in the town of Handan, the young man set about watching how the people there walked in the street. He was well indulged in the study all day long; sometimes he followed one this way and sometimes another that way.

As time passed, the young man felt more and more worried because he had not learned to walk as the natives there. And to make things worse, he found himself unable to walk in his own way in the end. So he had no choice but to crawl home.

13. Mend the Fold After a Sheep Is Lost

During the Warring States Period, the State of Chu was not very powerful. The king and the important court officials were dissolute and incompetent. They indulged in luxury and excessive pleasure. Zhuang Xin, one of the ministers, foresaw that the country was in danger. One day he remonstrated with the king: "Your Majesty, wherever you go, you're always surrounded by people who flatter you with what you like. They try everything to please you and you forget to tend to state affairs. If you go on like this, no doubt, the country will perish sooner or later."

The King of Chu flew into a rage. "How dare you! You even use such vicious words to curse my country and arouse resentment among the people!" Zhuang Xin explained, "I dare not curse the State of Chu. But I really have a premonition that Chu is facing great danger." Seeing that the king is especially fond of those corrupt officials and trust them in everything, the minister thought Chu is bound to extinct. So he asked the king to let him leave Chu. He wanted to go to the State of Zhao and stay there for a while.

The king gave him the leave.

Five months later, the King of Qin sent his troops to invade Chu and occupied a large tract of its territory. The King of Chu himself went into exile. Now, the king remembered Zhuang Xin's words. He sent his men to fetch him. When the king saw Zhuang Xin again, he asked him, "What can I do now?"

Zhuang Xin replied, "It's not too late if you mend the sheepfold when you find a sheep is missing." He then made some good suggestions to rehabilitate the state and recover the lost land. The king was very much pleased.

The idiom "mend the fold after a sheep is lost" has developed from Zhuang Xin's answer to the king.

14. Play the Tune to a Cow

In ancient time, there lived a musician named Gongming Yi. He was very good at playing the Zheng, a 21- or 25- stringed plucked instrument. But he also behaved foolishly sometimes.

One day, he saw a cow eating grass in the field near his house. He was inspired by the scene and ran outside to play a tune for the cow. Gongming Yi played beautifully and he himself was intoxicated by the music. But the cow paid no heed to the beautiful tune. It simply focused its attention on eating the grass. Gongming Yi was surprised and couldn't understand why the cow was so indifferent to his performance. Obviously, it is not because his performance is poor, but the cow could neither understand nor appreciate his elegant music!

From that story comes the idiom "play the tune to a cow" which implies that someone speaks or writes without considering his audience. Generally speaking, the speaker or writer has overestimated his listeners or readers. In these cases, the idiom mocks the audience rather than the speaker.

15. Draw a Snake and Add Feet to It

An official of the ancient State of Chu awarded a pot of wine to his men after the ceremony of Spring Sacrifice. One man said, "We have only one pot of wine. It's not enough for all of us but sufficient for one. Let's determine who'll have the wine by drawing a snake on the ground. He who finishes first will have the wine."

The others agreed. Very soon, one man finished his snake. He was about to drink the wine when he saw the others were still busy drawing. He said complacently, "How slow you are! I still have enough time to add feet to my snake." But before he finished the feet, another man finished his snake and grabbed the pot from him, saying, "Whoever has seen a snake with feet? Yours is not a snake. So the wine should be mine!" He drank the wine. The man adding feet to the snake had to give in and could only regret his foolishness.

Word Bank

allude	暗指，提及
savor	品尝，欣赏
encapsulation	压缩，节略
resourcefulness	足智多谋，机智
accredit	委任，派往
officious	好管闲事的
bout	回合，较量
convene	召集
railing	围栏
tadpoles	蝌蚪
trough	水槽
berth	安全距离，回旋余地
absolve	赦免，开脱
dissolute	荒淫
remonstrate	规劝
premonition	预感
tract	一片土地
sheepfold	羊栏
intoxicate	陶醉
heed	留意，注意
mock	嘲讽
allay	减轻

参考译文

汉语成语和寓言故事是中国语言文化和智慧宝库中耀眼夺目的璀璨明珠。事实上，每则成语皆有一段历史典故，内容丰富，语言精粹，寓意深刻，哲理经典。

寓言故事是人类最通俗的语言，是历史最形象的表述。每则寓言都是一个包含了某种道理的故事，有时这个道理是显而易见的常识，有时则需要我们去体会和感悟。寓言故事所具有的道德教育功能远胜于其文学价值。寓言故事短小简洁，经过千百年来的锤炼，已经精炼为成语，被人们普遍接受并广泛使用。无论讲话还是写文章，成语都能使谈吐焕彩、文章生辉、意味隽永。

本章中所提供的 15 则寓言故事亦为成语故事。这些故事反映了中国人的价值观，例如：正义战胜邪恶、智慧胜过力量和足智多谋的魅力等。这些都是中国重要的传统价值观，它们通过语言的代代相传而深入人心。

1. 狐假虎威

有一天，一只老虎正在深山老林里转悠，搜寻猎物，突然发现了一只狐狸，便迅速抓住了它。

狐狸生性狡猾，它知道今天被老虎逮住以后，前景一定不妙，于是就编出一个谎言，对老虎说："我是天帝派到山林中来当百兽之王的，你要是吃了我，天帝是不会饶恕你的。"

老虎对狐狸的话将信将疑，便问："你当百兽之王，有何证据？"狐狸赶紧说："你如果不相信我的话，可以随我到山林中去走一走，我让你亲眼看看百兽对我望而生畏的样子。"

老虎想这倒也是个办法，于是就让狐狸在前面带路，自己尾随其后，一道向山林的深处走去。森林中的野兔、山羊、花鹿、黑熊等各种兽类远远地看见老虎来了，一个个都吓得魂飞魄散，纷纷夺路逃命。

转了一圈之后，狐狸洋洋得意地对老虎说道："现在你该看到了吧？森林中的百兽，有谁敢不怕我？"

老虎只得点头说："对，你是林中之王。"

2. 黔驴技穷

过去贵州(黔)这个地方没有驴。有好事者用船运来了一头驴，运来后却没有什么用处，就把驴放到山脚下。

一只老虎看见了驴，以为这个躯体高大的家伙一定很神奇，就躲在树林里偷偷观察着，后来又悄悄走出来，小心翼翼地接近驴，想看看仔细。

这时，驴叫了一声，老虎大吃一惊，远远躲开，以为驴要咬自己了，非常恐惧。然而，老虎反复观察以后，觉得驴并没有什么特殊本领，而且越来越熟悉驴的叫声了。

老虎接着走到驴的周围，在它身边转来转去，还不敢上去攻击驴。后来，老虎慢慢逼近驴，越来越放肆，或者碰它一下，或者靠它一下，不断冒犯它。驴非常恼怒，就用蹄子去踢老虎。

老虎心里盘算着："你的本事也不过如此罢了！"非常高兴。于是，老虎腾空扑去，咬断了驴的喉管，啃完了驴肉，才离去。

人们常用这个故事来比喻某人有限的本领已经用尽，再没有别的办法了。

3. 郑人买履

郑国有个人想去买一双鞋，他先量了自己的脚，然后画了一个底样的尺码。

他匆忙走到集市上，看中了一双鞋子，却突然想起："我忘了拿量好的尺码来了。"于是，赶紧跑回去拿底样。等到他赶回来时，集市已散了，鞋子也就没有买成。

有人问他："你用自己的脚去试鞋子不就行了吗？为何还要跑回去看鞋样呢？"

他说："我宁可相信自己量好的尺码，也不相信自己的脚。"

4. 滥竽充数

战国时代，齐国的国君齐宣王爱好音乐，尤其喜欢听吹竽，手下有 300 个善于吹竽的乐师。齐宣王喜欢热闹，爱摆排场，总想在人前显示做国君的威严，所以每次听吹竽的时候，总是叫这 300 个人在一起合奏。

有个南郭先生听说了齐宣王的这个癖好，觉得有机可乘，是个赚钱的好机会，就跑到齐宣王那里去，吹嘘自己说："大王啊，我是个有名的乐师，听过我吹竽的人没有不被感动的，就是鸟兽听了也会翩翩起舞，花草听了也会合着节拍颤动，我愿把我的绝技献给大王。"齐宣王听后很高兴，不加考查，很痛快地收下了他，把他也编入那支 300 人的吹竽队。南郭先生就这样靠着蒙骗混过了一天又一天，一直没有被识破。

可是好景不长，过了几年，爱听竽合奏的齐宣王死了，他的儿子齐湣王继承了王位。齐湣王也爱听吹竽，可是他和齐宣王不一样，喜欢听独奏。于是齐湣王发布了一道命令，要这300个人好好练习，做好准备，他将让他们一个个地轮流吹竽给他欣赏。乐师们知道命令后都积极练习，想一展身手，只有那个滥竽充数的南郭先生急得像热锅上的蚂蚁，惶惶不可终日。他想来想去，觉得这次再也混不过去了，只好连夜收拾行李逃走了。

5. 画龙点睛

南北朝时期的梁朝，有位很出名的大画家名叫张僧繇，他的绘画技术很高超，得到当时的皇帝梁武帝的大力赞赏。

传说，有一年，梁武帝要张僧繇为金陵（现江苏省南京市）的安东寺作画，在寺庙的墙壁上画四条金龙。他答应下来，仅用三天时间就画好了。这些龙画得栩栩如生，惟妙惟肖，简直就像真龙一样活灵活现。

张僧繇画好后，吸引很多人前去观看，都称赞画得好，太逼真了。可是，当人们走近一看，发现美中不足的是四条龙全都没有眼睛。大家纷纷请求他，把龙眼睛点上。张僧繇解释说："给龙点上眼珠并不难，但是点上了眼珠这些龙会破壁飞走的。"

大家听后谁都不相信，认为他这样解释很荒唐，墙上的龙怎么会飞走呢？日子长了，很多人都以为他是在说谎。

张僧繇被逼得没有办法，不得不答应给龙"点睛"。这一天，在寺庙墙壁前有很多人围观，张僧繇当着众人的面，提起画笔，轻轻地给两条龙点上眼睛。奇怪的事情果然发生了，他刚点上第二条龙的眼睛，突然间天空乌云密布，狂风四起，雷鸣电闪。在雷电之中，人们看见被"点睛"的两条龙震破墙壁凌空而起，张牙舞爪地腾云驾雾飞向天空。

过了一会，云散天晴，人们吓得目瞪口呆，一句话都说不出来了。再看看墙上，只剩下了没有被点上眼睛的两条龙，而另外两条被"点睛"的龙已不知去向。

6. 井底之蛙

一口废井里住着一只青蛙。有一天，青蛙在井边碰上了一只从海里来的大龟。

青蛙就对海龟夸口说："你看，我住在这里多快乐！有时高兴了，就在井栏边跳跃一阵；疲倦了，就回到井里，在砖洞边睡一觉。或者只留出头和嘴巴，安安静静地把全身泡在水里，或者在软绵绵的泥浆里散一会步，也很舒适。看看那些虾和蝌蚪，谁也比不上我。而且，我是这口井里的主人，在这井里极其自由自在，你为什么不常到井里来游赏呢！"

那海龟听了青蛙的话，倒真想进去看看。但它的左脚还没有整个伸进去，右脚就已经被卡住了。它连忙后退了两步，把大海的情形告诉青蛙说："你看过海吗？海的广大，哪止千里；海的深度，哪止千丈。夏朝禹王时，十年里有九年大水，海里的水，并没涨多少；商朝汤王时，八年里有七年大旱，海里的水，也未见浅多少。可见大海是不受旱涝影响的。住在那样的大海里，才是真的快乐呢！"

井蛙听了海龟的一番话，吃惊地待在那里，再也没有话可说了。

7. 自相矛盾

有一个楚国人在街头贩卖盾和矛，他自我吹嘘说："我所卖的盾坚固无比，任何武器都不能刺穿它。"

然后又继续大放厥词："我所卖的矛锋利无比，任何东西都能够刺得进去。"

有人问他："用你的矛刺你的盾，会怎么样呢？"

能抵挡任何武器的盾和能刺进任何东西的矛是不可能同时存在的。

8. 东施效颦

春秋时代，越国有一位美女名叫西施。

西施患有心口疼的毛病。有一天，她的病又犯了，只见她手捂胸口，紧蹙双眉，流露出一种娇媚柔弱的女性美。当她从乡间走过的时候，乡里人无不睁大眼睛注视。

乡下有一个丑女子，名叫东施。这一天，她看到西施捂着胸口、皱着双眉的样子竟博得这么多人的青睐，因此，也学着西施的样子，手捂胸口、紧皱眉头，在村里走来走去。哪知这丑女的矫揉造作使她原本就丑陋的样子更难看了。

结果，乡间的富人看见丑女的怪模样，马上把门紧紧关上；乡间的穷人看见丑女走过来，马上拉着妻子、带着孩子远远地躲开。

这个丑女人只知道西施皱眉的样子很美，却不知道她为什么很美，而去简单模仿她的样子，结果反被人讥笑。

9. 刻舟求剑

楚国有个人乘船渡江。剑从船上掉进水里了。这个人便急忙在船边刻下一个记号，说："这是我的剑掉下去的地方。"然后就悠闲地等着船靠岸。等船靠岸之后，他就从刻记号的地方跳进水里去找剑，可是再也没有找到剑。

船开走了，而剑没有动，这样的寻剑方法又怎么行得通？

10. 塞翁失马

战国时期，靠近北部边城，住着一个老人，名叫塞翁，以养马为生。一天他发觉有一匹马离群走失，越界跑到北边的胡国去了。当时知道这件事的人，都认为损失一匹马很可惜，跑来安慰他。

塞翁见有人劝慰，笑了笑说："丢了一匹马损失不大，没准会带来什么福气呢。"

数月之后，从前越界到胡国去的那匹马，不但自己认路跑了回来，还带回胡国的一匹骏马。人们知道了这件事情，于是接踵而来向塞翁道贺说："还是您有远见，马不仅没有丢，还带回一匹好马，真是福气呀。"但是塞翁却说："白白得了一匹好马，不一定是什么福气，这件好事或许带来灾祸也未可知。"

塞翁有个独生子，非常喜欢骑马。他很爱那匹骏马，时常骑它出去。一天，他从马背上跌下来，摔断了腿。邻居听说，纷纷前来慰问。

塞翁说："没什么，腿摔断了却保住了性命，或许是福气呢。"

不久，匈奴兵大举入侵，青年人被应征入伍，塞翁的儿子因为摔断了腿，不能去当兵。入伍的青年都战死了，唯有塞翁的儿子保全了性命。

11. 杯弓蛇影

晋朝有个叫乐广的人，爱喝酒。一天，他邀请朋友到家里来对斟对饮。忽然，朋友看见酒杯里有条蛇影在游动。

他受了惊吓，回去便一病不起。请医服药，都无起色。乐广跑来看他，问明生病的缘由。乐广听后一把拉起朋友往家走。

他让朋友坐在原处，斟满酒问："有蛇影吗？"杯子里还有"蛇影"！乐广随手取下墙上的弓。这次，"蛇影"不见了！"杯子里原来是弓影呀！"朋友的病顿时好了！

12. 邯郸学步

战国时，赵国都城邯郸以人们走路的姿势闻名。邯郸人的步伐充满活力，非常优美。其他地方人都很羡慕这一点，他们认为邯郸人的走路姿势是天底下最优美的。

燕国寿陵有个少年，听说邯郸人走路很好看，就赶去邯郸跟人家学习步法。可是，折腾了许多年，他不仅没有掌握邯郸人走路的独特技能，而且忘记了自己原来走路的步法，结果只好爬着回家了。

13. 亡羊补牢

战国时期，楚襄王统治楚国时，国势不振。楚王和重要的大臣都荒淫无能。他们一直沉溺于奢侈享乐之中。大臣庄辛预见到楚国会发生危险。一天他劝谏楚王说："陛下，无论你走到哪儿，身旁总是那些奉承您的人，他们想尽办法让您高兴，您就忘了处理国事。长此以往，国家迟早会灭亡的。"

楚王大怒："大胆！你居然用这样恶毒的话来诅咒我的国家，蓄意挑起人民的不满！"庄辛解释说："我不敢诅咒楚国，但我可以预言楚国正面临着巨大的危险。"庄辛见楚王如此宠信那些腐败的大臣，相信楚国必定要亡国。于是他向楚王请求离开楚国，到赵国居住一段时间。

楚王同意了，他便到赵国去了。五个月之后，秦君果然派军入侵楚国，占领了大片土地。楚王被迫流亡。这时，他想起了庄辛的劝谏，于是派人接庄辛回来。楚王见了庄辛，便问："现在我该怎么办呢？"

庄辛回答说："丢了羊，就把羊圈修好，不算迟。"然后他提出许多如何重振国家，收复失地的好谋略。楚王非常高兴。

成语"亡羊补牢"就是由庄辛对楚王的回答而来的。

14. 对牛弹琴

古时候，有个著名的音乐家公明仪。他弹筝技艺很好，但有时会做些傻事。

有一天，他看到一头牛在他家附近的田里吃草。他一下子有了灵感，就跑出去为这头牛弹琴。公明仪弹的曲子非常优美，他自己也陶醉在音乐之中。可是那头牛根本不理会那美妙的音乐，只顾着吃草。公明仪感到十分奇怪，不明白为什么牛对他的演奏无动于衷。很明显，牛不理会他并不是因为他的演奏很糟糕，而是因为牛听不懂也欣赏不了这种高深的曲调。

"对牛弹琴"这个成语就是从上述故事演化而来的，指那些说话或写东西不考虑听众或读者的人。一般来说，是说话人或作者高估了听众或读者。所以，这则成语嘲讽的主要是听众或观众，而不是说话者。

15. 画蛇添足

楚国有一个官员，在春天祭祖之后，便将一壶酒赏给他的办事人员。有人提议："我们只有一壶酒，肯定不够我们大家喝的，一个人喝倒是绰绰有余。我们每人在地上画一条蛇，谁画得最快，就把这壶酒给他。"大家都同意了。有一个人很快就把蛇画好了。他正打算喝这壶酒时，看见别人都还忙着画呢，就得意扬扬地说："你们画得好慢呀，等我再画上几只脚吧！"他的蛇脚还没画完，另一个人已经把蛇画好了。那人把酒壶夺了过去说："有谁见过长脚的蛇？你画的不是蛇，这壶酒应该是我的了。"说罢，就喝起酒来。那个给蛇画脚的人没办法，只能懊悔自己的愚蠢。

Exercises

Section A Thought-provoking questions

1. What is a fable?
2. What does the idiom about dotting the eyes of the dragon mean now?
3. When is the idiom in the first story usually used?
4. What does "塞翁失马,焉知非福" mean in English?

Section B Fill in the blanks with the idioms introduced in this chapter

1. ________ is used to describe the psychological state of being frightened caused by taking illusions as reality.
2. The expression ________ is now usually adopted to indicate the case that a person can make his speech or composition smartly lively just with only a few pointed key words or expressions.
3. The story ________ describes the case in which the spurious is mixed with the genuine.
4. The fable ________ tells us that man should not stick stubbornly to his own opinion, instead he should make changes according to specific conditions.
5. The idiom ________ is saying that we have to let things go in its natural course. Being too anxious to help an event to develop often results in the contrary to our intent.
6. A loss may turn out to be a gain is what the fable ________ wants to tell us.
7. Cheap tricks never last is the theme of the fable ________.
8. The story ________ warns us not to formally copy the way of others.
9. If someone is ________, he is addressing the wrong audience or talking over somebody's head.
10. We still use the metaphor ________ to advise someone that even when he has made a mistake and suffered losses, he can still remedy it by drawing lessons from the mistake.

※ **There are three kinds of beneficial friends and three kinds of detrimental friends: It is beneficial to make friends with people who are upright, honest, and well informed. It is detrimental to make friends with people who are crooked, dishonest, and fast-talking.**

From *Analects of Confucius*

(益者三友,损者三友。友直、友谅、友多闻,益矣。友便辟、友善柔、友便佞,损矣。)

——《论语》

※ **To commit a transgression and not reform is the real transgression!**

From *Analects of Confucius*

(过而不改,是谓过矣!)

——《论语》

Chapter 8

Chinese Food Culture

中国饮食文化

1. A Brief Introduction to Food Culture

1) Importance

As a common saying goes, there are three luxuries in one's life: an American house, a Japanese wife and Chinese food. That is to say Chinese food is most delicious, nutritious and inviting. In China, food culture not only has developed highly, but also has a great social importance. In the first place, customarily, in important events, such as wedding, festivity celebrations, etc., feasting is often an indispensable arrangement. Secondly, cuisine is an important means in social life. When a good friend comes from afar, he is entertained with rich and various foods by the host. Thirdly, business agreements may be achieved more efficiently and satisfactorily on the dinner table than elsewhere.

2) Range of Edibilities

Chinese people are expert at eating. In the light of regimen and nutrition, they eat a greater variety of food than the Westerners. They eat certain animals' viscera that the Westerners don't. They consider that liver is nutrimental for blood; kidney is nutrimental for kidney, etc. with the Cantonese in particular. Cantonese are said to be gourmets. The catalogue of delicious foods for them is very extensive and varied. There is a popular joke among people saying that the Cantonese eat practically everything that walks on the ground except cars, that swims in the water except ships, and that flies in the sky except airplanes.

In addition, Chinese people eat a lot of vegetable dishes, which are prepared often as meat dishes. In the Chinese vegetable restaurants, you can discover on the menu "vegetable pig's kidney", "vegetable pig's intestines", "vegetable fish", "vegetable chicken", etc. These are mostly bean products. Bean curd is popular among all people, rich or poor. Soy sauce is a Chinese industry, which is a delicious, appetizing and nutritious condiment. Soy sauce manufacture is a great contribution to nutrition and health.

3) Variety of Cookery

Chinese food is widely known for its variety and abundance. According to data on the subject, the number of well-known ancient and modern Chinese dishes amounts to

8,000. The ingredients may be roughly classified into 600 categories. There are 48 different basic ways of cooking, including pan frying, stir-frying, brewing, deep-frying, stewing, roasting, grilling, instant boiling, steaming, braising (with soy sauce), broiling, baking, etc.

4) Requirement in Cookery

Generally speaking, the Chinese cooking lays emphasis on the "complete presence of color, aroma and taste". "Color" refers not only to the color but also to the modeling of foods. Foods are often carved by the chef into various artistic designs. Their modeling is often exquisite and symbolic. For example, a fish dish symbolizes "surplus" (In Chinese language, "fish" and "surplus" both are pronounced "yu"). "Aroma" refers to the fragrant and appetizing smell of the dishes served on the table before eating. The Chinese people knew very early to use spices to prepare strongly fragrant dishes. "Taste" involves proper seasoning and fine slicing techniques. These three essential factors are achieved by careful coordination of a series of delicate activities: selecting ingredients, mixing flavors, timing and cooking, adjustment of the heat, and laying out the food on the plate. Thus every dish on the Chinese dinner table looks like a piece of art, good-looking and delicious.

What is worth mentioning is that there's a lot of cultural background knowledge involved in the naming of Chinese dishes. Often, it's hard, even for the Chinese people themselves, to tell what is actually in a certain dish by the name of it until it is served on the table. Of course, one can always turn to the waiter or waitress for explanation. In most cases, waiters and waitresses are ready to satisfy anyone's curiosity.

Apart from having regard for the above-mentioned three essential factors — "color, aroma and taste", Chinese cuisine attaches great importance to nutrition. As a matter of fact, Chinese cuisine has long been closely related to traditional Chinese medicine. Ginseng, walnut, Chinese angelica and the fruit of Chinese wolfberry are often used as ingredients in certain Chinese dishes.

2. Four Major Groups of Chinese Cuisine

China is a vast country with a wealth of local specialities for the cooking, and in different places, there are different ways for preparing dishes. So it is believed that its history and its unique cookery as well as the geographical location, climatic features, natural resources and eating habits of a specific area is inevitably indispensable to the formation of certain cuisine. Many different cuisines unique to certain areas are formed, for instance, Shandong cuisine, Beijing cuisine, Shanghai cuisine, Sichuan cuisine, Jiangsu cuisine, Zhejiang cuisine, Anhui cuisine, Hunan cuisine, Hubei cuisine, Fujian cuisine, Shannxi cuisine, Henan cuisine, north-eastern China cuisine, royal style cuisine, Muslim style cuisine and vegetarian cuisine. But generally speaking, the Chinese cuisine can be divided into four major groups, based on the localities of their origin (Of course, they can be further divided into eight groups). The four major groups are: Yue (Guangdong) group, Chuan (Sichuan) group, Lu (Shangdong) group and Su (Suzhou, Yangzhou and Hangzhou) group. Below is a brief introduction to their features:

1) Yue (Guangdong) Cuisine or the Canton School

Yue Cuisine includes Guangdong and Guangxi cooking. It is characterized firstly by its wide and strict selection of ingredients. Seafood and game food are the first-rate courses. Besides chicken, duck and goose, pigeon, partridge and squail also make delectable dishes. For seafood, the Cantonese take to grouper, pomfret, hairtail, conger eel, turtle, prawn and crab. Their favorite game foods include reptiles and amphibians: terrapin, tortoise and snake. Yue Cuisine holds fastidious norms in selecting ingredients.

Secondly, Guangdong people favor light, delicious, refreshing and slippery tastes. Their cooking methods are mostly steaming, boiling, sauté and stir-frying with thick gravy. Dishes are lightly cooked and not as highly spicy and hot as the other three groups. Due to the long duration of summer, they favor light and refreshing foods and aquatic food, and like to taste the original flavor of sea foods and fresh foods. Only in winter do they eat fatty foods and strongly flavored foods, such as dog meat, stewed pork chunks, fried oyster, braised eel, pig's knuckle, etc.

The third characteristic of Guangdong cuisine is plenty of supportive vegetables, due to the substantial scope of local produce. In the north of Guangdong are grown plenty of mushrooms and bamboo shoots. With the favorable climate, the province abounds also in rich varieties of fruits, such as pineapple, litchi, plum, cocoa nut, banana, Chinese chestnut, etc. All these can make hygienic dishes.

The fourth characteristic is the many kinds of porridges and refreshments. The long summer and the lot of perspiration require meat porridges to replenish the nutriments and water lost. Porridge shops (including some canteens affiliated to "five or four-star" hotels) prepare a stock of base porridge (called "taste porridge") with ingredients of hens, pig bones, dried scallops and soybean rolls. When a certain kind of porridge is required, the cook adds to the base porridge some other suitable, ready-made ingredients such as fish, shrimp, crab, meat ball, pig's giblets, beef, chicken, duckling, etc., as well as ginger, Chinese onion and pepper powder. Located at the junction of international exchanges, Guangzhou has amalgamated both the overseas and domestic merits in preparing refreshments. Every teahouse or hotel provides hundreds of cakes and refreshments, which are worth trying.

2) Chuan (Sichuan) Cuisine

World-famous Chuan Cuisine traces back to the ancient Ba Kingdom (modern Chongqing) and Shu Kingdom (modern Chengdu) and is distinguished for its oily and hot and spicy taste. Their uniquely hot, pungent flavor is created by a mixture of spices and condiments, including red pepper, garlic and ginger. This is due to the foggy, cloudy and damp climate in the Sichuan Basin. Hot food is useful for dispersing dampness. Sichuan folks are keen for hot and spicy oxen's giblet pot, hot and spicy beancurd and other hot and spicy foods.

Another characteristic of the Chuan cuisine is its preparation of different dishes with the same raw material. With a piece of half-fat, half-lean pork, Sichuan cooks can prepare a number of different dishes with different flavors, such as salted-fried pork slices, re-cooked pork slices, sweet and hot shredded pork, fried pork cubes, sliced pork cooked with rice crust, sweet steamed pork chunks, salty steamed pork chunks, pork steamed with ground glutinous rice, white cut hot pork, etc.

The third characteristic of the Chuan cuisine is the tasty snacks, including hot ox-head meat, spiced chicken, tea-stewed ducking, marinated rabbit meat, pickled vegetables, dumplings, eight-treasure rice puddings, etc.

3) Lu (Shandong) Cuisine

Lu Cuisine enjoys a long history and wide popularity and is the crystallization of the Qi and Lu culture of the ancient China. It has traces of palatial cuisine. Its first characteristic is its strongly flavored dishes made of costly ingredients such as petrel nest, shark fin, abalone, fish tripe, sea cucumber, deer meat, mushroom, white fungus, clam, etc.

Due to the long duration of the cold weather in north China and shortage of vegetables, the cooks in Shandong are skilled in making high-calorie and high-protein dishes. It is the second characteristic of the Lu cuisine. Typical Shandong delicacies are: skin-crisp roasted duck (Peking Duck), nine-bends pig intestines, bone-detached braised chicken, in-wok-fried Yellow River carp, conch braised in soy sauce, and deep-fried oyster.

Lu cuisine cooks used to keep a wok of flavoring broth (with old hen and pig knuckles, etc., as ingredients) and sprinkle it into the pan as a substitute for gourmet powder. It is the third characteristic as well as a tradition of the Lu cuisine. The Lu cuisine cooks are also expert at preparing milk soups. The vegetable milk soup in Jinan has enjoyed a fame.

4) Su Cuisine

Su Cuisine originated from Suzhou and later from Yangzhou and Hangzhou too, these places being known as a land flowing with milk and honey. Its first characteristic is the combination of relishes of both the Southerners and the Northerners. This region was the abode of the emperors during the Six Dynasties and the Southern Song Dynasty. The Great Canal flowing through the region has facilitated the exchanges between the South and the North. The Su cuisine chefs, on the one hand are dexterous in cooking southern style dishes, which are tasty and refreshing, and on the other hand are dexterous in cooking high-heat and high-protein dishes, such as stewed pig knuckles with ham, braised "Lion's Head" (pork balls) and stir-fried eel pastry. In the menu of the Su cuisine can be found a long list of dishes suiting both the Southerners and the Northerners.

Plenty of lake produce and seafood constitute the second characteristic of the Su cuisine. Such dishes include the Crab-yellow Lion's Head, crab-yellow petrel nest, shark fin in shrimp soup, West-Lake sweet-sour fish, steamed hilsa herring (produced in the Fuchun River), meat-stuffed lotus root, spicy Tai-Lake crucian carp soup, lotus-seed duck broth, etc.

The third characteristic of the Su cuisine is its exquisite refreshments and snacks, such as pine-nut-crystalline-meat sweet cake, crab-yellow-soup bun, crab-yellow steamed dumpling, Ningbo dumpling, etc., which are famed throughout China.

It is interesting to note that the four categories of cuisine are described as four kinds of persons: Su Cuisine is a Southern beauty, graceful and elegant; Lu Cuisine a Northern man, simple and robust; Yue Cuisine a pampered son of a wealthy family, refined and romantic; and Chuan Cuisine a celebrity, talented and versatile.

3. Chopsticks

1) Eating Utensils

When food is mentioned, it is highly necessary to say something about the eating utensils. It is said that there are generally three ways for people of picking up food to eat: 40% of people grasp or tear food with their bare hands, 30% use knife and fork, and 30% make use of chopsticks. It is the Chinese who first used chopsticks thousands of years ago.

So chopsticks can be said to be a great invention by the Chinese. They are regarded as the extension of fingers, which are not afraid of extreme heat and coldness. But exactly when the Chinese began to use chopsticks, as an eating instrument is anybody's guess. It is said that people began using chopsticks during the Shang Dynasty. They were first mentioned in *Liji* (*The Book of Rites*), a work compiled nearly 2,000 years ago. Likewise they were initially in the form of twigs, which the primitive Chinese possibly used to pick up a roast after they began to use fire. The twigs evolved into the wooden, tapering sticks, as we know them today. It is generally held that chopsticks began to be called *kuaizi* since the Ming Dynasty. But in the documents of the Ming and the Qing dynasties, *kuaizi* was seldom used, instead, *zhu* was often used to refer to chopsticks, especially in literary works.

2) Materials of Chopsticks

Zheng Chuanyin and Zhang Jian made a succinct summary about the invention and development of chopsticks in the *Dictionary of Chinese Folk Customs*, "Chopsticks, a food picking utensil made of bamboo or wood, is widely used by the Hans and some minority ethnic groups. In remote ages, they were made of branches, bamboo or natural animal bones. Later they were made of scraped bamboo or wood. Ivory and jade chopsticks appeared during the Xia and Shang dynasties; bronze and iron chopsticks emerged during the Spring and Autumn Period. Lacquer chopsticks did not appear until the Han Dynasty. Later silver and gold chopsticks were made. Among all kinds of chopsticks, the ones made with rhinoceros horns, jade or ebony inlaid with gold were the rarest."

Chopsticks may be made of several materials: bamboo, wood, gold, silver, ivory, pewter, and plastics. In the cross-section, they may be either round or square. Some of them are engraved with colored pictures or calligraphy for decoration. Ordinary chopsticks used in Chinese homes are made of wood or bamboo; those for banquets are often ivory, whereas gold ones belonged only to the royalty and aristocracy.

3) Holding of Chopsticks

Whatever their shapes or their material, chopsticks should go in pairs, and the pair must be identical to each other. The correct way to use chopsticks is to hold the pair in the hollow between the thumb and forefinger of your fork hand. The one closest to your body should rest on the first joint of the ring finger and stay relatively immobile. Hold the other one with the forefinger and middle finger, which manipulate it like pinchers to pick up the food. The strength applied by the fingers should vary with the things to be taken hold of. The skill to pick up, with speed and dexterity, small things like beans and peanuts and slippery things like slices of preserved eggs can only come from practice and coordinated action of the fingers.

4) Chopsticks — Dexterity and Intelligence of the Chinese People

Incidentally, using chopsticks has a great deal in common with wielding a brush to write Chinese characters. Those who write with a good hand, some scholars have observed, are invariably those who handle the chopsticks correctly. One holds the writing brush in the same way as one would the moving chopsticks and, while writing, one must achieve coordination in the movement of the shoulder, arm, wrist and fingers in order to write well. Westerners are very much fascinated at the skills the Chinese display at chopsticks and it is said that there are training centers established specially to teach people how to handle chopsticks.

The invention of chopsticks fully displays the dexterity and intelligence of the

Chinese people. According to some Japanese scholars, to properly handle chopsticks requires the coordination of over 80 joints and 50 muscles; what's more, certain cranial nerves are also involved. Therefore, using chopsticks can help make people more dexterous and intelligent.

Westerners are often impressed with the cleverness of the Chinese hand that makes embroideries and clay sculptures with such consummate skill. Couldn't this skill be attributed to the constant use of chopsticks?

Chopsticks are initially used in China, but the first museum in the world of chopsticks is established in Germany, where are exhibited, from various countries and regions and periods in history, more than 10,000 pairs of chopsticks that are made of gold, silver, jade, animal bones, etc.

Word Bank

vegetable pig's kidney 素腰花
vegetable pig's intestines 素肠
vegetable fish 素鱼
vegetable chicken 素鸡
vegetable restaurant 素菜馆
taper 使逐渐尖细
ivory 象牙
pewter 白镴,锡镴(一种以锡为主要成分的合金)
royalty 皇室
aristocracy 贵族

参考译文

1. 饮食文化简介

1) 饮食的重要性

有句话说得好:"人生有三大奢望:拥有一栋美国别墅,家有日本娇妻,享用中国美食"。意思是说中国饮食味道鲜美,营养丰富,香味诱人。在中国,饮食文化发展迅速,而且被赋予重要的社会意义。首先,在举行婚丧嫁娶、节日庆典这类大事时,总是以宴席为其重要形式甚至是活动的高潮部分。其次,它是中国人社交的重要手段。如果有朋友自远方来,主人会尽地主之谊,准备丰盛的美味佳肴招待宾客。第三,在餐桌上,在筷箸斛盏交错之间,商务洽谈往往能够更容易达到理想的效果。

2) 可食之物

中国人在吃的方面是很擅长的。从养身和营养的角度来看,中国人吃的食物种类比西方人要多得多。西方人不吃动物内脏,而中国人却认为"吃啥补啥",肝可以补血,肾可以补肾,对于注重美食的广东人来说更是如此。广东人吃的东西真是千奇百怪,形形色色。怪不得民间流传着这样一句玩笑话："广东人地上跑的除了小车、水里游的除了船只、天上飞的除了飞机不吃，什么都吃。"

中国人也吃各类蔬菜或素菜。比如素菜馆里常有"素腰花""素肠""素鱼""素鸡"等菜供应，其实它们均为豆制品。中国的豆腐，无论贫贱老幼，无不爱食。制酱业也是中国的一项特殊成就，生产的酱类制品不仅是一种优良的调味品，能增强食欲，而且含有多种发酵制成的酶，能促进人体复杂的化学变化。它的出现，对营养和保健，都是一大贡献。

3）烹饪方法

中国菜肴的花色之多、菜式之众、制作之繁，是世界闻名的。有数据表明，中国古今著名菜品有 8 000 种之多，采用的食材可粗分为 600 种，不同的基本烹饪方法也有 48 种，其中包括煎、炒、烹、炸、炖、烤、烧、涮、蒸、焖、炙、烙等。

4）烹饪要求

中国饮食的要求颇为严格，要求"色、香、味"俱全。"色"既指菜肴的颜色，也指食物的造型。厨师会把各类菜肴雕刻设计成风格独特的艺术造型，令人赏心悦目。这些菜肴的造型通常精美绝伦，并深藏一定的寓意。比如说，"鱼"象征着"年年有余"（汉语中，"鱼"和"余"发音相同）。"香"指的是菜未上桌其香气已经扑鼻而来，让人胃口大开。中国人早就知道用香料烹调香气四溢的菜肴了。"味"指的是食物的味道，还有精细的刀工。要做到"色、香、味"俱全，选料、调料、火候、烹炒、摆盘等无一不在考虑之列。正因为如此，中国的每一道菜看上去都是一件造型精美、美味可口的艺术品。

值得一提的还有中国菜的菜名蕴含的深厚文化底蕴。通常中国人自己都很难根据菜名说出某盘菜是什么，直到菜端上了桌。诚然，有疑问可以随时向服务生询问，而服务生们都会随时乐意满足人们的好奇心。

除了达到上面所说的"色、香、味"的要求外，中国菜还很注重菜品的营养。事实上，中国菜很早就同传统中医的养身之道联系起来了，人参、核桃、当归、枸杞等也常用于菜肴的烹制。

2. 四大菜系

中国地大物博，为适应各地不同的特产、口味，便逐渐出现了各种不同的调制方法。后来，在长期的实践过程中，又逐渐形成了各种具有地方特色的饮食体系。一个菜系的形成和它的悠久历史与独到的烹饪特色是分不开的，同时也受到这个地区的自然地理、气候条件、资源特产、饮食习惯等影响。因此，不同地方便出现了不同菜系，比如鲁菜（山东菜）、京菜（北京菜）、沪菜（上海菜）、苏菜（江苏菜）、浙菜（浙江菜）、川菜（四川菜）、徽菜（安徽菜）、粤菜（广东菜）、湘菜（湖南菜）、鄂菜（湖北菜）、闽菜（福建菜）、陕菜（陕西菜）、东北菜（东北地区菜肴的总称）、豫菜（河南菜），以及仿膳菜（仿制的宫廷菜）、清真菜（回族菜的总称）、素菜（由佛教寺院所创、由僧厨执鼎、以非动物原料烹制的菜肴）等。广义上，中国菜可粗分为四大地方菜系，即粤菜、川菜、鲁菜和苏菜。现粗略地介绍一下四大菜系的特色。

1）粤菜（潮粤风味）

粤菜的范围包括广东和广西。它的第一个特点是用料广、选料精，以海鲜和野味为上馔。如禽类，除了普通的三禽（鸡鸭鹅）以外，还常以鸽子、山鹑、鹌鹑等入馔。海鲜最推崇石斑、鲳鱼、带鱼、海鳗、乌龟、明虾、螃蟹等。野味最欣赏爬行动物和两栖动物，如：水龟、甲鱼和蛇。粤菜很讲究选料。

粤菜第二个特色是口味偏重清、鲜、爽、滑，做法以蒸、煮、炒、溜居多。这与气候有一定关系。岭南酷暑时间长，需要清爽的口感，因此岭南人长期惯食海鲜和其他鲜活料，形成追求原味的传统嗜好。食物只是稍加烹制，而且也不像其他 3 种菜系那么辛辣。岭南人多在冬令进食浓香型及油气重的菜，如开堡狗肉、炖扣肉、炸生蚝、红焖白鳝（海鳗）、红炖猪肘等。

粤菜第三个特色是配菜丰富，这和物产丰富有关。粤北盛产各类蘑菇、竹笋等食物。而因气候适宜，四季各式鲜果不断，菠萝、荔枝、梅子、椰子、香蕉、风栗等，都是做菜的良好材料，也符合饮食卫生。

粤菜第四个特色是粥品点心特别丰富。由于岭南炎热的时间长，人们流汗多、消耗大，需要及时补充水分及易被吸收的养料，各类肉粥是较理想又较方便的食品。粥店（不少大饭店都兼有粥品）以老母鸡、猪骨、干贝、腐竹等熬好一大锅底粥，称为味粥，然后随时把味粥舀进小锅里，用鱼、虾、蟹、肉丸、虾丸、猪杂、牛肉、鸡、鸭等预先备好的粥料，配以姜、葱、胡椒粉等，生滚出多种粥品，随时供应顾客。岭南人善仿善创，广州又是长期中外交通的要道，粤式点心也特别丰富，吸取了中外许多点心的做法，各大茶楼饭店都有数百款点心的底单，很值得一尝。

2）川菜

四川烹饪（川菜）世界闻名，独具特色。川菜发祥于巴（今重庆）蜀（今成都），特色是重油重味，偏爱麻辣，将红辣椒、蒜、姜等香料和调味品混合在一起，做出当地人喜欢的独特辣味。这与四川盆地的气候有关，雾多，阴天多，湿气重，麻辣的食物使体表的湿气容易发散。四川人爱吃的“毛肚”（以牛肚、牛杂为主料的重味麻辣火锅）、“麻婆豆腐”（这个菜具有麻、辣、油、烫、咸、嫩、滑 7 个特点）和其他一些麻辣菜式，都具有川菜的传统色彩。

川菜另一个特点是善于运用一种普通食材制成多种美味菜肴。如拿起一块五花肉，在四川厨师手里，可以做出美味的盐煎肉、回锅肉、萸（鱼）香肉（用泡菜、泡辣椒等为配料做成的香辣菜）、酱爆肉丁、锅巴肉片、甜烧白（豆沙、薯片夹扣肉）、咸烧白（香芋、芽菜夹扣肉）、粉蒸肉、咕噜肉、白煮麻辣肉等。

四川人还善于做小吃，如麻辣牛头肉、怪味鸡、漳茶鸭子、酱兔肉、泡菜、赖汤圆、八宝糯米饭等，这是第三个特色。

3）鲁菜

鲁菜历史悠久，广受欢迎，是古代中国齐鲁文化的体现之一。它带有宫廷菜的余韵，第一个特点是用料讲究，善于以燕窝、鱼翅、鲍鱼、鱼肚、海参、鹿肉、蘑菇、银耳、蛤干等高档食材，做出厚味大菜。

由于华北地区寒冷时间较长，蔬菜品种又较少，练就了鲁菜厨师善于做高热量、高蛋白菜肴的本领，这是鲁菜的第二个特点。如脆皮烤鸭、九转肥肠（烧炸出来的猪大肠，可与烤鸭媲美）、脱骨烧鸡（酥香离骨的烧鸡）、锅烧黄河鲤鱼、红烧海螺、炸蛎黄等，都是鲁菜的佼佼者。

善于以汤调味，是鲁菜的第三个特点。鲁菜厨师的传统习惯是在炒锅旁边备好一锅味汤（以老母鸡、猪蹄等为汤料），无论炒、溜、烧、扒，都以味汤溅锅，以代替味精，这是一个好传统。鲁菜厨师也善于做奶汤，济南的奶汤蒲菜，就久负盛名。

4）苏菜

苏菜的发祥地是苏州，随后扬州和杭州的菜系也并入这一系列。由于六朝和南宋的都城都在苏菜的地域，加上南北大运河通航一千多年，华东各大城镇成了南北人民长期交汇的地点，为适应南北人的口味，苏菜的第一特点是味兼南北。苏系厨师既能做出清炒、清溜的南方爽口菜，又能做出像火腿炖肘子、狮子头、炒鳝糊等高热量、高蛋白的美馔。苏菜的菜目中，让南北人都能接受的折中菜肴也特别多。

由于盛产湖蟹海鲜，所以河鲜菜特别突出，这是苏菜的第二个特点。如蟹黄狮子头、蟹黄燕窝、虾羹鱼翅、西湖糖醋鱼、清蒸鲥鱼(富春江特产)、鲜藕肉夹、浓汁太湖鲫鱼汤、莲子鸭羹等,都是苏系菜肴中著名的河鲜菜。

苏式点心和小吃也很精美,这是第三个特点。如松子水晶肉甜糕、灌汤蟹黄包、蟹黄烧卖、宁波汤圆等都全国驰名。

有人把"四大菜系"用拟人化的手法描绘为:苏菜好比清秀素丽的江南美女;鲁菜犹如古拙朴实的北方壮汉;粤菜宛如风流典雅的公子;川菜就像内涵丰富充实、才艺满身的名士。

3. 筷子

1) 食具

说到吃,就不得不提到吃的工具。据说,世界上共有三种吃东西的方式:直接用手拿东西吃的占40%,用刀叉的占30%,还有30%则用筷子。中国人几千年前便开始使用筷子。

筷子,是中国人的一大发明。筷子是人类手指的延伸,手指能做的事,它都能做,且不怕高热,不怕冰冻,真是高明极了。然而,中国人到底从什么时候开始使用筷子作为取食工具只能靠推测了。最早提到筷子是2 000多年前编纂的《礼记》。筷子是如何发明的呢?有人推测,远古人学会用火烤东西吃时,随手折两根树枝或竹枝,用来夹着吃,这样既不烫手,又能趁热吃到美味,于是就演变成了木质的上粗下尖的筷子。据说早在3 000多年前的殷商时代就开始使用筷子,一般认为从明代开始这个取食工具有了"筷子"一名,而在明清时期的文献中,尤其在文学作品中,"筷子"一词很少提到,大多用"箸"一词来代替。

2) 制筷材料

郑传寅、张健在《中国民俗辞典》中对筷子的形成、发展作了较精练的概括:"筷子,以竹木等材料制成的挟食器具,广泛流传于汉族和某些少数民族地区。远古时,用树枝、竹棍或天然的动物骨角制成,后改为竹、木刮削后制成。夏、商有象牙筷、玉筷问世。春秋战国,又有铜筷和铁筷。汉魏六朝,始生产漆筷。稍后,又出现了银筷和金筷。以犀角筷、乌木镶金筷和各种玉筷最为名贵。"

筷子可以由各种不同材料做成,如竹、木、金、银、象牙、白镴、塑料等。从横截面的形状来看,可以有圆形或方形。有的筷子上面刻有彩色图案或书法作品用作装饰。中国普通百姓家中的筷子大多用竹木材料;重要宴会等场合会用象牙筷;而金筷银筷多为皇室和贵族所用。

3) 学用筷子

无论筷子是用什么材料制成的,用时必须两根一起用,而且应该成双成对。正确使用筷子的方法是:拿筷子的手掌心呈虚空状,一根放在中指和无名指之间,另一根置于食指和中指之间,大拇指压住两根筷子,由中指和食指掌控,像钳子一样夹食物。夹不一样的食物各手指用的劲也不同。要想掌握灵活快速地夹食物的技巧,比如夹豆子、花生那样的小东西,还有像切成一片片的皮蛋之类滑溜溜的东西,必须训练各手指间的协调配合。

4) 筷子——中国人的灵巧与智慧

用筷子吃饭同用毛笔写字有很多共通之处。有学者注意到,写得一手好字的人无一例外都很擅长使用筷子,因为运笔和用筷方法是一样的,要想写好字就必须做到肩、臂、手腕、手指的协调配合。中国人用筷子的技巧,常常吸引了许多外国人,甚至还有专门教人使用筷子的"培训中心"。

筷子的发明充分显示了中国人的灵巧和智慧。有些日本学者曾经测定,人在使用筷子夹取食物时,需要80多个关节和50条肌肉的协调运动,并且与大脑中枢神经有关。因此,用筷子吃饭可以使人心灵手巧。

西方人历来对中国人刺绣和泥塑方面精美绝伦的工艺印象深刻,这些巧夺天工的手艺难道与经常使用筷子有关吗?

中国是筷子的故乡，但是世界上第一家“筷子博物馆”据说在德国。这家博物馆展出了一万多双以金、银、玉石、兽骨等不同材料制成的筷子，这些筷子来自不同的国家和地区，出自不同的历史时期，可谓洋洋大观。

Exercises

Section A Thought-provoking questions

1. How would you respond to the challenge by the Westerners that “You Chinese are very cruel because you eat your best friends — dogs”?
2. How would you explain the display of anyone's dexterity by cleverly using chopsticks?

Section B Translate the following ways of cooking into Chinese

1. to deep-fry
2. to stir-fry
3. to saut
4. to assort
5. to pan fry (to fry in boiling oil)
6. to boil in soy sauce, or in light brine
7. to broil, to grill
8. to braise, to fricassee
9. to cook in boiling oil
10. to quick fry
11. frying and simmering
12. twice-cooked
13. soft deep-frying
14. crisp deep-frying
15. scalding

※ **The man of wisdom delights in water; the man of humanity delights in mountains. The man of wisdom is active; the man of humanity loves tranquility. The man of wisdom enjoys happiness; the man of humanity enjoys long life.**

From *Analects of Confucius*

(智者乐水，仁者乐山。智者动，仁者静。智者乐，仁者寿。)

——《论语》

※ **Those whose care extends not far enough will find their trouble at hand.**

From *Analects of Confucius*

(人无远虑，必有近忧。)

——《论语》

Chapter 9

China's Tea Culture
中国茶文化

China, the homeland of tea, is the first country to grow, produce and drink tea. The discovery of tea, one of the 3 beverages of the world, is a great contribution to the history of human culture. Throughout the dynastic history of China, the enthusiasm of the Chinese people in tea drinking has remained unchanged. This is probably due to the fact that tea is a health drink. In *Guide to Chinese Medical Herbs* by Li Shizhen of the Ming dynasty, tea is described as a drink good for our digestive system and the brain. Recent scientific analysis has also verified that tea is a salutary beverage.

Over the long history of tea drinking, a special Chinese tea culture came into being. Tea is indispensable in the life of the Chinese people. It is not simply a type of drink, but a transmitter of culture, representing the philosophy, aesthetic views and way of life of the Chinese people, from which the spiritual world of the Chinese people can be discerned.

Chinese tea culture not only refers to the methods of preparing tea, the equipment used to make tea and the occasions on which tea is consumed, but also includes articles, poems, pictures about tea, the art of making and drinking tea, and some customs about tea. This chapter relates the rich knowledge about Chinese tea and Chinese tea culture in terms of the origin of tea, its history, the methods and customs of drinking tea and tea drinking vessels, the Chinese tea ceremony, legends about tea, and the literature and art closely connected with tea.

1. Tea Sage of China

When we talk about Chinese tea culture today, we shouldn't miss an important figure in Chinese history — Lu Yu (733 - 804), who was respected as a "Tea Sage" for his contribution to Chinese tea culture. During the Song Dynasty, Lu Yu wrote the *Tea Scripture* (also translated as *The Classic of Tea*).

1) Lu Yu

Born in A.D. 733 in the Tang Dynasty, Lu Yu was an orphan adopted by a scholarly monk named Jigong in modern day Hubei Province. At that time, drinking tea became a nationwide tradition. Tea drinking originally appeared in Southern China, and in the mid-Tang Dynasty it started to gain favor with Northern Chinese.

The widespread distribution of tea can be attributed to the extensive practice of Zen Buddhism in the whole country. Because sleeping and eating were strictly prohibited for Buddhists practicing meditation, they could only drink tea. Many monks were tea connoisseurs at the same time.

Jigong was a well-known monk and a tea lover. Lu Yu learned from him how to read and write and how to prepare tea for him from childhood. As the years passed, Lu Yu developed a great interest in the brew. However, he rebelled against the discipline of priestly training which had made him a skilled observer. At the age of 11, he fled the temple and joined a theatrical troupe. Although he was a stammer and was not handsome, his fame as a performer increased with each year due to his wit and humour. However, he felt his life lacked meaning. In his late years, Lu Yu withdrew from the outside world into seclusion and concentrated on research into tea. The fruits of his research were written down in his masterpiece — *Tea Scripture*.

2) *Tea Scripture*

Lu Yu began to develop a love of tea during his boyhood in the temple. He picked and prepared tea himself, discovering a new world in the tea leaves. His *Tea Scripture* was a systematic summation of the scientific knowledge and people's experience of tea in the Tang Dynasty and before. It was based on first hand information he got from his own practice as well as his extensive study of related books, and his learning of tea-making experience from other people. It is divided into three sections and ten chapters, including the origin of tea, tea tools, tea picking, tea cooking, tea ceremony, tea events in history, famous tea producing areas, etc. Perhaps of most historical value is the seventh chapter, entitled "Tea Events" which records incidents concerning tea over thousands of years, from legendary times to the Tang Dynasty, introducing the history of Chinese tea in a systematic and comprehensive way.

3) The Discovery of Tea

According to Lu Yu's *Tea Scripture*, tea drinking in China can be traced back to the Zhou Dynasty: "Tea was discovered by Shennong and became popular as a drink in the State of Lu because of Zhou Gong." Shennong (the Divine Farmer) is a legendary ruler, the 2nd of the Three August Ones and the God of Sun. He is supposed to have invented the plough and discovered the curative virtues of plants. The most well-known work attributed to Shennong is *The Divine Farmer's Herb Classic* in which Shennong is said to have tasted hundreds of herbs to test their medical value. He was poisoned seventy-two times in a day and saved by tea.

Legend has it that in Shennong Period before 2700 B.C., Shennong often went to the remote mountains to pick herbal medicines in order to cure his patients. He carried out an investigation of hundreds of wild plants to see which were poisonous and which were edible, so as to prevent people from eating the poisonous plants. His approach to each plant helped him to experience its unique taste and discern its properties. It is said that one day he was poisoned seventy-two times and was luckily saved by chewing some tea leaves. The green leaves, with a faint scent, were carried to him by a gust of wind. He picked up two leaves and put them in the mouth. Chewing the tender leaves made him feel refreshed and energetic. Out of curiosity, he picked up some more leaves and observed them carefully. He also found nearby the evergreen plant from which the leaves came. He picked some leaves from the plant and brought them home for further study. Later he named the plant " Cha"(tea). Therefore, in early times, tea was used as a magic medicine for all sorts of diseases. The curative plant later became a popular beverage for the Chinese people.

2. Tea Drinking and Appreciation

We Chinese give great attention to our tea and the way they drink it. People have high requirements for the quality of the prepared tea leaves, the water they use to brew tea and the wares they use to prepare and serve tea.

1) Tea Appreciation

Generally, appraisement of tea leaf is based on four principles, namely, appearance of the infused leaf, color of the liquid, aroma and taste. There are many different characteristics to the shape of the leaf. For instance leaves can be curly or flat, needle-like or flower-like. The appearance of the leaf is important, but the aroma and taste are the more important factors in judging the quality of a kind of tea.

The Chinese emphasize water quality and water taste, so people select their water carefully. Fine water must be sweet, cool, clean, and flowing. Water from good springs is always considered best, as is rainwater from autumn and the rainy seasons. Tap water may have a perceptible odor or taste, which will be imparted to the infused brew, and will compromise the quality of the tea.

Chinese people take great delight in sampling tea. By sampling, one is not only discriminating the quality of the tea, but also experiencing the intoxication and enjoying being lost in reverie. One would snatch a little leisure from the busy life, make himself a nice cup of tea at home and imbibe slowly in small sips. One could also secure a serene space outside, for example, a teahouse tucked away in a park or nestled in a hill. Tea-drinking will be sure to relieve one's weary and release one's worry until one's spirit soars up and up into a sublime aesthetic realm.

2) Teapot Appreciation

In China, people think different teas look and taste better in certain tea wares than others. For example, green tea should be matched with glass tea ware; scented tea is poured into porcelain ware; and oolong tea is best presented in purple clay tea ware. Chinese prefer pottery wares to wares made of metal or other materials. The best choice is the purple clay wares made in Yixing, Jiangsu province. The purple clay of this region gives the wares their internationally-known purple color.

Yixing has been famous for the production of purple clay teapot (see picture 19-1) since the Northern Song Dynasty. Purple clay ware is made from purple clay or red clay found in Yixing region. It is delicate and hard in nature, but is also able to have air penetration at the same time. The aroma of the tea can be stored in purple clay ware teapot, and will then be absorbed by the clay. As the purple clay ware is fairly heat insulated, it is good for tea drinking both in winter and summer. The most attractive thing about this kind of ware is that it looks shiny through time and the often used pot can release a kind of aroma when it is just filled with hot water without tea. This is the reason why purple clay ware is regarded as invaluable object by most collectors.

3) Tea Drinking Customs

Tea plays an important role in Chinese people's social and emotional lives. Tea is always made and offered to a guest or friend immediately upon that person's entering a Chinese home. Serving a cup of tea to the guest is a common practice in China. "To invite the guest to stay longer with a cup of tea" demonstrates hospitality and traditional etiquette. Serving tea is more than a matter of mere politeness; it is a symbol of togetherness, a sharing of something enjoyable and a way of showing respect to visitors.

When the guest arrived, the host would use the best quality tea leaves and tea utensils to prepare the tea. Normally a host would only fill a teacup to seven-tenths of its capacity. It is said that the other three-tenths would be filled with frendship and affection. For the guest, not to take at least a sip might be considered rude in sone areas. When the host is accompanying the guest and sees that the guest's cup is already half empty, he should add more hot water for him immediately.

Here are three special circumstances in which tea is prepared and consumed:

A. A Signal of End of Talk

We normally think of tea drinking as an invitation to stay and socialize. Starting from the Qing Dynasty, however, the drinking of tea could signal the close to the social encounter. This was particularly true when one visited one's superior. When the guest reached the host's home, the host would offer his guest a cup of tea. They would then talk. When the host wanted his guest to leave, he would signal this by holding his own cup of tea and drinking it. The guest would then know that the host wanted him to leave and would ask to leave. With the end of the feudal society, this practice is outdated and can only be seen in literary works reflecting the old times.

B. A Sign of Respect

In Chinese society, the younger generation would show its respect to the older generation by offering a cup of tea. In the past, people of lower rank served tea to higher ranking people. Today, as Chinese society becomes more liberal, sometimes at home parents may pour a cup of tea for their children, or a boss may even pour tea for subordinates at restaurants. The lower ranking person should not expect the higher ranking person to serve him or her tea in formal occasions, however.

C. A Gesture of Apology

In Chinese culture, people make serious apologies to others by pouring them tea. That is a sign of regret and submission.

3. Chinese Tea Ceremony

China boasts a sophisticated tea culture. Tea ceremony rituals collectively represent the spirit of the "Way of Tea" with four basic principles: thrifty, harmony, respect and beauty.The Chinese tea ceremony emphasizes the tea — what the tea tastes like, smells like, and how one tea tastes compared to the previous tea, or in successive rounds of drinking. Ceremony doesn't mean that each server will perform the ritual the same way. Each step is meant to be a sensory exploration and appreciation.

The most famous tea ceremony in China is that of *gongfu* tea. *Gongfu* tea is a technique of preparing tea. The term "*gongfu*" denotes any skill that is developed through great practice such as Chinese painting, martial arts or Chinese tea making. It generally refers to the more formal preparation of Chinese tea using tiny cups to match the small unglazed purple clay teapots. The drinking of *gongfu* tea is an old custom of Chaoshan area in Guangdong Province where almost every family is equipped with *gongfu* tea utensils. People there drink several rounds of *gongfu* tea a day. Even after moving to other places of the country or emigrated to foreign countries, they still maintain this custom.

Word Bank

salutary	有利健康的,有治疗作用的	treatise	(专题)论文
discern	辨别,识别	infuse	注入,泡(茶)
scripture	经书,经文	impart	把……分给
connoisseur	鉴赏家,行家	imbibe	喝,饮
brew	沏茶	sublime	庄严的,崇高的
seclusion	隔离,隐居	sensory	传递感觉的

参考译文

中国素有“茶的故乡”之称，是世界上最早种植茶、制作茶、饮用茶的国家。茶是世界三大饮料之一，茶的发现和利用是中国人对人类文化史的一大贡献。几千年以来，中国人品茶的热情始终未减，因为茶是一种有益健康的天然饮品。在明朝李时珍所著的《本草纲目》中，茶是一种有利于消化系统和大脑的饮品。现代科学研究也证明了茶是有利健康的饮品。

中国悠久的饮茶历史，形成了颇有特色的中华茶文化。茶成为人们生活中不可缺少的一部分，它不仅是一种饮品，而且是文化的传播者，代表了中国人独特的哲学思想、美学观点和生活方式，它能体现中国人的精神世界。

中国茶文化不仅指泡茶的方法、茶具和饮茶的场合，还包括茶诗、茶画、茶艺及茶俗。本章主要介绍茶的起源与种类、品茶用具、中国茶道以及相关的神话传说和文学作品等。

1. 茶圣陆羽

谈及中国茶文化，不能不提及中国历史上的一位重要人物——陆羽(733 年-804 年)。陆羽，以撰写了世界第一部茶叶专著《茶经》而闻名于世，对中国茶文化的发展做出了卓越贡献，被奉为“茶圣”。

1) 陆羽

陆羽生于公元 733 年，原是一个被遗弃的孤儿，被现河北境内当时有名的积公禅师收养。当时饮茶的习惯正从南方向全国传开。饮茶习惯的广泛传播可以归功于僧侣，因为僧侣坐禅时严禁睡眠与进食，只能饮茶。因此，许多僧侣深谙品茶之道。

积公为唐代名僧，喜好品茗。陆羽在寺院里跟他学文识字，习诵佛经，还学会煮茶等事务。但他不愿皈依佛法，削发为僧。十一岁那年，他乘人不备，逃出龙盖寺到一个戏班里学演戏，做了优伶。他虽其貌不扬，又有些口吃，但却幽默机智，演丑角很成功。晚年的他隐居苕溪，闭门著书，使《茶经》得以问世。

2)《茶经》

陆羽自幼在寺庙与茶结缘，然后自己采茶、制茶、煮茶，从茶叶中发现新天地。陆羽的《茶经》，是唐代和唐代以前有关茶叶科学知识和实践经验的系统总结，是陆羽躬身实践、笃行不倦取得茶叶生产和制作的第一手资料，也是他遍查群书、广采博收茶叶采制经验的结晶。《茶经》共分上、中、下三卷，包括茶的本源、制茶器具、茶的采制、煮茶方法、茶艺茶道、历代茶事、茶叶产地等十章。其中第七章“茶之事”，辑录了自上古神农氏到唐代中叶数千年间有关茶事的记录，系统而全面地介绍了中国古代茶的发展演变，尤具史料价值。

3) 茶的发现

据陆羽《茶经》载：“茶之为饮，发乎神农氏，文于鲁周公。”神农氏，即远古三皇之一的炎帝，远古传说中的太阳神。传说神农发明了耕田的犁并发现了植物的药用价值。著名的《神农本草经》记载：“神农尝百草，日遇七十二毒，得茶而解之。”

相传在公元前 2700 年以前的神农时代，神农为了给人治病，经常到深山野岭去采集草药，他调查了数百种野生植物，亲口尝试，识别有毒植物和可食植物，以防止人们误食有毒植物，体会、鉴别草药的功能。据说有一天，神农尝百草，日遇七十二毒，得茶而解之。一阵风吹来几片绿油油的带着清香的叶子，神农拣了两片放在嘴里咀嚼，没想到一股清香油然而生，顿时感觉舌底生津，精神振奋。他感到很奇怪，于是，再拾起几片叶子仔细观察，并在附近找到了该植物，采集了一些带回去细细研究。后来，就把它命名为"茶"。因此，早期的茶，是作为一种能医治百病的神药，后来逐渐演变成中国人的日常生活饮料。

2. 品茶和赏壶

中国人非常注重茶和饮茶方式，历来对选茗、取水、备具、烹茶、奉茶以及品尝方法都颇为讲究。

1）品茶

茶叶的好次，主要从色、香、味、形四个方面鉴别，即一看色泽、二闻香气、三观外形、四品滋味。不同种类的茶叶有不同的外形特点，或条索卷曲，或扁平挺直；或形似针状，或状似花朵。茶叶的外形虽重要，但决定茶叶品质的关键因素还是内质，即香气和滋味。

中国茶文化讲究水质水源，因此人们选取泡茶用水时非常用心。好水须甘、清、净、活。据说称得上好水的是山中乳泉水，或是秋天和雨季的雨水。自来水因含有漂白粉，使得人们已经很难再喝到真正的茶味了。

中国人饮茶，注重一个"品"字。"品茶"不但是鉴别茶的优劣，也带有神思遐想和领略饮茶情趣之意。忙里偷闲在家中泡上一壶好茶，细啜慢饮，舒适惬意；或择雅静之处，如园林或自然山水间的茶室，自斟自饮。饮茶可以消除疲劳、涤烦益思、振奋精神，达到美的享受，使精神世界升华到高尚的艺术境界。

2）赏壶

中国人饮用不同的茶往往会选用不同的茶具。例如：绿茶用玻璃茶具，花茶用瓷茶具，乌龙茶用紫砂茶具。中国人还认为陶器茶具佳于金属的或其他质地的茶具，而最佳的选择便是产于江苏省宜兴市的紫砂茶具。

自北宋起，宜兴即已以产紫砂壶闻名（见图 19－1）。紫砂壶由紫泥或红泥等当地天然泥料烧制而成，质地坚硬而透气性佳，泡茶不易变味，容易吸收茶汁，留下浓郁香味，且隔热性能好，冬夏使用皆宜。最吸引人的是紫砂壶经日积月累的茶汁浇洗涤揩日愈光亮。经常沏茶的紫砂壶偶尔不放茶叶，其水也有茶香味。这也是它深受大多数收藏爱好者青睐的原因。

3）茶事礼俗

茶在中国人的社会和情感生活中都有着重要的作用。凡客人、朋友到来，沏茶、敬茶的礼仪是必不可少的。客来敬茶是中国较为普遍的茶俗。"一杯香茗暂留客"体现了中国人的重情好客和传统礼节。敬茶不只是出于对客人的礼貌，而且是一种亲近的象征和快乐的分享。

当有客来访时主人会选用家里最好的茶叶和最佳茶具待客。倒茶通常以斟七分为敬，据说杯中空着的三分将被友情填满。在有些地方，客人至少要喝一口茶，否则会被认为不礼貌。主人在陪客人饮茶时，如看到客人杯中被已喝去一半，就要及时添加开水。

以下是敬茶的三个不同场合：

A. 端茶送客

我们往往认为喝茶意味着留客，但从清朝开始，端茶成为一种送客的暗示。尤其是当下属拜见上司时，主人家会上一杯茶，然后开始谈话。如果主人想客人离去，主人会举起茶杯说："请喝茶"，这时客人会识趣地赶快告辞。随着封建社会结束，这种礼节也成为历史，只存在于反映旧时生活的文学作品中。

B. 表示尊敬

在中国社会，当晚辈要向长辈表示尊敬时，会向他们奉上一杯茶。以往，下属要为上级准备茶水。但如今，社会变得开放自由，这种传统不但消失，还倒过来出现家长为孩子冲茶或老板为下属冲茶的情况。不过，在正式场合下属不应该期望上司为自己倒茶。

C. 斟茶道歉

在中国的传统中，人们正式道歉时要向对方敬茶，以示自己的后悔和顺服。

3. 中国茶道

中国的茶文化博大精深。中国"茶道"是一种和美仪式，其基本精神为："俭、和、敬、美"。中国茶道注重的是茶的本身——茶的口感和味道、此杯茶与前杯茶的比较和与后杯茶的异同。茶道不同敬茶者的方法也有所不同。茶道的每一步都是一种感官的探索和欣赏。

中国最著名的茶道是功夫茶道。所谓功夫茶，是一种泡茶的技法。之所以叫功夫茶，是因为这种泡茶的方式操作起来需要一定的功夫，此功夫，乃为沏泡的学问，品饮的境界，正如中国画与武术，皆为功夫。功夫茶的茶具是紫砂茶壶和与之配套的几个小茶盅。品功夫茶是广东潮汕地区很出名的风俗之一。在潮汕本地，家家户户都有功夫茶具，每天必定要喝上几轮。即使是侨居外地或移民海外的潮汕人，也仍然保存着品功夫茶这个风俗。

Exercises

Section A Thought-provoking questions

1. Why is tea indispensable in the life of the Chinese people?
2. How to ensure the greatest enhancement of the taste of tea?
3. What is your understanding of tea and tea drinking?

Section B Fill in the blanks in the following tea quotes

1. Love and scandal are the ________ sweeteners of tea. — Henry Fielding, *Love in Several Masques*
2. Drink your tea slowly and reverently, as if it is the axis on which the world earth ________ slowly, evenly, without rushing toward the future. — Thich Nat Hahn
3. The best quality tea must have creases like the leathern boot of Tartar horsemen, curl like the dewlap of a mighty bullock, unfold like a mist rising out of a ravine, gleam like a lake touched by a zephyr, and be wet and soft like a fine earth newly swept by ________. — Lu Yu
4. If you are cold, tea will warm you. If you are too heated, it will cool you. If you are depressed, it will ________ you. If you are excited, it will calm you. — Gladstone, 1865
5. Tea is drunk to ________ the din of the world. — T'ien Yiheng
6. There is a great deal of poetry and fine ________ in a chest of tea. — Ralph Waldo Emerson, *Letters and Social Aims*
7. Strange how a teapot can represent at the same time the comforts of solitude and the pleasures of ________. — Author Unknown
8. Tea, though ridiculed by those who are naturally coarse in their nervous sensibilities ... will always be the ________ beverage of the intellectual. — Thomas De Quincy (1875 - 1959)
9. Each cup of tea represents an ________ voyage. — Catherine Douzel

10. Drinking a ________ cup of tea will surely starve the apothecary. — Chinese Proverb

※ **One whose words are shameless will have difficulty carrying them out.**

From *Analects of Confucius*

(其言之不怍，则为之也难。)

——《论语》

※ **To be poor without complaint is difficult; it is easier to be rich without conceit.**

From *Analects of Confucius*

(贫而无怨，难；富而无骄，易。)

——《论语》

Chapter 10

Chinese Plants and Their Cultural Connotations

中国植物文化意象

Plants have countless ties with the traditional culture, national psychology and national spirits of a country. Due to different cultural backgrounds and natural environment, plant culture varies from country to county. In China, the symbolic meanings of plants have been merged into the essence of the ideology of Chinese Taoism, Buddhism and Confucianism. Therefore, the Chinese plant culture, a component of Chinese traditional culture, has its unique national features which differ from those of other nations.

1. Top Ten Flowers in China

China particularly loves its native lotus flowers, camellia, azalea, peony, chrysanthemums, etc. Perfumed and exquisite, these flowers are symbols of purity, perseverance, renewal and devotion. Being the favoured subject of poets and painters, they are frequently reproduced, along with other favoured national themes, in art and literature.

The Chinese Top Ten Famous Flowers were nominated in 1987. They are the plum blossom, peony, chrysanthemum, orchid, Chinese rose, azalea, camellia, lotus, sweet-scented osmanthus and narcissus. These flowers are not only loved for their floriated beauty but also favored for their ample and lucky meaning.

1) Plum Blossom — Flower No.1

Plum blossom (see picture 10 - 1) is evaluated as the No. one of the Chinese Top Ten Famous Flowers. The five petals of the plum blossoms symbolize happiness, good luck, longevity, smooth sailing and peace.

When a whirling snow obscures the sky and all other flowers wither and fall, only plum trees stand upright proudly and bloom in rich colors bringing people the news of early spring. With the characteristic of cold resistance, plum blossom stands for courage, hope and new life.

2) Peony — King of Flowers

Beautiful and graceful, peonies (see picture 10 - 2) have been renowned for their noble beauty ever since the Tang Dynasty. The flamboyancy of peony exceeds any flowers, so people have named it "the king of flowers" and regarded it as a symbol of happiness, prosperity and spring in China. Peony is also an omen of good fortune, an emblem of love and affection, wealth and distinction, feminine beauty, and the sign of spring.

Peony cultivation in China can date back to 1,600 years ago. Peony is regarded as the most beautiful and charming flower and has prestigious reign in the flower world of China. Chinese people have been enthralled by the beauty of the flower and it has been the favorite flower from the imperial down to the common in Chinese history. The flowers are colorful, fragrant and very elegant-and-pleasant-looking in appearance with a variety of over 500.

3) Chrysanthemum — the Hermit

Chrysanthemum (see picture 10 - 3) is a famous traditional flower of China. Some varieties of chrysanthemum are effective to treat some diseases, and some are edible, both delicious and nourishing. Chinese people have the convention of viewing and admiring chrysanthemum in autumn. In late autumn, there are chrysanthemum exhibitions in many places of China. Chrysanthemum is described by Zhou Dunyi, a literary man of Song Dynasty, as a hermit because it was regarded as keeping a low profile and not fighting with other flowers for attention.

Peony, lotus, chrysanthemum and plum represent the four seasons in China. Chrysanthemum is also a symbol of long life or duration since its Chinese name "ju" sounds similar to the words meaning "remain, nine, and long time".

4) Orchid — the Gentleman

Ancient Chinese favored the fragrance of the orchid (see picture 10 - 4) and cherished it as the "Supreme Fragrance" and the "Sweetest Fragrance under the Sun".

Orchid conveys the image of a flower of such fragrance and beauty that it makes its surroundings seem plain by comparison. It thus tends to be lonely, perhaps content in its solitude. The orchid thus became a symbol for the true gentleman in ancient China where it was revered for its esthetic and artistic value. Mention of this orchid in poetry might suggest the image the author would like to convey of himself, or of the subject of his poem.

Confucius was a great lover of orchid. He compared the orchid flower to the superior man and its scent to the pleasures of friendship. Confucius deemed it extremely important to nurture one's spirit. He associated the good qualities of people with orchid. One of Confucius' famous quotes is "The association with a superior person is like entering a hall of orchids."

5) Chinese Rose — Queen of Flowers

China is the homeland of the monthly rose (see picture 10 - 5) with a fairly long history of its cultivation. Chinese rose was recorded in *A Record of Flowers* early in the Ming Dynasty as "Permanent Spring Flower", "Every-Month Red" and "Four-Season Flower".

The character of permanent blooming, beautiful looking and delicate fragrance of the rose bring it the reputation of "Queen of the Flowers". It stands for spring, and magnificence. Many Chinese poems in praise of Chinese rose have been written by men of letters and well-known personages throughout ages.

6) Azalea — the Beauty of Flowers

Originated in China, azalea (see picture 10 - 6) is one of the Chinese traditional famous flowers. Nicknamed "Red on the mountain" and "Mountain Pomegranate", azalea enjoys the reputation of being the crown or Xi Shi (one of the four ancient Chinese beauties) of flowers. China has a giant treasure-storage of azalea resources with the most varieties and greatest number in the world.

Azalea blooms in early spring when cuckoo cuckoos ceaselessly. So the ancient people thought the bird ululates to return home and believed that it is changed from cuckoo's blood.

7) Camellia — Treasure in Flowers

Camellia (see picture 10 - 7) is an evergreen and broad-leaved shrub originated in China where it is also known as "Shan Cha". Wild camellias are found blooming in profusion in mountains and valleys of Zhejiang, Jiangxi, Sichuan, Yunnan and Guangdong Provinces and the offshore islands in the country. In Rui'an County, Zhejiang Province, grows a camellia tree of 1, 200 years old.

Camellia blooms during the time between winter and spring with elegant petals and rich colors. It symbolizes serenity.

8) Lotus — Fairy of Flowers

The lotus (see picture 10 - 8) is also known as "Lian Hua" and "Water Lilly". The lotus displays its elegant beauty when it blooms in summer. In 1973, fossil pollen of lotus was unearthed in Hemudu Cultural Relic, Yuyao County, Zhejiang Province, which further proves that there was lotus pollen existing 7,000 years ago. In the same year, two carbonized lotus seeds were unearthed in Yangshao Cultrual Relic, Zhengzhou, Henan Province, which shows again that there were lotus seeds existing more than 5,000 years ago.

The lotus comes out of the mire but stays pristine. It is inwardly empty yet outwardly upright. Its noble image is very much respected and admired by people. Among all the flowers, the lotus is the most represented in poems, paintings and dances. The Lotus is also the flower dedicated to Buddha. It is one of the Eight Auspicious Symbols of Buddhism.

The lotus is of unique importance in Chinese folklore and symbolism as the symbol of peace, purity, sincerity and perfection and an emblem of summer.

Chinese people compare the conjugal love to two lotuses growing in one root, blossoming around one center, which contains profound cultural meanings.

9) Sweet-scented Osmanthus — Fragrant Smell from Far Away

Also known as "Nine-li-fragrance" (4.5 kilometers Fragrance), the sweet-scented osmanthus (see picture 10 - 9) is only native to China. Its cultivation by the Chinese people dates back to 2,500 years. In Hanzhong, the "home of osmanthus" is located in the south of Shaanxi Province, where there are many ancient osmanthus trees. In the courtyard of the Shenshuisi Temple in Nanzheng County, 7 kilometers away from Hanzhong in the southeast, there is an ancient Osmanthus blooming in profusion every autumn. It is said that this tree was planted by Xiao He, the Chancellor of Emperor Liu Bang of the Western Han Dynasty in 206 B.C. Thus, it is named Han Osmanthus. Ascertained by measuring, the tree is 1840 ± 350 years old. The tree trunk is 232 centimeters in diameter and its crown covers 400 square meters. It blooms twice a year with sweet golden flowers.

10) Narcissus — Fairy Walking over Ripples

Narcissus (see picture 10 - 10) is deeply loved by Chinese people who give it a lot of lovely aliases, for example, "Golden Calyx and Silver Desk", "Fairy Walking over Ripples" etc. It is also known as "Heavenly Onion", "Elegant Garlic". Many poems praise of the firm and unadorned character of the narcissus. The most well-known laudatory title for narcissus is from Huang Tingjian's poem (Song Dynasty): "Lingbo Goddess treading the waves, gracefully under the soft moonlight". The alias of "fairy walking over ripples" has hence been used. In modern history, the famous woman revolutionist Qiu Jin intoned in her poem named "Narcissus": "Delicately white as snow, exceeding the faint scent of the plum blossom." The poem highly praises the beauty and fragrance of the flower.

Late winter and early spring witness the flowering of the years' first narcissus. Being the messenger of spring, narcissus is cherished by many people for her elegance and her full-bodied aroma. Chinese people consider narcissus a good omen on New Year's Day. Many overseas Chinese regard it as a holy flower of the native land. Hence narcissus proves to be the best choice as a gift for relatives and friends for the New Year.

2. Symbolic Meanings of Plants

Apart from the top ten flowers, quite a lot of plants have deep symbolic meaning in them over the long history of China. Due to their individual properties, certain plants can symbolize longevity, wealth and prosperity. For example, the peach is the symbol of immortality, the bamboo as the famous symbol of resilience, the pomegranate as symbol of fertility, the grapes as symbol of abundance and many more.

1) Bamboo

Always green in color and hollow inside, bamboo (see picture 10 - 11) is a symbol of longevity and modesty. It is often depicted with pine trees and plum blossom altogether as "three friends in severe winter". Ancient literary men often depicted bamboo in their writings and paintings.

In traditional Chinese culture, bamboo is one of the four favorite plants along with Chinese plum, orchid and chrysanthemum, the so-called Four Men of Honor, the characters of which are highly admired by the Chinese people so they want to be just like the four plants.

2) Mandarin Orange

The pronunciation for "orange" in Chinese is similar to that of "auspicious". Therefore, orange symbolizes good luck. Tradition has it that you must bring a basket of mandarin oranges together with a red packet when visiting family or friends anytime during the Chinese New Year celebrations. Mandarin oranges are symbols for abundant happiness and good fortune.

3) Peach

For longevity, the peach is the most symbolic of any tree or fruit in Chinese culture. Hence it has the name of "immortal peach" and "longevity peach". According to ancient text, peach has a cultivation history of over 1,000 years in China. It was the tribute to the imperial families of past dynasties. It is believed in ancient China that its tree wood and color can keep demons at bay.

There are many stories about peach in Chinese mythology. One of them is about the peach tree of immortality planted in Yaochi by the West Queen Mother. The tree was said to blossom once every 3,000 years and the fruit of eternal life took another 3,000 years to ripen. If one ate one of those peaches, he could live 600 years longer. Therefore, the peach is also known as the "immortal fruit" which can give immortality to people, so it is the traditional benison gift in China.

Arriving in spring as they do, they symbolize life, growth and prosperity. Should the peach blossom bloom during New Year celebrations, it is a sure sign that the year ahead will be one of good fortune!

4) Chinese Parasol Tree

Wutong, the Chinese parasol tree, is a beautiful tree which figures prominently in literature. It is an emblem of strong affection between husband and wife. Ancient myth has it that "wu" is male and "tong" is female. "Wu" and "tong" grow in the same tree to live and die together. As the Chinese saying goes, "Wu and tong treat each other, mandarin ducks die together." The euphonious Chinese name "wutong" is often left untranslated as in the poem of Wen Tingyun, the well-known poet of Tang Dynasty: "Wutong trees, third watch rain, care not for utter bitterness of separation sorrow."

5) Pine and Cypress

Pine is often mentioned together with cypress. Both trees remain green and stand upright in spite of the severe cold in winter. Chinese people favor pine tree for its quality of cold resistance and being evergreen. This natural property of pine is regarded by Chinese people as the moral character — being firm and unyielding. Pine, the favorite tree of Chinese painters, symbolizes longevity and brawniness and epitomizes self-discipline and steadfastness.

6) Pomegranate

The pomegranate, being full of seeds, is an auspicious emblem of fecundity and family prosperity and, therefore, is well loved by Chinese people. Its red color represents joy and happiness, so in some places there is the custom of eating pomgranate at weddings to bless the bride and groom and to wish them a bright future. Because its many seeds represent numerous progeny to the Chinese, pomegranate is widely represented in art works symbolizing fertility, abundance, prosperity, numerous and virtuous offspring and a blessed future.

7) Peanut

The peanut, also named groundnut, represents the birth of prosperity and signifies continuous growth and multiplication in wealth and good fortune. One would also notice the presence of peanuts during the festive Chinese New Year season among Chinese families to generate luck associated to health and longevity.

The groundnut is unique because it grows with its roots expanding in a wide area in the form of nodules. This symbolizes stability and prosperity. Peanuts are a must at traditional wedding for blessing the newly weds with fertility so that they would have lots of children, both boys and girls.

Word Bank

floriated	花形的	unadorned	朴素的,不加渲染的
ample	足够的,丰裕的	laudatory	表示赞美的,颂扬性的
obscure	使隐晦,掩盖	intone	吟咏
flamboyancy	艳丽	resilience	韧劲,适应力
enthrall	迷住,吸引住	benison	祝福
pomegranate	石榴	euphonious	好听的,悦耳的
ululate	哀鸣,悲泣	brawniness	强壮
pristine	纯洁的,未受玷污的	epitomize	概括,集中体现了
conjugal	婚姻的,夫妇之间的	fecundity	多产,富饶,生育力
alias	别名	progeny	子孙,后裔
calyx	花萼,杯状结构	nodule	节,块

参考译文

大自然中的花草树木与一个国家的传统文化、民族心理和民族精神有着千丝万缕的联系。由于文化背景和自然条件的不同，各民族的植物文化不尽相同。在中国，各种植物所具有的象征意义融入了道教信仰、佛教精神和儒家思想的精髓。因此，中国植物文化，作为中国传统文化的一部分，具有不同于其他国家的特点。

1. 中国十大名花

中国人特别喜爱荷花、茶花、杜鹃、牡丹、菊花等本土花木，它们象征了纯洁、坚韧、新生和奉献，是诗人和画家喜爱表现的主题，因此在文艺作品中时常可以见到它们。

1987 年评选出的中国十大名花，分别为梅花、牡丹、菊花、兰花、月季、杜鹃、茶花、荷花、桂花和水仙。上述十大名花，不仅因为它们的色彩和姿态能在众花中取胜，而且由于它们丰富的内涵以及吉祥的寓意，使人们倍加钟爱。

1) 梅花——花魁

梅花（见图 10－1）是中国十大名花之首，其花五瓣，是五福的象征：一是快乐，二是幸运，三是长寿，四是顺利，五是和平。

在万木萧瑟、风雪飘零的严冬中，梅花展现着一花独放的孤傲，给人们透露早春的信息。梅花以其不畏严寒的坚贞不屈的品性，代表了勇气、希望和新生。

2) 牡丹——花中之王

"国色天香"的牡丹（见图 10－2），自唐朝以来，一直被视为荣华富贵的象征，同时获得"花中之王"的美誉。牡丹也代表了好运、爱情、财富、美貌和春天。

牡丹在中国的栽培历史可以追溯到 1 600 年前，其花大色艳，独傲群芳，上至帝王将相，下至平民百姓，无不喜爱，广泛栽培。牡丹花容端妍，花色绚丽，品种多达 500 余个。

3) 菊花——花中隐士

菊花（见图 10－3）是中国传统名花之一。菊花中有些种类具有药用价值，有些种类可以食用，而且味道鲜美，营养丰富。中国人有赏菊的传统。每到秋菊绽放之时，许多地方都会布置菊展，供人们观赏。宋代诗人周敦颐称："菊，花之隐逸者。"其不与众花争俏的隐逸风骨受世人赞赏。

牡丹、荷花、菊花和梅花则是四季的代表。菊花还是长寿的象征，因为"菊"字的发音近似于"九"或"久"。

4) 兰花——花中君子

兰花（见图 10－4）香气清幽，有"香祖"之誉，古人尊其香为"天下第一香"。

兰花的芬芳与美丽，使之所置身的环境相形逊色。因此，它是孤独的，然其不为无人而不芳。在中国古代，兰花的审美价值和艺术价值使之成为真正君子的象征。诗人在诗中提及兰花时，往往意在表露自己美好的理想和高尚的情操。

孔子十分喜欢兰花，他用兰花比喻高尚的人，并以兰的馨香喻交友的愉悦。孔子特别重视个人思想品质的修养，在兰花身上寄托了深切的感情，曰："与善人居，如入芝兰之室。"

5）月季——花中皇后

中国是月季（见图10-5）的故乡，月季花在中国已有相当长的历史，早在明朝的《群芳谱》中就有以"长春花"、"月月红"和"四季花"为名的记载。

月季花四季盛开，色彩绚丽、香味浓郁，被誉为"花中皇后"，代表了春天和美丽。在历代文人的诗篇中，有多首咏月季诗篇。

6）杜鹃花——花中西施

源于中国的杜鹃花（见图10-6），是中国传统名花之一。有"皇冠"和"花中西施"之称，别名"映山红"和"山石榴"。中国杜鹃花科植物种类丰富多样，数量居世界之首，是宝贵的植物财富。

杜鹃花开早春。杜鹃鸟啼鸣之时，正是杜鹃花如火如荼之际。因此，古人相信杜鹃鸟口中血滴成枝上花。古人认为，杜鹃啼鸣不已，是在呼唤游子归来。

7）茶花——花中珍品

源于中国的茶花（见图10-7）亦称"山茶"，是一种四季常青的阔叶灌木。中国野生山茶古树集中地分布在浙江、江西、四川、云南、广东等省以及沿海岛屿等地。浙江省瑞安县生长着一株树龄为1 200年的山茶。

茶花绽放于冬春，花瓣优雅、花色鲜艳，象征宁静安详。茶花又名曼荼罗花，是佛教中的吉祥花。

8）荷花——花中仙子

荷花（见图10-8）又称莲花或水芙蓉。盛夏花开之际，众美纷呈。1973年，浙江余姚河姆渡文化遗址出土了荷花花粉化石，距今7 000年。同年，河南郑州仰韶文化遗址发掘出两粒炭化莲子，距今5 000年。

荷花出淤泥而不染，中空且直。因其高贵圣洁的形象，自古以来深受人们的青睐，是人们诗歌、绘画和舞蹈等艺术创作中最常涉及的花卉。荷花还有着佛教因缘，是佛教八宝祥之一。

在中国民间传说和象征中，荷花寓意和平、纯洁、真诚和完美，同时也是夏日的象征。

人们常用荷花中的并蒂莲来比喻夫妻间的婚姻和爱情，蕴含着极其丰富的文化内涵。

9）桂花——九里飘香

桂花（见图10-9）俗称"九里香"，是中国特有的植物，种植史可追溯到2 500年前。位于陕西省西南部的"桂花之乡"汉中，有许多参天古桂。汉中市城东南7千米的南郑县圣水寺庙内，有一棵最古老的桂花树，花开繁茂。相传这棵桂花树为西汉初年汉高祖刘邦的大臣萧何于公元前206年亲手栽植，故称"汉桂"。经科学测定，树龄在1840±350年。这棵汉桂，树干直径232厘米，树冠覆盖面积400平方米，花色金黄，每年开花两次。

10）水仙——凌波仙子

水仙（见图10-10）花深受中国人喜爱，人们给了它许多别称与雅号，如"金杯银盏"和"凌波仙子"，还有"天葱""雅蒜"。

许多诗人写过咏水仙诗，盛赞水仙朴素无华的品行。最有名的是宋朝黄庭坚的诗句："凌波仙子生尘袜，水上轻盈步微月。"自黄诗一出，"凌波仙子"这一水仙雅号美称，便一直流传至今。近代女革命家秋瑾赋诗《水仙》，诗中咏道："嫩白应欺雪，清香不让梅。"诗句高度赞颂水仙的美丽与馨香。

水仙花开冬末春初，是春的使者。人们珍爱水仙花，爱它优雅告诫，芳香袭人。中国人认为水仙花若新年开放，来年必有好运。许多海外华侨视水仙花为家乡的圣花。水仙花是新年赠送亲友的最佳礼品。

2. 植物的文化意象

除了十大名花，自古以来，中国人在许多花木上赋予了深刻的精神意义。根据植物自身的特点，可以象征长寿、财富和繁荣等。比如，桃象征长生，竹象征韧性，石榴象征多子，葡萄象征充裕等。

1）竹

绿意葱茏、茎秆空心的竹子(见图 10－11)象征着长寿和谦虚。竹子与松树、梅花合称为“岁寒三友”，古代的文人墨客常以咏竹、画竹为趣。

在中国的传统文化中，竹与梅、兰、菊并称为“四君子”。许多中国人都以“四君子”所代表的高尚品质激励自己洁身自好。

2）橘

橘谐音“吉”，所以象征吉利。春节上门拜年时除了送红包还要带上一篮橘子，这是传统习俗。橘寓意大吉大利。

3）桃

在中国文化中，桃最能代表长寿，因而有“仙桃”、“寿桃”之美称。据古籍载，桃已有千年栽培历史，为历代皇室贡品。桃木常被古代中国人视为为避邪之物。

中国关于桃的传说很多，其中一则源自神话中西王母瑶池所植的蟠桃：“天上有蟠桃园，三千年一开花，三千年一结果。食一枚园中仙桃可增寿 600 岁。”故桃被喻为长寿象征，给老人祝寿便用寿桃。

桃花春天绽放，象征着生命、生长和繁荣。如果桃花新年即开，预示着来年吉祥如意。

4）梧桐

梧桐树在中国的文学作品中时常见到。传说中，梧为雄，桐为雌，梧桐同长同老、同生同死。于是，梧桐便成为伉俪深情的象征。我国有“梧桐相待老，鸳鸯合双死”之说，因此，诗文中常以梧桐表示男女之间至死不渝的爱情，如唐朝诗人温庭筠的诗句：“梧桐树，三更雨，不道离情正苦。”

5）松柏

松常与柏并称，且都四季常青，历严冬而不衰。中国人将其耐寒而又常青的自然特性理解为一种抗击环境变化而保持自身不变的社会品格，有坚强不屈的精神。因此，古人把松柏看作长生、坚强、自律和坚定的象征，它也成了画家笔下经常出现的主题。

6）石榴

石榴深受中国人喜爱，因为它丰硕多子，是象征多子多孙、家庭兴旺的吉祥之物。石榴花花红似火，表示热情和欢乐的喜庆，因此有些地方有在婚礼上吃石榴以示对新郎新娘的祝福的习俗。石榴还因多子多福的寓意，常被绘入吉祥图案，称作“榴开百子”。

7）花生

花生俗称“落花生”，它代表财富兴旺、好运不断。过年时每家每户都要准备花生，意喻来年有好运、健康和长寿。

花生的特点还在于其根绵绵不断，果实累累，象征稳定与多产。花生是中国传统婚礼上用来祝愿新人的必备之物，祝愿姑娘出嫁后能“花着生”，既生男也生女。

Exercises

Section A　Thought-provoking questions

1. What is the role that bamboo plays in our life?
2. What is most likely to be the national flower of China? Why?
3. What do you know about the "lotus effect"?

Section B　Translate the following expressions with names of plants

1. 灿若桃花
2. 胸有成竹
3. 桃红柳绿
4. 桃腮杏眼
5. 莲步轻移
6. 桃李满天下
7. 桃李不言，下自成蹊。
8. 出淤泥而不染，濯清涟而不妖。

※ The orchid originates in the deep valleys, but its obscurity does not discourage it from exuding its fragrance. A gentleman cultivating himself is not to change his moral because of poverty.

From *Analects of Confucius*

（芝兰生于深谷，不以无人而不芳；君子修道立德，不为困穷而改节。）

——《论语》

※ A gentleman does not recommend people based on what they say; or disregard what is said based on the speaker.

From *Analects of Confucius*

（君子不以言举人，不以人废言。）

——《论语》

Chapter 11

Wedding Traditions in China

中国传统婚俗

Chinese marriage became custom during the Warring States period. Due to the vast expanse of the territory, different practices are followed in different places, although they all generally adhere to similar guidelines. Traditional marriage customs lost their popularity due to their complexity and the collapse of feudal society. However, traditional marriage can still be witnessed in the countryside. Especially recently, traditional marriage customs are being revived in some places and they are attracting many prospective couples.

1. Wedding Procedures

According to the old wedding custom of China, parents and matchmakers arranged the marriage. Especially for a woman, she had to "follow the man she married, in whatever ways". She must obey her husband and abide by the decisions of her parents-in-law. The old wedding custom usually included the following procedures.

1) Engagement

The engagement was an indispensable procedure for the old marriage tradition. The process began with an elaborate marriage proposal and acceptance. The important parties in proposal and betrothal negotiations were the parents of the prospective bride and groom, rather than the bride and groom themselves. Marriage was considered too important a duty to be left in the rash hands of the young. This process was placed in the hands of a go-between, who acted as a buffer between the two parties — a role similar to that of a real estate agent today.

A. Bringing Together

Before the engagement, the matchmaker would go between the two families to communicate the conditions of both, such as the family estate, family members, the appearance, age and temperament of both parties, etc. Generally speaking, the bridegroom's side would favor a literary family and the bride's side a rich one. Only if parents of both sides were satisfied with each other was it possible to go on to the next procedure.

B. Consensual Marriage

"Consensual Marriage" means that the eight characters about both parties' birthday were taken to the fortune-teller by the matchmaker to reckon whether they were right for each other as far as their birth signs were concerned and whether the union would yield a lucky result. Then the matchmaker would notify the results to the parents of both parties. For some discreet parents, they would see the other party at the appointed place when the fortune-telling results were thought lucky. If both parties were satisfied with each other, the "betrothal gifts" might be given.

C. Give Betrothal Gifts

It was the object matter of engagement to give betrothal gifts. The matchmaker wrote out the betrothal card and negotiated with the bride's family to decide the items. Then the bridegroom's side gave the betrothal gifts according to the betrothal card in three times. The betrothal gifts consisted of gift list, gifts and monetary gifts. The gift list was the most important because it was the attestation of a formal betrothal. After giving the betrothal gifts, the wedding day could be decided.

2) Preparation for Wedding

A. Installation of Bridal Bed

Preparation on the part of the groom involved the installation of the bridal bed on the day before the wedding. At a propitious hour on a selected day before the wedding day, a "good luck man" and a "good luck woman", that is a man and woman with many children of both sexes, were selected to install a newly purchased bed. The "good luck man" would help to install the bridal bed in the correct place in the bridal chamber. The installation ceremony consisted of merely moving the bed slightly. The actual work was done earlier by servants or friends. The "good luck woman" would come to arrange the bridal bed. Then nobody is allowed to touch the bed until the couple entered the bridal chamber after the wedding ceremony.

Children were then invited onto the bed to bless the couple with fertility — the more children, the merrier. For the same reason, the bed was scattered with red dates, lotus seeds, peanuts, pomegranates and other kinds of fresh or dried fruits. Part of the fun was watching the children scramble for the fruits.

B. Dowry

Usually the bride's dowry shall be sent to the bridegroom's family by the day before the wedding day. Apart from jewellery, embroidered beddings, kitchen utensils and furniture, the traditional dowry normally consisted of such symbolic items as scissors, a pair of pillows, shoes, clothes, chopsticks tied in red ribbon and bowls were musts in a traditional marriage.

3) Wedding Ceremony

A. Cry-of-Marriage

Before the bride left for the bridegroom's home, the "good luck woman" would lead her to the sedan chair. On her way to the chair, one of her sisters would shield her with a red parasol, while another sister would throw rice at the sedan chair. At the back of the sedan hung a sieve and a metallic mirror that were believed to protect the bride from evil.

Before she got on the bridal sedan chair bound for her new home, the bride had to cry to show that she did not want to leave her parents. She would cry over the love and care her parents had given her for so many years. At this moment, the bride's mother would pass on to her daughter the secrets of how to be an adequate wife and daughter-in-law, how to handle the household with thrift and decency as well as make herself pleasant to every one of the new family, etc.

B. Escorting Bride to Groom's House

It was the prelude of wedding ceremony to send a party for escorting the bride to the bridegroom's house. On the day before the wedding, the bridegroom was supposed to visit the bride's family and salute to all the family members of the bride but he couldn't meet the bride. On the day of wedding, the bridegroom should send an honor guard to the bride's house. On the way to the bridegroom's home, the honor guard would take the lead, followed by the bride's sedan.

After various rules of rites, the bride would be carried to the sedan chair by her father or elder brother with the bridegroom standing by. When everything was all right, the bridegroom could take leave. The bride was still unseen to the bridegroom at this time with a piece of red silk veil covering her head and face (see picture 11 - 1). Usually a crowd of friends would escort the bridegroom and musicians would play joyful tunes during the entire trip. Dancing lions, if any, preceded the troop. In ancient times, a bridal sedan chair (or a decorated donkey due to poverty or bad traffic) would be used to transport the bride.

C. Performing Formal Bows

After the sedan reached the bridegroom's bridal chamber, an elder woman who had many offspring would support the hand of the bride and help her come out of the sedan chair in the wedding march. The woman would feed boiled rice dumplings to both bridegroom and bride because the round shape of the dumplings signify harmony and union. Then the candles and the incenses were lighted and the bridegroom and the bride held the two ends of a red ribbon respectively and met on the red carpet. They would bow to each other and then drink from the nuptial cups. Now came the climax of the wedding ceremony. The bride and bridegroom were led to the family altar, where the couple kowtowed to Heaven and Earth, the family ancestors and parents successively. They then bowed to each other and were led to the bridal chamber. The ceremony proceeded under a director's prompts and applauses of the audience.

D. Teasing Games in the Bridal Chamber

The teasing games started when the newly wed couple entered their bridal chamber after the wedding ceremony. Usually all young men could participate except for the bride's brothers-in-laws. The funny and silly games help ease the tension, since in ancient times the newlyweds never met each other before the wedding! The teasing games varied with regions.

E. Bridal Chamber

By the evening of the wedding day or, failing that, the next day, the bride should salute the uncles-and aunts-in-law. Then she would be led by the younger aunt or other female elder to salute all the elders. Next evening the new couple might have their supper (known as "Bridal Chamber Supper") together in their bridal chamber for the first time. On the third day, the bride and the bridegroom would salute the memorial tablets of ancestors, which meant to show that marriage was not only for the bridegroom, but more importantly, for continuing the ancestral life.

F. Bride's Return to Parents' Home

Traditionally, the newlyweds were to return to visit the bride's parents three days after the wedding. It is an indispensable etiquette. A month after the wedding the bride would visit her parents' home again accompanied by her husband bringing many kinds of gifts. The bridegroom went home on the same day after the escort mission, leaving his wife staying at her parents' home for several days.

2. Related Knowledge about Ancient Marriage Customs

1) Three Letters and Six Etiquettes

A. Three Letters

Betrothal Letter: This was the formal document of the engagement, a must for a marriage.

Gift Letter: This would be given to the identified girl's family. Within the letter would be a list of the types and quantity of gifts designated for the wedding once both parties accepted the marriage.

Wedding Letter: The Wedding Letter was prepared and presented to the bride's family on the day of the wedding and was a document that confirmed and commemorated the formal acceptance of the bride into the bridegroom's family.

B. Six Etiquettes

Proposing: If an unmarried boy's parents identified a girl as their potential future daughter-in-law, they would then locate a matchmaker. Proposals were the specialty of the matchmakers. The matchmaker would formally present his or her client's request to the identified girl's parents.

Birthday matching: If the potential bride's parents did not object to the marriage, the matchmaker would then ask for the girl's birthday and birth-hour to assure the compatibility of the potential bride and bridegroom. If the couple's birthdays and birth-hours did not conflict according to astrology, the marriage would continue onto the next stage. If there was any sign of astrological conflict, which meant the marriage would bring disasters upon both families, the proposed marriage was immediately quashed.

Presenting betrothal gifts: Once both birthdays matched, the bridegroom's family would then arrange for the matchmaker to present betrothal gifts and the betrothal letter to the bride's family.

Presenting wedding gifts: After the betrothal letter and betrothal gifts were accepted, the bridegroom's family would later formally send wedding gifts to the bride's family. Usually, gifts may include money and food.

Picking a wedding date: An astrologer would be consulted by the bridegroom's family in order to help select an auspicious date for the holding of the wedding ceremony.

Wedding ceremony: On the selected day, the bridegroom departed with a troop of escorts and musicians, playing cheerful music all the way to the bride's home. After the bride was escorted to the bridegroom's home, the wedding ceremony began.

2) Ningbo Bridal Sedan Chairs

Bridal Sedan Chair (see picture 11-2) is also called Wan Gong Jiao, famous for its delicate technique. The bridal sedan chair in the picture has a height of 3 meters, a length of 1.5 meters, and a width of 95 centimeters. It has delicate wood-carving and splendid golden decoration, which reveals its golden elegance to people who see it.

According to the legend, in Southern Song Dynasty, Zhao Gou, Song Gaozong, was once in danger as he was chased after by the Jin soldiers. Fortunately, he was saved by a local girl. The emperor decided to see her and pick her up to the court. But their meeting signals were revealed. Then the emperor ordered that all the girls in the east of Zhejiang province be queens. When they got married, they could dress themselves in queen's phoenix decorations and could sit in the bridal sedan chairs. When officials met them, they had to get off their chairs or horses. Therefore, since the Southern Song Dynasty, the custom of Ningbo girls sitting in bridal sedan chairs on their marriage was getting more and more popular, and the technique of making the bridal sedan chairs was also getting more and more delicate. One might often hear a married woman say proudly, "I'm carried here by the bridal sedan chair on the wedding day".

3) Red — Color for the Wedding

Unlike Western tradition, the color red dominates traditional Chinese weddings. Chinese people tend to use or wear red to add a joyful atmosphere to such a festive occasion.

At dawn on the wedding day, the bride would put on new clothes and a pair of red shoes after bath and waited for the so-called "good luck woman" to dress her hair in the style of a married woman. Her head would be covered with a red silk veil with tassels. She waited for her future husband to escort her home, with married women talking around her about how to be a good wife.

On the other hand, the bridegroom was preparing himself to receive his wife. He was dressed in a long gown, red shoes and a red silk sash with a silk ball on his chest. The groom knelt at the ancestral altar as his father would declare his adulthood and his family responsibility.

Then the bridegroom set out to receive his bride. The most interesting part of the reception really took place at the doorstep of the bride's residence, which was heavily guarded by the bridesmaid or the bride's sisters. It was customary for the bridesmaid to give the bridegroom a difficult time before he was allowed to enter. Usually wisdom, courage and his friends could help the bridegroom to succeed in his "trial". However, there was one more situation he had to negotiate with the bridesmaid and sisters of the bride — to distribute among them red packets containing money — in order to take his bride home.

Word Bank

betrothal	订婚，许婚
go-between	中间人，媒人
buffer	缓冲物
matchmaker	媒人，红娘
consensual	双方同意的
fortune-teller	算命先生，星象术士
discreet	谨慎的，审慎的
attestation	证明，证据
propitious	吉祥的，顺利的
dowry	嫁妆
sedan	轿车，轿子
parasol	阳伞
nuptial	婚礼的，婚姻的
altar	祭坛
tablets	碑，匾额
quash	废止，撤销
sash	肩带，腰带

参考译文

中国婚姻风俗始于战国时期。由于中国幅员辽阔，各地结婚的程序及仪式虽基本相似，却又不尽相同。传统的婚俗烦琐复杂，早已随着封建社会的消亡而不再流行。然而传统的婚礼在农村仍时有所见，特别是近来，传统的婚俗似乎在复苏，正吸引着许多准备结婚的年轻人。

1. 结婚程序

往昔的婚姻是包办婚姻，以“父母之命，媒妁之言”为定。尤其是妇女，“嫁鸡随鸡，嫁狗随狗”，以夫为纲，婚后更受公婆管束。旧式婚姻通常包括以下几个步骤。

1）订婚

订婚是传统婚姻中一项必不可缺的手续。订婚始于提亲，在提亲和订婚过程中，男女双方父母扮演主要角色，而非当事人自己。婚姻被看作是人生头等大事，不能让年轻人自己草率决定。媒人则似双方之间的一个缓冲物，其功能正如现今的房产代理商。

A. 说合

“说合”即在订婚前，媒人往来于双方家长之间沟通情况，主要是了解双方门户是否相当，家庭财产情况如何，其次是家庭成员情况，然后才是当事人的相貌、年龄、性情等。男方多要求女方是书香门第，女方则要求男方家境殷实。如果双方家长认为合意，才可以继续进行下一步。

B. 合婚

所谓“合婚”，即将男女双方生辰八字由媒人送算命先生处推算吉凶，再由媒人通报双方家长。有的家长为郑重起见，还要在合婚得吉之后约定地点互看人选。双方认为满意，便可办理“行聘”之礼了。

C. 行聘

行聘是订婚的主要内容，由媒人开彩帖与女方家商议，议定目录，然后由男家正式行聘。行聘还需分三次进行。聘礼有礼帖、礼物和礼金三部分，其中最重要的是礼帖，因为它是正式婚约的证据。聘礼行过，然后才可以选定婚期迎娶。

2）备婚

A. 安床

新郎需要在婚礼前一天准备好婚床。之前要择定良辰吉日，请一位“好命佬”和“好命婆”（即父母健在、子孙满堂、婚姻和睦的男子和女子）帮忙准备婚床。“好命佬”将新床搬至新房适当位置。安床仪式实际上只是象征性地移动一下已经让仆人或朋友放置好的床。床安置好之后，由“好命婆”负责铺床，将床褥、床单及龙凤被等铺在床上。安床后任何人不得进入新房及触碰新床，直至新人于婚礼当晚进房为止。

新人进新房后会让小孩爬到床上，俗称“压床”，取其百子千孙之意，孩子越多越好。床上撒着各式喜果，如红枣、莲子、花生、石榴等水果或干果。看孩子们抢食喜果也是颇有乐趣的。

B. 嫁妆

女方家的嫁妆须最迟于结婚前一天送到男方家。嫁妆除珍贵的珠宝首饰、绣花的床上用品、厨房用品和家具以外，主要是一些象征好兆头的东西，如：剪刀、一对枕头、鞋、衣服以及两双用红绳捆着的筷子及碗等。

3）婚礼

A. 哭嫁

新娘离开家之前，“好命婆”将她引上花轿，上轿前，由大姐或伴娘撑着红伞护着新娘，另一个姐妹将米撒向花轿。轿子后面挂着一面筛子和一面金属制的镜子用来为新娘除恶避邪。

姑娘出嫁，上轿前在娘家必哭一场，以示对父母家人的依恋。哭后，做娘的便要对女儿传授女儿经，如何为妻为媳，如何勤俭持家，如何待人接物等，一一指点。

B. 迎娶

迎娶为结婚大典之前奏。迎娶前一日，新郎须至女方家会亲，然只能谒见新娘的父母，并与女方亲友一一行相见礼，但不能与新娘相见。迎娶当日，新郎须亲自迎亲，以鼓乐仪仗为先行、新娘之彩轿随行。

彩轿到达女方家后，经过一系列仪式，新娘由父兄抱入彩轿，俗称“抱轿”。新郎侍立在侧，挽新娘登轿后，便“请轿”辞行。此时，新娘顶着红盖头(见图 11-1)，与新郎仍未会面。花轿在迎归男方家的路上，前呼后拥，好不气派。有时在前面开道的是舞狮队。古时姑娘出嫁时，根据女方家境贫富，或骑毛驴或坐花轿。

C. 拜堂

新娘所乘彩轿到男方家时，彩轿入门，鼓乐并奏。一位多子多孙的妇人，把新娘扶出轿来，先喂汤圆给新郎新娘吃，以取和气团圆之意，然后拜堂。堂前明烛点香，新郎新娘各牵着红缘巾的一端，在红地毯上相会，然后行交拜礼，饮交杯酒。接下来是婚礼的高潮，新人被带到祖宗牌位前，一拜天地，二拜高堂，然后夫妻对拜，最后新人被送入洞房。婚礼进行过程中，由司仪说颂词，亲朋好友在一旁喝彩。

D. 闹房

结婚仪式告成，新婚夫妇同入洞房，亲朋好友开始闹房。一般说来，除了新娘的姐夫，年轻人都可以参加闹洞房。闹房可以缓解新婚夫妇对彼此的紧张感觉。因为在过去，很多新人婚前互相并不熟悉甚至不相识。各地的“闹房”有不同的方式。

E. 洞房花烛夜

结婚当夜或第二天，新娘拜见叔姑。姑姑引导新妇向尊长们一一见礼，如果没有姑姑则由族中的女尊长为引导。第二天晚上，新夫妇可以在新房中第一次同桌饮食，俗称“洞房夜饭”。婚后第三天，行庙见礼，以示男子娶亲不专为个人，也是为家族的繁衍。

F. 回娘家

按照中国婚俗习惯，结婚三天后，新娘便要偕同新郎一起回娘家，也称“回门”。这是必不可少的礼节。新娘出嫁满月后要再次回娘家，女婿准备多种礼物陪同前去，以示孝敬。当日，女婿返回，新娘则在娘家小住几日。

2. 古代婚俗相关知识

1) 三书六礼

A. 三书

聘书：定亲之书，男女双方正式缔结婚约。婚约必备之物。

礼书：过礼之书，即礼物清单，详尽列明礼物种类及数量。

迎亲书：迎娶新娘之书。结婚当日接新娘过门时用，是男方家接受新娘的证明和纪念之书。

B. 六礼

纳采：男方父母属意女方时，延请媒人做媒，谓之纳采，今称“提亲”。

问名：男方探问女方之姓名及生日时辰，以卜吉兆，谓之问名，今称“合八字”。

纳吉：问名若属吉兆，遣媒人致赠薄礼及聘书，谓之纳吉，今称“过文定”或“小定”。

纳征：奉送礼金与礼物等，即正式送聘礼，谓纳征，今称“过大礼”。

请期：由男家请算命先生择日，谓之请期，又称“乞日”，今称 “择日”。

亲迎：新郎乘礼车，赴女家迎接新娘，谓之亲迎。

2) 宁波花轿

宁波花轿(见图 11-2)又称“万工轿”，以其做工精细而著称。图中的花轿高 3 米、长 1.5 米、宽 95 厘米，木质透雕，漆朱贴金，给人金碧辉煌之感。

传说南宋高宗赵构被金兵追杀，幸得一位宁波村姑相救。赵构脱险后，约好来年接村姑入宫，但两人所约暗号泄露，于是赵构下旨浙东女子皆封后，出嫁时可穿戴凤冠霞帔，乘坐龙凤花轿，官员遇见，文官下轿，武官下马。于是从南宋开始，宁波姑娘出嫁坐花轿的民风愈来愈盛，花轿制作也愈来愈考究。"我是花轿抬来的"这句话自然成为往日媳妇们的豪语。

3）红色——婚礼的颜色

与西方传统不同的是，红色是中国传统婚礼的主导色。中国人喜欢用红色来为这个喜庆的日子增添欢快的气氛。

婚礼当日的清晨，新娘在沐浴后穿上新嫁衣，红色绣鞋，等待"好命婆"为她梳妇人头。新娘的头上要披上带有流苏的红色真丝盖头，然后静静地等待新郎把她娶回家。此时，一些已婚妇女会教她到了婆家如何做一个好媳妇。

新郎那边正准备着迎娶新娘，他身穿长衫，脚着红鞋，肩披红带。新郎跪拜于先辈的灵位前，其父宣布儿子独立成人和他即将担负的家庭责任。

接着新郎出门迎接新娘。迎娶时最有趣的是在新娘的家门前，门口由伴娘或新娘的姐妹们严把紧守。伴娘往往会刁难新郎，不让他轻易进门。新郎要过这道关，需要智慧、勇气以及小兄弟们的帮助。此外，还要给她们发红包，否则休想接得佳人归。

Exercises

Section A　Thought-provoking questions

1. Why is red the favorite color of bride in old China? What about in China today?
2. What is the significance of wedding traditions?
3. What kind of wedding ceremony would you choose? Why?

Section B　Cloze

At a traditional Chinese wedding, the bride is often seen with a red veil on her head. It covers the bride's face. Chinese people call the veil, made of a laced silk square, red head cover.

This practice dates__1__ to the Qi Period of the Northern and Southern dynasties. The head cover was used by women farmers to protect their heads against cold wind or hot sunshine while working in the fields. It could be a cloth of any color and was big enough to cover the head top. For its practical use and ornamental function, the head cover became a widespread custom.

By the beginning of Tang Dynasty, the cover had become a long veil down to the shoulder. And it was no longer a __2__ of working women. Later, Emperor Li Longji made a decision. He demanded that all maids-in-__3__ in the palace add a piece of gauze to the head covers to cover their faces. It soon became a fashion among the commons. But the commons made a difference of the cover's function. In those days, women's faces were thought of as a lure to men. A husband did not want his beautiful wife to be an attraction to men. He wanted her to behave bashfully and look too shy to see men. A veil could realize his __4__. And the wife readily accepted the veil to show her __5__ to her husband. Gradually the veils became popular among both married and unmarried women who were eager to demonstrate their virtues. Veils are not unique in China. Even today veils can still be seen in some other places in the world.

Chapter 12

Chinese Traditional Folk Entertainments

中国传统民间游艺

As an important part of Chinese folk customs, traditional folk entertainments consist of children games, intellectual games, athletic games, gambling games, seasonal games and festive activities. It is said that the card game, a game which enjoyed high popularity in the Tang and Song Dynasties, spread across Europe in the following Yuan Dynasty by the ambitious Mongolian cavalrymen during the period of Yuan's territory expansion to Europe in the west. After absorbing foreign traditions and cultures, card games came back to China at the beginning of the 20th century. Now the game of cards, in a constant new guise, still prevails among Chinese. The process of this game's development proves that entertainments and traditions are always handed down from generation to generation according to the transmission law of tradition. They mix with other cultures harmoniously and are in constant renovation. People have endowed traditional entertainments with vitality and, in return, are benefited by the relaxing and refreshing entertaining activities.

1. Children's Games

1) Playing Hide-and-Seek

Hide-and-seek, also known as "*zhuoxi*" or "*cangmeng*", is a most common game for children. The game can be played as long as there are at least two people. It is recorded in the works of Qing Dynasty, "One child is blindfolded with silk before starting to seek others. This is called *zhamangmang*." In addition, there are "*moxiayu*" (seeking blind fish), "*xiazimoxiang*" (blind men feel an elephant) and many other similar favorite games of children.

It is said that Emperor Xuan Zong of Tang Dynasty is a master-player of hide-and-seek. In the reign of Qian Long and Jiang Qing, there was an imperial artist Shen Qinglan, who once produced a painting "Children-Playing", in which 6 children are playing hide-and-seek.

2) Rope Skipping

Rope skipping in the Ming and Qing Dynasties was called *tiaobaisuo* (skipping ropes or skipping white ropes). In the Tang and Song Dynasties, it was recorded that rope skipping was called *tousuo* (through the rope), *tasuo* (jumping across the rope) and other names. In the Ming Dynasty, group rope skipping vigorously flourished as one of the Lantern Festival entertainments. Even adults joined the children to take part in this game. In the Qing Dynasty, the ropes used for this game fell into two kinds: a short rope and a long one. The former was used by one or two persons; the latter by a group of people. While skipping, one often sang or recited nursery rhymes: "A peace drum sounds rab-a-dub and a white light looks like a turning wheel. One child swings the rope, one sings and one jumps in the turning wheel."

3) Shuttlecock Kicking

Shuttlecock kicking is otherwise known as *tiyanzi* (kicking swallow) or *zanhua*. Traditional shuttlecock is made of a coin covered in cloth and fitted with cock feathers upward. In the Northern Dynasty, a Tianzhu (India in ancient Chinese) monk came to Luoyang to emancipate those who had predestined relation with Buddhism. He saw a child standing by a well ring on a very limited space and kicking shuttlecock. The child kicked five hundred rounds at a stretch. This proved that the technique already reached a very high level in the Northern and Southern Dynasties. Till the Tang Dynasty, it became more popular than ever before. It is said that the monks in the Shaolin Temple took it as a supplementary exercise for practice of martial arts. The imperial concubines were also keen on this game and all practiced and competed with each other.

As for its history, the Southern and the Northern Song Dynasties were an important phase in which its name became fixed and the way of making shuttlecock and its structures were almost identical to those of today. At the same time, many diversified techniques came out, such as walking while kicking, playing with shuttlecock on the knee, the abdomen and the head. Shuttlecock playing, inferred from research, can at least be traced back to the Han Dynasty two thousand years ago.

2. Intelligence-benefiting Games

1) Seven-piece Puzzle

A seven-piece puzzle, otherwise known as a seven-piece picture, is a famous jigsaw, which enjoys high popularity all over the world and gains the title of Tang Pictures. A seven-piece puzzle is invented out of inspiration from yanji of the Tang Dynasty, a kind of table used in ancient times with a distinguished feature of easy assembling and separation according to the number of guests.

The seven-piece puzzle made considerable progress during the Yuan and Ming Dynasties. During the period from the end of Ming Dynasty and the beginning of Qing Dynasty, a unit of seven pieces or sets made of wooden chips or cardboard was popularly known as seven-piece card. In the reign of Jiaqing of the Qing Dynasty, retired Scholar self nicknamed Lay Buddhist wrote a book *Seven-piece Picture* based on his comprehensive study and extensive practice of this game. Thenceforth, the structure and design of seven-piece puzzle were fixed.

The seven-piece puzzle is easy to solve even for a child. However, it is very interesting to play with. Even adults get fascinated with it. In the last one hundred years, special books on the game have come out in the western countries.

2) Riddle Guessing

Riddle guessing may be accounted as the most ancient intelligence-benefiting game. In the ancient books of the Zhou and Qin Dynasties, it is recorded that riddles were named *yinyu* (enigma) that employed such techniques as metaphor, analogy and implication to hide what riddles refer to. In the Han Dynasty, *yinyu* developed towards two directions: one is characterized by portrayal and the other is mainly about the meaning and form of words, with the former being popular among folks and the latter being the main way of intelligence racing among men of letters.

What's more, in the Song Dynasty, there appeared professional artists who were specialized in making riddles, who were called commercial riddle makers. They put up stands at such public places of entrainment as *wazi*, attracting people to participate in riddle guessing. He who guessed rightly got the prize; he who guessed wrongly paid money. Meanwhile, this game was combined with the lantern show on the Lantern Festival. Therefore, lantern riddles pasted on the lanterns for amusement and enjoyment were produced.

3) Untying a Chain of Rings

Untying a chain of rings is a traditional intellectual game. The rules go like this: first, one ties a number of rings together into a chain and then he who unties them is the winner. The chain of rings has various structures: five-ringed, seven-ringed, nine-ringed, eleven-ringed and even thirteen-ringed. Among them, the nine-ringed is the most popular. This game made its first appearance in the Warring States Period. Thenceforth, it remained prevalent through dynasties. Su Shi, a famous poet in the Song Dynasty, writes: "It is easy to untie a chain of rings as if with the help of a god's hands." This indirectly reflects the complexity and difficulty of untying a chain of rings. In the reign of Emperor Jiajing of the Ming Dynasty, Karl Dane, an Italian mathematician came to China. He could not admire more the Chinese chain of rings.

4) Practising *Guqin*, *Qi*, *Shu*, and *Hua*

Qin, a seven stringed-plucked instrument in some ways similar to the zither, originally was called *qin* or seven stringed *qin* (see Chapter 17). Since the Tang and Song Dynasties, it was called "*guqin*" which was used as a musical instrument for offering sacrifices, entertainments and performance.

Qi specially refers to *weiqi* with a history over four thousand years. In the Spring and Autumn period and Warring States period, *weiqi* was beginning to take shape. A *weiqi* board has 19 vertically and horizontally parallel lines, 361 crosses, 180 black pieces and 180 white ones.

Shu (calligraphy) refers to the writing in brush. It resorts to the change of lines to express the style of writing and the mood of the writer.

Hua means painting in brush, ink and painting coloring on specially made *Xuan* paper, a high quality paper made in Xuancheng in Anhui Province, or on silk. As for its skill and technique, there are *gongbi* (traditional Chinese realistic painting characterized by fine brush and close attention to details), *yibi* (focus on the mood instead of details), sketching, boneless technique (painting without outline but with forms achieved by washes of ink and color), etc.

Qin, *qi*, *shu* and *hua* not only act as entertainments for traditional scholars, but also exert immeasurable influence on the character of traditional scholars and creation of the Chinese cultural heritage. Enjoying *guqin*, *weiqi*, calligraphy and painting are regarded as literary pursuits by scholars. He Yanzhi of the Tang Dynasty records in his *Lanting Account*: "One is elegant, erudite and good at writing and obtains the essence of *qin*, *qi*, *shu*, *and hua*."

3. Athletic Games

1) Tug-of-War

Tug-of-war was also known as pulling a hook or tugging a hook in the ancient times. It can be traced back to late Spring and Autumn Period and early Warring States Period when the army of Chu employed a rope with a hook on one end to train soldiers to catch hold of their enemy's war chariots and boats. Later, it developed into a sport and popular folk custom.

Tug-of-war was initially prevalent in the middle and lower reaches of the Yangtze River. While playing tug-of-war, both sides extend their utmost efforts in time with drum beating. Both participants and audience joyously shout to boost the pullers' morale, presenting a grand and liveliest scene. A flag stuck in the ground as the demarcation, the party who pulls the rope over the demarcation to its own side is the winner.

2) Dragon-Boat Racing

A bronze drum of Spring and Autumn Period was unearthed in the Yin County, Zhejiang Province, on which racing boat lines were found. It can be inferred that dragon-boat racing has its origin from the Spring and Autumn Period in the South. Archaeological researchers also found racing boat pictures on the bronze drum of the Han Dynasty unearthed at Stone Village Mountain in Yunnan Province. According to ancient records, the dragon boat in the Ming and Qing Dynasties was 10 *zhang* (about 33 meters) in length with 16 oars on either side.

On the racing boat, drums are arranged to boost up the morale of the race attendants and the atmosphere. Bladders of pig, live ducks or geese afloat on the surface of the river work as live marks instead of fixed poles of the dead marks. Many fleeting boats struggle for them, making the race more interesting and appealing.

Legend goes that Qu Yuan, a senior official in Chu, was unfortunately slandered and forced to exile and took his own life by jumping into the Miluo River on the 5th day of the 5th lunar month. People in Chu were in great sorrow after hearing the news and they drove boats to rescue him. The custom of dragon boat racing on that day was then formed and has gradually become a sport event.

3) Other Sport Games

Various sport activities exist in almost every historical period and the background of each culture. The long standing Chinese civilization has given birth to its own culture of Chinese sports. When ancient Greeks hosted the Olympic Games, some of the sport activities were similar to what existed in the ancient times of China, such as: horsemanship, skills of penetrating, resisting skills, military skills in martial arts, hunting, running, jumping and some water sports. Meanwhile, such sport games as *cuju* (ancient Chinese football), *nongwan*, cockfight, dog racing, etc. were also getting popular in the developed areas of China.

When the Western countries held spearing, racing and other matches, the most popular sport in the old China was the "*lishe*". Its scale, form and organization enjoyed a high recommendation like any other forms of the sport competitions. Even today, it has a high value of research in the area of the sport literature. Through the display of *lishe*, people will certainly have a deeper understanding of the ancient Chinese sports culture and they may have a brand new expectation for the culture of sports to reach the "harmonious" realm.

4. Gambling Games

1) Mahjong

Chinese gambling arts have a distant resource and a long stream through ages. They are synthesized and brought to a highest realm, i.e. the almost everyone known "the game of square city" — playing mahjong. Mahjong is also known as sparrow pieces or horse pieces. It grew out of *Yezige* game — a card game and evolved into a new game of bone cards in the Song Dynasty and was imperially named *Xuanhe* Cards by Gaozong of the Southern Song Dynasty. Until the Ming Dynasty, it adopted a new rule that the game should be played by 4 people. Because of this, it got the name of *madiao* with the meaning that a horse could not walk without 4 legs. As the father-in-law of Emperor Chongzhen of the Ming Dynasty, Tian Hongyu was the very No. One *madiao* veterinarian. In the Qing Dynasty, besides "tong", "suo" and "wan", "north", "south", "east" and "west" were added. What's more, "yaotou" was changed into "zhong", "fa" and "bai". Thus a new gambling art — mahjong — eventually took shape.

2) Cricket Fight

A cricket has many alternative names, among which "qiong" is a comparatively refined one. Because cricket produces sounds like quick weaving, it gets other names of *jizhi*, *quzhi* and *cuzhi* (hurry weaving). It is absurd that history saw high officials Jia Shidao, the Cricket Prime Minister and Ma Shiying, the Cricket Xianggong. Their craziness about cricket fighting often resulted in their dereliction of duty.

In the Qing Dynasty, government had once supervised cricket raising. In addition, special cricket fighting venues were established and managers made profits by taking a percentage from the winnings. Influenced by the Han culture, the royal family of the Qing Dynasty and the Eight Banners descendants also took to playing this game. Later, even Empress Dowager Cixi was listed among the players.

The earliest historical records about cricket can be found in the *Cricket Classic* by Jia Shidao in the Southern Song Dynasty. It was called the encyclopedia of cricket, which has long been lost.

5. Seasonal Activities

1) Swinging

Swing, as a traditional sport and program on festive occasions, is very popular among the Hans and other minorities such as the Korean nationality and the Lahu nationality. In the Han and Wei Dynasties, swing already evolved from a military training program into an entertainment enjoyed by both the imperial palace and the ordinary families, especially on the Beginning of Spring (the first of the 24 solar terms), Cold Food Festival and many other festivals. It became an indispensable program among the diversified celebrating activities. Swinging was so popular on Cold Food Festival that it was even referred to as Swinging Festival.

It is said that swinging originated from the reign of Wudi of the Han Dynasty. It was invented as a game for the imperial palace to celebrate his birthday and wish him long life of one thousand years. Therefore, at that time, it was called qianqiu (one thousand years) which was falsely rumored as qiuqian in later ages.

In the Tang Dynasty, this sport, prevalent in the imperial palace, was called half immortal game. Beautiful imperial concubines were gorgeously dressed up and richly ornamented and then sat or stood on swings with two hands gripping the ropes, swinging gracefully, dizzily pleasant as immortals. Hence the vivid name — half immortal game.

2) Kite Flying

Like many age-old cultural fruits, kites initially showed up in China. The northerners call it *zhiyuan* (paper sparrow hawk), while the southerners call it *yaozi* (sparrow hawk) (see Chapter 17). With *muyuan* (wooden sparrow hawks) as its original shape, a kite is a primitive aircraft made by ancestors. It is a pity that this kind of craft has been lost. Until the Han Dynasty, bamboo slips were chosen for the frame structure with paper or thin silk stuck together in shape of birds attached with a slanting line. Gripping the line, people flew the kite onto the sky with the help of the wind. Hence, it derived the name *zhiyuan*. Usually a bamboo flute is banded on a kite and gives forth sounds similar to those of *zheng* as a result of the blowing wind. *Zheng* is a 21- or 25- stringed plucked instrument in someway similar to zither. This is why kite is called *fengzheng* (wind zither).

The legend behind it is that the master carpenter Lu Ban once cut a piece of bamboo and make it into a magpie shape. He called it wooden magpie. It kept flying on the sky for three days and nights. Therefore, if *muyuan* were taken as the earliest kite, then Lu Ban would be the inventor of kites.

Kite flying is a favorite pastime to people all over the world today. According to kite lore, the first kite was flown in China about 3,000 years ago. In modern China, kites are used not only as toys, but also as exquisite handicrafts worthy of collection. Tianjin has long enjoyed a great reputation as a kite provider. "Kite Wei" is a famous brand of kites in Tianjin, originated by folk craft master Wei Yuantai (1872 - 1961). Kite Wei products once won a gold medal at San Francisco's Panama Pacific International Exposition in 1915. The city of Weifang, Shandong Province, hosts the Weifang International Kite Festival annually in mid-April.

6. Acrobatic Games

1) Playing *Kongzhu*

Kongzhu (meaning empty bamboo), known abroad as diabolo or Chinese yo-yo outside of China, is originally a Chinese folk toy in which a round wooden box, dotted with several holes, is set at one end of a bamboo cylinder(single-domed) or both ends of it (double-domed) and when played with using a string, the box revolves quickly and produces a buzzing sound through its holes. The oldest records of the *kongzhu* appear in ancient Chinese literature written 1,700 years ago. It is considered to have been practiced for more than 2,000 years and to be one of the 3 major traditional folk games originated from China along with the shuttlecock and the kite.

The *kongzhu* is widely popularized among common people throughout China, hence the many and different names of it in dialects of regions such as *kongzhu* in north China; *cheling* or *chetuoluo* in the south of Yangtze River and in Taiwan; *xianghuang* in Sichuan Province, and so on. It is used for athletic pastime or for performance on festive occasions, and is later introduced into acrobatic show. It is possible to perform an enormous variety of tricks with the *kongzhu*.

2) Walking on Stilts

It is said that stilt walking (see picture 12 - 1) is originated from the ancient times when the primitive people bound sticks onto their legs to make them taller so that they could reach the wild fruits on the trees.

Walking on stilts is called "*zougaoqiao*" as well as "*tagaoqiao*". According to historical records, it has been more than 2,500 years since walking on stilts showed up in China.

Walking on stilts has become a popular performance. In the northern part of China, stilt-walking performers usually play the roles of fisherman, matchmaker, foolish son of a high official, Taoist nun, monk, etc. in a very funny way. In the southern part of the country, the roles of Guan Gong (Lord Guan), Daoji (commonly known as Ji Gong), fairy He Xiangu, immortals and clowns are usually played. The performers sing and walk at the same time, acting vividly in an amusing way.

7. Festive Activities

1) Lion Dance and Dragon Dance

Lions live in Africa and South America. After the Han Dynasty, it was introduced into China. It is generally accepted that Lion Dance came into being as long ago as in the Three Kingdom, which was initially prevalent in the army and spread among the ordinary people afterwards.

Lion dance is a game very popular with the ordinary people. It usually appears in towns and villages on the Spring Festival and idolatrous processions, adding much to the joyous festive air.

The folk lion dance falls into the Northern Lion Dance (violent lion dance) and the Southern Lion Dance (gentle lion dance). Violent lion dance attaches importance to the martial arts with nimble movements and high techniques. While gentle Lion dance focuses on facial expressions with exquisite movements which strives to depict lion's docile and lovely bearings and dynamic, frolicsome character.

Dragon dance is the vestige of totem worship in ancient times. The performance was not only to pray for rain and offer sacrifices but also to entertain.

During the Tang and Song periods, dragon lantern dance already became ordinary artistic forms in the performance of traditional programs of *shehuo* (a religious procession) and team dance. Dragon dance, in the Ming and Qing Dynasties, was listed among folk festival entertainments with peculiar flavor.

2) Waist Drum Dance

Waist-drum dance (see picture 12 - 2) boasts a long-standing tradition and enjoys great popularity in Ansai, northern Shaanxi Province. Characterized by a variety of drumbeats and accompanied with folk songs, percussion instruments and wind instruments, the unique Ansai drum dancing can be generally classified into "soft-swing dancing" and "martial arts dancing". The performance scene is quite impressive with diversified arrays which integrate dance, song, gymnastics and vigorous martial arts movements. It serves as a display of the traits in the character of northern Shaanxi villagers, who are known far and wide as being valiant and heroic. Sometimes the number of performers may reach several hundred. The imposing scene is full of grandeur with great momentum.

It is a traditional custom for young people in villages in northern Shaanxi to do the waist drum dancing to greet Spring Festival and Lantern Festival. A dancer with a red drum tied to his waist holds a drumstick with red silk, beating the drum while dancing. The rhythmical drum beats are full of power and grandeur and the dance is vibrant and vigorous, reflecting the straightforward and uninhibited character of villagers in northern Shaanxi Province. At the climax of the dance, dancers beat drums while jumping into the air, shouting "Haihai" excitedly. It is an expression of their happy and passionate feelings.

3) Setting off Fireworks

Almost every country sets off fireworks on important festivals. This traditionally ceremonial entertainment originates from China. The Dynasties of Sui and Tang saw the earliest fireworks which fell into two categories. One is gun-powered wire firework: figures, objects, birds, flowers, pavilions, buildings and many other varied patterns were made of metal wires on which gunpowder is coated. They present varied fantastic scenes against the background of dark night. The other is tube firework with gunpowder put into a paper tube. After it is lighted, it will spurt multicolored flames.

In the Ming Dynasty, gun-powered wire fireworks changed from plane into three-dimensional ones. Different layers of gun-powered wires were vertically and horizontally arranged and designed. Then it was put into a big box to be hung on a stand. Ignited, the wires in the box catch fire and fell slowly layer by layer, demonstrating magical and dimensional sights.

Word Bank

cavalrymen	骑兵	enigma	谜语
emancipate	解放,使不受束缚	erudite	博学的
predestined	(命中)注定的	chariot	战车
stretch	一段连续的时间	demarcation	边界,分界

slander	诽谤	valiant	骁勇的
dereliction	玩忽职守	imposing	壮观的
magpie	鹊,喜鹊	grandeur	宏伟
cylinder	滚筒,圆柱体	vibrant	生机勃勃的
idolatrous	崇拜偶像的	uninhibited	不受约束的
frolicsome	嬉戏的	spurt	喷射

参考译文

民间游艺是中国民族文化的重要组成部分。中国传统游戏包括儿童游戏、益智游戏、竞技游戏、博弈游戏、时令游戏和节日娱乐活动。相传中国唐宋时期非常盛行的卡片游戏在随后的元朝随着蒙古骑兵的西进传到欧洲,与异邦的民族文化杂交、融合,形成了扑克牌。20 世纪初叶,又传回中国,至今花样翻新,盛行不衰。这说明,民间游艺总是按照民族传统传承的法则在民众中代代相传,与世界文化交融并不断推陈出新。民众赋予了民间游艺以顽强的生命力,同时又在游艺中获得放松和休息。

1. 儿童游戏

1) 捉迷藏

捉迷藏是最普通的童稚游戏,亦称“捉戏”或“藏朦”。只要不少于两人,便可玩起来。清人的著作中称:“儿童以绸扎眼相扑捉,谓之‘扎盲盲’。”其他还有“摸瞎鱼”“瞎子摸象”等与之类似的儿童喜爱的游戏。

相传唐代皇帝唐玄宗是捉迷藏的大玩家。清代乾隆、嘉庆时期宫廷画家沈庆兰曾创作了一幅《戏婴图》,画中即 6 名儿童在玩捉迷藏游戏。

2) 跳绳

跳绳在明清时期叫“跳百索”或“跳白索”。唐宋时期的跳绳有“透索”“踏索”等名词记载。明代盛行集体跳绳,是正月闹元宵期间的节令游艺,大人孩子均可参加。清朝时,“跳白索”有短绳和长绳之分,短绳可单人跳或双人跳;长绳为集体跳。跳时一边唱歌或吟诵儿歌:“太平鼓,声咚咚,白光如轮舞索童。一童舞索一童唱,一童跳入光轮中。”

3) 踢毽子

踢毽子,也称“踢燕子”,又叫“攒花”。传统的毽子是用铜板做底座,上面插上公鸡尾巴上的毛。北朝一天竺(旧时中国对印度的称呼)僧人去洛阳度“有缘”时,见一小儿站在井栏极为有限的平面上,用脚外侧一口气反踢了 500 下毽子,足见踢毽子的技巧在南北朝时已有很高的水准。唐代时,踢毽子愈加风行,据说河南少林寺僧人曾把踢毽子作为习练武术的辅助功。皇宫嫔妃亦爱此游戏,莫不竞相练习。

两宋时期是踢毽子游艺史上的一个重要发展阶段,那时这项游艺不仅名称已定型,且制作方式也和现在的毽子结构基本相同,并产生了边走边踢和以膝部、腹部、头部要弄毽子的诸多技巧方式。根据相关研究,踢毽子的历史至少可以追溯到 2 000 多年前的汉朝。

2. 益智游戏

1）七巧板

七巧板也称“七巧图”，是中国著名的拼图玩具，现已风行世界，号称“唐图”。七巧板的发明受唐代“燕几”的启发而发明。“燕几”是古代的一种桌子，可按坐客的人数拼装、拆卸，十分方便。

七巧板在元明两代有了长足发展。在明末清初，用薄木片或厚纸板做成的七件套组合，俗称“七巧牌”。嘉庆年间有位号为“养拙居士”的名人在结合拼玩实践的基础上写成《七巧图》一书，其形制乃成定式。

七巧板较容易拼搭，即便是孩子也能拼出。七巧板虽然简单，但非常有趣，连大人都会玩得入迷。在过去的 100 年中，西方出版了一些关于七巧板的书籍。

2）猜谜

猜谜语大约可称为中国最为古老的益智性游艺。周、秦的古籍中，人们则称猜谜或谜语为“隐语”，即出谜者借用隐喻、形似、暗示等手法，将所欲表达的事物隐藏其间。汉代，隐语开始朝两个方向发展，一是以特征描写为主的事为谜，二是以文字形义为主的谜语。前者是民间猜谜的主要模式，后者则成为文人斗智的游戏。

宋代还出现了靠制谜为主的专业性艺人，称“商谜”，他们在“瓦子”等娱乐场所设摊，聚众竞猜。猜中者获奖，猜不中则由猜客付钱。同时，这项游艺又同繁盛的元宵灯会相结合，产生出粘贴在灯笼上供赏灯者猜的谜语——灯谜。

3）解连环

解连环是中国传统的智力游戏，玩法是：把若干金属制成的圆环连成串，然后以解开为胜。连环的形制有 5 环、7 环、9 环、11 环乃至 13 环等多种，其中最流行的是九连环。解连环的游戏起源于战国时代，此后历代不衰。宋代大诗人苏轼云：“连环易解如神手。”这从侧面反映了当时连环形制的繁复和开解之难。明代嘉靖年间来华的意大利数学家卡尔丹对“中国之环”推崇备至。

4）琴棋书画

“琴”为弦拨乐器，与齐特琴有某些类似的地方，原称琴或七弦琴（见第 17 章），唐宋以后称作古琴，是古人用来祭祀、娱乐和表演的乐器。

“棋”在古代专指围棋，已有 4 000 多年历史，春秋战国时已成规模。围棋棋盘纵横各 19 条平行线，361 个交叉点。棋子分黑白两色，各有 180 枚。

“书”指毛笔字的书写方法。它以线条的变化来表现风格和意境。

“画”以毛笔、墨及中国书画颜料，在特制的宣纸或绢上作画（宣纸是安徽宣城出产的高质量纸张），在技法上有工笔、意笔、勾勒、没骨等技法形式。

琴、棋、书、画不仅是传统文人娱乐、消闲的模式，而且对传统文人人格的塑造、对中华文化遗产的创造都有不可估量的作用。琴棋书画是古代学者提高文化修养的方式。唐代的何延之在《兰亭记》中写道：“辩才博学工文，琴棋书画皆得其妙。”

3. 健身游戏

1）拔河

拔河，古名“牵钩”“拖钩”等，源于春秋晚期。当时楚国军队用绳子一头拴上铁钩，训练士兵甩出绳子钩住敌人的战车和船只。后来，这个军事训练项目逐渐演变成体育活动和流行的民间习俗。

拔河最初在今长江中下游一带流行。操作时还要“鸣鼓”以整齐双方角力的节奏，场面恢宏。

双方参与者和观众大声呼喊，为己方加油，气氛热烈。拔河时，一面旗子插在地上作为分界线，拔河的两队哪一方将绳拉过界线便赢。

2）赛龙舟

在浙江鄞县出土的春秋时代的铜鼓上，绘有竞渡船纹，可见赛龙舟的习俗起源于春秋时代的江南地区。考古工作者在云南石寨山发现的汉代铜鼓上，也有划船竞渡的图像。有典籍记载，明清时南方的龙舟长10丈(约33米)，两边各有木桨16支。

舟中设有锣鼓以振士气并渲染气氛，还常以漂在水面上的猪尿泡或鹅、鸭等“活标”取代位置固定的竹竿“死标”，由飞驰的龙舟竞夺目标，从而增强竞赛的娱乐性。

据传说，楚国大臣屈原遭到谗言，被流放到沅、湘流域，在阴历五月初五投汨罗江自尽。楚国百姓得知消息，十分悲痛，急划小船前往搭救。从此有了五月五赛龙舟这个民俗，后来逐渐普及为一项体育运动。

3）其他体育活动

几乎在所有历史时期和每一种文化背景中，都存在着各种各样的体育活动。源远流长的中国古老文明孕育了中国特有的体育文化。在古希腊人举办奥运会时，有些项目与中国古代存在的体育活动类似，如：骑术、射术、御术、军事武艺、田猎、跑、跳跃及水上活动等项目。同时，蹴鞠(古代中国足球)、斗鸡、走狗等体育娱乐活动也在当时中国发达地区流行起来。

当西方世界大规模举办投枪、赛跑等项目的比赛时，中华大地最盛行的体育项目是“礼射”，它的规模、形式与组织不逊于任何形式的体育竞赛，即使在现代也具有很高的体育文化学价值。通过礼射的展现，人们必定会对悠久的中国古代体育文化有深层的理解，并对体育文化最终达到“和谐”之境产生新的期待。

4. 博弈游戏

1）麻将

中国博弈游戏源远流长，集大成者，就是无人不知的“方城之战”——搓麻将牌。麻将牌又称麻雀牌、马将牌。它形成于一种卡片游戏——“叶子格”，在宋代演变为一种新的牌戏——骨牌，并被南宋高宗明诏颁行天下，号称“宣和牌”。明代形成4人合局的定式，并产生出“马吊”的名称，取“马凭四条腿才能行走”之意。明朝崇祯皇帝的老丈人田弘遇就是天下第一“马吊郎中”。清代，人们在“筒”“索”“万”三门之外又加进“东”“南”“西”和“北”四种，并把三种“幺头”改为“中”“发”“白”。于是，一种新的牌型博弈——麻将，最终成型。

2）斗蟋蟀

蟋蟀的别名很多，比较古雅的是“蛩”，因其鸣声如“急织”，故又有“趋织”“促织”之名。荒唐的是历史上出现了官居高位、为玩蟋蟀小虫而把军国大事置之不顾的“蟋蟀宰相”贾似道和“蟋蟀相公”马士英。

清朝养斗蟋蟀，一度为官府所主持。此外民间也设有斗场，专门组织斗会从中抽头。由于受汉文化影响，清皇室贵族及八旗子弟也开始玩蟋蟀。后来，甚至连慈禧太后也加入其中。

关于蟋蟀的最早记录见于南宋贾似道的《蟋蟀经》，被称为蟋蟀百科全书，但是该书已经失传。

5. 时令游戏

1）荡秋千

荡秋千，是中国传统竞技游戏，在汉族和北方的一些少数民族中流行，朝鲜族、拉祜族等同胞还将其作为欢庆节日的竞赛项目。汉魏时代，秋千已从军训项目演化为游艺，不仅宫人以此戏乐，也是民间在立春、寒食等传统节日中必不可少的娱乐形式。荡秋千之于寒食节非常普遍，以至于寒食节又被称为“秋千节”。

据说秋千源于汉武帝时代，宫人为给汉武帝庆寿并祈求他千秋之寿发明了这个游戏。当时被称为“千秋”，后讹传为“秋千”。

秋千在唐朝时盛行宫中，被叫作“半仙之戏”。容貌端丽、衣饰华贵的嫔妃手握两根悬绳，或坐或立在绳下所系的横板上，凌空荡逸，飘飘欲仙，故而得名“半仙之戏”。

2）放风筝

像许多古老文化成果一样，风筝首先出现在中国的上空。中国北方称之为“纸鸢”（纸雀鹰），南方则称之为“鹞子”（见第17章）。纸鸢的前身是春秋战国时期的木鸢，其实是古人所制的早期飞行器。可惜这种技艺久已失传。直到汉朝，由于制作技术的进步和造纸术的出现，木鸢才改用细竹为骨，用纸或薄绢粘贴成鹊鸟的形状，再斜坠一线，可以引线乘风而上，所以人们就称之为纸鸢。纸鸢上还拴上竹笛，微风吹动，嗡嗡有声，宛如乐器——筝（21弦或25弦乐器，与齐特琴有相似之处），“风筝”由此而得名。

相传鲁班曾将竹子劈开削光滑，用火烤弯曲，做成了喜鹊的样子，称为“木鹊”，在空中飞翔达三天三夜。因此，如果说木鸢是最早的风筝，那么鲁班就是风筝的鼻祖。

放风筝是今天世界各地的人们都喜爱的一种娱乐活动。对风筝历史的研究表明，风筝起源于中国，已有3 000多年历史。现今在中国，风筝不仅是一种玩具，还是一种有收藏价值的精美工艺品。天津作为风筝产地之一，久负盛名。“风筝魏”是天津风筝的著名品牌，为民间工艺大师魏元泰（1872年-1961年）所创。他制作的风筝曾于1915年在旧金山举行的巴拿马—太平洋国际博览会上获得金奖。而山东省潍坊市每年四月中旬举行潍坊国际风筝节。

6. 杂技游艺

1）抖空竹

空竹，在国外被称作“迪亚波罗”或“中国悠悠”，它原是中国的一种用竹木制成的民间玩具，在竹制圆柱的一端（单头）或两端（双头）安上周围有几个小孔的木制圆盒，用绳子抖动圆柱，圆盒就迅速旋转，发出嗡嗡的声音。有关这种游戏的最早记述见于1 700年前的文学作品中，一般认为至少已有2 000年的历史，跟踢毽子、放风筝同为起源于中国的三大民间传统游戏项目。

空竹在中国民间相当流行，因此各地方言中，空竹有不同的名称。如在北方叫空竹，在江南和台湾地区叫车铃或车陀螺，在四川叫响簧等。空竹平日用来健身，节日可用于表演，现在空竹已成为杂技表演项目，用空竹可以表演展示许多技巧。

2）踩高跷

据说踩高跷（见图12-1）这种形式，原是古人为了采集树上的野果为食，在自己的腿上绑两根长棍而发展出来的一种跷技活动。

踩高跷，也称走高跷或踏高。据史书记载，中国人踩高跷的历史，至少也有2 500年以上。

踩高跷，是民间盛行的一种群众性技艺表演。北方的高跷秧歌中，扮演的人物有渔翁、媒婆、傻公子、道姑、和尚等，表演者扮相滑稽。南方的高跷，扮演的多是戏曲中的角色，关公、济公、何仙姑、神仙、小丑皆有。他们边演边唱，生动活泼，逗笑取乐，如履平地。

7. 节日活动

1）舞狮与舞龙

狮子生活在非洲和南美，汉朝以后传入中国。一般认为，舞狮起源于三国时代，开始时流行于军中，后来传至民间。

舞狮是中国民间普遍流行的一种游戏活动。每逢春节或迎神赛会，它常出现于城镇和乡村，为佳节增添了浓郁的欢乐气氛。

中国民间舞狮有北方武狮和南方文狮之分。武狮着重于武功，动作矫健，技巧性高；文狮着重于表情动作细腻，着意刻画狮子温驯可爱的神态和表现狮子活泼好动、善于嬉戏的性格。

舞龙源于古代的图腾崇拜思想。其演出目的主要是用于观赏，而不仅仅是祈雨和祭祀。

在唐、宋时期的"社火""舞队"表演中，舞龙灯已是常见的表演形式。舞龙在明、清时，更以其独特的风韵出现在民间娱乐活动之中。

2）打腰鼓

腰鼓舞(见图 12－2)历史悠久，在陕北安塞十分流行。陕北安塞腰鼓鼓点花样多，分文鼓与武鼓两种。表演时鼓舞与武术、体操、民歌、打击乐、吹奏乐结合于一体。表演场面雄浑，队形多变，以体现陕北汉子剽悍、英武的风格而闻名遐迩。有时表演者多达数百人，场面十分壮观。

陕北青年打腰鼓迎接农历新年和元宵节是传统习俗。鼓手腰系红色小鼓，手拿系着红绸带的鼓槌，边击鼓边舞蹈。节奏激昂、气势磅礴的鼓点和着刚劲奔放、豪迈粗犷的舞姿，高潮时边击鼓边跳跃，同时口中高喊"嗨嗨"。场面壮阔，气魄震撼人心，表现了陕北农民憨厚朴实、悍勇威武而又开朗乐观的性格。

3）放烟花

世界各国每逢节庆之夜都要燃放烟花，这种传统的庆典性游艺发源于中国。隋唐时期产生了中国最早的烟花：一类是药线烟花，先用金属丝编排成人物花鸟、亭台楼阁等各式图案，金属丝上涂药剂后称"药线"。点燃药线，各式图案在夜幕的衬托下幻丽奇生。另一类称"筒子烟花"，即把烟花药剂装入纸筒内，点燃后往外喷射五彩火焰。

明代，药线烟花由平面转为立体，把多层"药线"纵横编排放入大盒子里，再悬在架上。点燃后，盒子药线逐层脱落燃烧，可以幻演出多层形象。

Exercises

Section A Thought-provoking questions

1. What are the basic materials needed to make a traditional shuttlecock?
2. How can games of shuttlecock and rope skipping benefit children physically?
3. What are the four arts of the old Chinese scholars?
4. What do you know about Jia Shidao?

Section B Cloze

Shuttlecock kicking is a popular folk game. Some records __1__ its origin as far back as the Han Dynasty. This game prevailed during the Tang Dynasty, when shops __2__ in shuttlecocks __3__ appeared. In the Ming Dynasty, formal competition of shuttlecock kicking was __4__. In the Qing Dynasty, shuttlecock kicking reached its __5__ in terms __6__ both making techniques and the kicking skills.

As a traditional game unique __7__ China, shuttlecock kicking is fun to do and provides vigorous physical exercise as well. There are endless variations to the styles and methods of ___8___, some of ___9___ include kicking the shuttlecock back and ___10___ between two people. Those who ___11___ to a high ___12___ of mastery can perform some truly impressive feasts. The challenge of the increasingly difficult levels of shuttlecock kicking has made it a popular game ___13___ Chinese children. This game helps them ___14___ their legs and enhance their concentration.

In the 1930s, the sport of shuttlecock kicking was in ___15___ for a time. After the establishment of new China, it ___16___ vitality and the first formal National Shuttlecock Kicking Competition was held in Guangzhou in 1956.

To ___17___ a shuttlecock, a piece of cloth wrapped around a coin is needed, and then a ___18___ of feathers from cock's tails is inserted into a tube ___19___ to the coin base, which retards the ___20___ and descending of the shuttlecock.

※The one who merely knows the value of study is not so good as the one who takes an interest in studying. The one who takes an interest in studying is not so good as the one who delights in studying.

From *Analects of Confucius*

(知之者不如好之者，好之者不如乐之者。)

——《论语》

※A young man should be respectful to his parents in the home, and to his elders outside. His words should be cautious and trustworthy. He should care for people in general and seek the company of benevolent men. If having accomplished these he still has energy to spare, he should study.

From *Analects of Confucius*

(弟子入则孝，出则悌，谨而信，泛爱众，而亲仁。行有余力，则以学文。)

——《论语》

Chapter 13

Ancient Chinese Martial Arts

中国古代武术

1. Chinese Martial Arts

1) History

Ancient Chinese martial arts (or Wushu in Chinese) are different from modern ones. The ancient martial arts were developed for military use. Not until after the Spring and Autumn Period did martial arts begin to incorporate sophisticated aspects of ancient Chinese culture.

The precise origin of martial arts is too remote to identify. When the Qin Dynasty conquered contending states and united China, the ruler ordered all weapons be put in storage. Discouraged by the Qin government, Chinese martial arts developed very little during this period.

Martial art development picked up during the Han Dynasty, a period noted for its advanced political, economic and cultural development. During the Western and Eastern Jin and Northern and Southern Dynasties, warfare was rampant. Minority ethnic groups such as the Huns, Xianbei, Jie, Di and Qiang from northern China were constantly invading the Central Plains. The battlefield provided a good environment for the development of martial arts.

The Sui and Tang Dynasties were politically stable and economically strong and flourished with foreign trade and cultural exchanges. This period saw modifications of martial arts and improvement in the appearance of demonstrative exercises. The prevailing imperial examination system of the Tang Dynasty was also adapted for the selection of martial arts champions. Soldiers with outstanding martial arts skills were honored with commendation and titles. Martial arts were encouraged and promoted among ordinary people.

By the Song Dynasty, martial arts had become an art separate from military drills. Routine and apparatus exercises developed quickly, and many theoretical works were published. Practitioners studied both fighting skills and theory and introduced the theory of "yin" and "yang" into martial arts.

During the Yuan Dynasty, the Mongol ruling class and soldiers practiced martial arts as well as horse riding, and wrestling. There martial arts skills were performed on stage and were gradually more artfully refined.

During the Ming Dynasty, different martial arts schools flourished. The Qing Dynasty outperformed the previous dynasties in developing martial arts skills. Many exercises that are still famous today, such as Taijiquan (Taiji Boxing) and Baguazhang (Eight-Trigram Palm Exercise), were created during the period.

2) Characteristics

Literally, *wu* means military while *shu* means art, thus Wushu the art of fighting or martial arts. Wushu is an important and unique component of Chinese cultural heritage with centuries of cultural history attached. Wushu not only includes physical exercise but also Chinese philosophy, and aesthetics.

With vigorous, graceful and somewhat laborious movements, Chinese martial arts provide the exercisers with beauty and strength. The persistent exercises will build up their body and strength. Martial arts involve methods and skills for fighting. They incorporate highly practical consecutive movements including jumping, falling, passing through, somersaulting, retreating, shaking, turning, kicking, hitting, wrestling, seizing, etc.

The consecutive movements should be done in close sequences so as to overcome the movements of the opponent. Any slight neglect in the gestures of hands, legs and body and in the timing will result in favoring the opponent. So, the Chinese martial arts emphasize the gestures and timing.

To attain the true essence, the Chinese martial arts stress guidance by masters, and conscientious practice. The exerciser should practice diligently until he can carry out the movements unhesitatingly and very naturally.

The Chinese martial arts stress perfection. From the angle of the art of attack and defense, there are three grades of martial arts: the inferior-grade exerciser does not master the arts at all; the middle-grade exerciser is skilled in the art, and concentrates his attentions in fighting; the senior-grade exerciser has a high degree of dexterity and carries out his movements very naturally to beat the opponent. His arts attain perfection.

2. Chinese Martial Arts and Other Fields

1) Martial Arts and Ancient Chinese Philosophy

Martial arts were developed under the great influence of ancient Chinese culture and they have benefited a lot from ancient Chinese philosophy. The Spring and Autumn Period was a golden age of academic study and resulted in different schools of philosophical thinking that would lay a solid foundation for the subsequent formation of Chinese culture. Ancient Chinese philosophy advocated the theory of Dao, and held that the Dao was connected with both the heaven and the earth and was the source of everything. Martial arts practitioners begin with the irregularity and infinity of Dao and seek to reach a stage in which he or she blends harmoniously with nature. The arts teach practitioners to train the inner spirit and mind as well as the external muscles, bones and skin. Martial arts stress the combination of the physical being with the mental being and emphasize a close relationship between physical exercises and the surrounding environment. Practitioners are advised to use different methods of exercises according to the changes of natural environment and the conditions of the body. These practices reflect martial arts understanding of the ancient philosophy: let the mind swing freely in Dao and the oneness of man and nature.

2) Chinese Martial Arts and Ancient Chinese Aesthetics

Ancient Chinese aesthetics advocated a balance between hardness and softness, voidness and solidness, notion and stillness, and negative and positive, as well as the expression of the spirit of an object through its form. Under this influence, Chinese martial arts have formed their own aesthetic standards that incorporate a stage of conceptual contentment, harmony, and nature, as well as beauty and elegance. For example, Changquan (Long Boxing) features fully extended, elegant and unrestrained movements; Nanquan (South Boxing) demonstrates steadiness and momentum of movements; Shaolin Boxing expresses resolution and strength in its quick and rhythmical movements; and the beautifully and smoothly stringed movements of Taiji Boxing remind viewers of floating clouds and flowing streams.

A distinct aspect of Chinese martial arts is the advocacy of morals and emphasis on benevolence, fidelity and sincerity. Benevolence is the core of Confucianism. It includes love and generosity. As a result, practicing martial arts implies not only building health and strength, but also purifying one's soul. Chinese martial arts work for those who are benevolent, brave, and courageous. The arts stress that the moral level of a practitioner is as important as his or her martial arts skills.

3) Martial Arts and Morality

Traditional Chinese schools of martial arts, such as the famed Shaolin monks, often dealt with the study of martial arts not just as a means of self-defense or mental training, but as a system of *wude*, which can be translated as "martial morality" and is constructed from two Chinese characters, "wu" which means martial and "de" which means morality. Wude deals with two aspects: "morality of deed" and "morality of mind". Morality of deed concerns social relations; morality of mind is meant to cultivate the inner harmony between the emotional mind (Xin) and the wisdom mind (Hui). The ultimate goal is reaching no extremity (Wuji) (closely related to the Taoist concept of wuwei), where both wisdom and emotions are in harmony with each other.

3. Three Main Boxing Schools in China

1) Shaolin Wushu (or Shaolin Boxing)

Chinese Martial arts are divided into two main categories: the Northern and the

Southern. Shaolin leads the Northern category. It combines both external and internal, and "hard" and "soft" exercises.

Boxing is the foundation of Wushu and Shaolin Boxing serves as the basis of other kinds of Wushu. The Shaolin Boxing has compactly designed routines. Its movements are quick, powerful and flexible, both practical for defense and attack.

The most outstanding characteristic of Shaolin Boxing is that the practitioner works on one straight line. It means that his movements of advancing, retreating, turning around, sideways, or jumping are restrained on one line. His arms are kept slightly bent so that he can stretch out to attack or withdraw for self defense freely.

Another characteristic of Shaolin Wushu is to maintain the body in perfect balance, as stable as a mountain. The practitioners should keep a tranquil mind but strike with great force and speed. He should be good at "borrowing" force from the opponent. That is, he should take advantage of the striker's force and go along with it to bring him to ward off a force of a thousand weights. He should know how to make feigned strikes and when striking, hit the vital parts of the opponent. His movements should be as dexterous as a cat, his shaking as a tiger, his moving as a dragon, his advancing as lightning and his yelling as thunder.

The practice of Shaolin Wushu does not need a large space. It is said that *Shaolin* Boxing can fight within an area where a cow can lie down. It is not affected by weather, or the kind of weapons used. So Shaolin Wushu has become a very convenient sport.

In 1982, a feature film "Shaolin Monastery" was released on the mainland China, in Hong Kong, Macao and abroad. Due to its popularity, the number of visitors to Shaolin Monastery to learn *Wushu* or for sightseeing increases day by day. Wushu teaching schools have been set up. In 1985, there were more than 40 of them, with students from 20 provinces, municipalities and autonomous regions. In early 1986, the county government combined the schools into five in order to guarantee their quality. In the past several years, many students from these schools have gone on to join professional Wushu teams or sports colleges, and some have become coaches of Wushu teams in other provinces and cities.

Shaolin Wushu got its name from the Shaolin Monastery, and the Monastery became famous for Shaolin Wushu.

2) The Eight-Trigram Boxing

The Eight-Trigram Boxing is characterized by changing positions of the palms and changing paces. Its fighting principle is the "combination of attack and defense". It stresses the stratagem: "I move before my opponent moves, halt before my opponent halts; when my opponent attacks, I defend; when my opponent exhausts himself, I keep energetic; when my opponent retreats, I advance; when my opponent moves, I watch my opponent while he is moving, and discover and make use of opportunities; when my opponent is near, I attack him; I extricate myself and then attack my opponent, and while my opponent is not moving, I move." The stratagem prefers sideways attack to frontal assail.

3) Taiji Boxing

Taiji Boxing, named after the term "*tai ji*" (supreme ultimate from the *Book of Changes*), was believed to be composed of by King Wen of the Zhou Dynasty. The term means that the universe was an entirety before it divided into heaven and earth. The Taiji Boxing has been sourced from many forms of folk boxing, and has been improved on through several generations.

Taiji Boxing is characterized by the unification of mind, breath and motions (body), requiring concentration of mind and calmness of motions. Mind works as a commander and body a soldier. When in motion, all of the body moves. When at rest, all of the body rests. Calmness is required for motion. Simple force is not preferred. Force is like a wheel and waist is its axis. The motions are continuous as a circle. The breath is deep and controlled by the diaphragm. Be concentrated, gentle and natural. Be stable as a mountain when not moving, and be flowing as a river when moving. The moves are characterized by roundness, softness, slowness, stability and evenness. They are extended but very well coordinated, and all are an antithetical unity of Yin and Yang (negative and positive). These principles are the same for all schools of Taiji Boxing, though their types are different. There are mainly five types: Chen-Type, Yang-Type, Sun-Type, Wuu-Type, and Wu-Type.

4. Martial Arts' Prospect

In the past, Wushu was developed for the sake of military prowess and physical well being. Wushu was seen as crucial to a soldier's survival in the time of hand-to-hand combat. Today, military function has faded and it has been organized and systematized into a formal branch of study in the performance arts by the Chinese. Its physical welfare and athletic functions become dominant. Hence Wushu is popular among the whole nation of China, practiced by men and women, young and old alike. Today many people practice Wushu to pursue health, defense skills, mental discipline, entertainment and competition.

Recently, Chinese Wushu has been modernized. Training and competing standard systems have been set up. Continuing its fighting function, Wushu becomes a more athletic and aesthetic performance and competitive sport. More and more foreigners come to learn the mysterious Wushu. In order to promote Wushu internationally, China Zhengzhou International Shaolin Wushu Festival will be held twice annually.

Among the many styles are *Changquan* (long boxing), *Nanquan* (southern boxing), *Taijiquan* (shadow boxing or supreme ultimate boxing), *Xingyi quan* (mind boxing), *Baguaquan* (eight-trigram boxing). The former two belong to the external style which emphasizes physical strength and abilities while the latter three belong to the internal style that depends upon internal power — qi.

Wushu was last seen at the Olympics in 1936 when a small Chinese team performed during the Berlin Olympics. Wushu is known to many people around the world but has yet not become as popular as Japan's judo and Korea's taekwondo. To push for Wushu to become an Olympic competing item, China has much to learn from Japan and South Korea in promoting the martial arts to International Olympic Committee (IOC) members and the world. Japan successfully pushed for judo's inclusion at the Tokyo Olympics in 1964, while South Korea's taekwondo made it to the Olympics 12 years after the 1988 Seoul Olympics.

IOC president Jacques Rogge told Chinese media during the 10th National Games that the IOC had agreed in principle to allow the Beijing Organizing Committee to hold a Wushu tournament on the sidelines of the 2008 Games. The IOC has tried to streamline the summer Olympics and freeze the number of sports.

Chinese sporting authorities say Wushu is part of China's 5,000 years of civilization and its presence at the Olympics is in line with the spirit of a "Humanity Olympics", one of the three themes for 2008. Besides, only two of the 28 competition sports at the Olympics originated, and were modernized, in the east. Therefore, the inclusion of Wushu in 2008 will help promote cultural exchanges between East and West.

Chinese sports officials began pushing for Wushu's inclusion as a competition sport in the Olympics in the late 1990s and lodged a formal application with the IOC in December, 2001. But the IOC postponed a decision at an assembly in Prague in July, 2003.

The International Wushu Federation (IWF) passed a new set of rules for Wushu tournaments at the 8th World Wushu Championship in the Vietnamese capital of Hanoi. The rules were more scientific and objective. In rehearal for the Beijing Olympic Games, the 9th world Wushu Championship was held at Beijing in November, 2007. But Wushu's acceptance into the Olympics still needs time. However, we are expecting it!

Word Bank

incorporate	将某事物包括进去，包含，整合，合并
modification	改变，改型
routine	武术套路，舞蹈中的成套动作
apparatus	器械，设备
practitioner	习艺者，实习者
consecutive	连续的
somersault	翻滚，翻跟头
sequence	次序，顺序
voidness	虚，空
momentum	冲力，势头
advocacy	拥护，提倡，主张
compactly	严实地，紧凑地，严谨地
feigned	假装的，虚假的
dexterous	灵巧的，手巧的
restrain	抑制，约束，管制
extricate	释放
assail	猛攻，猛击
comprise	包括，组成
prowess	勇猛，英勇

参考译文

1. 中国武术

1) 中国武术的历史

中国古代武术不同于现代武术。古代武术缘起于军事目的，但从春秋战国时期开始，它就融入中国博大精深的古代文化之中。

中国武术起源何时，尚无定论。秦始皇统一中国后，他下令收缴兵器，在朝廷的打压控制下，武术发展缓慢。

随着汉朝政治、经济和文化的发展，武术也发展起来。魏晋南北朝时期，战争频繁，北方少数民族如匈奴、鲜卑、羯、氐、羌等不断侵扰中原，战争促进了武术的发展。

隋、唐两个时期都具有政治稳定、经济繁荣、中外交往频繁的特点，中国的武术也不断完善和改进。武术作为当时非常盛行的科举考试的内容之一被用于选拔武官。武艺杰出的士兵会被授予嘉奖和官衔。民间的武术也得到了促进和发展。

宋朝的武术不同于军事技能，已经发展成为一门艺术。武术套路不断完善，器械得到改进，并且也出现了有关武术的理论著作。习武者不仅练习武技，还研究理论，将中国传统的"阴""阳"理论运用到武术中。

元朝的统治者和士兵既练骑马、摔跤，又要习武。那时的武术日臻完美优雅。

明、清时期涌现出很多武术学校，武术技艺在清朝时期的发展超过以往任何朝代，现在还很盛行的太极拳、八卦掌等就是在那时发展起来的。

2) 中国武术的特点

从词汇意义上讲，"武"即"武力"，"术"即"艺术"，合在一起即"武术"。武术有着很长时间的文化历史，是中国传统文化的重要组成部分。它不仅是一种体育锻炼，而且也包含着中国的哲学、美学思想。

中国武术刚劲有力、动作优美，是力与美的完美结合。坚持不懈地习武可以强身健体。中国武术包括搏击的方法和技巧。它包括跳、倒、插、翻、退、闪、转、踢、击、摔、拿等一系列连续动作。这些动作要求一气呵成，如行云流水，这样才能克敌制胜。任何小的失误，无论是手部动作、腿部动作，还是时机选择，都可能使对手有利，让自己处于不利的地位。因此，中国武术十分强调动作与时机的协调。

领会中国武术的精神实质，需要师傅的指导和坚持不懈的操练。各种套路要能运用自如，炉火纯青，非下苦功不可。

中国武术讲究完美。从攻、防角度来讲，武艺可分三等：初级、中级和高级。初级习武者根本谈不上掌握了武艺；中级习武者技术娴熟，专心武术。高级习武者动作流畅自然，处险不惊，从容应对，这样的武艺就称得上完美。

2. 中国武术与其他领域

1）中国武术与中国古代哲学

中国武术深受中国文化的影响，尤其是中国古代哲学的影响。春秋战国时期，百家争鸣，学派林立，为中国文化奠定了扎实基础。中国古代哲学崇尚“道”，“道”强调“天人合一”，中国武术深受道教这一思想的影响，每一个习武者都在追求这种精神境界。武术的目的不仅在于强身健体，而且也在于陶冶性情、磨炼意志。它强调身体健康，也强调心灵健康，强调个人与环境的和谐关系，做到人的心性与自然的和谐统一。习武者根据环境的变化和不同的身体条件采用不同的操练方法。这反映了中国武术所包含的传统哲学思想即道家思想：天人合一。

2）中国武术与古代中国美学

古代中国美学注重刚与柔、虚与实、动与静、阴与阳以及神与形的平衡、统一。在这些观念的影响下，中国武术形成了自身的审美标准和尺度，中国武术刚柔相济、动静结合、自然优美。如长拳舒展、雅致，灵活多变；南拳稳重，动作有力；少林拳刚劲有力，动作敏捷，节奏分明；太极拳舒缓优雅，行云流水。

中国武术另一个审美特点是强调“仁、忠、孝”。“仁”是儒家的核心，包括爱和宽容。中国武术不仅强调强身健体，还注重心灵的净化。武术是为那些“仁、忠、孝”之人服务的。一个习武者的道德水平与他的武术技艺同样重要。

3）武术与道德

传统的武术流派，像有名的少林武术，不仅认为武术是防身的手段或精神强化，而且强调习武者必须讲究武德。汉语中“武德”由“武”（武术）和“德”（道德）组成，这里的“德”既包括“德行”，也包括“德心”。前者是从社会关系层面上来讲的，后者是指达到心和智的和谐。终极的目标是“无极”（与老子“无为”的观点很类似），即心智统一。

3. 中国三大武术流派

1）少林武术

中国武术分为南、北两派。北派的代表是少林武术。它融内外、刚柔于一体。

拳术是武术的基础，少林拳术又是其他武术的基础。少林拳套路严谨，动作敏捷有力，灵活多变，攻防结合。

一个显著特点是习武者走直线即前进、后退、转身、侧移、跳远等必须沿一条直线运动。手、背稍有弯曲，攻守有力自由。

少林武术的另一个特点是身体必须完全平衡，稳如泰山。习武者头脑冷静，攻击出其不意，凶狠有力。习武者擅长借助对方的力量，出奇制胜。他的动作“秀如猫，抖如虎，行如龙，动如闪，声如雷”。

练习少林武术不需要很大的地方，据说只要一头牛可以躺得下的地方就可以习武。它不受天气的影响，也不受任何器械的影响。因此，它现在变成了一种非常方便的体育运动。

1982 年，功夫片《少林寺》在中国大陆、港澳和海外地区同时上映。少林寺一时间红遍大江南北，游客纷至沓来，有的来习武，有的来观光。武术学校也应运而生。1985 年成立了 40 多所武术学校，学员来自 20 个省、市、自治区。1986 年，为了保证武术学校的办学质量，政府出面合并重组为 5 所学校。毕业生一般都加入了专业武术团体，或进入体育院校，有的成为武术教练。

少林武术因少林寺而得名；而少林寺则因武术而闻名。

2）八卦拳

八卦拳是以掌法变换为主要手法，搏击原则是攻防结合。战术强调：对手动，我先动；对手停，我先停；对手攻，我防守；对手筋疲力尽，我斗志昂扬；对手退，我前进；对手移动，我趁机行事；对手靠近，我进攻；对手不动，我动。这种战术强调侧面进攻，而不是正面进攻。

3）太极拳

太极拳中的“太极”得名于《易经》。太极指宇宙的本原。在盘古开天地之前，宇宙是一个整体。据说太极拳是周文王开创的。太极拳始于民间各种拳术形式，又通过一代又一代的发展完善，延续至今。

太极拳要求心、神、气、运统一，注意力集中，动作平稳，“心到手到”“动，则全身动；静，则全身静”。太极拳需要平心静气，光有力量还不行。力如轮，手如轴。步法呈弧线运动，凝神静气，自然放松。静则稳如泰山，动则行云流水。太极拳圆润、轻柔、和缓、平稳，既舒展又协调，以慢生柔，以匀求活，柔极生刚，刚柔相济，阴阳结合。这是所有太极拳的共同特征。太极拳流派很多，主要分为五派：陈式、杨式、孙式、吴式、武式。

4. 武术的前景

过去，武术出于军事的目的和强身健体的需要。在赤手空拳的肉搏中，武术是古代战士们必不可少的技能和本领。现在的武术不是出于军事的需要，而更多地演变为一种有组织的、系统性的表演艺术。武术的健身功能和审美功能居主导地位。武术深受中国人的喜爱，无论男女老幼，都喜欢这项运动。如今，人们练武的目的是健身、防身、自律、娱乐和竞赛。

当前，武术逐步现代化，训练、竞技标准已经确立。现代武术继承了传统武术的搏击功能，已经成为融体育、审美、表演、竞技于一体的体育活动。越来越多的外国人士都来中国学习武术。为了让武术走向世界，中国郑州每年举行两次国际少林武术节。

受人们喜爱的现代武术包括长拳、南拳、太极拳、形意拳和八卦拳等。前两者是外功，注重力量、技能。后三者是内功，内修心神意气。

武术出现在奥运会上是在 1936 年的柏林，中国武术队首次亮相国际舞台。武术虽然世界闻名，但没有日本的柔道、韩国的跆拳道受人欢迎。要让中国武术列入奥运项目，中国还得向日本、韩国学习。1964 年，日本成功地使柔道进入东京奥运会；韩国在 1988 年汉城奥运会之后 12 年，使韩国的跆拳道列入奥运赛事。

国际奥委会主席罗格在第 10 届全国运动会上对媒体说，国际奥委会原则上同意北京组委会举办武术锦标赛，但不直接列入 2008 年奥运会。因为国际奥委会一直在努力谋求优化奥运赛事，削减奥运项目。

中国体育界的权威人士认为，武术是中华五千年文明的一个重要组成部分，它的精神体现了“人文奥运”的宗旨。况且，在当前 28 个奥运项目中，只有 2 项源于东方，并得以发展。武术进入奥运会有助于东西文化的交流。

20 世纪 90 年代，中国开始推动中国武术进入奥运会。2001 年 12 月提出正式申请。但在 2003 年 7 月的布拉格会议上，国际奥委会迟迟没有做出决定。

在越南首都河内举行的第 8 届世界武术锦标赛期间，国际武术联合会确定了一套新的武术规则。这套规则更科学、客观。当时为了迎接 2008 北京奥运会，第 9 届世界武术锦标赛于 2007 年 11 月在北京举行。但是，武术走进奥运会仍需时日。我们期待着！

Exercises

Section A Thought-provoking questions

1. When did Chinese martial arts incorporate sophisticated aspects of ancient Chinese culture?
2. How did ancient Chinese philosophy influence martial arts?
3. What aspects of ancient Chinese aesthetics influenced Chinese martial arts?
4. What are the typical characteristics of Shaolin Wushu?
5. What is the core of the technique of the Eight-Trigram Boxing?
6. What are the main characteristics of Taiji Boxing?

Section B Decide whether the following statements are true or false

1. People know the precise origin of martial arts.
2. The imperial examination system of the Tang Dynasty was used to select martial arts champions.
3. Martial arts stress the importance of the physical being but neglect the importance of the mental being.
4. It can be inferred that martial arts also stress the balance between hardness and softness, voidness and solidness, notion and stillness, and negative and positive.
5. Chinese martial arts pay much attention to morals, benevolence, fidelity and sincerity.
6. Shaolin Boxing combines both external and internal, and "hard" and "soft" exercises.
7. Shaolin Boxing objects to "borrowing" force from the opponent.
8. In 1982, a film made Shaolin Monastery known to people all over the world.
9. It was said that Taiji Boxing was composed in the Zhou Dynasty.
10. Taiji Boxing is characterized by the unification of speed, strength and techniques.

Chapter 14

Chinese Calligraphy and Painting

中国书画艺术

1. Chinese Calligraphy

1) Writing Medium

The "writing" of Chinese characters first requires a medium. As today's writings are mostly on paper, one may wonder: What came before that?

In the Shang Dynasty, characters were carved on oracle bones or bronze wares. The Spring and Autumn Period was a time when the amount of writings and characters increased in great number. Hence new mediums emerged. Before paper was invented, bamboo and wood slips were important writing mediums while silk was used by aristocrats for writing.

2) Writing Instruments

Knives were first used as carving tools in the early phases of Chinese script. With the emergence of other specialized tools like brushes, knives began to serve as "erasers" — to scratch off writing mistakes.

Among the various calligraphic tools, the writing brush is special to China. It represents one of the four treasures of the study, which also include paper, ink and ink stone. A writing brush comprises two parts: the head and shaft. The head is made of goat, wolf, rat or rabbit hair, which is softer than a quill pencil, or ballpoint pen. The shaft can be made of bamboo, wood and porcelain, as well as some precious materials such as ivory and jade.

"Four treasures of the study" are the key instruments for writing Chinese characters. When the inkstone is filled with water, it is used as a base to grind solid ink sticks into liquid ink. Inkstones are usually made of stone or bricks. As the brush hair is made of soft animal fur, this instrument is very flexible and adaptive in writing.

The Chinese writing brush boasts a long history. According to the *Records of the History*, the brush was invented by Meng Tian (? —210 B.C.), a general under the First Emperor of the Qin Dynasty, using rabbit hair. Therefore, Meng Tian has been regarded as the father of the writing brush. However, primitive painted pottery unearthed in Yangshao, Henan Province, contains decorative designs painted by tools resembling a brush. Clearly visible stains or brush marks remain in certain places on the pottery. This evidence suggests that the brush may have predated written language itself.

Brushes became the major writing instrument of Chinese characters in the Spring and Autumn period. Among the cultural relics unearthed in Zuojiagong Mountain of Changsha, Hunan Province in 1954 were different kinds of ancient writing brushes and relics related to writing. This is the first time that our imagination of the writing brushes before the Han Dynasty got proved.

3) Knife-carved Scripts: Seal Cutting

Seal cutting is, in other words, "writing" with knives on materials like stone, wood and metal. It is a traditional graphic, calligraphic and engraving art of China. Before the invention of paper, official documents were written on bamboo or wooden slips and sealed with clay. A lettered seal was then stamped on the clay envelope.

Before the Ming Dynasty, seals were generally made for practical uses such as identification. Since the Ming Dynasty, calligraphers and painters have begun to treat seals as artistic creations. Through deliberate choice of material and application of cutting and arranging, the inch-long seals became genuine art of interest.

4) The Art of Writing: Chinese Calligraphy

Chinese calligraphy is an art of self-cultivation and self-expression. It reflects the mindset and mood of the writer, and fully embodies the unique beauty of Chinese script. Today, Chinese calligraphy is enjoyed by people throughout the world. There are five writing styles of Chinese calligraphy: ① *Xiaozhuan* (Lesser Seal) — with standardized shape, strokes and structure, this script established the basic formation for all Chinese characters created since; ② Clerical script — simpler and more regular in shape, it established the basic structure of most Chinese characters; ③ Standard script — evolved from Clerical script, it is straight in line, square in shape, and easy to write; ④ *Caoshu* script — an easy-to-write form for greater efficiency; and ⑤ *Xingshu* script — a simple and smooth script between Standard script and *Caoshu* script.

Chinese calligraphy dates from the earliest day in history, and has been widely practiced throughout China to the present day. Different from paintings, Chinese calligraphy uses Chinese characters as its vehicles of expression to communicate the spiritual world of the artist. One does not have to know Chinese to appreciate its beauty since calligraphy, in essence, is an abstract art. It is so abstract and sublime that in Chinese culture it is universally regarded to be the most enlightening art form.

Just as one person's appearance differs from others, so one person's handwriting differs from the others'. Through its unique word structures, writing styles and way of handling the brush, calligraphy, as work of art, conveys the moral integrity, character, emotions, esthetic feelings and culture of the artist to readers and charms them with appealing beauty. So it is believed among a lot of people that we can tell a person's character through his or her handwriting.

Chinese characters evolved from pictures and signs, and Chinese art of calligraphy developed naturally from its unique writing system. Great calligraphers developed representative calligraphic styles of their times through the ages. The love of calligraphy is deeply ingrained in Chinese scholars and has been handed down to the present day.

Just like Chinese *qigong*, the Chinese brush calligraphy can temper a person into a state in which one can apply intuition got from the daily practice to control the concentration of ink and the size of each stoke or word. Calligraphy is considered an active way of keeping oneself fit and healthy, for the practice is relaxing and self-entertaining. Historically, many calligraphers were well known for their longevity.

The modernization of writing tools has given rise to many types of calligraphy other than the traditional brush-writings. Some contemporary western artists also assimilated Chinese calligraphy into abstract art, yielding many excellent works. Today, Chinese calligraphy is still considered an elegant art form even in neighboring countries. As Chinese culture spread to Japan, Korea, Singapore and Vietnam, calligraphy has become a unique feature of Oriental art.

2. Chinese Painting

1) Ancient Chinese Painting

A. Painted pottery

Chinese traditional painting dates back to the Neolithic Age about 6,000 years ago. The excavated colored pottery with painted human faces, fish, animal and plants reflect various aspects of the life of primitive clan communities. The line patterns on unearthed pottery ware resemble ripples, fishing nets, teeth. The animal and human figures, succinct and vivid, are proofs to the innate sensitivity of the ancient artists to the nature.

B. Rock painting

Paintings or engravings found on precipitous cliffs in Sichuan, Yunnan and Guizhou in Southwest China, Fujian in East China, Mount Yinshan in Inner Mongolia, Heihe in the far north and Altai in China's extreme west are even more ancient. Strong visual effects characterize the bright red cliff paintings in southern China that depict scenes of sacrificial rites, production activities and daily life. In comparison, hunting, animal grazing, wars and dancing are the main themes of cliff paintings in northern China.

C. Silk painting

Silk painting is the work painted on silk. The painting unearthed in 1949 from a tomb of Chu of the Warring States Period in the southern suburb of Changsha, Hunan

Province, was painted on silk with human figures, dragons and phoenixes. It is the earliest work on silk ever discovered in China and measures about 30 centimeters long by 20 centimeters wide. From this and other early paintings on silk showing vigour and elegance, it can be seen that the ancients were already familiar with the art of the writing or painting on silk with brush. Silk painting kept developing before the invention of paper and reached its artistic peak in the Western Han Dynasty.

D. Paper painting

Paintings on paper appeared much later than those on silk for the simple reason that the invention of silk preceded that of paper by a long historical period. In 1964, when a tomb dating to the Jin Dynasty was excavated at Astana in Turpan, Xingjiang, a coloured painting on paper was discovered. It shows on the upper the sun, the moon and the Big Dipper and at the lower a man with a fan in his hand. The portrayal, 106.5 centimeters long and 47 centimeters wide, is the only known painting on paper of such antiquity in China.

2) Famous Painters of Different Dynasties

A. Painter of Northern and Southern Dynasties

Northern and Southern Dynasties were an important period in the history of painting. China plunged into a situation of divided states from the third to the sixth century, where incessant wars and successions of dynasties sharpened the thinking of Chinese artists which, in turn, promoted the development of art. Grotto murals, wall murals in tomb chambers, stone carvings, brick carvings and lacquer paintings flourished in a period deemed very important to the development of traditional Chinese painting. The scroll paintings of Gu Kaizhi, known as the founder of traditional Chinese painting, represented the painting style of the period.

B. Court Painters of Tang Dynasty

The Tang Dynasty witnessed the prosperity of figure painting, where the most outstanding painters were Zhang Xuan and Zhou Fang. Their paintings, depicting the life of noble women and court ladies, exerted an eternal influence on the development of *shi nü hua* (painting of beautiful women), which comprise an important branch of traditional Chinese painting.

C. Four great painters of Yuan Dynasty

During the Yuan Dynasty the "Four Great Painters" — Huang Gongwang, Wu Zhen, Ni Zan and Wang Meng — represented the highest level of landscape painting. Their works immensely influenced landscape painting of the Ming and Qing Dynasties.

D. Wumen Painting School of Ming Dynasty

Suzhou in south China is called "*Wumen*" in history. Many well-known painters gathered in Suzhou in the Ming Dynasty which saw the rise of the *Wumen* Painting School. Keen to carry on the traditions of Chinese painting, the four *Wumen* masters

Shen Zhou, Wen Zhengming, Tang Ying and Qiu Ying blazed new trails and developed their own unique styles. The technique and way of expression exerted great influence on later generations.

E. Four Monk Masters of Qing Dynasty

When the Manchus came to power in 1644, the then-best painters showed their resentment to the Qing court in many ways. The "Four Monk Masters" — Zhu Da, Shi Tao, Kun Can and Hong Ren — had their heads shaved to demonstrate their determination not to serve the new dynasty, and they soothed their sadness by painting tranquil nature scenes and traditional art.

F. Eight Eccentrics of Yangzhou

The eight painters of Yangzhou were all with strong characters. They refused to follow orthodoxy. They were proud, aloof and unrestrained, hence their name. They used freehand brushwork in their paintings with the main subjects of flowers and birds, bringing a pleasant change in painting style. Although they were not well accepted and even criticized for being heterodox, they broadened the horizon of flower-and-bird painting and expanded the future for flower-bird paintings.

G. Shanghai Painting School

By the end of the Qing Dynasty and the beginning of the Republic of China, Shanghai, which gave birth to the Shanghai Painting School, had become the most prosperous commercial city and a gathering place for numerous painters. Following the spirit of the Eight Eccentrics of Yangzhou, the Shanghai School played a vital role in the transition of Chinese traditional painting from a classical art form to a modern one.

3) Founders of Chinese Painting

A. Gu Kaizhi — Originator of Painting

Gu Kaizhi, a painter of Eastern Jin Dynasty, was born into an official family in Wuxi, Jiangsu Province, and served as a government officer at a young age. Having toured many beautiful places, Gu was proficient in writing poetry and essay. Chinese art history abounds in anecdotes about him with the following being one of them.

At 20, he was already a well-known painter, When the construction of Waguan Temple was built on the outskirt of for Jiankang (Nanjing), the monks and abbot could not collect enough money for the decoration. One day, a monk saw Gu Kaizhi and asked him to donate some money for decorating the figure of Buddha. Gu offered to donate a large sum of money. He suggested he would draw a picture of the Buddha on the wall and, in the process, collect donations from curious passersby. For three consecutive days, thousands of people flocked to see the young man at work. By adding the final touches to the picture, the Buddha seemed to come alive, and the viewers cheered and applauded the young man's artistry. Hence, the money needed for the consummate construction of the temple was obtained.

The young man who paid great attention to the details that revealed the characteristics of his subjects was none other than Gu Kaizhi. He was once asked to paint Pei Kai's portrait, a man with three, long, fine hairs on his face that had been ignored by other painters. Gu laid great emphasis on the three hairs to depict his unique feature and Pei was very satisfied.

Another time, Gu painted a man named Xie Kun standing in the midst of mountains and rocks. When asked the reason for the setting, Gu explained that Xie loved to travel and see beautiful mountains and rivers. Such stories demonstrate Gu's skill of creating atmospheres that enhanced the characteristics of his subjects.

The theme of the *Luoshen Appraisal Painting* was drawn from the article, Luoshen Appraisal (Luoshen Fu), written by Cao Zhi, son of Cao Cao. The painting depicts with wild imagination the meeting between Cao Zhi and the Goddess Luoshen at Luoshui River, vividly capturing the mood of their first meeting and eventual separation. Gu emphasized his subjects' facial expressions, with the stones, mountains and trees having an ornamental purpose. Gu's paintings, which greatly influenced later traditional Chinese paintings, are similar in style to the Dunhuang murals.

Gu also made great advances in summarizing painting theories. His theoretical works included *Painting Thesis* and *Notes on Painting Yuntai Mountain*. Gu paid considerable attention to the vivid expressions of his subjects to expose their spirit. His Graphic Theory later became a basic theory for traditional Chinese painting. According to historical records, Gu created more than 70 paintings based on historical stories, Buddha, human figures, birds, animals, mountains and rivers. His three existing scroll paintings include the *Nü Shi Zhen Painting*, *Luoshen Appraisal Painting* and *Lienü Renzhi Painting* — the earliest examples of scroll paintings.

B. Wu Daozi — Sage in Chinese Painting

In Chinese ancient art history, three people are revered as sages: the calligrapher Wang Xizhi of the Eestern Jin Dynasty, the poet Du Fu of the Tang Dynasty and the painter Wu Daozi, also of the Tang Dynasty.

Wu's most prolific period was during the Kaiyuan and Tianbao eras (713 - 755) in the Tang Dynasty. Born in Yangzhai (Yu County in Henan Province now), Wu lost both his parents at a young age and lived a hard life in his early years. He learned how to make a living from folk painters and sculptors. Because his diligence and talent in art, Wu earned himself a good reputation as a painter by the time he was 20 years old. Emperor Xuanzong invited Wu as an imperial painter in the court, naming him Daoxuan. As an imperial painter, Wu only painted at the emperor's request, which was a big restriction for a civilian painter. On the other hand, the court provided the best living conditions and was an outlet for artistic creativity.

Wu's character was unrestrained, direct and indifferent to trivial matters, and it is known that he always drank while painting. It is also said that when Wu drew the halo around Buddha's head in a mural, he used his brushes without drafting the measurements first; when he was painting at Longxing Temple, the temple was always packed with observers. Wu moved his brush quickly, and most of his works were accomplished in a single session. Chang'an (present day Xi'an), capital of the Tang Dynasty, was the cultural center of the time where many famous men of letters and artists lived. Wu had many opportunities to stay with them, which helped improve his painting skills.

Wu mainly created religious murals and his abundant works had a wide range of subjects. According to records, Wu painted over 300 murals and more than 100 scrolls. While many of them involved Buddhism and Taoism, Wu also drew pictures of mountains, rivers, flowers and birds and animals. *The Presentation of Buddha* is his most representative work. Unlike his predecessor Gu Kaizhi, whose line strokes were slender and forceful but lacked variety, Wu's strokes were full of change and vigor, expressing the internal world of his subjects. Wu was always in great ferment when he was painting, and his works exhibit an expressionist style.

C. Zhang Yanyuan — Art Historian

Zhang Yanyuan, styling himself Aibin, was the art historian of the Tang Dynasty. Born into a chancellor family in Yishi of Puzhou (present Linyi County of Shanxi Province), Zhang once took office. He was a learned scholar and excellent painter and calligrapher.

Zhang's works include *Fashu Yaolu*, *Collection of Poems on Color Paper* and the first general history of art — *Records of Historical Famous Paintings* which gave a summation of achievements in ancient painting history. Following the tradition of combining historical facts and painting critics, Zhang initiated the style of general art history. By using abundant materials, Zhang's research focused on the development and internal relations of art history, using systematic historical painting materials to support his theories. The book extensively covered the development and significant theories of Chinese painting history. The biography section consisted of comprehensive records of painters' lives, thoughts and works. Zhang passed equitable judgments on painters by quoting predecessors, yet still developed his own ideas. From the point of view of the whole process of art creation and appreciation, Zhang brought recording, appraising, collecting, circulating and even mounting to the list of indispensable components, which gave rise to the integral research system of Chinese painting history. For a long time, the book was regarded as China's first publication on the general painting history and an encyclopedia of painting of the period. It had a unique position in the development of Chinese painting as a link between the past and the future.

In general, there are several features to Zhang's artistic theory. Apart from confirming Xie He's theory that painting had moral and political functions, Zhang put more emphasis on the meaning of painting itself. Opposing dull and stereotyped painting styles, Zhang stressed that painting needs ingenious creation and that the basic skill of painting lay in conception and stroke. He also emphasized that a painter's cultural taste and personality were also very important to painting. Zhang was the first to forward the theory that painting was a career of moral scholars who had knowledge and unique personalities. As one of the earliest art theorists and critics, Zhang contributed many achievements to the theory of ancient painting history.

3. Chinese Calligraphy and Painting Share the Same Origin

Since similar tools and lines were used for the earliest painting and writing, painting is said to have the same origin as calligraphy. Chinese paintings usually integrated poetry and calligraphy with themes that include figures, landscapes, flowers, birds and other animals, offering more profound aesthetic connotations. Many Chinese painters are poets and calligraphers at the same time. A painter often adds a poem to the painting, which invariably carries an impression of his or her seal. The resulting piece of work is usually an integrated whole of four branches of Chinese art — poetry, calligraphy, painting and seal-carving.

Like Chinese writing brushes, Chinese paintbrushes are mainly made of animal hairs glued into a bamboo handle. New brushes are stiffened with glue, which must be soaked before their first use to remove the glue. Once they are soaked, the brushes swell. Most brushes have loops at the end of the handle, which can be used to hang the brushes with their bristles downwards. To hang the brushes like this allows them to dry without letting the water from the bristles affect the brush handles.

There are two main types of brushes: hard brushes made from brown wolf hairs and soft brushes made from white goat hairs. Chinese brushes tend to be larger than typical European watercolour brushes. One reason for this is that the brushes can be loaded with several colours at the same time (usually with darker colours towards the tip of the brush), so that leaves or petals may be painted in a single stoke with a blend of colours by using the side of the brush instead of just the tip.

Different from western painting, traditional Chinese painting has its unique way of expression. As an important part of Chinese cultural heritage, traditional Chinese painting is distinguished from Western paintings in that it is executed on *xuan* paper or silk with the Chinese brush, Chinese ink and mineral and vegetable pigments. *Xuan* paper is the most suitable for Chinese painting. It is of the right texture to allow the writing brush wet with Chinese ink and held in a trained hand, to move freely on it, making stokes varying from dark to light, from solid to hollow. These soon turn out to be vivid human figures, plants and flowers, birds, fish and insects.

Word Bank

oracle bone	卜骨	mural	墙壁上的
stele	石柱,石碑	abbot	(大寺院的)住持
shaft	杆子	consummate	圆满的,巧妙的
quill	鹅毛笔	outlet	机会,途经
mindset	思想形式	chancellor	宰相,大臣
clerical	办公室工作的,誊抄工作的	equitable	公平的,公正的
sublime	庄严的	conception	思想的形成,概念
assimilate	吸收,同化	bristle	(刷子等的)毛
innate	与生俱来的,天生的	pigment	颜料
the Big Dipper	北斗七星		

参考译文

1. 中国书法

1) 汉字的书写材料

汉字是“写”出来的。今天,我们的文字大都写在纸上。但在发明纸张之前,汉字是写在什么材料上面的呢?

商代的汉字,刻写在甲骨、青铜器上。春秋战国时期,随着汉字不断增多,书写内容不断丰富,新的书写材料不断出现。竹、木简是纸发明前最主要的书写材料。贵族们还会把字写在丝制品上。

2) 汉字的书写工具

最早的汉字是用刀刻的。毛笔等专门的书写工具出现后,刀不再用于写字,而是用于刮掉人们写在竹、木简上的错字,其作用就像今天的橡皮。

在林林总总的笔类制品中,毛笔可算是中国独有的品类了。毛笔是文房四宝之一,另外三宝是墨、纸、砚。文房四宝是书写汉字的主要传统工具。毛笔由两部分组成:笔头和笔杆。笔头用羊毛、狼毛、鼠毛或兔毛等动物毛加工制成,相当柔软。制作笔杆可用竹、木和陶瓷以及象牙和玉等贵重材料。

“文房四宝”是书写汉字的主要工具。用毛笔写字时,先在砚中放入清水,然后用墨条研成黑色的墨汁,再用毛笔蘸上墨汁来写字。砚台通常由石或砖制成。因为毛笔笔头由动物的软毛制成,运笔可轻可重,线条可粗可细,相当灵活。

毛笔历史悠久,据《史记》记载,毛笔由秦始皇手下的大将军蒙恬取兔毛造之。因此,我们通常称蒙恬为毛笔的史祖。但是根据对河南省已出土的仰韶彩陶花纹的研究,发现这些花纹可能是由类似毛笔的工具绘制而成,可见当时已有毛笔的存在。

毛笔在春秋时便已成为主要的书写工具。1954 年在湖南长沙郊外的左家公山出土的文物中,已有多种古毛笔及与其相关的书写文物,第一次印证了我们对汉朝以前的毛笔形象的想象。

3) 用刀"写"的汉字:篆刻

篆刻,就是镌刻印章,也就是用刀在石头、木材和金属等硬质材料上写汉字,是中国传统的汉字造型艺术。纸发明前,人们用竹木简牍书写公文信件,然后用泥封缄,在泥上加盖印章,叫作"封泥"。

明代以前,印章只是人们在交往中表明身份的凭信工具。明代以后,专供艺术欣赏用的印章出现了,其用料考究,刀工细腻,布局精致。小小印章所呈现的篆刻艺术从此大放异彩。

4) 汉字的书写艺术:书法

书法,是借助文字的书写来陶冶性灵、抒发情感的艺术,是汉字独有的艺术,也是深受中国和世界人民喜爱的艺术。书法根据书写风格分为五类:①篆书(小篆)——笔画粗细匀称,确立了当时所有汉字的基本构成部分;②隶书——更简洁,形状规整,确定了大部分汉字的结构;③楷书——由隶书演变而成,书体规整方正,笔画平直,书写简易;④草书——一种笔画简省、字形连绵的书体;⑤行书——介于楷书和草书间的一种书写简洁、流畅的书体。

中国书法这种艺术形式历史悠久,直到今天仍在广泛运用。因为从本质上讲,书法是一种抽象的艺术,不像画画,它用汉字来传达艺术家的精神世界。虽然书法以汉字为表达工具,但欣赏书法并非必须懂得中文。在中国文化中,书法因其抽象和庄严,被公认为是最具有启迪性力量的。

正如千人千面,各人的笔迹各不相同。书法作为艺术作品,通过字的独特结构、字体和运笔的方法,表达了艺术家的道德、性格、感情、审美和文化观,给读者以美的享受。因此,许多中国人认为"字如其人"。

中国汉字是从图画、符号逐渐演变而来的,汉字独特的书写方式发展成了后来的书法艺术。中国历代都有大书法家,其书法艺术和风格成为所在朝代书法的典型代表。人们对书法的喜爱一直流传到今天。

书法和中国气功一样,可以调节人的性情,让人在写字时不自觉地运用平日的练习来控制墨的深浅、笔画粗细和字体大小。书法被认为是一种保持健康的有效方法,因为它可以使人放松,也可以让人自娱自乐。历史上,很多大书法家都非常长寿。

随着书写工具的更新,除传统毛笔书法之外,硬笔书法及其他书法艺术蓬勃兴起。当代西方艺术家将中国书法与西方艺术相结合,创造出许多杰出的艺术品。中国书法作为一种高雅的艺术形式已随着中国文化传播到日本、韩国、新加坡和越南等周边国家,成为东方艺术独有的特点。

2. 中国绘画

1) 古代中国绘画

A. 彩陶

中国传统绘画可追溯到 6 000 年前的新石器时代。现已出土的彩陶之上的人面、鱼类、动物和植物反映了原始氏族社会生活的方方面面。出土彩陶器皿上描绘着水波纹、网纹或锯齿纹等抽象的图案。而那些动物纹和人物纹线条简练,形象生动,显示了远古艺术家对大自然质朴的敏感。

B. 岩画

中国岩画分布很广，见于西南部的四川省、云南省和贵州省，东部的福建省，北部内蒙古的阴山、黑河以及西部的阿尔泰山等。南部地区岩画普遍用炽热的血红色调表现人们的祭祖及生产生活场面，具有强烈的视觉效果；北部地区岩画多表现狩猎、游牧、战争、舞蹈等题材。

C. 帛画

帛画是一种在丝布上创作的绘画作品。1949 年出土于湖南省长沙南郊一座战国时期的楚墓中的帛画《人物龙凤图》是中国迄今发现的最早的帛画作品。该画长约 30 厘米，宽约 20 厘米。从中国出土的早期帛画可以看出，这个时期的绘画生动优美，人们已经能充分运用毛笔在丝帛上写字作画。在纸张出现之前，帛画不断发展，到西汉时，技法纯熟，达到高峰。

D. 纸画

纸画的出现晚于帛画，这是因为纸的发明晚于丝绸的缘故。1964 年在新疆吐鲁番市阿斯塔一座晋代的古墓中，发现了一幅彩绘纸画，画面上部是日、月、北斗七星，下部的正中是墓主人安闲地坐在上，手执团扇。这幅画长 106.5 厘米、宽 47 厘米，是中国迄今发现的最早的纸画。

2）历代代表画家

A. 南北朝画家

南北朝是中国绘画史上一个十分重要的时期。从公元 3 世纪到公元 6 世纪，中国当时许多地方各自为政，连年的战乱与频繁的朝代更替，使当时的学术思想分外活跃，促进了艺术的发展。这一时期石窟壁画、墓室壁画、石刻、砖刻及漆画均具有相当规模，对中国传统绘画的发展起了很重要作用。被尊为画祖的顾恺之和他的卷轴画极具这一时期的代表性。

B. 唐朝宫廷画家

唐朝是人物画的繁盛时期。擅长描绘宫廷女性的张萱和周昉是这个画派的代表人物，他们是贵族女性风俗画的先驱，对此后中国仕女画的创作具有重大影响，仕女画成为了中国传统绘画中的重要部分。

C. 元朝四大画家

元代山水画四大家黄公望、吴镇、倪瓒和王蒙代表了山水画的最高水平，他们的作品对明代和清代的山水画家影响很大。

D. 明代吴门四家

江南苏州，史称“吴门”，这里人杰地灵，文人荟萃，明朝时许多著名画家在这聚会，形成了一个强大的画派，人称“吴门画派”。吴门画派领袖沈周、文征明、唐寅和仇英，统称“吴门四家”。他们开拓了新的绘画风格，并形成了自己独特的一面。吴门画派的笔墨技巧和表现手法，对后代影响很大。

E. 清代高僧画家

清朝初年，作为明朝遗民的朱耷、石涛、髡残和弘仁，为反抗清朝政府先后削发当僧人，被后人称为四大高僧画家。他们利用传统艺术形式，创作山水风景画作，来平息自身的伤感情绪。

F. 扬州八怪

著名的“扬州八怪”之所以被人称为“怪”，是因为这些画家作画不墨守成规。他们大都很有个性，孤傲清高，行为狂放，所以被人称为“八怪”。他们的作品很多取材花鸟，以写意为主要表现方式，作品令人耳目一新。尽管当时并不完全被人理解，甚至被认为旁门左道遭到非议。事实上，正是他们开创了画坛新局面，为中国花鸟画的发展拓展了前途。

G. 上海画派

清代末年民国早期，上海成为中国最繁荣的商业城市，因而吸引了当时很多的绘画高手的到来，形成了在“扬州八怪”之后中国近代绘画史上最后一个画派——上海画派。海派画家既吸收传统，又贴近现实生活，是中国古典绘画向现代绘画过渡的一个重要环节。

3）中国绘画奠基者

A. 画祖——顾恺之

顾恺之是东晋时期的画家，江苏无锡人。出生在一个官僚家庭，年轻时做过官，有机会游览各地的风景。他精通诗文，历史上记载了不少关于他的轶事。

顾恺之20岁即蜚声画坛，成为远近闻名的画家。当时，建康（南京）城郊的瓦官寺刚落成，寺里的住持与和尚们募捐不到足够的银两用以寺庙的装修。一次，寺院里的和尚碰到顾恺之，请这位年轻的画家多少捐些银两，装点佛像。顾恺之认捐一大笔银两，提出在寺庙的墙上画一幅佛像，让驻足观看的过往行人募捐。三天内，有数千个行人观看他作画，在画上添上最后几笔后，整个佛像栩栩如生，围观者顿时欢呼鼓掌，而寺庙也募集到了所需的银两。

顾恺之还特别注意表现人物的特点。有一次，他为一个叫裴楷的人画像。此人脸颊上有三根长汗毛，别人为他画像时，都不画出来，顾恺之却把这三根汗毛画得特别突出来强调对象的特征，裴楷对此十分满意。

还有一次他为谢昆画像时，衬以山岩为背景，并解释这样更能体现人的神韵，因为谢昆爱好旅游，钟情山水。这两个例子，都是以形来传达人物的神，以氛围烘托主题，加强表现人物的特征。

《洛神赋图》是根据三国时期曹操的儿子曹植所写的《洛神赋》来创作的。《洛神赋图》描绘了曹植与洛神在洛水上相逢又相别的情节，发挥了高度的艺术想象力。顾恺之注重对人物情态的刻画，山石、树木都富有装饰性。他的作品与同一时期的敦煌壁画风格相近，对后世中国画产生了深远的影响。

顾恺之在绘画理论方面也很有成就，他留下来的论著有《论画》《画云台山记》等。他主张作画要形神兼备，他提出的“传神论”成为中国绘画的基本理论之一。根据记载，顾恺之的作品有七十余件，他画过历史故事、神佛、人物、飞禽走兽、山水等题材。可惜，现在能看到的只有《女史箴图》、《洛神赋图》和《列女仁智图》三幅卷轴画摹本了，它们是现在所知道最早的卷轴画。

B. 画圣——吴道子

在中国古代艺术史上，有三位艺术家被称作“圣”人：一位是东晋王羲之，被称为“书圣”；一位是唐代杜甫，被称为“诗圣”；还有一位被誉为“画圣”，那就是唐代的吴道子。

吴道子一生主要活动在唐朝开元、天宝年间（713年-755年）。吴道子出生在阳翟（今河南禹州），自幼失去双亲，生活贫困，为了生计向民间画工和雕匠学习。由于他刻苦好学，才华出众，20岁时就已经很有名气。唐玄宗把他召入宫中担任宫廷画师，为他改名道玄。成了御用画家的他，没有皇帝的命令，不能擅自作画。这样，一方面，对他这样一个平民意识很强的艺术家是一种约束和限制；另一方面，他得到了最优厚的生活条件，不再到处流浪，可以施展自己的艺术才华。

吴道子性格豪爽，不拘小节，喜欢在酒醉时作画。传说他在描绘壁画中佛头顶上的圆光时，不用尺规，挥笔而成。在龙兴寺作画的时候，观看者水泄不通。他绘画时速度很快，像一阵旋风，一气呵成。当时的都城长安是中国的文化中心，汇集了许多著名的文人和书画家。吴道子经常和这些人在一起，相互促进、提高技艺。

吴道子主要从事宗教壁画的创作，他创作的作品题材广泛，数量很大。据说寺廊壁画有三百余件，有记录的卷轴画有一百余件。其中以佛教、道教题材为多，还有山水、花鸟、走兽等。《送子天王图》这幅画反映了吴道子的基本画风，他打破了长期以来历代沿袭顾恺之的那种游丝线描法。吴道子用笔讲究起伏变化，富有生气，表现出内在的精神力量。他在创作的时候，处于一种高度兴奋与紧张状态，很有点表现主义的味道。

C. 美术史论家——张彦远

唐代时期的张彦远，字爱宾，蒲州猗氏（今山西省临猗县）人，是一位美术史论家。他出生在宰相家庭，学问渊博，擅长书画，曾任官职。

张彦远编写的著作有《法书要录》《彩笺诗集》和中国第一部绘画通史《历代名画记》。《历代名画记》总结了古人有关绘画的成果，继承发展了史和论相结合的传统，开创了编写绘画通史的体例。作者运用丰富资料，探讨绘画史的发展和内在联系，并以系统的绘画史料来支持自己的理论认识。全书用大量的篇幅阐述绘画史的进程，讨论重大的理论问题。传记部分比较全面地汇集了画家生平、思想和作品，充分引证古人的评价，但又不受前人的局限，有分寸地评价画家的得失。此外，他从绘画创作与欣赏的全过程着眼，把著录、鉴藏、流传，以至装裱也纳入研究画史的必要组成部分。这本书长期以来被认为是中国第一部系统完整的绘画通史，具有当时绘画"百科全书"的性质，在中国绘画史学的发展中，具有独特的地位和承先启后的里程碑的意义。

张彦远的艺术观点主要有几项特征。他除了肯定谢赫等人关于绘画具有道德、政治功能的观点以外，更重视绘画本身的意义。张彦远强调绘画是灵巧创作，反对呆板的死画，他强调绘画技巧的根本在于立意和用笔。他还强调绘画艺术的文化品位。他最早提出绘画是有学问和有独立人格的读书人的事业。作为最早的美术理论家和批评家之一，张彦远对古代绘画史理论贡献重大。

3. 书画同源

由于最早的绘画和写字均使用同样的工具，故有"书画同源"之说。中国绘画作品在描绘人物、山水、花鸟与走兽时，通常将诗、书、画汇合成一个艺术整体，予以更加丰富的美学内涵。不少中国画家，既是诗人又是书法家。他们常常在作品上写上一首诗，盖上印章，使诗、书、画、印融为一体，这就是中国画的"四绝"。

与书法用的毛笔一样，中国画笔主要是用动物的毛黏在竹竿上制成的。新笔的笔头用胶水或糨糊黏住，第一次使用前，必须浸泡笔头以去除糨糊。一旦浸水，笔头就会张开。毛笔的笔杆上一般都有一个挂笔的环，可以将毛笔笔尖向下挂起晾干，并防止水把黏笔头和笔杆的胶水泡坏。

中国画笔主要有两种类型——硬毫和软毫。硬毫主要以棕狼毛制成，软毫以白山羊毛为主。中国的毛笔比典型的欧洲水彩画笔大一些，一次可蘸多种颜色（通常越接近笔尖颜色越深），这样像树叶或花瓣之类可以用笔的侧面而非单用笔尖一笔挥就，且混合了多种色彩。

不同于西方绘画，中国绘画有其独特的表现形式。作为中国文化遗产的一个重要组成部分，传统的中国画与西方作品的不同之处在于：中国画运用毛笔、墨汁以及从矿石植物中提炼出的色素，在宣纸或丝帛上进行创作。宣纸最适合画中国画，它有吸墨的特性，正适合一个老练的画家，握一支饱蘸墨汁的毛笔，在纸上任意游走，画出深浅不一、虚虚实实的线条，组成的人物、树木和花鸟鱼虫栩栩如生，意趣无穷。

Exercises

Section A Thought-provoking questions

1. What are the four main tools for Chinese painting and calligraphy? What are they considered

as by Chinese people?
2. What do you know about figure painting in the Tang Dynasty?
3. What are the main themes of traditional Chinese painting?

Section B　Decide whether the following statements are true or false

1. *Gongbi* style is characterized by simple and bold stokes to represent the exaggerated likeness of the objects.
2. To attain proficiency in Chinese painting calls for assiduous exercises and a good control of the brush.
3. Chinese paint brushes are the same as European watercolor brushes.
4. The May 4th Movement of 1919, or the New Culture Movement, inspired the Chinese to learn from western art and introduce it to China.
5. According to painting techniques, Chinese painting can be divided into two styles: *xieyi* (freehand brushwork) and *gongbi* (detailed brush work).
6. *Gongbi* is marked by exaggerated forms and freehand brushwork.
7. Inscriptions and seal cuttings have stopped since the invention of papers.
8. The Hu Writing Brush produced in Huzhou City, Jiangau Province, is regarded as the best-quality brush and the most exquisite handicraft.
9. Without the writing brush, Chinese painting and calligraphy could not have achieved such distinct features.
10. "Painting in poetry and poetry in painting" has been a criterion for excellent works.

※ **A person who is not benevolent cannot live long in hardship. Nor can he be happy for long. A benevolent person takes refuge in benevolence. A wise person sees benevolence as advantageous.**

From *Analects of Confucius*

（不仁者，不可以久处约，不可以长处乐。仁者安仁，智者利仁。）

——《论语》

※ **Only a benevolent person is able to like people who deserve to be liked and dislike people who deserve to be disliked.**

From *Analects of Confucius*

（唯仁者，能好人，能恶人。）

——《论语》

Chapter 15

Chinese Carving

中国雕刻

Carving art has a long history in China and it reflects the culture of Chinese nation. The carving remains and cultural relics kept till now are the precious artistic pearls in the treasure house of Chinese art. There are many types of carving, mainly four types in China, that is, jade carving, wood carving, stone carving and bamboo carving.

1. Jade Carving

Jade is understood in China as the collective name for most precious stones, and the love of jade ware has been one of the cultural features of China. The Chinese regard carved jade objects as intrinsically valuable, and they metaphorically equate jade with human virtue due to its solidity, durability and (moral) beauty. Jade can be divided into many categories such as white jade, yellow jade, agate, and turquoise, etc. The jade carved into different shapes is called jade carving which is one of the oldest carving types and constitutes an important part of Chinese arts and crafts.

Many countries boast a jade ware culture, but none of them can match China's long jade ware history. In China, jade ware underwent a long process of development beginning from the Neolithic Age 10,000 years ago. The earliest jade ware found in China was a piece of serpentine stoneware unearthed at the Immortal Cave in Haicheng, Liaoning Province, dating back more than 12,000 years ago.

The second jade ware was a small hanging jade article excavated at Hemudu in Zhejiang Province dating back more than 7,000 years ago. Jade ware from that period was mainly used for personal decoration. A large number of exquisite jade objects were produced 4,000 years ago. At the time, jade ware was mainly used for witchcraft and as an emblem of privilege.

The three dynasties of Xia, Shang and Zhou were significant periods in the development of Chinese ancient jade articles. There were few jade articles found of Xia Dynasty. During the Shang Dynasty, with the development of society, craftsmen used metal tools to make progress in jade ware models and sculpture. During Zhou Dynasty, ancient jade art had achieved a high level and jade carving had become an independent trade.

In the Spring and Autumn Period and the Warring States Period, all the kingdoms paid special attention to the producing of jade carving articles; as a result, well-carved, initiative and exquisite works were left and the coherent and undulating patterns of the dragon, phoenix and *panli* (a figure of Chinese folklore) on the jade decorations are still treasured today.

In Han Dynasty, Chinese jade carving art experienced its prosperous golden time, putting an end to the development of the ancient jade art of Shang and Zhou dynasties, and actively exploited new schools succeeding the techniques of the Spring and Autumn Period and the Warring State Period. During this period, jade ware became more practical and objects such as jade tablets became obsolete. At that time, people began to believe in the power of jade ware to increase longevity: they thought they would live forever like gods if they possessed jade ware. Therefore, the practice of burying the dead with jade ware became common. Invaluable jade figures and clothes sewn with golden thread have been found in tombs dating back to the Han Dynasty.

After the advanced Han jade art, jade carving met its low tide in the following 300 years. In Sui and Tang Dynasties, jade carving became flourishing again, but people didn't take jade carving as something mysterious. A large number of jade carving articles were collected as treasures by royal families, aristocrats and the rich, thus made jade carving articles mainly as rare curios, as well as a kind of complementary decorum.

Song Dynasty was a period in which Chinese craft got highly developed, and jade articles also began to develop in a worldly, decorative manner. Jade carving in Yuan Dynasty also gained big achievement.

Jade carving craft in Qing Dynasty was highly advanced. Jade carving articles in Ming Dynasty were often inlayed with silver and gold, or embedded with gems. White jade vessels with golden holders and white jade bowls with golden lids, which were unearthed in the Ming Tombs, reflected the Dynasty's peak level in jade carving. A wide range of jade was employed in making jade carving articles in this period, and the articles were delicate, diversified in form. The most flourishing period of jade carving craft was the 60 years under the reign of Emperor Qianlong (1736 - 1795). After Emperor Daoguang (1821 - 1850), jade carving craft began to decline.

2. Wood Carving

Wood carving can be divided into many different categories due to its wide range in application and decoration, diversity in methods of representation and difference in wood texture. In terms of application and decoration, there are three types of wood carving: architecture carving, furniture carving and display art ware carving, which will be explained in detail in this part; in terms of representation, there are carvings such as piercing carving, basso-relievo, solid tondo, piercing decal, etc.; in terms of different wood texture, there are two types: hard (often called rosewood carving) and soft wood carving (ash wood carving).

1) Architecture Carving

Architecture carving refers to the wood decoration of architecture. Wood decoration of ancient architecture occupies a very important position in the history of world architecture. The methods that are applicable to ancient architecture are basso-relievo, piercing carving, solid tondo, etc.

2) Furniture Carving

Furniture carving refers to the carving of wood furniture and it can be called the most widely applied practical art. The furniture decorated with wood art shows simple and elegant nature of itself. Owing to the difference in customs and aesthetic value, furniture carving varies from one place to another in pattern of woodwork, design of carving decoration, and carving technique. For example, both rosewood carving furniture in Suzhou, Jiangsu Province and Dongyang wood carving furniture in Zhejiang Province are world-famous, but they differ with each other on the former being elegant and luxurious and the latter being exquisite and unique. Below please find two good examples of these two types of wood carving.

3) Art Ware Carving

Art ware carving boasts two types: appreciative display art ware and practical art ware.

A. Appreciative Display Art Ware

Appreciative display art ware refers to the small and single art ware that is put on the closet, window, desk or shelf for decoration purpose. As a traditional type of wood carving art, it is carved with the solid tondo technique. Modern display art ware has broken the limit on subject and pattern, bringing about a new situation on the development of display art ware.

B. Practical Art Ware

Practical art ware is the kind of art ware that combines practicality with art of wood carving technique. It is divided into two types: woodwork carving such as wood palace lantern, floor lamp, wall lamp, lacquer folding screen, woodcarving folding screen, mirror shelf, pen shelf and wood clock seat, and other art ware carving such as desk, table, seat and shelf, etc.

3. Stone Carving

Stone carving is an ancient activity where pieces of rough natural stone are shaped by the controlled removal of stone. Owing to the permanence of the material, evidence can be found that even the earliest societies indulged in some stone carving activities.

1) History

Beginning in New Stone Age, Chinese stone carving art developed rapidly and became more and more mature during Shang and Zhou Dynasty. The stone chimed with tiger engraving unearthed at Anyang, Henan Province in 1950 displayed the beautiful sculpt, skillful cutting technique, and graceful and natural lines of stone carving. From Qin Dynasty to Tang Dynasty, stone carving art reached the peak, with many good stone carvings produced showing the simple, rough characteristics of Qing and Han stone carvings as well as the delicate and perfect characteristics of stone carving art in Tang Dynasty. The strong and lively Qin tombs with their pottery warriors and horses, exquisite Bodhisattva statue, tall and splendid Six Stone Steeds at the Zhaoling Mausoleum of the Tang Dynasty, etc. are all world famous and are regarded as the pearl in the treasure-house of human history.

2) Characteristics

Stone carving is mainly used for the base and tablet inscription of arch and civilian residence. It has a wide variety of ways to set up its modeling and composition. It can be divided into two types in terms of its characteristics: one is decorative, being fully developed, compact, well-organized and finely divided; the other is artistic, being simple, concise, and equally densified.

The carving methods are being perfect. Some carvings, overdone in carving either too deep or too shallow, are so interesting and impressive that till now under hundreds of years of wind and rain they still look attractive and are admired by people, especially those carving with three to four levels of architrave or railing board. The exquisite carvings are highly graded and combine different carving methods and techniques to extend the limited space, creating greater literary and artistic heights.

The manifestation of stone carving art is always limited by the nature and practicality of material, which determines the carving strategy. Not only is stone carving art limited by the nature of material but also it is limited by the function of construction components. Besides, it has high requirements for adaptability of composition, modeling and carving methods. Carving technique must meet the art form and content which is the principle of stone carving art. Differences existing in content and aesthetic value during each period propel the development of stone carving technique from single and shallow to complex and changeable and then to single and shallow again. The latter is not just the repetition of the former; it actually develops from original simple and naive form of art to complicated and neat form of art.

4. Bamboo Carving

China, the hometown of bamboo, boasts the richest resource of bamboo forest in the world, hence its title as the "kingdom of bamboo" and it is also one of the first nations to use bamboo. Since ancient times, bamboo has been widely used in the daily life of the Chinese people, and it has great influence on the development of Chinese history and culture.

1) History

Bamboo formed the earliest ties with Chinese characters, which can be traced back to 6,000 years ago. The pictographic symbol of "bamboo" was found on the potteries unearthed in the Yangshao cultural relics of Banpo Village, Xi'an in 1954, and the symbol was also discovered in oracle bone inscriptions and inscriptions on ancient bronze objects. During the period from the Warring States Period to the Jin Dynasty, people carved characters on the bamboo slips to keep records. Later, books made of bamboo slips were created to convey cultural information. Many of the earliest Chinese historical documents, such as *The Book of History*, *The Book of Rites and Analects of Confucius*, were recorded on such material, making great contributions to the development of Chinese culture. After the papermaking technique was invented by Cai Lun, bamboo slips were replaced by paper gradually.

2) Bamboo Carving

Bamboo carving, also called bamboo engraving, has a long history in China. Archeologists once unearthed a painted dragon-pattern bamboo spoon from the Western Han Dynasty at the No.1 Han tomb of Changsha Mawangdui in Hunan Province which shows that as early as 2,000 years ago people carved bamboo into elaborate utensils.

Bamboo slips can be regarded as the earliest form of bamboo carving. Although bamboo slips were replaced with the development of papermaking technology, the bamboo carving was still loved by people and is still today. Very few bamboo carvings pre-dated the Ming Dynasty, but mid-Ming-Dynasty bamboo carvings have become a professional industrial art, and more and more artists have taken it up, shifting its role from practical use into an art form.

Bamboo carving has two classifications based on the technique it adopts: bamboo board carving and three-dimensional round bamboo carving. The former can be further divided into positive and negative, each containing deep and surface carving. Negative carving includes line, deep and sunken round deep carving, while positive carving includes thin ground mass with positive relief, low relief carving, carved in high relief and openwork. Incense tube, bamboo brush pot, arm rest and fan rib belong to this category. The latter is three-dimensional carving in the round, or called bamboo root carving, which carves bamboo into different shapes like birds or animals.

There are two major schools of bamboo carvings: Jiading School and Jinling School.

The initiator of Jiading School was Zhu Songling, and the major feature and traditional skill of Jiading Bamboo Carving is "to use knife instead of brush and carve the bamboo in the same way as calligraphy".

Pu Zongqian's Jinling School featured another style, which pursued natural tastes with minimal cut and polish. The major carving skill is shallow carving, which is also called intaglio carving. This carving skill not only carves lines and surfaces, and the figures carved could demonstrate writing sentiments on the drawings.

Chinese carving is precious artistic heritage in Chinese industrial arts and it benefits enormously from the four types of carving, that is, jade carving, stone carving, wood carving and bamboo carving. With the importing of other elements from other countries, Chinese carving is sure to have a bright future.

Word Bank

relics	遗物	privilege	特权
collective	总的	obsolete	过时的
intrinsically	内在的	longevity	长寿
metaphorically	比喻性的	aristocrat	贵族
turquoise	绿松石	inlay	镶嵌
serpentine	蛇纹的，蛇状的	basso-relievo	浮雕
immortal	神仙	practicality	实用性
excavate	出土	adaptability	适应性
exquisite	精致的		

参考译文

雕刻艺术在中国有着悠久的历史，闪耀着古老民族不朽的文化光芒。保留至今的雕刻遗迹、文物数不胜数，是中国文物中的瑰宝。雕刻的种类有很多，主要有玉雕、木雕、石雕和竹雕等四种雕刻形式。

1. 玉雕

玉，实际是优质石头的总称。中国人自古就爱玉，因此玉是中华文明的一个重要组成部分。由于玉具有坚贞、不屈和灵秀等特性，因此人们常将玉石的品质比喻人。玉石的种类非常多，有白玉、黄玉、玛瑙、绿松石等，玉石经加工雕琢成为工艺品，称为玉雕，玉雕是中国最古老的雕刻品种之一，是中国传统工艺的重要组成部分。

玉文化是很多国家引以为豪的，但没有一个国家可以与中国的玉文化相媲美。在中国，玉器的发展大概要追溯到距今约1万年前的新石器时代。中国新石器时代的玉器，最早的见于距今

1.2 万年的辽宁海城仙人洞遗址的一件蛇纹石质地的石器。

第二件是距今 7 000 余年的浙江河姆渡遗址的项间挂饰小玉璜。这段时间的玉器主要是用于个人装饰。但在距今约 4 000 年前大量生产的玉器大多用于巫术或作为身份的象征。

夏朝、商朝和周朝是中国古代玉器发展史的重要阶段。夏朝的玉器特别少。在商朝，由于社会的发展，特别是青铜制工具的使用，使得玉器数量增加，品种增多。到了周朝，玉器艺术达到了很高的水平，玉雕变成一门独立的商业。

春秋战国时期，各诸侯国特别注重玉雕产品的生产，玉石雕刻技术发展迅速，出现很多雕刻精美的玉器，诸如龙、凤凰及蟠螭等形状的玉器现在仍被人们视为珍品。

到了汉朝，玉雕艺术进入了黄金时期，结束了商周时期古代玉器艺术的发展模式，在春秋战国时期技术的基础上，开创了新的雕刻形式。这个时期的玉器更注重实用性，像玉碑之类的东西已过时。这个时期的人们开始相信玉器能够延年益寿：人们相信拥有玉器就拥有了长生的法宝。所以，人死后用玉器陪葬成了非常普遍的事情，在汉朝古墓中就出土过用金线缝制的玉衣。

汉朝以后的 300 年，玉雕工艺的发展进入低谷期，一直到隋唐时期，玉雕工艺才重新开始繁荣，但在这个阶段玉雕并不是什么神秘的东西。皇室、贵族和富人收集了大量玉雕，使玉雕成为古玩，变成一种风俗。

宋朝期间，中国工艺得到高速发展，玉器逐渐向装饰方向发展。玉雕工艺在元朝也有一定的发展。

到了明朝时期，玉雕有了很大的发展，工艺上也有很大改进，人们开始在玉雕上镶嵌金、银或宝石等。明陵中出土的带金架的玉容器和带金盖的玉碗是玉雕发展到鼎盛时期的见证。在这个时期，多种玉被用来雕刻成玉器，工艺精细，品种多样。玉雕艺术最繁荣的时期是清朝乾隆统治的那 60 年间。但从道光帝之后，玉雕工艺开始走向衰落。

2. 木雕

木雕，由于其应用及装饰的范围广泛、表现形式的多样以及雕刻木材质地的不同，所以它分出许多类型。从应用及装饰的范围来讲，可分为建筑雕刻、家具雕刻、陈设工艺品雕刻三大类。从表现形式来分，有镂空雕刻、浮雕、立体圆雕、镂空贴花等。因木材质地的不同，又分硬质木雕与软质木雕两大类（习惯上称硬质木雕为红木雕刻，软质木雕称白木雕刻）。

1）建筑木雕

建筑木雕是指建筑的木雕装饰。中国古建筑上的木雕装饰，在世界建筑史上占有很重要的地位。适用于古建筑的木雕表现形式大致可分为浮雕、镂空雕刻、立体圆雕等。

2）家具雕刻

家具雕刻指的是对木制家具进行雕刻，这可以说是应用木雕艺术最广泛的一种大型的实用艺术。用木雕艺术装饰的家具，具有古朴、典雅的风味。在中国，由于各地区风俗习惯的不同及人们审美趣味的差异，因而各地的木雕家具无论从木工制作的造型及雕刻装饰的图案花纹和雕刻技艺都各具特色。比如，虽同为红木雕刻家具，但江苏苏州的红木雕刻家具和浙江东阳的木雕家具却大不相同，苏州的红木雕刻家具端庄、豪华，而东阳的艺术雕刻家具则精美、别致。

3）工艺品雕刻

木雕工艺分观赏性的木雕陈设工艺品和木雕实用工艺品两类。

A. 木雕陈设工艺品

所谓陈设工艺品，就是陈列摆设于橱、窗、桌、架之上，供人欣赏的小型的、单独的艺术品。木雕陈设工艺品属木雕工艺中的一个传统类别。它是利用立体圆雕的工艺技术雕制的。现代的木雕陈设工艺品，无论是造型制作，还是题材内容，都打破了历史局限，开创了新时代的新局面。

B. 木雕实用工艺品

木雕实用工艺品指利用木雕工艺装饰的实用与艺术相结合的艺术品。木雕实用工艺品又分木制品木雕装饰和其他工艺品的木雕装饰两类。木制品木雕装饰比较多，如木制宫灯、落地灯、壁灯、漆器屏风、木刻屏风、镜架、笔架、木刻钟座等木雕装饰。木雕主要是为其他工艺品配制装饰的有几、案、座、架。

3. 石雕

石雕是一项古老的活动，是根据预先设计，去除粗糙石头上的多余部分后，在石头上进行雕刻的艺术。所以有证据表明，石头具有持久性，在人类早期社会中，石雕这种活动就存在了。

1）历史

中国石雕艺术起源于新石器时代，商周时期的石雕艺术发展迅速，日趋成熟。1950 年在河南安阳殷墟，发掘出商朝的虎纹石磬，此石雕造型优美，刀法纯熟洗练，线条流畅自然。秦汉至唐代是石雕艺术的高峰阶段，从纯朴粗犷的秦汉时期石雕到精致完美的唐代石雕艺术，诞生了许许多多的石雕精品。雄壮威武的秦陵兵马俑、精致完美的菩萨立像、高大雄健的昭陵六骏等均闻名世界，被誉为人类历史宝库中的明珠。

2）特点

石雕多用于牌坊、民宅的底基、碑刻等处。石雕艺术无论造型或构图，方法多种多样。论其特点可分为两类：一类书面充盈，紧凑饱满，层次分明，错落有致，富于装饰性。另一类书面简洁大方，疏密相同，构图大势开合，如同书画艺术。

石雕的雕刻方法也比较趋于完美。有些作品正是由于深雕浅刻过度，显得意趣无穷。因此，虽经数百年风雨剥蚀，至今看上去仍然十分耐人寻味。特别是那些雕筑有三至五层的额枋或栏杆华板，雕刻精丽，层次分明，综合运用了各种雕刻方法与技巧，方使有限的层面能表现出无限的空间，创造出较高的艺术境界。

石雕艺术的表现形式自始至终受到材料特性和实用性的制约。石雕艺术不仅受限于材料性能，而且受到建筑构件功能的约束，加之各种石质性能不同，要求构图、造型、雕刻方法具有极大的适应性，只有因地制宜，才能因材施艺。雕刻技巧必须以服从艺术形式和内容为原则。由于不同时代有不同的内容和审美要求，从而不断促进石雕技法的发展。石雕技法从平浅单一到复杂多变之后，复为平浅单一，后者并不是前者的重复，而是由当初的古朴稚拙发展到繁褥工整。

4. 竹雕

中国是竹的故乡，因其拥有世界上最丰富的竹林资源而被称为“竹子王国”。中国也是世界上最早使用竹制品的国家，自古以来，在中华民族的衣食住行中到处可见竹的影子，竹子对中国历史和文化的发展产生了巨大影响。

1）竹子历史

1954 年在西安半坡村发掘了距今约 6 000 年左右的仰韶文化遗址，其中出土的陶器上可辨认出“竹”字符号，而甲骨文和古青铜器的铭文中都发现了代表竹的符号。在战国到晋朝期间，人们将字写在竹片（有时是木片）上，再把它们用绳子串在一起就成了“书”。竹简等材料为我们保存了大量早期历史文献，如《尚书》《礼记》和《论语》等都是写在竹简和木简上的，对中国文化的发展做出了巨大贡献。直到蔡伦发明了造纸术后，竹简才逐渐被纸代替。

2）竹雕

竹雕，也称竹刻，在中国也由来已久。现知最早的竹刻是湖南省长沙马王堆 1 号西汉墓出土的彩漆龙纹竹勺。这证实早在 2 000 多年前人们就将竹子雕刻成各种精美的用具。

竹简可以说是竹雕的最初的形式，后来随着造纸业的发展，竹简被渐渐取代，但竹雕一直深受人们喜爱。明朝以前竹雕作品较少，但从明朝中期开始，竹雕发展成为一门专业艺术，越来越多的艺术家涉足竹雕，使其功能从实用向艺术欣赏转变。

竹雕大体分两类。一类为竹面雕，如香筒、笔筒、臂搁、扇骨等，竹面雕刻又可分阴文、阳文，两者又各有深刻、浅刻。如阴文则有毛雕、线刻、深刻、陷地深刻；阳文有薄地阳文、浅浮雕、高浮雕、透雕。另一类为立体圆雕即竹根雕，可塑造出鸟兽等立体形象之物。

当时的竹雕工艺发展形成了各具特色的两大派：一是“嘉定派”，二是“金陵派”。以朱松邻为创始人的“嘉定派”的主要特点和传统技艺是“以刀代笔，以书法刻竹”。濮仲谦开创的金陵派根据竹材的自然形状和特征，用简洁的刀法，略加雕琢，随形施刻，自然成器。金陵派竹雕以浅刻、简刻为主要特征。

雕刻是中国工艺美术中一项珍贵的传统艺术遗产。玉雕、石雕、木雕及竹雕对这个艺术形式的发展壮大起了很大的推动作用。从别国引进的新的技术及新的理念，肯定会对雕刻未来的发展产生极大的影响。

Exercises

Section A　Thought-provoking questions

1. What do you think contributed to the development of jade carving and stone carving?
2. Why do people metaphorically equate jade with human virtue?
3. How many types can wood carving be divided?

Section B　Cloze

How is that jade is so ___1___? First, its value ___2___ in its scarcity. Precious stones are formed ___3___ long geological epochs and are hard to get, ___4___ green jade, white jade and agate. Ancient people on a ___5___ hunt had to trek on the back of yaks in mountainous regions to get at the unhewn rocks containing the gems, exposed or half exposed, ___6___ the stamping of the animal's hoofs.

Sometimes, precious stones were washed down by mountain torrents and were got ___7___ of midway by men. In any event, exposed stones grew ___8___ and people began to bore through the mountains to time for precious stones, making them even more difficult to get.

Secondly, the value of jade lies in its ___9___. Precious stones are divided by their hardness into two major groups: jadeites and nephrites. Jadeites are the ones with a solid texture and a hardness of degree 6 or above (on the basis of 10 for diamond). The more valuable varieties, such as green jade, may be as ___10___ as degree 8 or 9.

Chapter 16

Chinese Farmers' Painting

中国农民画

Chinese farmers' painting enjoys a unique status of its own in the world folk art circles. In China, farmers constitute a large portion of the Chinese population, so it is natural that they have their own form of art due to the differences in customs, living background and educational background. The paintings reflect both styles and scenes of their life in the vast countryside of China. The glamour of the paintings has conquered hundreds of people both at home and abroad. The paintings have become an established art form in modern Chinese culture.

1. History

Chinese farmers' painting or Folk Painting is both ancient and young. It is ancient because it originated from the thousand-year traditions of embroidery, batik, paper cutting and wall paintings. And it is young because it did not emerge as an art form until the 1950s when farmers were encouraged to engage in art.

"People need art, and art needs more people." It is this new understanding of art that stands at the cradle of Chinese farmers' paintings. Some communes pick it up, in the beginning for recreational purposes, or as a well-meant means of propaganda, or to express their dreams of a better life.

The farmers' painting's movements continued through 1960s. With the political and economic reforms at the beginning of the 1980s, farmer painting, as a genre of paintings, had developed gradually and has now become a very popular form of art. Moreover, the international exhibitions held at home and abroad and the coming of Western tourists to China in large numbers are sure to push this form of art to move forward. Today, there are more than 40 government recognized farmers' painters communities, organized in different artists associations on county, provincial and national level. The government promotes these activities and supports them by providing funds and various trainings.

2. Characteristics

The characteristics possessed by Chinese farmers' paintings in subjects, color and techniques make it rather a unique form of art.

1) Subjects

The subjects of Chinese farmers' paintings are taken from the experience of the daily life in rural communities. They show trivial activities like coming home from a market or having dinner; they display events like a marriage or a Spring Festival procession or they express the happiness of farmers or good wishes, such as a stable full of healthy cattle, happy children, sweet home, electricity, etc. With subjects focusing on simple and small things in the countryside, these paintings reveal farmers' understanding of life and their expectation for a better life.

2) Colors

The typical Chinese farmers' painting is hand-painted with gouache watercolors on paper. Different from sketches, farmers' painting should not be valued by the detailed accuracy. Farmers use color to show what they feel rather than what they see and they draw the pictures following their feelings. Therefore, the color of the grounding is mainly deep and colors like red, purple, blue are usually applied. These colors are rather brilliant and vibrant, which makes the whole compositions look naive. It may seem naive at first sight, but it should by no means be underestimated because they are the right style to show the rustic rural life.

3) Techniques

Generally speaking, farmers resort to intense colors, simple and clear line to detail their feelings and understandings of the world. Some of the farmers' paintings use the keyline technique which is adopted from ukiyoe, Japanese woodblock prints. The whole design is drawn with strong black outlines, and then the areas are filled with colors. Many of the Chinese poster designs use the same technique.

Some farmers use a more refined technique called gradation to draw paintings which is a passing by barely perceptible degrees from one color to another.

3. Major Types

Chinese farmers' painting mainly refers to the auspicious handmade or printed drawing, with strong rural characteristics. Since the 1950s several painting centers have came into being: Longmen (Guangdong Province), Huxian (Shaanxi Province), and Jinshan (Shanghai).

People often regard the farmers' painting of Longmen, Guangdong, representing the southern areas, the farmers' painting of Jinshan, Shanghai, representing the eastern areas, and the farmers' paintings of Huxian of Shaanxi representing the northern areas as the three major types of Chinese farmers' paintings. The three villages play very important roles in the development of farmers' painting.

In addition to the paintings in these three places, some other paintings like New Year Paintings, which are pasted onto doors, walls, cornice and furniture of homes, business establishments, and temples in Chinese villages and towns during the Spring Festival are also regarded as some of the most influential painting forms of farmers' painting.

1) Longmen

Longmen County is located in South China's Guangdong Province. Surrounded by picturesque scenery, the local people have kept up the fine tradition of drawing the dynamic scenes of their daily life. For their outstanding achievements in developing this folk art since 1970s, the State Ministry of Culture in 1988 awarded the region the honorary title of a "Village of Chinese Modern Farmers' Painting."

The most salient feature of Longmen Farmers' Paintings is their bright and contrasting colors. Using bright colors and exaggerated depictions, the artworks usually boast profound morals. The farmer-artists mainly take festivities, local customs and work scenes in the fields as their subject matter. The terse and crisp style vividly outlines the place's beautiful landscape, farmers' cozy family lives, lively atmosphere on the farmland, and jubilant festivals, fully demonstrating the modern artistic features.

The artworks demonstrate the heart and soul of the farmer artists. The composition, color, shape and pattern clearly show the profound cultural background of these works. While emitting the flavor of modern arts, the works also boast high value for academic researches and collection.

2) Huxian

Huxian County, with a population of only 500,000, has been commonly known as "Home of Painting", not only because the place has a picturesque landscape, but also everyone there loves painting and most of the painters are farmers. These farmers have stepped out of Shaanxi, as well as China, to the world.

Developing from traditional paper-cut, embroidery and other folk arts, farmers' painting in Huxian County, long-lasting, has come out with a great number of fine works in the last 50 years. The total works add up to 30,000, among which 1,500 pieces have been published in periodicals of the state level, 428 have gained reward in exhibitions of fine arts in the mainland, 4,500 have been selected to show to 48 nations and regions, and over 18,700 pieces of works have been collected by international friends and in overseas museums.

The expression techniques of the Huxian County farmers' painting bear an obvious local trace. Bright red and purple take a predominant place in the works of Huxian County farmers' painting. Peculiar and exaggerated in depiction, the works possess profound implication. They are concise and lively in style. The picturesque landscape, lifelike life in the rural area, grand scenes of working and the scenes of joyful festival celebrations are all covered, fully reflecting the characteristics of the modern folk art. Not only are their hands employed in their painting, but also their hearts. The design, sculpting and color all symbolize abundant cultural contents, brim with the taste of modern art, and possess high academic and collective value.

3) Jinshan

Jinshan District is located in the southwest of Shanghai and it is not until 1970s that local farmers developed folk painting in Fengjing town of this district, which combines elements from traditional arts, such as paper-cuts, embroidery and knitting. The works of Jinshan farmers have been exhibited around the world in more than 20 countries, and more than 200 pieces have been collected by the National Art Museum of China, the Research Institute of Chinese Paintings and the China Folk Arts Museum.

Drawing from their life experiences and romantic imaginations, the people of the land have created many paintings full of freshness and images of the Shanghai countryside. With simple subjects rendered in bold colors, these beautiful works of art have gained the name of "Jinshan Farmers' Painting" and the creative farmer artists are even considered "Chinese Picassos".

The "primitive" painters usually use a wide range of striking colors across the canvas. Instead of exploring modern urban reality, traditional rural themes such as fishing, cloth dyeing, spinning, and market scenes are preferred. Figures and objects are usually drawn in a way that most may consider "childish".

4. New Year Painting

New Year Paintings or *Nian Hua* are one form of farmers' paintings and are China-specific drawing genre. The paintings are pinned up on doors, walls, windows, cornices and furniture of homes during the Chinese Spring Festival for decoration as well as praying for blessing. They are an important part of the annual celebrations.

1) Content

New Year Paintings have a great variety of topics, the contents of which are well-wishing stories that could add to the festive atmosphere. Some come from fairy tales and classical novels. Therefore, images on the painting are of gods and deities, heroes and sages, to whom the Chinese prayed and worshipped in return for protection and blessing. The most popular characters appearing on painting are the door gods Qin Qiong and Yuchi Gong, the demon catcher Zhong Kui, the Three Star Gods of Happiness, Wealth and Longevity, the God of Wealth, and Guanyin — the Goddess of Mercy.

Some of them carry a moral message. At a time when education was not accessible to everyone, these paintings served as useful teaching tools. Some of the typical messages are loyalty, benevolence, kindness and retribution. Beautiful lady figurines are another favorite topic for these painting. Besides, some topics about people's everyday life are also quite popular and appear on the painting, the most common of which is a cartoon-like chubby child with short arms, short legs, a short neck, small eyes, and a big head. Playful, plump children symbolize the wish for many sons to come or a blessing for good fortune.

The iconography reflects traditional Chinese folk and popular cultures. In ancient China, people believed that numerous gods inhabited the Three Realms (heaven, earth, and the underworld) and ruled over human affairs and destiny. To fulfill their hopes for a bountiful harvest, a healthy male heir, official promotion, and other auspicious wishes, people sought the blessing of these deities by representing them graphically in a medium that has become a unique folk art tradition known as "paper gods" or "paper joss".

2) Types of New Year Painting

New Year Painting has a long history, recorded as early as the Song Dynasty. China's top three New Year Paintings are those developed in Taohuawu, Suzhou, Jiangsu Province, in Yangliuqing, Tianjin, and in Yangjiabu, Weifang, Shandong Province.

A. Taohuawu New Year Painting

Taohuawu New Year Painting was once one of the major paintings in China. The painting, originated at the end of the Ming Dynasty in a workshop on Suzhou's Taohuawu Street, was highly popular during the reign of the emperors Yongzheng and Qianlong (1723 - 1795) of the Qing Dynasty with annual publications up to one million. In the first half of the 20th century, New Year Painting's production declined because of constant warfare and turmoil. After the founding of new China in 1949, great efforts were exerted in Suzhou to restore this folk art, and over 200 representative draft drawings were collated and printed.

The painting, taking the form of door painting, central painting and hanging scroll, is made delicately with one color of woodblock print being used at one time. Therefore, the production of one single painting requires at least four-time prints, sometimes even more than 10 times. While maintaining simplicity, economy of means, and strong decorativeness of farm art, the craft in figure creation, cutting techniques and coloring has also been striven. The colors used are never confined only to those seen through the eye in real life; colors like scarlet, peach, yellow, green and purple are used, resulting in a gay, bright and striking style. Themes of Taohuawu Painting cover every aspect of life: stories of the Gods or heroes, customs, current news, beauty, babies, or even Kitchen God, etc. The characteristics listed above accounts for their popularity home and abroad for hundred of years.

B. Yangliuqing New Year Painting

Yangliuqing New Year Painting, which first appeared in the late Ming Dynasty, is another important genre of New Year Paintings throughout China. Because of the genre's delicate painting style and strong rustic flavor, such pictures are quite popular. The paintings, taking motifs from people's daily lives, display strong local features. They are an art incorporating carving and painting and are characterized by delicate delineations, bright colors, graceful figures and extensive motifs. They feature mainly figures, including the most popular old-style maids and babies.

The artistic characteristics of Yangliuqing New Year Painting are multi-facets and so are the reasons of forming them. The most prominent one is reflected on the production. The production of a New Year Painting consists of several steps, including outline tracing, woodblock distribution, woodblock cutting, printing, color painting and mounting. Compared with the other genres of New Year Painting, the first four steps have nothing special but follow exactly the same procedures as the others. It is different from others in that the painting of colors is very complicated by delicately combing knife carving with brush lines which brings the best in each other. Due to painters' different drawing styles, the same original painting can be polished into "decent painting" or made into "rough painting", making a striking contrast with each other in style and each possessing high artistic value.

C. Yangjiabu New Year Paintings

The production of Yangjiabu New Year Painting began during the Ming Dynasty over 400 years ago and thrived in the Qing Dynasty, when there were over 100 workshops producing copies of more than 1,000 pictures.

The Yangjiabu style was, to some extent, influenced by the Yangliuqing style, while at the same time maintaining its original flavor of being unsophisticated and vivid, forming its own unique style.

Yangjiabu New Year Painting is characterized by local flavor, artistic exaggeration and sharp color contrasts. The production of Yangjiabu Painting consists of outline drawing, cutting, printing, and mounting and every step is highly refined. The first plate finishes black outlines, which then is stuck to planed pear wood or planed birchleaf pear wood to carve the main line. The next step is to use color plates. Deep colors are printed first on small sections of a picture. Light colors are printed last on large sections of the picture. The main colors are red, yellow, purple, green, blue and black. The production is completed when the mounting is done.

The contents of Yangjiabu New Year Painting come from the lives of the local people. Their motifs cover flowers, birds, mountains, rivers, characters in traditional operas and fairy tales, etc. In a word, festivity and prosperity are the permanent motifs of Yangjiabu New Year Painting. The composition of the pictures is vigorous, the depiction is exaggerated, the lines are simple and smooth and the colors are gorgeous. The bright red, green and purple colors give prominence to the rustic flavor. The collocation of colors is usually exaggerated, bold, intense, and violent in contrast.

The wild lines also add a special touch of farmer style painting to the art form. The pictures highlight the bold and unconstrained character of farmers in northern China.

Chinese folk art reflects the long history of popular customs and traditions in Chinese culture. Deeply rooted in agriculture, people's daily life and rituals are inevitably connected with nature, the surrounding landscape. Therefore, paintings drawn by local people have the subjects, colors and techniques of their own. Chinese farmers' painting, growing out of the countryside, is the representative of farmer's aesthetic value and thinking, Therefore, Chinese farmers' painting is not only the works adorned by people but also a channel for people to know more about farmers and their way of life.

Word Bank

batik	蜡染	canvas	画布
gouache	树胶水彩画	benevolence	善行
rustic	乡村的	retribution	报偿
gradation	(颜色)渐渐变化	figurine	小雕像
salient	突出的	chubby	圆胖的
terse	简洁的	iconography	肖像画法
jubilant	喜悦的	motif	主题
sculpting	造型	delineation	描绘
primitive	朴实的		

参考译文

中国农民画这一艺术形式在世界民间艺术界享有特殊的地位,是中国独有的一种艺术形式。其出现的原因是中国农民占中国人口的很大一部分,由于风俗习俗、生活背景和文化教育背景的差异,中国的农民总是相对保持着他们自己特有的文化特性。中国农民画反映了中国广大农村农民的生活方式和生活场景,其独特的艺术魅力赢得了国内外友人的青睐。现在农民画已经成为现代中国文化的一种既定的艺术形式。

1. 农民画的历史

中国农民画可以说既古老又年轻。说它古老,是因为它以中国几千年传统的刺绣、蜡染、剪纸和壁画为基础。说它年轻,是因为直到 20 世纪 50 年代中国大力提倡农民投身艺术才可以称得上是农民画的初级阶段。

"人民需要艺术,艺术需要人民。"人民对艺术的这一新的理解成为农民画发展的根源。起初,很多人是怀着娱乐或宣传的目的来作画的,以表达他们的梦想或对美好生活的向往。

农民画在20世纪60年代的时候继续发展。20世纪80年代初的改革开放给农民画的发展提供了一个平台,使农民画有了长足的发展,越来越受到人们的欢迎。而在国内外举办的具有国际规模的农民画展览以及大批西方游客的涌入对农民画的发展起到推动作用。在农民画的发展方面,政府也提供了财力以及培训等方面的支持,迄今为止,全国已有40多个政府认可的农民画村。

2. 农民画的特点

农民画这一特殊艺术形式的特殊主要表现在主题选择、色彩及技巧应用等方面有鲜明的特色。

1) 主题

农民画的主题都和乡村生活有关。这些主题有的展现的是平常的活动,如从集市回到家中或吃饭等,有的展现的是婚礼、春节等节日场景,有的用来表达农民的欢乐心情或美好的心愿,如大群牛羊、快乐的孩子、温馨的家庭等。农民画作者通过描绘农村简单细小的事情,表达他们对生活对世界的理解以及对美好生活的向往。

2) 颜色

农民画大多是手工画的树胶水彩画。与素描不同,农民画不是通过精确性来衡量其价值。农民用颜色来表达他们所感觉到的,根据内心的感受来作画。因此,大多数农民画色彩鲜艳,对比强烈,底色多以红、紫、蓝等深色为主,这些特点使整幅画第一眼看起来非常纯稚,但其艺术价值决不应该被低估,因为他们是乡村田园生活的真实表现。

3) 技巧

总的来说,农民用鲜艳的色彩,简单清楚的线条来表达他们对世界的感受及认识。一些农民采用日本木版画的拼版手法来绘画,整幅画的轮廓用又黑又粗的线条来勾画,中间的部分用颜色来填充,很多宣传画的设计也用这种方法。

有的农民用另一种精细的"渐变"的手法来演绎农民画,这种手法主要通过色彩的浓淡以不可察觉的层次的变化来作画,以达到既定的效果。

3. 农民画的分类

农民画多系农民自己制作和自我欣赏的吉祥图案的绘画和印画,乡土气息很浓。自20世纪50年代以来,逐渐形成了广东龙门、陕西户县、上海金山等地的农民画乡。

人们常把代表中国南方的农民画——广东龙门农民画,代表中国北方的农民画——陕西户县农民画,还有代表中国东部的农民画——上海金山的农民画,并称为中国农民三大画乡。这三大画乡对农民画的发展起了不可低估的推动作用。

除了这三大画乡的农民画之外,农民自印的春节期间贴在自家门上、墙壁上、房屋屋檐角、家具上的年画以及贴在商业机构和乡镇寺庙里的年画,也是最有影响力的农民画的一种。

1) 龙门农民画

龙门位于中国南部风景秀丽的广东省,当地人有将日常生活的情景画下来的传统。鉴于龙门人民在民间艺术发展上所做的贡献,文化部于1988年授予龙门"中国现代民间绘画画乡"这一称号。

龙门农民画主要特点就是颜色非常鲜艳、对比鲜明。鲜艳的颜色和夸张的描述通常包含深刻的寓意。主要以节庆喜事、特色民俗还有田间劳作等为主题。简洁轻快的绘画风格生动地描绘出当地秀丽的自然风光、居民温馨的家园生活、农耕时活跃的气氛以及喜气洋洋的节日等,充分展现了农民画的艺术特点。

这些艺术作品表达了农民画家内心深处的愿望，作品无论在构图、色彩、造型、勾线等方面都带有浓郁的当地文化气息。农民画中散发出强烈的现代艺术气息，具有极高的学术研究和收集价值。

2）户县农民画

户县人口为50万，向来有“绘画之乡”的美称，获得这一美称的原因不仅因为户县风景如画，而且还因为户县人人喜欢绘画，爱好绘画。现在户县的农民画家已走出陕西，走出中国，走向世界。

户县农民画有一大部分作品来源于传统剪纸、刺绣和别的艺术形式。在过去的50多年来，户县农民画经久不衰，生机勃勃，成果丰硕，累计创作作品30 000余件。其中1 500多件作品在国家级刊物上发表，428件作品在中国美术展览中获奖，4 500多件作品应邀在48个国家和地区展出，18 700件作品被国内外博物馆和农民画爱好者收藏。

户县农民画的表现手法有着明显的地域特色，它多以大红大紫的色彩、夸张化的描述和简洁明快的风格来表现寓意深刻的主题。户县农民画勾画出了画乡户县美丽的田园风光、栩栩如生的农家生活、气氛热烈的劳动场面和欢天喜地的节日庆典，充分体现了现代民间艺术的特点。在绘画中，艺术家不仅运用手来作画，并且用心来作画。农民画的设计、色彩都被赋予丰富的文化内涵，富有现代艺术的韵味，具有极高的学术和收藏价值。

3）金山农民画

金山位于上海的西南郊。著名的金山农民画于20世纪70年代发起于金山县的枫泾镇。农民画家将剪纸、刺绣、编织等传统艺术巧妙地运用到绘画中去，形成独具特色的农民画。

金山农民画在20多个国家展出过，200多幅画被国家艺术博物馆、中国画研究机构和中国民俗艺术博物馆收藏。

金山人民从日常生活场景中选材，运用浪漫的想象力，创作出生动的农民画，充分展现了上海农村的生活习俗和劳动场景。运用深色来诠释简单的主题，使金山农民画成为农民画的一个派别，为这些农民画家赢得了“中国毕加索”之名。

纯朴的农民画家们经常采用大量对比鲜明的色彩，绘画的主题围绕着传统乡村生活的，诸如钓鱼、印染、纺纱及集市场景，而不是描绘现代城市生活。人物的刻画及实物的描绘都采用天真、纯朴的手法。

4. 年画

年画是农民画的一种，是中国特有的一种绘画体裁，大都用于春节时张贴在门、墙、窗、屋檐、家具上，装饰环境，含有祝福新年吉祥喜庆之意。春节贴年画是节庆活动的重要内容之一。

1）年画内容

年画多为祈福内容，以增添节日气氛。通常取材于当地的神话、传说故事，因此年画上的人物通常是神仙或英雄人物等，人们张贴他们的画像来祈福。门神秦琼和尉迟恭、捉鬼的钟馗、福禄寿三星、财神以及观世音菩萨等都是最受人们欢迎的神仙形象。

其中一些含有道德寓意，在教育不普及的旧时代，这些画起到了教育作用。一些年画以忠孝仁义、善恶有报等为内容。仕女图是另一个受欢迎的题材。除此以外，以人们日常生活为主题的年画也非常流行，其中以娃娃年画最为出名。娃娃画在造型上的特点是：短胳膊短腿大脑壳，小鼻子大眼睛没有脖子。可爱的胖娃寓意来年多子多孙或来年多福。

这些画是传统中国民间文化和大众文化的反映。古时候，人们相信神住在天堂、地狱和人间三界，掌管人类的一切事务及命运。因此，人们为了实现丰收、得子、升官等愿望或追求，向神仙的画像祈求，以求得到神的庇佑，这使得年画发展成为一种独特的民间风俗。

2）年画类型

年画历史悠久，据记载，最早始于宋朝，主要产地有江苏省苏州桃花坞、天津杨柳青和山东省潍坊杨家埠等。

A. 桃花坞年画

桃花坞年画是中国主要的民间年画之一。桃花坞年画始于明朝桃花坞街的手工作坊，清代雍正、乾隆年间为鼎盛时期，每年出产的桃花坞年画达百万张以上。20 世纪上半叶，由于连年战乱，桃花坞年画生产受到了严重的破坏，此后一直萎靡不振。直到新中国成立后，苏州大力恢复这一民族艺术，200 多种代表性的年画得以整理出版。

桃花坞年画，主要有门画、中画和屏条等形式，系用一版一色的木版套印方法印刷，工艺精美，一幅画要套印四五次至十几次。在人物塑造、刀法及设色上，具有朴实、稚拙、简练、丰富的民间美术装饰性特色；在色彩上，不局限于现实生活人眼所见过的颜色，多用大红、桃红、黄、绿、紫等色彩，创作出欢快明亮的风格；在主题上，涵括生活的各个方面，有神话故事、人情风俗、时事新闻、美人、娃娃、灶神等。因其风格独特，数百年来享誉海内外。

B. 杨柳青年画

杨柳青年画创始于明朝，是中国年画又一重要部分。由于绘制手法细腻，具有浓郁的乡土气息，因此深受人们喜爱。杨柳青年画多取材于百姓的日常生活，具有鲜明的地方特色，它巧妙地将雕刻与绘画融为一体，笔法细腻、色彩艳丽、人物造型秀美、内容多姿多彩，具有很高的艺术价值。杨柳青年画主要是以人物为主，其中仕女图和娃娃图是最受欢迎的。

杨柳青年画的艺术特点是多方面的，形成其艺术特点的条件也是多方面的。其中较为突出的则是表现在制作上。杨柳青年画的制作程序大致是：创稿、分版、刻版、套印、彩绘、装裱。前期工序与其他年画大致相同，都是依据画稿刻版套印；而杨柳青年画的后期制作，把版画的刀法版味与绘画的笔触色调巧妙地融为一体，使两种艺术相得益彰。而且还由于彩绘艺人的表现手法不同，同样一幅杨柳青年画坯子（未经彩绘处理的墨线或套版的半成品），可以分别画成精描细绘的“细活”，和豪放粗犷的“粗活”，艺术风格迥然不同，各具独特的艺术价值。

C. 杨家埠年画

山东省潍坊杨家埠年画兴起于明代，清代达到鼎盛期，杨家埠曾一度出现“画店百家，画种过千”的盛景。

杨家埠年画发展初期受到杨柳青年画的影响，但保持生动、简朴的特点，形成自己独特的风格。

杨家埠年画具有乡土气息浓厚、形象夸张、色彩鲜明等特点。杨家埠年画生产分为绘画、雕刻、印刷、装裱等几道工序，每一道工序都极为精细准确。做法是先将画稿勾出黑线稿，贴到刨平的梨木或棠木板上，雕刻出主线版。待印出主线稿后，再分别用不同颜色比如红色、黄色、紫色、绿色、蓝色和黑色，刻出色版，套色印刷，最后修版装裱而成。

杨家埠年画反映了当地人们的生活，其题材广泛，包括山水花鸟、戏剧人物、神话传说等，但喜庆吉祥是杨家埠年画的主题。杨家埠年画构图对称饮满、刻画手法大胆夸张、线条简单明了、色泽鲜艳明快。大红、大绿、大紫等颜色的运用，增加了年画的乡土韵味，而粗犷线条的运用，为农民画这一艺术形式增添了独特的表达方式。此类型的年画勾画出北方农民无拘无束的性格特征。

中国民间艺术反映了中国文化的悠久传统和风俗习惯。广大劳动人民根植于农村，因此他们的日常生活不可避免要和大自然、周围的秀丽风光联系起来。所以他们绘画作品的主题、色彩及技巧也必定会和他们生活的环境息息相关。在乡村成长起来的农民画,代表了农民的审美观点及观念,因此农民画不仅具有观赏意义,而且对于进一步了解农村、农民的生活习惯及方式提供了捷径。

Exercises

Section A Thought-provoking questions

1. Why did Chinese farmers' painting come into being and how did it make itself a unique art form?
2. What are the characteristics of Chinese Farmers' painting according to the passage?
3. In which aspects Huxian Farmers' Painting, Jinshan Farmers' Painting, and Longmen Farmers' Painting are in common?
4. Please list three types of New Year Painting and describe their characteristics in detail.

Section B Cloze

Fengjing has developed folk culture. Here is __1__ as the cradle of famous Jinshan farmers' paintings, which have borrowed the essence of other folk arts __2__ indigo print, furniture carving, kitchen mural, lantern, paper-cut, embroidery and weaving. Represented by the farmer painters in Fengjing, Jinshan farmers __3__ the unique art of Jinshan farmers' paintings with dense folk elements, which have made great influence at home and __4__. On Heping Street stands the ancestral home of Cheng Shifa, a master of traditional Chinese painting. And on the North Street is the cartoonist Ding Cong's works exhibition hall. In Fengjing Town, you can __5__ farmers' paintings, Ding Cong's cartoons, Cheng Shifa's Chinese paintings and famous go-player Gu Shuiru's. These international influencing arts and works can be seen in a town, which is really a __6__ regional culture phenomenon in China.

Huxian Peasant Paintings originated in the late 50s. Jinshan County style __7__ in the late 70s. Both styles show the ordinary aspects of __8__ life. The paintings explore all parts of daily life. Festivals, parades, harvest, weddings, village traditions, farm animals, and children are all depicted in their paintings. The style can be described as __9__, with child-like figures and __10__ colors which are often exaggerated.

※ **Study without contemplation leads to confusion. Contemplation without study is dangerous.**

From *Analects of Confucius*

(学而不思则罔,思而不学则殆。)

——《论语》

Chapter 17

Chinese Folk Musical Instruments
中国民族乐器

According to recent archaeological findings, ancient Chinese music was much more developed and sophisticated than is generally believed. During the Shang Dynasty, music had already been an important element in traditional ritualistic ceremonies, such as during a traditional Chinese funeral procession. It reached one of its greatest peaks during the Zhou Dynasty, featuring a great abundance of percussion instruments, several wind instruments, but only a few zither-type string instruments.

All the bowed string instruments and most of the plucked string instruments first came to China from Central Asia after the Han dynasty. The Tang dynasty saw the first wave of musical influence from Central Asia, which was a very important epoch in the evolution of Chinese music. However, it was during the Song Dynasty that Chinese music reached its maturity.

Traditional Chinese musical instruments were classified into eight groups (bayin) according to their materials: bronze, stone, silk and bamboo, gourd, earthenware, hide and wood, many of which have been lost or are obsolete today. Like modern music instruments, traditional Chinese instruments are generally grouped according to the way they are played: 1) bowed strings; 2) plucked strings; 3) woodwinds and 4) percussion.

1. Development of Folk Orchestral Instruments

More than 2,000 years ago, there were already quite a few musical instruments in China, namely, chime, drum, *xun* (an egg-shaped holed wind instrument), bell, etc. In the Zhou Dynasty and Spring and Autumn Period and Warring States Period, the number of musical instruments totaled over 80. During the period of Qin Dynasty, the Han Dynasty, the Three Kingdoms, the Jin Dynasty, the Southern and Northern Dynasties, Sui Dynasty and Tang Dynasty, there appeared such instruments as *hengchui* (like today's bamboo flute), *qiangdi* (a musical instrument of the Qiang Minority), *bi* (the present *guanzi*), bronze drum, waist drum, etc. They have all become key instruments in modern national orchestral music.

In the Five Dynasty, the Song Dynasty, the Yuan Dynasty, the Ming Dynasty and the Qing Dynasty, with the rising of folk art there appeared more instruments, such as *yunluo*, *bajiaogu*, *diangu*, *xiaomuyu*, *bangzi* (percussion instruments), *suona* (wind instrument); *sanxian* and *yangqin* (plucked instruments), and *erhu*, *banhu*, *jinghu*, *zhuihu*, ect. (bowed instruments).

Like musical instruments, national orchestral music was well developed in ancient times. The most influential orchestras in history were wind music (*Guchuiyue*) in the Han Dynasty and Yanyue in the Tang Dynasty. The former mainly consisted of percussion instruments while the latter focused on tender music.

The locations of the imperial capitals in ancient times are the centers of the transmission of orchestras and maestros of folk music today. For example, Xi'an percussion music dates from the days when Xi'an was the capital of the Tang Dynasty; the Daxiangguo Temple music of Kaifeng emerged when that city was the capital of the Song Dynasty; and the Zhihua Temple music of Beijing and the wind orchestra music of Hebei Province have associations with the days when Beijing was the capital of the Liao, Jin, Yuan, Ming and Qing Dynasties. Hebei's Chengde City, which is not far from Beijing, was the summer resort of the Qing emperors, and local musicians can still play the court music of that time, despite the fact that the dynasty disappeared long ago. This makes it easy to understand why so many farmer-musicians can have such comparatively high artistic attainments. This is an important component of the Chinese people's musical artistry.

2. Representatives of Folk Musical Instruments

1) Zeng Houyi Bells — Gem of Ancient Chinese Art

The set of bells, set of chimes and other instruments excavated from the tomb of Zeng Houyi, a Warring States duke, are the largest-scale ancient percussion instruments found so far.

The Zeng Houyi bells (see picture 17 - 1) are a three-tiered set which has 65 refined bronze bells. There were inscription of seal characters and his name on each bell.

The musical range of the Zeng Houyi bells, which can carry the main melody as well as the harmony, was five octaves, next only to modern piano. Modern scholars inferred that the set of bells could not only play melody, but also play in a musical ensemble.

All the musical instruments excavated from the Zeng Houyi tomb show superb craftsmanship and function surprisingly well. The bells has established itself as one of the wonders of traditional Chinese music.

2) *Zhuihu* — an Instrument That Can Speak and Sing

Zhuihu, a bowed string instrument, also known as *Zhuiqin* or *Zhuizi*, is altered from *sanxian* (a three-stringed musical instrument), can be used to perform solo and tutti. Since *Zhuihu* has a wide diapason, a soft sound and relatively high sound volume, performers can use it to imitate the voice of human and animals.

There is a legend about the origin of *Zhuihu*. In the Qing Dynasty, Emperor Kangxi forbad all the opera performances in the Forbidden City and artists had to earn a living on the street. One day, an artist's *sanxian* was bitten by mice and the covering leather of the sound box got a hole in it. In order not to miss the performance, the artist had to use piece of paulownia wood to replace the leather and used a bow from *huqin* (two-stringed Chinese violin) to play the *sanxian*. This musical instrument that could not only play music but also imitate human voice, was later called *Zhuihu*.

3) Bone Flute — Earliest Musical Instrument of China

There are various kinds of musical instruments in the world, including Chinese musical instruments, western musical instruments, special instruments, wind instruments, stringed instruments and so on. Among them, the earliest musical instrument is bone flute (see picture 17 - 2). However, in the 1980s, China did discover bone flutes of 8,000 to 9,000 years old. Excavations in 1986 and 1987 at the early Neolithic site of Jiahu Village, Wuyang County, located in central Henan Province, China, have yielded 6 complete bone flutes. Fragments of approximately 30 other flutes were also discovered. Three seven-hole dizi are now kept in Beijing Musemu, Henan Musemu and Henan Institute of Cultural Relics. The flutes may be the earliest complete, playable, tightly-dated, multi-note musical instruments.

4) *Liuqin* — Small Version of *Pipa*

Liuqin (see picture 17 - 3), with four strings which sound similar to mandolin, is played with a piece of plectrum, and is used to accompany other instruments for folk songs and local opera.

The *liuyeqin*, abbreviated to the *liuqin*, has got its name from the willow-leaf-sharped sound box. It is also called *tu pipa* (unrefined *pipa*) because of its appearance of a small *pipa*. It came into use in the music of the local operas, narrative singing (storytelling music) in north Jiangsu, south Shandong and Anhui provinces.

The folk type is made of willow wood, with 2 or 3 strings and 7 frets. The performer plays it with a slender bamboo tube on the forefinger as a plectrum. The professional type is made of red sandalwood or rosewood, and the performer plays it with a plastic pick (the same as guitar pick). In the modern type the front sides made of paulownia wood and the reverse side, of red sandal. The four strings are steel wires. The frets, increased from 7 to as many as 24, are arranged in half-step intervals. The plectrum is made of horn. The tone quality is clear, bright and more delicate.

5) *Qing* — Oldest Percussion Instrument

Qing(see picture 17 - 4) (musical stone) was a kind of stone or jade percussion instrument in ancient China. It was hung on shelf and played with wooden hammer. It was not only a kind of musical instrument, but also the symbol of power and status.

Historical records show that *qing* originated from stone tools used in daily life by Chinese ancestors. During their laboring, they found that these tools could produce pleasant sounds and therefore used them as musical instruments for entertainment.

Archeological findings show that *qing* came into being in the Xia Dynasty 4,300 years ago. By the Zhou Dynasty, a set of *qing*, pending from a rack and each with a different tone, emerged and these *qing* series were a native Chinese invention. The whole rack is called *Bianqing*.

6) *Erhu* — Queen of Chinese Folk Orchestra

Producing one of the most beautiful and haunting sounds in Chinese music, the *erhu* (see picture 17 - 5) is one of the most popular Chinese bowed-string instruments with a history of more than 1,000 years.

Hailed as a Chinese violin, the *erhu* is quite different from a western fiddle. There is a vertical post with a fingerboard crosses the sides of a resonator at its base. This resonator, made of either wood or bamboo, is covered with a piece of stretched python skin. The *erhu* bow is placed between its two strings called the inner and outer strings. Traditionally the two strings are made of silk, but metallic strings are more popular now. An *erhu* player usually sits with the instrument on his or her left upper thigh in front of the left hip. The *erhu* is played by moving the bow horizontally over the two vertical strings, with sound produced by the vibration of the strings.

The range of *erhu* spans over three octaves and the tune produced shares some qualities with the violin, although it produces a more nasal tone which is gentle but firm. The *erhu* resembles a human voice and can imitate many natural sounds, such as birds and horses. It is a very expressive instrument, most known for playing melancholy tunes, but also for its joyful melodies.

The *erhu* is almost always a must in national orchestras. In fact, the *erhu* plays the same role as the violin in Western orchestras. The *erhu* is extremely popular in China today as a medium for both traditional and contemporary music and plays an important role in both solo and orchestral performances.

7) *Dizi* — Bamboo Flute

Dizi is native to China with a very long history. It became popular as early as the Warring States Period. Two flute instruments were discovered in the relics excavated in Tomb No. 3 of Mawangdui in Changsha, Hunan Province.

This transverse bamboo flute has a blowing hole, a stop hole and six finger holes. Bamboo can be found in many places in China and it is very easy to make a bamboo flute. Therefore, bamboo flute is a very popular musical instrument in the country.

There are two basic kinds of *dizi* — *bangdi* and *qudi*. *Bangdi*, popular in northern China, got its name because it is used to accompany clapper-type operas. It is 40 centimeters long and has a strong and piping tone, suitable for expressing robust and lively emotions. *Qudi*, popular in southern China, is also named as *sudi* for its origin from Suzhou city. It is often used to accompany Kunqu Opera. *Sudi* is about 70 centimeters long and its tone is pure and mellow, making it suitable for expressing delicate and understated moods.

A large number of techniques are used when playing these wind instruments, such as tapping, tremolo, legato, flower tongue, augment, glide, trill, overtone. Famous *dizi* tunes include *Joyous Meeting*, *The Partridge Soars*, *The Bird in the Shade*, *Five Clappers* and *A Trip to Suzhou*.

8) *Guqin* — Representative Instrument of Chinese Music Culture

Guqin is (see picture 17 - 6) also called the seven-stringed *qin*. The body is a long and narrow sound box made of wood. Generally speaking, it is 130 centimeter long, 20 centimeter wide and about 5 centimeter thick. The surface is generally made of paulownia wood or China fir, and has seven strings stretched along it. Black is the common color for *guqin*. Sometimes brown or red ones can also be seen. On the edges are 13 inlaid jade/gold markers. Catalpa wood is used for the base, and there are two holes, one big and one small (called the "phoenix pool" and "dragon pond", respectively) to emit the sound.

Because it embodied the traditional cultural values of clarity, fineness, simplicity and far-sightedness, *guqin*, along with chess, calligraphy and painting, headed the list of four subjects scholars trained themselves in. Throughout history, philosophers and artists such as Confucius, Cai Yong and Ji Kang were all masters of the instrument. Old records contain a large number of treatises on *guqin*, and thousands of pieces of music for this instrument have been preserved.

In recent times, a dozen or so masters of *guqin* have emerged in China. They have mastered the strong points of the various schools of this instrument and grasped the interpretation of a large number of pieces of *guqin* music, manifesting not only their musical skill but also their deep esthetic appreciation.

9) *Konghou* — Chinese Harp

Konghou (see picture 17 - 7), also called *Kanhou*, is an ancient plucked stringed instrument in China. There are mainly three kinds of *konghou*: one is played lying flat, one is played upright and another one is the phoenix-headed *konghou*. As early as the Spring and Autumn and Warring States period, there appeared the rudiment of *konghou* played lying flat in the Chu Kingdom in southern China. *Konghou* was originally used in Yayue (court music), and was used in Qingshangyue (a music genre) in the Han Dynasty. It was used in Yanyue (music played in court banquets) in the Sui Dynasty, and gradually prevailed among the ordinary people and in places inhabited by ethnic minorities.

Konghou played upright appeared in the Eastern Han Dynasty and got popular in the Sui and Tang Dynasties. It was generally played in rites and ceremonies. The phoenix-headed *Konghou* was introduced from India to the Central Plains of China in the Eastern Jin Dynasty, and was prevalent in the Sui and Tang Dynasties.

Konghou, with its sweet timbre and wide diapason, can be used to play not only cantus but also chord and has many advantages in both solo and tutti performances. It was an indispensable instrument in China's ancient royal courts. From basso-relievo in the Yungang Grottoes of Datong and Dunhuang murals we can see persons playing *Konghou*. This shows that *Konghou* playing was very popular in China a long time ago.

10) *Pipa* — an Expressive Instrument

The earliest form of *pipa* (see picture 17 - 8) known appeared in the Qin Dynasty. It had a long neck, leather surface and circular sound box, and was held upright. Around the time the Qin was succeeded by the Han Dynasty, this instrument underwent a number of modifications and it evolved into the *ruan*, three-string (*sanxian*), *yueqin*, etc. All these forms of the *pipa* had the common characteristics of a straight neck and circular sound box.

Two major changes which took place in the course of its evolution were the practice of holding the instrument upright instead of horizontally while playing it and the use of 5 fingers to pluck the strings, instead of using a plectrum. The long-time history endowed *pipa* a rich collection of scores and a mature performing technique. In the 20th century, through the unremitting efforts of a large number of performing artists and composers, the amount of techniques and compositions developed quickly, with the result that the *pipa* is now one of China's most important national instruments for solo, accompaniment and ensemble recital.

11) Harvest Drum — A Special Instrument

Harvest drum, or peace drum, is popular among regions of Northeast China, Inner Mongolia, Hebei and Anhui provinces. It's a kind of feature instrument used mainly by the Han and Manchu people. It is said that the drum came into being in the Tang Dynasty and was named as harvest drum in the Ming Dynasty.

According to folk legends, the harvest drum was a tool used by Manchu hunters. Hunters were beating drums when they pursued an animal. And they kept beating drums to express their pleasure when they got back with their preys.

Harvest drums have many different features. Those used by Manchu are oval-shaped. The ones used by Han people are round, oblate or peach-shaped. The drum in Mongolia is only oblate-shaped. People like dancing accompanied by harvest drum playing, especially when they celebrate festivals.

12) *Xun* — One of the Oldest Music Instrument in China

The only earthen musical instrument is a kind of ocarina called *xun* (see picture 17 - 9), which was a very important wind instrument in ancient China. It can produce sound with a timbre similar to that of human voice, and is suitable for performing some lamenting aria. People in ancient times used the instrument to imitate bird sounds and ensnare them.

The oldest *xun* that has been discovered in China up to now was made about six thousand years ago. For instance, a conical *xun* was discovered in the Hemudu of the Hangzhou Bay in Zhejiang Province. The *xun* without holes and the one-hole *xun* were found in the Yangshao Culture site in Banpo Village in Xi'an and *xun* was also discovered in Wanrong County of Shanxi Province, Yumen Huoshao Gou of Gansu Province and Huixian County in Henan Province.

13) *Yangqin* — Adapted from a Foreign Instrument

Yangqin (see picture 17 - 10), the strike-stringed music instrument, was originated from west Asia and introduced to Europe in the 11th century. It was said to have been introduced to China from Europe in late Ming Dynasty. It has been combined into Chinese national music for more than 300 years and has become an important folk musical instrument.

To improve the traditional *yangqin*, Chinese musicians have tried very hard to make changes on its music scales, increase its harmony, augment its loudness and deepness, and improve its timbre. Moreover, many professional performing techniques have been developed to lift up on its expressions. Thus the instrument has been a dominant character in a modern Chinese ensemble as well as a powerful solo instrument for performing Chinese national pieces.

Word Bank

chime	编钟,排钟	trill	颤音
maestro	名作曲,名指挥,艺术大师	overtone	弦外音
ensemble	合奏	partridge	鹧鸪
tutti	合奏,合唱	catalpa	梓,梓树
timbre	音品,音色,音质	rudiment	雏形
diapason	音域	cantus	曲调,旋律
plectrum	拨子,弦拨,琴拨	basso-relievo	浅浮雕
fret	(弦乐器指板上定音的)品	recital	演奏会
resonator	共鸣体,共振器	oblate	扁平的,扁圆的
transverse	横的	ocarina	奥卡里那笛,陶制的卵形笛
tremolo	震音	aria	曲调,咏叹调
legato	连音	ensnare	使入陷阱
augment	强音		

参考译文

根据考古学家最近的发现，古代中国音乐远比人们所想的更为发达、复杂。在商朝，音乐已经成为如葬礼等传统仪式的一个重要部分。至周朝，音乐的发展就已经到达过一个高峰，打击乐器种类很多，也有吹奏乐器，筝类弦乐器较少。

拉弦乐器和大部分弹拨乐器在汉朝之后从中亚传入中国。唐朝是中国音乐史上一个重要时期，中亚音乐第一次大规模影响中国。到宋朝，中国音乐到达一个成熟阶段。

传统的中国乐器根据制作材料，按照周代的“八音”乐器分类法分为金、石、丝、竹、匏、土、革、木，其中不少乐器已经失传或者废弃。同现代乐器一样，传统的中国民族乐器一般也根据演奏方式分为四类：1）弹拨乐器；2）拉弦乐器；3）吹奏乐器；4）打击乐器。

1. 民族管弦乐器的发展

2 000 多年前中国就已有了许多乐器，如：钟、鼓、埙、铃等。到了周代和春秋战国时期，乐器发展到了 80 多种。秦、汉、三国、晋、南北朝和隋唐期间，由于各族人民的频繁交流，又出现了横吹（现在的笛）、羌笛（羌族的笛子，即现在的箫）、筚（现在的管子）、铜鼓、腰鼓等，这些都成为现代民族管弦乐器中的重要乐器。

五代、宋、元、明、清时期，由于民间文艺的兴起又增加了云锣、八角鼓、点鼓、小木鱼、梆子等打击乐器，唢呐等吹奏乐器，三弦、扬琴等弹拨乐器以及二胡、板胡、京胡、坠胡等拉弦乐器，乐器品种更为齐全。

同乐器一样，中国的器乐合奏在古代也很发达。在古代历史上，最有影响的乐队是汉代的鼓吹乐队和唐代的燕乐乐队。鼓吹乐以吹奏乐器和打击乐器为主，而燕乐乐队善于演奏细腻文雅的音乐。

不同朝代首都的所在地往往是音乐传播的中心，也是管弦乐队和音乐大师聚集的中心。例如，西安鼓乐始于作为唐朝首都的长安，开封大相国寺音乐出现于作为北宋首都的开封，北京智化寺音乐和河北管乐与北京曾是辽、金、元、明、清这几个朝代的首都有关系。离北京不远的河北省承德市是清朝皇帝的避暑山庄，当地的音乐艺术家现在还能演奏当时的宫廷音乐。因此不难理解为什么有这么多农民音乐家有如此高的音乐造诣，这是中国民族音乐史的一个重要组成部分。

2. 代表性民族乐器

1）曾侯乙编钟——“国之瑰宝”

曾侯乙是战国时期的一个诸侯，从其墓中出土的墓葬物品规模相当可观，仅仅乐器就足以令人瞠目结舌，其中最令人震惊的就是堪称“国之瑰宝”的编钟。

整套编钟上下三层（见图 17－1），共有 65 枚，全部由青铜铸造，异常精美。每件钟体上都镌刻有金篆体铭文，正面均刻有“曾侯乙乍（作）持”或“曾侯乙乍（作）持用终”。

曾侯乙编钟的总音域可以跨五个八度，仅次于现代的钢琴。现代学者推断这套编钟不但可以演奏旋律，还可以演奏和声。

曾侯乙墓出土的所有乐器，制作工艺精美，音乐效果惊人，尤其是编钟，是中国古代音乐史上的一个奇迹。

2）坠胡——能说会唱的乐器

坠胡(一种拉弦乐器)是由小三弦改制的，又名坠琴或坠子。这种乐器既能独奏又能合奏，它的音域非常宽，声音柔和，音量也比较大，与别的乐器有所不同的是它可以惟妙惟肖地模仿人唱歌说话的声音，甚至鸟兽的叫声等。

关于坠胡的起源有一个传说。在清代的康熙年间，皇帝下御旨，撤掉宫廷戏班，艺人们便流落到民间卖艺。有一天，一个艺人的小三弦被老鼠咬坏了蒙皮，可是马上就要演出了，情急之下，这位艺人就用薄薄的桐木板代替，又把胡琴的弓子夹在两根弦中间拉奏。于是，一个既可演奏乐曲，又近似人声的乐器就诞生了——这就是坠胡。

3）骨笛——中国最早的乐器

现在的乐器五花八门，中式乐器，西式乐器，特色乐器，吹的、拉的、弹的、打的、刮奏的，真是不计其数。但是最早的乐器是骨笛(见图 17－2)。20 世纪 80 年代，中国发现了距今有 8 000 到 9 000 年之久的笛子——骨笛！1986 年到 1987 年在河南省(中国中部)舞阳县贾湖村新石器遗址发掘出了随葬的骨头制成的笛子。目前，贾湖遗址中出土的骨笛达 30 多支，比较完整的有 6 支，其中 3 支七孔笛分别珍藏于北京故宫博物院、河南博物院和河南省文物研究所。这是迄今发现的最古老、完整、仍可吹奏的多调乐器。

4）柳琴——小琵琶

柳琴(见图 17－3)声音很像曼陀林。柳琴用拨片弹奏，主要用于民歌和地方剧种中为其他乐器伴奏。

因其音箱形状像柳叶，所以叫柳琴或柳叶琴，俗名土琵琶、金刚腿，是苏北鲁南一带的柳琴戏及安徽泗州戏的主要伴奏乐器。

民间柳琴用柳木制作。原来的柳琴是二弦或三弦、七品，用拨子弹奏。经过多次改革，专业柳琴用檀香木或红木制作，琴拨同吉他弦拨，塑料制。而现代柳琴前半部用桐木制造，后半部用红檀木，将二弦七品改为四弦二十四品，依半音排列，扩大了音域，便于转调；又将弦改为钢丝弦，增大了音量，使音色更加优美。柳琴琴拨用牛角制，发音刚劲清脆，锐利明亮。

5）磬——最古老的打击乐器

磬(见图 17－4)，是中国古代的石制打击乐器(也有用玉石雕刻成的)，悬挂在架子之上，用木槌敲击。磬不仅是乐器，还是权力和地位的象征。

根据文献记载，磬起源于中国人的祖先在日常生活经常用的一些片状的石制工具。他们在长期的生产过程中，发现这些工具能发出悦耳的声音，于是将它们当作娱乐的乐器使用。

考古学家们发现中国早在夏代(距今 4 300 多年)就有了这种乐器。到了周代，常有十几个大小成组的磬，每一个演奏不同的音调，这种磬被称为“编磬”。

6）二胡——民族管弦乐队的皇后

二胡(见图 17－5)音色优美迷人，是中国最普遍的弓弦乐器，已有一千多年历史。

被称作“中国的小提琴”的二胡，与西方的提琴结构造型区别很大。垂直的琴杆是支撑琴弦、接指操作的重要支柱。琴杆底部的琴筒是二胡的共鸣箱，由木或竹制成，一端蒙蟒蛇皮。二胡的拉弓夹于两弦之间拉奏。过去二胡大多用丝弦，现在钢丝弦的使用日益普遍。演奏时通常将二胡置于左大腿根部，水平方向拉动琴弦之间的琴弓，音响来源于琴弦的振动。

二胡的音域跨 3 个八度，演奏效果可以与小提琴相媲美。音质略带鼻音，但是温婉而坚定。二胡声近似人声，可模拟自然界的许多声音，如鸟鸣和马蹄声等。二胡表现力丰富，能演奏忧思的曲调，也能演奏欢快的乐曲。

二胡在民乐队中是不可缺少的。事实上，二胡在民族管弦乐团中的作用相当于小提琴在西洋管弦乐团中的作用。它既能表现传统音乐，又能演奏当代音乐；既能用于独奏，也是合奏中不可替代的乐器。

7）笛子——竹笛

笛子是中国的土产，历史悠久，源远流长。早在战国时期就很流行，在湖南长沙马王堆三号墓出土的文物中，就有两支笛类乐器。

横吹的笛子上有一个吹奏孔、一个笛膜孔和六个按音孔。竹子遍于乡野，而且竹笛易于制作，因此流传很广。

民间常用的笛子有两种，梆笛和曲笛。流行于北方的梆笛因为其给梆子腔伴奏而得名。梆笛长 40 厘米，声音非常清脆、嘹亮，擅长演奏一些欢乐的曲子，具有中国北方粗犷豪放的风格。曲笛流传于南方，因其是为昆曲伴奏的主要乐器而得名。由于这种曲笛产于苏州所以也叫苏笛。曲笛大约有 70 厘米长，声音柔和清新，甜美圆润，具有南方细腻、委婉的风格。

笛子的演奏技巧多样，有打音、叠音、连音、花舌、强音、滑音、颤音和弦外音等，表现力极其丰富。著名的笛子曲目有《喜相逢》《鹧鸪飞》《荫中鸟》《五梆子》和《姑苏行》等。

8）古琴——中国音乐文化的代表

古琴(见图 17－6)也叫七弦琴，琴身为一狭长木制音箱，一般长 130 厘米、宽 20 厘米、厚大约 5 厘米。面板用桐木或杉木，上有七弦。背板用梓木，下面有大小两个出音孔。大孔为“龙池”，小孔名“凤沼”。琴身通常为黑色，但也有少数用棕色或红色。琴的面板上有 13 个小圆徽，玉制或金制，用来标记音的位置。

琴、棋、书、画是中国古代文人的四个朋友，其中所谈到的琴，就是现代所说的古琴。古琴体现了中国传统文化价值的清、精、简和远。在中国历史上，著名的哲学家和艺术家如孔子、蔡永和嵇康都会弹奏古琴。古代大量关于古琴的论述和数千首古琴曲都被保存流传了下来。

近年来涌现出一批古琴演奏家。他们的演奏不仅表现出精湛的技艺，而且体现了对古琴曲的深刻理解和欣赏。

9）箜篌——中国的竖琴

箜篌(见图 17－7)，又名坎侯，是中国古老的弹拨乐器。箜篌有三种样式，卧箜篌、竖箜篌、凤首箜篌。远在春秋战国之时，中国南方楚国就已有了卧箜篌的雏形。箜篌最初用于雅乐，在汉代用于清商乐。隋代用于燕乐，并逐步流行于民间和少数民族地区。

东汉时期竖箜篌由波斯经西域传入中国，盛行于隋唐时代，一般多用于仪仗音乐中。凤首箜篌在东晋时经天竺传入中国中原地区，在中国隋唐时代使用广泛。

箜篌，音色明亮、音域宽广，不仅能演奏旋律，也能演奏和弦，在独奏与合奏中有着很多优越性，是中国古代皇室中不可缺少的乐器。从中国大同云冈石窟的浮雕上和敦煌壁画中的许多乐舞场面都可以看到弹奏箜篌的人像，可见在中国流传之广、之久。

10）琵琶——具有丰富表现力的乐器

琵琶(见图 17－8)最早出现于秦朝。细长的琴颈、皮革的表面、圆形的音箱，竖抱着弹奏。秦末汉初，琵琶经历了数次改良，衍生出了阮、三弦和月琴等近亲乐器。琵琶的这些不同形式都有两个共同点，即直琴颈和圆音箱。

琵琶经历了两大变革，一是由横弹改为竖弹，二是由拨片弹改为五指弹。由于人们弹奏琵琶的历史悠久，积累了大量的曲目和演奏技法。二十世纪，在许多表演艺术家和作曲家的不懈努力下，出现了大量新的技巧和作品。琵琶现在是民乐独奏、伴奏和合奏中的重要乐器。

11）太平鼓——特色乐器

太平鼓流行于东北地区、内蒙古、河北和安徽等地，是汉族、满族、蒙古族等民族经常使用的特色乐器。太平鼓的历史由来已久，相传在唐朝就已存在。到了明代，民间开始固定其名称为“太平鼓”。

民间传说太平鼓最早是满族人打猎的用具。猎人们在围剿猎物时，一边敲鼓一边围追，在缴获了猎物以后又边击鼓边载歌载舞，来表达人们喜悦的心情。

太平鼓在各族都有不同特点。满族的鼓是椭圆形，汉族的鼓有圆形、桃形和扁圆形，而内蒙古（中国北方）的鼓只有扁圆形。人们在舞蹈时也使用太平鼓，经常配合舞蹈，边敲边舞，尤其是喜庆节日，更是鼓乐喧天、热闹非常。

12）埙——最古老的乐器之一

乐器中唯一用土制作的是埙（见图 17-9）。埙是中国古代很重要的一种吹奏乐器，它有近似人声的音色，很擅长演奏一些抒情的哀婉曲调。在中国古代人们用这种乐器（当时是捕鸟的工具）模仿鸟叫，用来诱捕鸟兽。

目前发现最为古老的埙是在 6 000 多年前，比如浙江杭州湾河姆渡出土的圆锥形埙。西安半坡村仰韶文化遗址的无孔埙和一孔埙。而在山西万荣县、甘肃玉门火烧沟、河南辉县等地均有发现埙。

13）扬琴——洋为中用的琴

扬琴（见图 17-10）是击奏弦鸣乐器，相传扬琴起源于西亚，公元 11 世纪时传入欧洲。明代晚期扬琴传入中国，始称“洋琴”，流传至今已 300 余年，成为中国重要的民族乐器。

传统扬琴经近代中国扬琴演奏家和乐器制造家的不断改进，扩大了音域，提高了和谐度，增加了音量和厚度，美化了音色。加上专业演奏技巧的发展使得这一传统乐器更具备丰富的音乐表现力，成为乐团中举足轻重的独奏、重奏、合奏与伴奏乐器。

Exercises

Section A Thought-provoking questions

1. How are Chinese musical instruments divided?
2. What do silk instruments include?
3. Can you name the instruments included in the wind instruments category?
4. What do you know about Chinese percussion instruments?
5. What is the role of the musical instruments of the ethnic minorities?

Section B Fill in the blanks with the names of the musical instruments

1. The ________ is a dulcimer played using a pair of bamboo mallets rubberized on one end.
2. The ________ is a soprano range lute. It looks similar to the *pipa* but smaller with two sound holes on each side of the body.
3. Like *pipa* players, ________ players also have to wear synthetic nails, sometimes on both hands depending on the requirements of the piece.

4. A ________ is somewhat similar to the Western orchestral harp. Therefore, sometimes a Western harp is used as a substitute when it is not available.
5. The tone produced by ________ is loud, piercing and uplifting, thus it is usually used to perform vibrant and lively pieces.
6. ________ instruments produce sound by striking on the surface.
7. The ________, or Chinese gong, is made of high-tin bronze, hammered into the shape of a sifter.
8. The ________, mostly made of mulberry, was used originally to accompany Buddhist chants only. Since the Qing dynasty the instrument has appeared in folk ensembles.
9. The ________ means "gourd silk". "Gourd" is the material making the instrument while "silk" refers to its silky tone.
10. ________ is a musical instrument with five or six pipes of different pitches, played by such ethnic groups as the Dong and the Miao.

※ **The most important thing in governing is to utilize revenue intelligently and avoid waste.**

From *Analects of Confucius*

(政在节财。)

——《论语》

※ **In guiding a large country, serve respectfully and be trustworthy. Spend frugally and care for the people. And employ the people at appropriate times.**

From *Analects of Confucius*

(道千乘之国,敬事而信,节用而爱人,使民以时。)

——《论语》

Chapter 18

Appreciation of Chinese Folk Music

中国民族音乐

1. Famous Folk Music Pieces

1) *One Hundred Birds Serenade the Phoenix*

One of the best-known pieces of *suona* is *One Hundred Birds Serenad the Phoenix* (*Bainiao Chaofeng*), especially popular in Shandong and Anhui provinces in East China and Henan and Hebei provinces in the north. It is also an ensemble of traditional wind instruments. In the music, the orchestra settles down to a fixed accompaniment mode after a spirited introduction. With the background of the accompaniment, the *suona* section plays a vigorous piping tune in imitation of the chirping of birds in flight. The closeness of the mimicry expresses the people's love for nature and the careful observation of life by folk artists, as well as their virtuosity in performance. Such beautiful and auspicious tunes help to account for its the popularity.

The *suona* horn is the most widespread and popular folk musical instrument in northwest China. In shape, it is like a trumpet. It is conical with eight holes, seven forward and one at the back. The body part is made of wood. At one end there is a thin brass tube with a reed attachment and flares like a trumpet. Its sound is loud, bright and vigorous, especially good for expressing joy and creating a festive atmosphere.

2) *A Beautiful Moonlit Night by the River in Springtime*

This is one of the most famous Chinese traditional music pieces. It had been popular among ordinary people before the year 1875, and has become one of the masterpieces in the treasury of Chinese classical music.

Originally named as *Drums at Dusk* or *Xunyang Pipa Tune*, the music is a solo piece played by the *pipa*. It got its recent name from Zheng Jinwen, a famous folk musician, in 1930 after undergoing some adaptations. Since 1949 it has undergone many revisions until it becomes a highly polished piece now.

A Beautiful Moonlit Night by the River in Springtime (*Chunjiang Huayueye*) has been played thousands of times and is loved by millions. With gracefulness and romantic imagination, the music depicts the picturesque scene from a small boat on the river in the moonlight.

The intro has a background of musical harmony, and then a *pipa* is plucked faster and faster, producing drumbeat-like notes. The whole work is divided into ten sections, each under a different title. The understated melody, the fluid rhythmical meter and the ingenious subtlety of orchestration, combine to show a tranquil scene of a river on a moonlit night in spring, paean of praise to the beauty of the countryside south of the Yangtze River.

3) ***The Moon Reflected in Erquan Spring***

The most widespread music piece of *erhu* in China is *The Moon Reflected in Erquan Spring* (*Erquan Yingyue*) composed by the Wuxi folk artist Ah Bing, whose original name was Hua Yanjun. The work has two themes which gradually melt into each other subtly and smoothly. Step by step and variation upon variation, the two themes rise and fall effortlessly. The crescendos especially show the composer's steely and unyielding spirit in a very hard situation.

The profound range of feeling in this piece of music is incorporated by a tightly knit composition. The result of vigorous variations in bowing technique and the full use of the five hand positions is a fiercely emotional expression of the composer's suppressed grief at having tasted the full bitterness of life in the old society. *The Moon Reflected in Erquan Spring* is an exquisite example of a Chinese instrumental folk music piece. The world-famous Japanese conductor Ozawa Seiji was moved to tears when listening to this music piece and said "The most suitable term for describing this music piese is'the sense of heartbreak'.The music is so touching that one should kneel down to listen to it."

4) ***High Mount and Flowing Water***

During the Spring and Autumn Period, there was a man called Yu Boya, who was a famous music master with a good command of the temperament and superb skills in playing the *guqin*.

On the night of a mid-autumn day, the 15th day of the 8th lunar month one year, Boya was doing sightseeing. The moon was bright and a brisk breeze was blowing gently. With myriads of thoughts welling up in his mind, he went into a nearby pavilion and began to play the *guqin*, which he carried wherever he went. The melodious music was so beautiful that it attracted a woodcutter who came and sat down to listen. When Boya played a piece of music eulogizing the high mountains, the woodcutter said, "Wonderful! The melody is as magnificent and dignified as Mount Tai which reaches the sky!" When he played a piece of music depicting the turbulent waves, the woodcutter was very much immersed in the music and exclaimed, "Wonderful! The melody is as vast and mighty as the great rivers!" Boya knew that this man was keenly appreciative of his talents because he understood his music and his moods. They became very good friends and made an appointment — meeting again at the same time the next year. That woodcutter was Zhong Ziqi.

The next year, Boya went to meet Zhong Ziqi. He waited and waited but Zhong did not turn up. Later Boya found out that Zhong had passed away. Boya was so sad that he broke the strings and threw away the Guqin and quit playing forever.

The music played by Boya in the story is *High Mount and Flowing Water* (*Gaoshan Liushui*). It is later divided into two parts, one is *High Mountains*, and the other *Flowing Water*. It is still played now.

America sent out two spacecrafts ("Voyager 1" and "Voyager 2") on August 20,1977. Expecting to meet humankind in other planets, the spacecraft carried a gold-painted bronze record consisting of 27 pieces of world famous music. *Flowing Water* was chosen to represent Chinese music in the CD. Therefore, *High Mount and Flowing Water* is the first Chinese music piece in the outer space.

5) *The Butterfly Lovers*

Almost everyone in China can hum a few lines of the violin concerto *The Butterfly Lovers* (*Liang Shanbo and Zhu Yingtai*, abbreviated as *Liangzhu*), which can be traced to a Chinese folk legend with the same title.

In South China, there was a village called Zhujiazhuang. In the village there was a beautiful and clever girl named Zhu Yingtai who assumed a male identity so she could travel to study in Hangzhou, a southeastern city in China, where she met Liang Shanbo, a poor but kind-hearted young man. In the course of their 3-year study, Zhu and Liang became very close friends. When the time came for Zhu to return home, the pair was overcome with much suppressed sadness. Zhu proposed marriage to Liang for her younger sister and said her sister closely resembled her. She even entreated Liang to visit her home to discuss the issue with her parents. Liang was unaware that Zhu was female nor that she did not have a younger sister. (She was, in fact, offering her own hand in marriage.)

A year passed before Liang made his way to Zhu's residence. He was overjoyed to realize Zhu's true identity and that she was in love with him. However, happiness turned into sorrow as the two soon discovered that Zhu had been betrothed to another man. Upon his return to Hangzhou, Liang fell ill in his great misery and died. When Zhu heard of this on her wedding day, she fled from the wedding and went to his grave site. There, legend has it that her tears moved the heavens so much that the clouds themselves shed tears over Zhu's grief. Then, the earth beneath her cracked open and Zhu jumped into the open grave. Miraculously, the pair was transformed into butterflies. Arising into the sky, they fluttered and danced side by side among the flowers, never to be separated again.

The Butterfly Lovers (*Liangzhu*) was composed in 1959 by He Zhanhao and Chen Gang, who were studying at the Shanghai Conservatory of Music. The pair was exploring the feasibility of setting Chinese music to a western symphonic medium and incorporating borrowed devices from Chinese folk theatrical music as well as vocal techniques of Zhejiang's Yu Opera. The result was a concerto for the violin in one movement.

The music of *Liang Zhu*, or *The Butterfly Lovers*, romantic and touching, is most popular in China. It is also one of the few Chinese pieces that have often appeared on the international stage.

6) *Meihua Sannong*

Meihua Sannong is one of the earliest and most famous pieces of Chinese ancient music. Its origin went back to as early as the Eastern Jin Dynasty, in which period lived a famous general and musician named Huan Yi. Huan was a heroic General and a humble man. He knew music very well and was especially good at paying the flute. One day, he met a young man named Wang Huizhi, who admired Huan very much and invited him to play one piece of the *dizi* (bamboo flute) music. To the young man's surprise and delight, Huan accepted the invitation with no hesitation. What he played was *Meihua Sannong*, the most popular melody in that period.

Generally speaking, *Sannong* means the repetition of main melondy three times, in different musical forms. The slow tempo depicts the pure and noble peacefulness of the plum blossoms, and the rapid tempo represents the way the flowers sway in the wind showing their fearlessness of the severe cold. The whole piece deseribes the manner of the dauntless plum blossms that are fighting against the snow and frost. The ancient Chinese scholars' loftiness and self-admiration of their own purity find expression in the extolling of plum blossms in this music piece.

With time passing by, *Meihua Sannong* is fairly common with other kinds of musical instruments and this elegant melody is now one of the repertoires of the *guqin* music.

7) *Ambush on All Sides*

Ambush on All Sides (*Shimian Maifu*) is a famous ancient *pipa* score of China, which is always played on international concerts. A foreigner might be familiar with it just as a Chinese with the *Blue Danube*.

Ambush on All Sides pictured the battlefield of the ancient war in China. Its boldness and majesty have attracted lots of people. How amazing it is to demonstrate such a vivid picture by the *pipa* merely with four strings! We can hear drum beating and horse roaring which will bring us in the midst of the ancient battle.

What the *pipa* solo describes is the whole process of the decisive battle of Gaixia, a well-known battle between Chu and Han in 202 B.C.

According to historical records, this melody was already popular among the Chinese people before the 16th century. As early as the end of the 16th century, there was already written record of *Ambush on All Sides*. It is a treasure of the ancient historical scores of China.

8) *Adios at Yangguan*

Adios at Yangguan (*Yangguan Sandie*), a piece of music played with the *guqin*, is based on a poem written by Wang Wei, a famous poet in the Tang Dynasty.

Wang Wei wrote the poem when he saw off his friend Yuan Er who was to serve in the army at Weicheng, a small town in Yangguan at the border. Instrument players made it a see-off song based on Wang's farewell poem. It has become a masterpiece. Even today, some people would sing this song when they see off friends.

9) *Dance of the Yi People*

Dance of the Yi People (*Yizu Wuqu*), composed by Wang Huiran in 1960, is a classical *pipa* composition that airs a sense of happy life. This piece combines the spirit of the folk tradition and the best use of the *pipa* technique, which becomes the model for contemporary *pipa* compositions.

The 1st part is the introduction in which the music is slow and then it becomes faster. When listening to the music, we cannot help imagining that we are right there in a Yi people's village bathing in the tender moonlight.

In the 2nd part, the nice slow melody is beautiful and intoxicating. It is so soft, light and tender, giving us an impression of dancing Yi girls.

In the 3rd, 4th, 5th and 6th parts, the melody is more rapid and powerful and makes us think of bold and handsome Yi lads. Then the music tends to be tender, depicting the beautiful Yi maids who are like fairies coming from the heaven to join the lads in the dancing.

In the 7th, 8th and 9th parts, it's the reappearance of the first part to show that make people are filled with great happiness. Then the music fades away slowly, presenting a picture in which people are going back home after the happy gathering, losing themselves in the shadowy distance, accompanied by the sound of the music produced by the *lusheng* far away.

2. Historical Figures and Folk Music

1) Cai Yan and *Eighteen Songs on a Nomad Flute*

Eighteen Songs on a Nomad Flute (*Hujia Shibapai*) leaves its landmark in the history of Chinese *guqin* music. Its composer, Cai Yan, showed her musical talent at an early age. Yan had an ear for music. When she was only 7 or 8 years old, her extraordinarily acute hearing and distinguished music sense to identify the notes of different strings of the *guqin* surprised her father Cai Yi, a famous musician.

At the end of Han Dynasty, the society was chaotic with wars. When the Huns invaded the Central Plains, Cai Yan was captured and taken to the remote northern grassland of the Huns. The king of the Huns was deeply attracted by her artistic talent.

Cai became the king's wife and they had a son and a daughter. But year after year, Cai never stopped missing her hometown in the Central Plains. Finally the Huns were driven out of the Central Plains and Cai Yan was redeemed by Cao Cao and allowed to go home to help her old father sort out his scholar works. Tortured by parting from her husband and her children, Cai composed the famous melody *Hujia Shibapai*, a perfect reflection of her rough life and how she missed her children. Until now, this famous melody is still one of the repertoires of *guqin* concerts.

2) Cai Yi and Tail-Burnt Guqin

Among the Four Famous *Guqin* in Chinese music history, the one named Tail-burnt has its interesting legend.

Cai Yi, an outstanding historian and musician in the Han Dynasty, once found that a person was feeding a piece of paulownia wood to the fire to cook his meal. To everyone's surprise, Cai dragged the wood out of the fire with bare hands. He distinguished the fire on the wood, observed it carefully and exclaimed: "What a pity! What a pity!" The man was confused. Cai Yi then explained that paulownia wood was the first-class material to make *guqin*. The man said: "I see. If you like it, take it." Cai happily took the wood home and made a refined *guqin* with part of the burnt wood at its tail and named it Tail-burnt *guqin*.

3) Confucius Learning Music

Confucius, the greatest ancient Chinese thinker and educator in the Spring and Autumn Period, was also an outstanding musician. Confucius not only could play many kinds of musical instruments but also was good at composing and singing.

His valuable modest personality attributed to his achievement in music. After he learned *guqin* from the musician Shi Xiangzi for some days, the instructor said his performance was "good". Confucius, however, was not satisfied with the progress and said: "Although I know how to play the music, I can't play very well". So he kept training himself for a longer time. After practicing for another couple of days, his performance was regarded as "very well" by the instructor, but Confucius still did not believe that he had given a perfect performance because he could not feel the spirit of the melody when he was playing. It is not until he finally realized and showed the inner spirit of the melody that Confucius was satisfied. His perseverance deeply touched Shi Xiangzi. Even today, Confucius's idea of "Being insatiable in learning and tireless in teaching" is still regarded as a motto by most people.

4) Liu Sanjie, the Fairy Singer

Liu Sanjie (Third Sister Liu) and her stories are very popular among the Zhuang people in southwest Guangxi Zhuang Autonomous Region. According to the local tale, Liu Sanjie was born in a village along the Liujiang River of Guangxi in the Tang Dynasty. She was not only beautiful but also good at singing folk songs. At the age of

17, Liu Sanjie fell in love with a handsome young man who was also a good folk singer. The two lovers swore that they would never separate in their lives. The peaceful happiness was, however, broken by a hooligan in the village who had been for a long time attracted by Sanjie's beauty. This evil man decided to get her by force. He got his chance on a moonlight night when Sanjie and her lover were sitting on a big rock at riverside to appreciate the beauty of the moon. Suddenly, a gang of hooligans surrounded them. Sanjie and her lover had no way to escape. With no hesitation, the couple jumped into the roaring Liujiang River, hand in hand. Nowadays, on the day of March 3, local people will gather along the riverside of the Liujiang River, organizing a folk-song competition to mourn Liu Sanjie.

5) Suhe and the Horse-Headed Stringed Instrument

The top of the neck of the horse-headed stringed instrument (*matouqin*) is carved in the shape of a horse's head, hence the name. It is the representative instrument of the horse-riding Mongolian people.

The instrument has two strings and it is played with a horsetail-hair bow. The sound box is trapezoid in shape, and decorated with ethnic motifs. Its hazy tone color is suitable for expressing soft and mellow moods. Its haunting melodies can often be heard on the vast Mongolian grasslands.

Besides its unique enchantment of the tone, *matouqin* has its interesting legend associated with it. Long ago, there lived a robust young man in the Mongolian grassland. The young man was named Suhe and he was a good folk singer. When he sang, one of his white horses would neigh along with the melody of its master as if accompanying his singing. Its sound was very pleasant. Suhe liked his horse very much and they two thus became good friends. Wherever Suhe went, the horse followed. In a horse race, this white horse helped Suhe win the first prize. The landlord, however, also wanted to have this magical horse and finally succeeded in holding the horse as his own by force.

The white horse missed his former master so much that one day it escaped from the cruel landlord. Although it got the deadly shot of a poisonous arrow from the landlord, the horse kept running until it fell at the feet of Suhe. Suhe was very sad. He caressed the horse and wept. In memory of the white horse, Suhe made a musical instrument with the remains of the horse: its head bone as the sound box and the tail as the bow, and decorated it with a carved horse head. This is the first *matouqin*.

Word Bank

serenade	唱(奏)小夜曲	myriad	极大数量的
accompaniment	伴奏	eulogize	称赞,颂扬
mimicry	模仿,模拟(表演)	entreat	恳求
virtuosity	(音乐演技方面)精湛技巧	concerto	协奏曲
flare	(声音等的)爆发	repertoire	保留曲目
pluck	弹奏(弦乐)	score	乐谱,配乐
paean	赞美	paulownia	泡桐
crescendo	(音)渐强,向(高潮)渐进	insatiable	不知足的
steely	坚强的	trapezoid	不规则四边形,梯形

参考译文

1. 著名乐曲赏析

1)《百鸟朝凤》

《百鸟朝凤》是一首非常著名的唢呐曲,也是民间管乐的合奏曲,流行于中国东部的山东和中国北部的河南、河北等地区。乐曲在百鸟齐鸣的引子后是一段欢快的旋律,在这种旋律中,唢呐演奏的声音生动也模仿了各种飞禽的啼鸣。乐曲表现了人们对大自然的热爱,也体现出民间音乐家作曲家细致的生活观察和精湛的演奏艺术。乐曲美妙,寓意吉祥,因此这首民间乐曲很受听众欢迎。

唢呐是中国西北地区最普遍、最受喜爱的乐器。唢呐状似喇叭,在一锥形木管上开八个音孔,前七后一。木管上端装一细铜管,铜管上端安装一个苇制哨子,为演奏者吹奏所用。唢呐音量洪大有力,音色高亢明亮,尤其适于气氛欢乐的节日。

2)《春江花月夜》

《春江花月夜》是一首著名的中国古典乐曲。早在 1875 年前就已流传在民间,成为中国古典音乐宝库之中的经典作品之一。

这首乐曲原名叫《夕阳箫鼓》(也称《浔阳琵琶》),是一首琵琶独奏曲。后来经过数次更名,1930 年由著名民族音乐家、古琴家郑觐文改名为《春江花月夜》。1949 年以来,乐曲又经历了一系列改进,直到成为现在的形式。

《春江花月夜》已经被演奏了无数次,深受人们喜爱。它是一首抒情写意的乐曲,通过典雅温婉的曲调,描绘了月夜江上归舟的自然美景。

乐曲的引子歌调和谐,随后琵琶由慢而快地模拟阵阵低沉的鼓声。全曲共分为十个小节,每一节都有不同的标题。委婉的旋律、多变的节奏、巧妙的配器,共同描绘了一幅宁静的春江月夜之景,赞美了江南乡村的秀美。

3)《二泉映月》

二胡名曲《二泉映月》是中国无锡民间艺人阿炳(原名华彦钧)遗留下来的名作。乐曲属于双主题变奏曲式，两个主题音调及它们的变体不断地反复展开，跌宕起伏，相互交融，然后音乐渐强，表现了作者在逆境中坚强不屈的精神。

作品以紧凑的结构表达了丰富的情感。乐曲演奏中二胡弓法的变化和五个把位的充分利用，强烈地表达了作曲家饱尝人间痛苦后压抑在心头的悲愤情绪。《二泉映月》是中国民族乐曲的经典例子。世界著名指挥家小泽征尔先生听了这段乐曲后感动得热泪盈眶，他动情地说："用断肠之感形容真是再合适不过了，这首乐曲应该跪下来听。"

4)《高山流水》

春秋时期有一位著名的音乐家叫俞伯牙，弹得一手好琴。

一个中秋之夜，伯牙在游览河山。圆月和轻风引得伯牙心潮澎湃，于是就走到附近的一个亭子里取下琴袋开始弹起琴来。这时有一个樵夫路过此地，看见伯牙在弹琴，于是就坐在一旁静静地听。当伯牙的弹奏意在描写巍峨耸立的高山时，坐在一旁的樵夫自言自语地感叹："善哉乎鼓琴，巍巍乎若泰山。"当伯牙意在流水时，樵夫沉醉在音乐之中，又自言自语地说："善哉乎鼓琴，汤汤乎若流水。"伯牙所弹的乐曲意境，所寄托的情感，他都能心领神会，伯牙知道遇见了知音。二人一见如故，结为知交。约定第二年此时再相会。樵夫名钟子期。

第二年，伯牙如期赴约，可是总不见子期到来。后来伯牙打听到原来子期已经故去。伯牙悲痛欲绝，绝望之中当即弄断琴弦，摔坏宝琴，从此不再弹琴。

这个故事中伯牙弹的乐曲就是《高山流水》。后来分为《高山》、《流水》两部分。这个曲子几经流传直到现在还在演奏。

1977 年 8 月 20 日，美国发射了两艘"航行者"太空船，科学家希望有朝一日能有幸遇到地球以外的"人类"，因此在太空船上有一张喷金铜唱片，唱片上共录有 27 段世界名曲，其中代表中国的就是用古琴演奏的这首古曲《高山流水》中的《流水》。因此，《高山流水》成为中国第一首遨游太空的乐曲。

5)《梁山伯与祝英台》

家喻户晓的小提琴协奏曲《梁山伯与祝英台》(简称《梁祝》)所表现的内容来自中国古老的民间传说。

以前在中国南方的村庄里有一个祝家庄。村里有一个美丽聪明的姑娘名叫祝英台，她女扮男装到杭州去求学。在学堂里，她结识了善良淳朴但家境贫寒的书生梁山伯。两人同窗三年，建立了深挚的友情。在学成分别的路上，两人都很伤感。祝英台说想把长相酷似自己的小妹许配给他，请他去她家与她父母商量婚事。可是，老实诚笃的梁山伯却一直没有领悟祝英台的心思，他并不知道祝英台是女子。

直到一年以后梁山伯得知祝英台是个女子才恍然大悟，立即到祝英台家求婚。可是祝英台已经被父亲许配给了一个豪门子弟。这个不幸的消息，如五雷轰顶，击倒了梁山伯。他悲愤而死。祝英台得知这一噩耗，在出嫁的路上来到了梁山伯的坟墓前，向苍天哀诉对梁山伯的思念和自己不幸的命运。祝英台的倾诉感动了上苍，梁山伯的墓突然裂开，祝英台毅然投入墓中，随即两人化作一对美丽的蝴蝶，形影不离，在花丛中上下翻飞，嬉戏其中……

《梁祝》是作曲家何占豪和陈钢于 1959 年创作的。当时，他们是上海音乐学院的青年学生。为探索交响音乐的民族化，选择了这一家喻户晓的民间传说为题材，吸取了越剧中的曲调为素材，成功地创作了这部单乐章小提琴协奏曲。

如今，这首绚丽浪漫的、抒情动人的作品广受国人的喜爱，也是国际舞台上经常演奏的为数不多的中国乐曲之一。

6)《梅花三弄》

《梅花三弄》是中国古代音乐保留下来的比较早而且很有名的一首曲子。关于这首曲子的传说，最早出现在东晋时期。相传东晋时期有一位大将名叫桓伊，他虽是战功赫赫的名将，但非常谦逊。他同时又精通乐律，尤其擅长吹笛子。有一天，桓伊在路上遇见了一个年轻人名叫王徽之，他非常仰慕桓伊的音乐才能，于是斗胆请桓伊吹奏一首曲子。没有想到桓伊欣然应允。他吹的曲子相传就是当时最流行的《梅花三弄》。

泛泛地说，"三弄"是以不同的形式将主旋律反复表现三次。缓慢的节奏用于描写梅花高洁安详的静态，急促的曲调则是表现梅花不畏严寒、迎风摇曳的动态。整首乐曲表现了梅花凌霜傲雪铮铮铁骨的神态。乐曲通过赞颂梅花的高贵品质来烘托文人那种超凡脱俗孤芳自赏的思想境界。

随着时间的推移，人们又用其他的乐器来演奏这首高雅的传世名曲，至今已成为古琴的保留曲目。

7)《十面埋伏》

《十面埋伏》是著名的琵琶古曲，也是民乐团出国演出时的一支必弹曲目。外国人就像中国人熟悉《蓝色的多瑙河》那样熟悉这首乐曲。

这是一首描写古代战争场面的音乐作品。乐曲雄伟的气势、壮观的场面震慑了很多人。琵琶只有四根弦，却能把古战场上的战争场面表现得淋漓尽致，生动地再现了战鼓齐鸣、金戈铁马的决战场景。

传统琵琶古曲《十面埋伏》描写的是一场大战的全过程，取材于公元前 202 年楚汉相争、垓下大战的历史事件。

据史书记载，该乐曲在 16 世纪以前就已广为人知。16 世纪初时已出现了该乐曲的书面记录。《十面埋伏》这首乐曲是中国古代历史宝库中的一件宝物。

8)《阳关三叠》

《阳关三叠》是古琴曲，根据唐朝大诗人王维写的一首诗所创作的。

王维送自己的友人元二去关外服役，最后送到渭城这个地方，依依不舍，并写下了一首送别诗。乐师们在王维送别诗的基础之上创作了这首送别曲，后来成为一首传世佳作，也成为人们送别朋友时的送别歌。

9)《彝族舞曲》

《彝族舞曲》是王惠然 1960 年所作，是一首体现幸福生活场景的琵琶乐曲，融合了民乐传统和琵琶演奏技巧，已成为当代琵琶乐曲的典范作品。

引子(第一部分)由慢到快地展开。聆听着音乐，仿佛看到了在朦胧月色下轻雾缭绕的彝族山寨。

乐曲的第二段是一支优美抒情的慢板旋律，柔美、轻巧、富于弹性，塑造了彝族少女婀娜多姿翩翩起舞的音乐形象。

乐曲的第三、四、五、六段是快板，这段音乐节奏欢快，刚劲有力，它描绘了彝族青年粗犷、热情爽朗的形象和健美剽悍的舞姿。随着音乐逐渐趋向柔和，引出一段优美、抒情、悠扬的旋律，仿佛是彝族美丽的少女们，像天仙一般自天而降，飘然汇入群舞的行列。

乐曲的第七、八、九段，是引子的再现，表现人们心头涌起的无限幸福感。渐渐地乐曲进入尾声，音乐又回到了所描绘的意境，尽兴的人们渐渐远去，只有远方还有芦笙在隐隐吹响……

2. 历史名人与民乐

1) 蔡琰和《胡笳十八拍》

《胡笳十八拍》是流芳百世的古琴名曲，作者蔡琰是一位女音乐家。蔡琰自小就显示了很高的音乐天分，对音乐有很高的悟性和极其敏锐的听力。早在七八岁时，她非凡的敏锐听觉和对古琴的辨音能力使其父惊诧不已。

汉末大乱，连年烽火。匈奴入侵中原时，蔡琰与家人失散，被匈奴掳走。匈奴的左贤王非常欣赏她的艺术才华，就把她留下来做了自己的王妃，并且生了一男一女两个孩子。可是，年复一年，蔡琰在遥远的他乡一直思念自己的故乡。后来，中原终于平定了，曹操用金帛把她赎回，让她回去帮助整理她父亲的文稿。蔡琰又要被迫与儿女离散，生离死别的痛苦折磨着她。她只有寄托于音乐，于是写了著名的词曲《胡笳十八拍》。词曲之音都表达了她坎坷的人生之路以及对儿女刻骨铭心的思念之情。这首名曲至今仍是古琴音乐会的保留曲目。

2) 蔡邕与焦尾琴

中国古代有“四大名琴”之说，其中，蔡邕的焦尾琴有一段有趣的故事。

蔡邕是汉朝末年一个大学问家和出色的音乐家。有一次，蔡邕看见有一个人正在烧火做饭，他忽然发现一块上好的梧桐木正在燃烧，于是不顾火势正猛，连忙把这块木板抽了出来，掸灭上面的火，一边仔细端详着这块烧焦的木头，一边连声说：“可惜，太可惜了”。他这种举动把烧火的人弄懵了。蔡邕解释说：“桐木是做琴的好材料。”烧火的人笑道：“原来如此！既然您这么喜欢，就拿去好了。”蔡邕高高兴兴地把这块木头拿回家，精心地制作了一张古琴，他把烧焦的部分放在琴的尾部，并给它取了一个极为雅致的名字“焦尾琴”。

3) 孔子学琴

孔子是中国春秋时期著名的思想家、教育家，同时还是一位杰出的音乐家。他会弹奏许多乐器，会作曲、唱歌。

孔子的虚心好学使他在音乐方面颇有造诣。有一次孔子随师襄子学古琴。孔子苦练多日，师襄子说：“可以了。”孔子却不满足，他又练了很多日子，师襄子又说：“可以了，你已于其数。”可是孔子仍说：“不可以，未得其志。”他反复钻研、直到体会琴曲的内涵才罢休。他的钻研精神深深地感动了师襄子。直到现在，许多人仍将孔子的名言“学而不厌，诲人不倦”作为座右铭。

4) 歌仙刘三姐

提起歌仙刘三姐，广西壮族的乡亲们无人不知，无人不晓。她生于唐朝，是广西壮族人，生活在柳江流域。她不仅人长得漂亮，歌也唱得好。刘三姐 17 岁那年爱上了一位英俊小伙子，也是一个唱歌能手。两人私订终身。然而好景不长，村里的一个恶霸对刘三姐的美貌垂涎多时，决意要把刘三姐抢到手。一个月光皎洁的晚上，刘三姐正和心上人坐在柳江边的岩石上看月亮，倾诉衷肠，忽然，一群恶棍包围了他们。刘三姐和小伙子望望无路可走的高山，又望望柳江，两人手拉着手毅然双双跳进了波涛滚滚的柳江里。人们怀念这位民间歌手，因而每年三月三这天，村民都会到柳江边上赛歌，悼念刘三姐。

5) 苏和与马头琴

马头琴的名称来自乐器本身，因为乐器的顶端有一个端庄生动的马头雕像而得名。马头琴是爱好骑马的蒙古族的代表乐器。

马头琴有两根弦，琴弓以马尾制作。音箱为四边形，上面装饰的图案颇具民族风格。马头琴朦胧的音色适合表现柔和的心绪，在内蒙古草原上时常能够听到马头琴深沉并带有伤感的旋律。

马头琴除了它的声音具有独特的魅力以外，还有一段动人的传说。相传在很早很早以前，在中国内蒙古草原上有一个健壮的小伙子叫苏和，歌唱得很好，他的马群里有一匹雪白的高头大马。每当小伙子唱歌时它都在一旁跟着嘶鸣，声音非常悦耳，好像是给小伙子伴奏一样。苏和非常喜爱这匹白马，他和白马成了好朋友。苏和走到哪里，白马都会寸步不离地跟随左右。在一次赛马会上，苏和骑着这匹白马获得冠军，小伙子非常高兴。可是王爷也看上了这匹马，他派了一群打手把白马抢走了。

白马离开了小伙子，日夜思念它的主人，终于有一天白马挣脱缰绳跑了出来，但被王爷的毒箭射中。它仍然坚持着，一直跑到了苏和面前才倒地而死。小伙子流泪了。他哭着抚摸着他的马。为了使白马一直陪伴着他，苏和用白马的头骨做了音箱，把马皮蒙在琴箱上，并用马尾做成了弓子，并根据白马生前的模样，在琴头上雕刻了一个同样的马头，于是就产生了草原上第一把马头琴。

Exercises

Section A　Thought-provoking questions

1. What poem is *A Moonlit Spring Night on the River* based on? Who wrote it?
2. What do you know about the composer of *The Moon Reflected in the Erquan Spring*?
3. What does the expression "like moving clouds and flowing water" mean when referring to music?

Section B　Match the music piece with the musical instrument.

1. *Shimian Maifu*	A. *guzheng*
2. *Erquan Yingyue*	B. *suona*
3. *Liangzhu*	C. *pipa*
4. *Yuzhou Changwan*	D. *erhu*
5. *Gaoshan Liushui*	E. *dizi*
6. *Gusuxing*	F. *guqin*
7. *Bainiao Chaofeng*	G. *hulusi*
8. *Liangxiao*	H. *yangqin*
9. *Saima*	I. violin
10. *Yangguan Sandie*	J. *lusheng*

Chapter 19

Chinese Folk Art and Handicraft

中国民间工艺

1. Paper-cutting

Paper-cutting is one of the most popular forms of Chinese traditional folk art. Its materials are easy to get and low in cost. Paper-cuttings not only reflect the aesthetic interest of the folk artists, but also represent the national mentality of Chinese people.

1) History of Paper-cutting

Paper-cuts are patterns cut on paper by scissors or engraving knife. Among the many traditional handicrafts, the history of paper-cutting is very long and can be dated back to Han Dynasty. It became quite popular in Northern and Southern Dynasties and prospered during the Qing Dynasty. Traditional paper-cuts mostly come form rural areas and are made by women in small hamlets of the countryside. Paper-cutting is an art form that is very suitable for country women who can do the cutting whenever they are free from farm work and use it for both practical and decorative purposes.

2) The Use of Paper-cuts

Paper-cuts were used as the ornament of the offerings to sacrifice ancestors and supernatural beings. Nowadays, paper-cuts are mainly used for interior decoration. People paste paper-cuts on walls, doors, windows, poles, mirrors, lamps and lanterns at wedding ceremonies or festivals to beautify the surroundings and enhance the festive atmosphere.

Gift paper-cuts are often seen as decorations on cakes, birthday noodles, eggs and other gifts. In Shandong Province, people attach gift paper-cuts to the symbolic "happy egg" to celebrate a baby's birth. Paper-cuts themselves are popular presents for friends and family. There are some special paper-cuts of traditional design used as patterns for embroidering clothes, shoes, hats, pillowcases, curtains and door curtains.

Chinese paper-cutting is rich in content and usually has symbolic meanings. The auspicious designs symbolize good luck and the avoidance of evil. For example, paper-cut based on Chinene character "福" (see picture 19 - 1) means happiness and luck. The designs of child, lotus and bottle gourd suggest a happy family with a large number of children and grandchildren. Tortoise-patterned paper-cuts symbolize longevity, which are commonly seen in the countryside of Fujian Province. Domestic birds, livestock, fruit, fish and worms are also familiar objects depicted by Chinese folk paper-cutting artists.

3) Regional Features of Paper-cutting

Paper-cutting can be seen all over the country. Different places feature their very unique style, though. Shaanxi window paper-cuts are simple and bold; Hebei and Shanxi paper-cuts are bright in color; Shandong paper-cuts are exquisite and great care is paid to details. Paper-cuts from Jiangsu are delicate and fine; paper-cuts from Guangdong are rich in color and various in cutting techniques. Generally speaking, the paper-cuts of the south are delicate and beautiful and those of the north are bold and straightforward.

2. Chinese Knot

1) Development of Chinese Knot

Chinese people have known how to tie knots with cords ever since they began to learn how to use animal pelts to cover their bodies to keep warm at the end of the Palae Age 70,000 years ago. All sorts of knots have been developed since. As civilization advanced, Chinese people used knots for more than just fastening and wrapping. Some knots were also used to record events, while others had a purely ornamental function.

Traditional Chinese decorative knots, also known as Chinese knots (see picture 19 -2), are typical local arts of China with a very long history. Appeared in ancient time, developed in Tang and Song Dynasties and popularized in Ming and Qing Dynasties, Chinese knot has now become a kind of elegant and colorful arts and crafts from its original practical use.

2) Significance of Chinese Knot

In Chinese, "knot" means reunion, friendliness, warmth, marriage, love, etc. Beside, the Chinese character "结" (knot) is close in pronunciation to "吉" which means anything auspicious including happiness, wealth, longevity, peace and health. Therefore, Chinese knots are often used to express good wishes, including happiness, prosperity, love and the absence of evil. With the pursuit for auspicious things, Chinese knot has been passed down from generation to generation as a folk handicraft with a long history and profound cultural connotations.

The characteristic of Chinese knot is that every knot is made of a single rope and named according to its specific form and meaning. By combining different knots or other auspicious adornments skillfully, a unique auspicious ornament which represents beauty, idea and wishes is formed. For example, "Full of Joy", "Happiness & Longevity", "Double Happiness", "Luck and Auspiciousness as One Wishes" and "Wish You a Fair Wind" are Chinese traditional pleasant phrases expressing warmest regards, best wishes and finest ideal.

The Chinese knot, with its classic elegance in design and ever-changing variations, is both practical and ornamental, fully reflecting the grace and depth of Chinese culture. It is of great significance to inherit this traditional cultural asset.

3) Features of Chinese Knot

The Chinese knot is based on over a dozen basic knots named according to their distinctive shapes, usages, or origins. The Two Coins Knot, for example, is shaped like two overlapping coins once used in ancient China representing double happiness. The Button Knot functions as a button, and the Swastika Knot was derived from the Buddhist symbol.

Almost all basic Chinese knots are symmetrical, which has set certain technical limitations on the design and creation of new patterns and themes. Symmetry is consistent with time-honored ornamental and aesthetic standards in China. Visually, the symmetrical designs are more easily accepted and appreciated by Chinese people.

The knots are pulled tightly together and are sturdy enough to be used for binding or wrapping, making them very practical. Furthermore, the complicated structure of the Chinese knot allows all kinds of variations and enhances its decorative value. Crafting the Chinese knot is a three-step process which involves tying knots, tightening them and adding the finishing touches. Knot-tying methods are fixed, but the tightening can determine the degree of tension in a knot, the length of loops (ears) and the smoothness and orderliness of the lines. Thus, how well a Chinese knot has been tightened can demonstrate the skill and artistic merit of a knot artist. Finishing a knot means inlaying pearls or precious stones, starching the knot into certain patterns, or adding any other final touches.

4) Candidature Logo for Olympic Games

The candidature logo for the 2008 Olympic Games features a stylized traditional Chinese handicraft pattern — "Chinese folk knot". It is known as the "knot of one heart" or, using the typical colors of the five Olympic rings. The design depicts a dynamic human figure in a stance that portrays someone doing "taiji" or shadow boxing. The simple gesture lines symbolize the graceful, harmonious and dynamic movements that connote the unity of, cooperation among, exchange between and development for the peoples all over the world.

3. Kite

Kites were invented by the Chinese people over 2,000 years ago. In the 12th century, Chinese kite spread to the West. Oriental and western kite cultures were formed after years of development. The traditional Chinese culture integrated legends and auspiciousness with the kite craft and finally formed Chinese kite culture with unique characteristics.

1) Development of Kite

Uses of kite have been changed several times in history. According to historical record, kite was first used in military. In the mid Tang Dynasty, the society was stable and peaceful so the use of kites was gradually changed from military to entertainment. With the innovation of papermaking, the raw material of kite changed from silk to paper. Kite became popular among civilians with a richer variety of forms in the Song Dynasty. Participated by the literary, the making and the decoration of kites underwent great development. Due to the great demand, kite making became a profession during that period.

The Ming and Qing Dynasties saw the peak of the development of Chinese kite. The kites underwent great development in size, design, decoration and flying skills. In recent years, kite flying has publicized as a sports activity as well as entertainment.

2) Crafting and Categories of Kites

To make a kite, the right kind of bamboo strips must be selected for the frame first. The regular paper or silk is used to cover the frame. Silk kites, especially, are more durable and generally of higher artistic value.

China has a large area of territory. As a traditional culture and folk art, kite has formed unique style of different regions during its development, among which the most famous ones are the styles of Beijing, Tianjin, Weifang in Shandong Province, Sichuan and Guangdong Province.

Kites could be generally divided into two categories: the Hard Wing and the Soft Wing. The Hard Wing can endure more air pressure and competitively fly higher, whilst the soft wing can fly farther, although it can not fly as high. In patterns, besides the traditional ones of animals, birds, worms, fishes, new patterns of human images emerged in modern times.

3) Poets and Kites

Quite a few men of letters in different dynasties made kites by themselves and sent them to relatives and friends as gifts, regarding it a literary pursuit. There are many classic poems written about kite flying from Tang Dynasty to Qing Dynasty. "Kite" by the Tang poet Gao Pian, "Flying kites" by Li Shizhen, a famous doctor of Chinese traditional medicine of the Ming Dynasty, "Spring" by Guo Lin, a well-known poet of Qing Dynasty, "Song of Jin City" by Yang Xie, the well-known poet of Qing Dynasty, "Country Life" by poet Gao Ding of Qing Dynasty and "Silly Slang" by Wu Haoshan of Qing Dynasty — all vividly and poetically depict the mood, the joyous kids, the delightful scenes of kite-flying.

4. Embroidery Art

The Four Famous Embroideries of China refer to the Su embroidery in eastern

China's Jiangsu Province, Xiang embroidery in central China's Hunan Province, Shu embroidery in western China's Sichuan Province and Yue embroidery in southern China's Guangdong Province.

1) Su Embroidery

With a history of more than 2,000 years, Su embroidery (see picture 19 - 3) is the general name for embroidery products in areas around Suzhou, Jiangsu Province. The craft, which dates back to the Three Kingdoms Period, became a sideline of people in the Suzhou area during the Ming Dynasty when almost every family kept silkworms and did silk embroidery.

Well known for its smoothness and delicateness, Su embroidery won Suzhou the title City of Embroidery in the Qing Dynasty. In the mid and late Qing, Su embroidery experienced further developments with the invention of double-sided embroidering. There were as many as 65 embroidery stores in Suzhou City at that time. During the Republic of China period, the Su embroidery industry was in decline due to frequent wars and it was restored and regenerated after the founding of new China. In 1950, the central government set up research centers for Su embroidery and launched training courses for the study of embroidery. Stitching methods have developed from 18 to the present 40 kinds.

Su embroidery features a strong folk flavor and its needling techniques are characterized by the following: the product surface must be flat, the rim must be neat, the needle must be thin, the lines must be dense, the color must be harmonious and bright and the picture must be even. Su embroidery products fall into three major categories: costumes, decorations for halls and crafts for daily use, which integrate both decorative and practical values. Double-sided embroidery is an excellent representative of Su embroidery.

2) Xiang Embroidery

Xiang embroidery (see picture 19 - 4) is well known for its time-honored history, excellent craftsmanship and unique style. The earliest piece of Xiang embroidery was unearthed at the No.1 Tomb of Mawangdui, Changsha City of the Han Dynasty. The stitching technique was almost the same as the one used in modern times, which demonstrated that embroidery had already existed in the Han Dynasty.

In its later development, Xiang Embroidery absorbed the characteristics of traditional Chinese paintings and formed its own unique characteristics. Xiang embroidery experienced its heyday at the end of the Qing Dynasty and in the early Republic of China (early 20th century), even surpassing Su embroidery. After the founding of the People's Republic of China, Xiang embroidery was further improved and developed to a new level.

Xiang embroidery uses pure silk, hard satin, soft satin and nylon as its material, combined with colorful silk and wool threads. Absorbing the spirit of Chinese paintings, the embroidery reaches a high artistic level. Xiang embroidery crafts include valuable works of art, as well as articles for daily use.

3) Shu Embroidery

Shu embroidery (see picture 19 - 5), also called Chuan embroidery, is the general name for embroidery products in areas around Chengdu, Sichuan Province. Shu embroidery enjoys a long history, too. As early as the Han Dynasty, Shu embroidery was already famous. The central government even designated an office in this area for its administration. During the Five Dynasties and Ten States periods, a peaceful society and large demand helped the rapid development of the Shu embroidery industry.

Shu embroidery experienced its peak development in the Song Dynasty, ranking first in both production and excellence. In the mid-Qing Dynasty, the Shu embroidery industry was formed. After the founding of the People's Republic of China, Shu embroidery factories were set up and the craft entered a new phase of development, using innovative techniques and a larger variety of forms.

Originated among the folk people in the west of Sichuan Province, Shu embroidery has been influenced by the geographical environment, customs and cultures and has formed its own unique characteristics of being smooth, bright and neat. Altogether, there are 122 approaches in 12 categories for stitching. The needling characteristics lie in the even stitches, bright threads, closeness and softness in texture.

The works incorporated flowers, birds, fish, worms and human figures and landscapes, as their themes. Its craftsmanship is a combination of fine arts and practical uses. Its products include quilt facing, pillowcases, clothes, slippers, scrolls, etc.

4) Yue Embroidery

Also called Guang embroidery, Yue embroidery (see picture 19 - 6) is a general name for embroidery products of the regions of Guangzhou, Chaozhou and Shantou, Zhongshan, Fanyu and Shunde in Guangdong Province. According to historical records, in the first year of Yongzhen's reign (805) during the Tang Dynasty, a girl named Lu Meiniang in Nanhai County, Guangdong Province embroidered the seven volumes of the *Fahua Buddhist Scripture* on a piece of thin silk about 30 centimeters long, making Yue embroidery famous all over the country. The prosperous Guangzhou Port of the Song Dynasty promoted the development of Yue embroidery and its products began to be exported. During the Ming Dynasty, folk embroidery artists employed animal hair as the raw material for Yue embroidery, which made the works more vivid. During Qianlong's reign of the Qing Dynasty, the first Yue embroidery industrial organization was established in Guangzhou. At that time, a large number of craftsmen devoted themselves to the craft, inciting further improvements to the stitching technique. Since 1915, the work of Yue embroidery garnered several awards at the Panama Expo.

Influenced by national folk art, Yue embroidery formed its own unique characteristics. The embroidered pictures are mainly of dragons and phoenixes and flowers and birds with neat designs and strong, contrasting colors. Floss, thread and gold-and-silk thread embroidery are used to produce costumes, decorations for halls, hanging screens and works for daily use.

Word Bank

hamlet	小村庄
pelt	兽皮
swastika	卍字饰,万字饰（相传为象征太阳、吉祥等的标志）
candidature	候选者的身份(或资格)
sideline	兼职,副业
heyday	全盛期
satin	缎子
incite	激励,促使
garner	收集,积蓄,得到

参考译文

1. 剪纸

剪纸是中国最普及的民间传统艺术形式之一。剪纸材料易得、成本低廉。剪纸不仅表现了民间艺术家的审美爱好,而且蕴含着民族的社会深层心理。

1) 剪纸的历史

剪纸,就是用剪刀或刻刀把纸剪刻成图形。在众多的传统工艺中,剪纸艺术历史十分悠久,最早可追溯到汉朝,至南北朝时期剪纸技术已发展得相当精熟,然而真正繁盛却是在清朝中期以后。古老的剪纸多在乡间,出自农家妇女之手,趣味纯朴天然。它最适合农村妇女闲暇制作,既可作实用物,又可美化生活。

2) 剪纸的用途

剪纸过去曾被用作祭祀祖先和神仙所用供品的装饰物。现在,剪纸大多用于室内装饰,在婚庆时或节日里贴在墙面、门窗、柱子、镜子以及灯笼上,美化环境,增添节日气氛。

剪纸可为礼品作点缀之用,装饰在蛋糕、生日面、鸡蛋以及其他礼物上。山东人有把剪纸放在庆祝婴儿出生的喜蛋上的风俗。剪纸本身也可作为礼物赠送朋友。剪纸还常作为绣花的纸样,用于服装、鞋帽、枕套、窗帘和门帘上的刺绣花样。

剪纸艺术一般都富有象征意义。吉祥图案寓意吉祥避邪。例如,"福"字(见图 19－1)剪纸意味着幸福和好运,娃娃、莲花、葫芦等象征多子多福。福建农村常以乌龟形象的剪纸象征长寿。

家禽家畜、瓜果鱼虫是农民熟悉的对象，也是农民剪纸艺术家在他们的作品里表现的主要内容。

3）剪纸的地域特色

全国各地都能见到剪纸，而且形成了不同地方的风格流派。陕西窗花风格粗朴豪放；河北和山西剪纸色彩亮丽；山东剪纸细腻精巧；江苏剪纸华丽工整；广东剪纸色彩富丽、手法多变。总的说来，南方剪纸纤巧秀逸，北方剪纸浑厚苍劲。

2. 中国结

1）“中国结”的发展

距今七万年前，旧石器时代的末期，当时的山顶洞人就已经知道使用骨针和线的缝补技巧，将兽皮缝合起来穿在身上蔽体御寒。从此，各式各样的绳结就逐渐发展出来了。随着文明程度的提高，绳结不仅是人们日常生活中的必备用具，同时还具有记载历史的重要功用，有的还用于装饰作用。

“中国结”（见图 19－2）是一种中华民族特有的手工编织工艺品，具有悠久的历史。它起始于远古，发展于唐宋，流行于明清。“中国结”已经由原先的生活实用品发展为制作精巧、配色考究的工艺品。

2）“中国结”的意义

在汉语中，“结”字有团聚、友谊、温暖、婚姻和爱情等意味。“结”又与“吉”谐音，“吉”有着丰富多彩的内容，福、禄、寿、安、康无一不属于吉的范畴。中国结经常被用来表示良好的祝愿，包括幸福、繁荣、爱情和避邪。“绳结”这种具有生命力的民间技艺也就自然作为中国传统文化的精髓，兴盛长远，流传至今。

“中国结”每一个结从头到尾都是用一根丝线编结而成，并根据其形和意来命名。把不同的结饰互相结合在一起，或与其他具有吉祥图案的饰物搭配组合，就形成了造型独特的中国传统吉祥装饰物品，用来代表美丽、理想和心愿。如“吉庆有余”“福寿双全”“双喜临门”“吉祥如意”“一帆风顺”等组配，都表示热烈浓郁的美好祝福，赞颂以及传达衷心至诚的祈求和心愿。

中国结造型典雅，富于变化，既实用又美观，展示了中国文化的雅致与精深。因此，对“中国结”这个传统文化财富的继承和发展是极有意义的。

3）“中国结”的特点

中国结的基本结法有十多种，其名称是根据绳结的状、用途或者原始的出处来命名的。例如，双钱结的形状像两个古铜钱半叠的式样，象征“好事成双”；纽扣结常用以扣紧衣服，因其功能而命名；万字结的结体线条走向如同佛门的标志（卍）。

几乎所有的中国结都是对称形的，符合中国传统的装饰和审美标准。也因为中国结具有紧密对称的特性，所以在感观上容易被人所喜爱。

“中国结”紧实牢固，作为绳结非常实用，而且结构复杂，变化无穷，装饰性强。“中国结”的制作包括三个步骤：打结、抽紧、点缀。打结的方法是固定的，但结的松紧程度决定结的长度和平整程度，也可显示结绳者的技巧和艺术水平。最后完成一件“中国结”艺术品需要添加珍珠或宝石，然后上浆定型。

4）申奥标志

北京申奥标志是一幅中国传统手工艺品图案，即“同心结”或“中国结”，它采用的是奥林匹克五环标志的典型颜色。图案表现了一个人打太极拳的动感姿态，其简洁的动作线条蕴涵着优美、和谐及力量，寓意世界各国人民之间的团结、合作、交流和发展。

3. 风筝

风筝是中国人发明的，距今已有 2 000 余年的历史。大约在公元 12 世纪，中国风筝传到了西方，此后经过不断发展，逐渐形成各具特色的东西方风筝文化。在风筝的发展过程中，具有悠久历史的中国传统文化开始与风筝工艺相融合，将神话故事和吉祥寓意等表现在风筝上，从而形成了独具地方特色的风筝文化。

1) 风筝的发展

在历史上，风筝的用途曾有过多次转换。根据史书记载，风筝最初用于军事。到了唐代中期，社会进入了繁荣稳定的发展阶段，风筝的功用开始从军用转向娱乐。同时由于纸业的发展，风筝的制作材料也由丝绢转向纸张。风筝逐渐走向民间，类型也丰富起来。宋代风筝的流传更为广泛。当时由于文人的参加，风筝在扎制和装饰上都有了很大的发展。同时由于社会上对风筝的需求，制作风筝发展为一种专门的职业。

明清时代是中国风筝发展的鼎盛时期，明清风筝在大小、设计、装饰和放飞技艺上都有了巨大进步。近年来，放风筝开始作为体育运动项目和健身娱乐活动普及开来。

2) 风筝的制作

制作风筝要选择合适的细竹扎成骨架，再糊以纸或绢。绢制风筝更为结实，艺术价值也更高。

中国地域辽阔，风筝作为中国的传统文化和民间艺术，在长期发展过程中，产生了许多具有不同地域特色的种类、样式和流派。其中以北京、天津、山东潍坊、四川、广东所制的风筝最为著名。

风筝的种类主要分硬翅和软翅两类。硬翅风筝翅膀坚硬，吃风大，飞得高。软翅风筝柔软，飞不高，但飞得远。在样式上，除传统的禽、兽、虫、鱼外，近代还发展出了人物风筝等新样式。

3) 风筝诗话

古代文人对风筝也是情有独钟，他们亲手扎绘风筝，除自己放飞外，还赠送亲友，并认为这是一种极为风雅的活动。从唐朝到清朝都留下了不少关于风筝的脍炙人口的精美诗篇。唐诗人高骈的《风筝》，明医学家、药学家李时珍的《放风筝》，清著名诗人郭鳞的《潍县竹枝词》，清著名诗人杨燮的《锦城竹枝词》，清朝诗人高鼎的《村居》以及清朝诗人吴好山的《笨拙俚语》等无不把风筝和放风筝描绘得形神兼备，绘声绘色，寓意颇深。

4. 刺绣艺术

在中国的传统刺绣工艺中，常常将产于中国东部江苏省的苏绣、中部湖南省的湘绣、西部四川省的蜀绣和南部广东省的粤绣合称为中国四大名绣。

1) 苏绣

苏绣(见图 19－3)是以江苏苏州为中心的刺绣产品的总称。苏州刺绣至今已有 2 000 余年的历史，早在三国时期就有了关于苏绣制作的记载。到明代时，苏绣已成为苏州地区一项普遍的群众性副业产品，形成了家家养蚕，户户刺绣的局面。

清代的苏绣以精细雅洁而闻名，当时的苏州更有了“绣市”的誉称。清代中后期，苏绣在绣制技术上有了进一步发展，新出现了精美的双面绣，仅苏州一地专门经营刺绣的商家就有 65 家之多。民国时期由于常年战乱，苏绣业曾一度衰落。新中国成立后，苏绣得到进一步的恢复和发展。1950 年后，国家专门设立了苏绣研究所，并开办刺绣训练班。苏绣的针法由 18 种发展到 40 余种。

苏绣地方特色浓郁，绣技具有平、齐、细、密、和、光、顺、匀等特点。平，指绣面平展；齐，指图案边缘齐整；细，指用针细巧，绣线精细；密，指线条排列紧凑，不露针迹；和，指设色适宜；光，指光彩夺目，色泽鲜明；顺，指丝理圆转自如；匀，指线条精细均匀，疏密一致。苏绣作品的种类主要可分为戏衣、挂屏和零剪三大类，装饰性与实用性兼备，其中以双面绣作品最为精美。

2）湘绣

作为中国四大名绣之一的湘绣(见图 19－4)，向来以历史悠久、工艺精湛、风格独特而闻名海内外。迄今为止发现最早的湘绣制品，是长沙马王堆一号汉代墓葬出土的一件丝织品，它所使用的针法与现代湘绣相差无几，说明早在汉代，湘绣工艺就已经产生了。

此后，经过漫长的发展，湘绣逐渐将国画传统特点引入其中，从而形成了自身的独特风格。至清末民初(20 世纪初期)，湘绣的发展达到鼎盛时期，甚至超越了苏绣，在中国刺绣业中独占鳌头。新中国成立后，湘绣工作者在继承传统的基础上致力创新，使湘绣工艺提高到一个崭新的水平。

湘绣主要以纯丝、硬缎、软缎、尼龙等为原料，配以各色的丝线、绒线绣制而成。它以中国画为神，达到了很高的艺术境界。绣品中既有名贵的欣赏艺术品，也有美观适用的日用品。

3）蜀绣

蜀绣(见图 19－5)也称川绣，它是以四川成都为中心的刺绣产品的总称。蜀绣也具有悠久的历史。早在汉代，蜀绣之名就已誉满天下，汉朝政府还在成都专门设置了“锦官”进行管理。汉代以后至五代十国时期，四川相对安定的局面为蜀绣的发展创造了有利的条件，社会需求的不断增大，刺激了蜀绣业的飞速发展。

到了宋代，蜀绣的发展达到鼎盛时期，绣品在工艺、产销量和精美程度上都独步天下。清朝中叶以后，蜀绣逐渐形成行业。新中国成立后，四川设立了成都蜀绣厂，使蜀绣工艺的发展进入了一个新阶段，技术上不断创新，品种日益增多。

蜀绣起源于川西民间，在长期的发展过程中，由于受地理环境、风俗习惯、文化艺术等方面的影响，逐渐形成了严谨细腻、光亮平整的独特风格。针法包括 12 大类共 122 种，针脚整齐，线片光亮，紧密柔和。

蜀绣作品选材丰富，有花鸟鱼虫和人物山水等。绣品的种类繁多，包括被面、枕套、衣、鞋和画屏等，是观赏性与实用性兼备的精美艺术品。

4）粤绣

粤绣(见图 19－6)也称广绣。它是出产于广东省广州、潮州、汕头、中山、番禺、顺德一带的刺绣品的总称。据史料记载，唐代的永贞元年(公元 805 年)，广东省南海县一位名叫卢媚娘的少女曾在一块一尺左右的绢面上绣出七卷《法华经》，粤绣从此名扬天下。宋元时期，广州港的繁荣促进了粤绣工艺的飞速发展，粤绣品开始输出国外。明代，广州的刺绣艺人已经能够娴熟地运用各色丝绒线刺绣，并创造性地使用动物的尾羽缠绒作线，使绣品更加自然生动。到清代的乾隆年间，第一个粤绣行业组织“粤绣行”在广州成立，当时从事刺绣的艺人众多，粤绣在工艺和针法上都得以不断发展完善。1915 年后，粤绣作品在巴拿马国际博览会等国际赛会上多次获得大奖。

粤绣受到各民族民间艺术的影响，在兼收并蓄、融会贯通的基础上，逐渐形成了自身独特的艺术风格。绣品主要取材于龙凤、花鸟等，图案构图饱满、均齐对称，色彩对比强烈、富丽堂皇。在种类上粤绣可分为绒绣、线绣、金银线绣三类，品种包括戏服、厅堂装饰、挂屏和各种日用绣品。

Exercises

Section A Thought-provoking questions

1. What are paper-cuttings?
2. What are the main characteristics of Chinese knot?
3. What have you learned about Chinese folk art?
4. What other Chinese handicrafts do you know?

Section B Decide whether the following statements are true or false

(1) Purely hand-made, each knot is woven out of one entire silk thread, and bestowed a name in tune with its shape and implied meaning.

(2) In Chinese characters, "knot" and "luck, felicity" have exactly the same pronunciation.

(3) Today, people are fond of Chinese Knot for its characteristic form, colorfulness and profound meaning.

(4) The Ming and Qing dynasties witnessed the heyday of the development of the Chinese kite.

(5) Su embroidery, Xiang embroidery, Shu embroidery and Yue embroidery are the only 4 types of embroidery in China.

(6) Machine-embroidered products are more precious and expensive than hand-embroidered products.

(7) Weifang has earned itself a proud name of the International Capital of Kites.

(8) The Weifang Kite Festival has become an annual feature of the city, drawing thousands of participants each May from home and many foreign countries.

※ **A gentleman is contented but not conceited; a lesser man is conceited but not contented.**

From *Analects of Confucius*

(君子泰而不骄，小人骄而不泰。)

——《论语》

※ **A gentleman gets along well with others but does not agree to unprincipled actions; a lesser man agrees to unprincipled actions but does not get along with others.**

From *Analects of Confucius*

(君子和而不同，小人同而不和。)

——《论语》

Chapter 20

China Wisdom

中国智慧

1. China — A Nation of Discoveries and Inventions

In more than a millennium from the Qin Dynasty to the Yuan Dynasty, Chinese science and technology took the lead in the world, and contributed greatly to the progress of the human civilization. Bernard, an English science historian, said, "For many centuries China was one of the great centers of human civilization and science." Joseph Needham, another English science historian, pointed out, "In many important respects the Chinese made scientific and technological inventions ahead of the legendary figures who created famous 'hopeful miracles'. The Chinese were abreast with the Arabs when Arabs possessed all the cultural wealth of the Western world. Between the 3rd century A.D. and the 13th century A.D., the Chinese kept scientific knowledge at a level far above that of the western world."

Robert Temple, a British scholar, stated in his work *China — A Nation of Discoveries and Inventions*: Probably over half of the inventions the modern world bases on have originated from China. Beside the four Great Chinese Inventions of compass, gunpowder, printing and paper making, many discoveries and inventions with respect to modern agriculture, navigation, petroleum industry, meteorological observation, music, decimal arithmetic, paper money, multistage rocket, submarine torpedo, poisonous gas, gun and cannon, parachute, brandy, whisky, and even the core design of steam engine were made first by the Chinese in the face of nature. These inventions have been the crystallization of Chinese wisdom.

The Four Great Inventions are the very great contributions of the Chinese people of ancient times to the development of the world's civilization. They reflected and represented the brilliance and prosperity of the ancient Chinese civilization.

2. The Four Great Inventions

1) Paper Making

Paper making stemmed from the necessity of cultural development and exchange. Prior to its invention, the Europeans wrote on sheep skin (and it is said that the copy of the Bible needed 300 or more pieces of sheep skin), the Egyptians wrote on thin barks of stalks of papyri, and the Chinese resorted to animal bones, tortoise shells and bronze and stone wares in the Shang Dynasty and later on silk, wood and bamboo. The earliest Chinese books were made from flat strips of bamboo or wood, inscribed and then threaded together. They were heavy and bulky, inconvenient for reading and carrying. Necessity is the mother of invention.

In the Western Han Dynasty, inspired by the process of silk-reeling, people learned to process silk fiber into thin pieces, called silk fiber paper (which is called "bo"), which was rudimentary paper making. Because silk was very scarce and expensive, people began looking for a new kind of writing material that is both cheap and available in large quantities.

It was generally believed that paper was first made by a man called Cai Lun, a court eunuch during the Eastern Han Dynasty, which was not exactly true. It should be precise to say that Cai Lun assimilated the previous experiences, and, based on them, carried out many experiments and improved paper-making technique. Eventually he succeeded in inventing a new kind of plant fibre paper, making full use of scrap materials including bark, ramie combings, worn cloth, fishing nets, and other raw materials which were, comparatively speaking, cheap, light, thin and durable. Thus, the source of raw materials was enlarged and the cost was reduced. He popularized this papermaking process throughout the country, thus giving an impetus to the papermaking industry. His new technique spread quickly, and he was recognized by the later generation as the inventor of paper.

By the Jin Dynasty, paper was widely used, taking the place of bamboo slips and silk cloth. At the beginning of the third century, the Chinese paper making technique was introduced into Korea, India, Vietnam, and Japan. It was during the reign of Tang Xuanzong that it reached Arabia, and from Arab countries into Europe and the rest of the world, thus putting an end to the history of writing on sheep skin for the Europeans. In 1150, the first European paper factory was established in Spain, lagging behind Cai Lun's invention by over 1000 years.

The importance of the invention of paper can hardly be exaggerated. It gave a great impetus to cultural progress not only in China but throughout the world. "No matter how highly the effect of the invention of paper making upon the whole course of later Western inventions is evaluated, the evaluation is never an overestimation." (Derk Bodde: *The History of the Westward Spread of Chinese Articles*) In the medieval Europe, parchment was still the main carrier of information. Cultural information spread very slowly due to the scarcity of carrier material. The production of paper provided a most advantageous condition for the flourishing of education, politics, commerce, etc., in Europe at that time. In this sense, "The world has benefited more from Cai Lun than from other more well-known celebrities."

2) Compass

The compass is an instrument showing the direction. In the process of mining ores and smelting copper and iron, people chanced upon lodestone, which attracted iron and pointed fixedly in a north-south direction. The magnetic property of the lodestone was known to the Chinese as early as the Warring States Period. Making use of its special property, people then invented a variety of south-pointing instruments. The primitive compass was invented in the shape of a spoon cut from an intact piece of natural magnetite. The spoon was put in the center of a level tray and rotated. When the spoon stopped, its handle pointed to the south, its head to the north.

Then the Chinese learned to magnetize the iron and invented the "Pointing-to-the-South Tortoise or Fish", a piece of thin iron sheet cut into the shape of a tortoise or fish, magnetized in a geomagnetic field and put into water, floating and lying north-to-south.

Another method was that people made iron needles and rubbed them on a piece of natural magnetite, so that they would become magnetized. Then one such needle was hung with a thin thread, or put on something light that floated on the water in a bowl. It pointed south when floated on water or suspended. This was the earliest compass. And finally, the round compass came into being after constant improvements. The legendary compass-guided vehicle in which Emperor Huang Di rode was most probably the result of using the compass on a chariot. Later it was used extensively in navigation and military operations.

The invention of compass was epoch-making in navigation. In the Northern Song Dynasty the mariner's compass was invented. It was made by putting a magnetic needle on a wooden disk called *luopan*. In the Northern Song Dynasty *luopan* compass was widely used on merchant vessels plying between China and the Malay Archipelago or India.

Before the compass was invented, people had to determine direction by the position of the sun in daytime and the stars at night. When it was cloudy and rainy, this had become impossible. The problem remained unsolved until the invention of the compass. The use of the *luopan* compass overcame many difficulties connected with navigation on the high seas. In the early Ming Dynasty, the navigator, Zheng He, made seven voyages going as far as the east coast of Africa. For each voyage he brought with him a fleet of 100 – 200 boats. The compass played an important role in the long distance voyages in ancient China. It is said that China was the first country in the world to use the compass on seagoing ships. Historical records show that in 1099 – 1102 compass was used on ships sailing to or from Guangzhou.

Compass spread to Arabia in the 12th century, where it was known as "friend of sailors". The Arabic people learned to use the compass from trading with China, and through the Arabians the compass spread to Europe in the 13th century. From the end of the 15th century to the beginning of the 16th century, European navigators opened many new routes. Without the invention and the application of the compass, the epoch-making ocean voyages, such as the voyage to India by Vasco da Gama of Portugal, Christopher Columbus' discovery of the Western Hemisphere, Ferdinand Magellan's earth-round voyage, and Zheng He's 7 voyages to the "western ocean", all would be inconceivable. To some degree, the invention of the compass has helped bring about economic and cultural exchanges between various countries of the world.

3) Printing

Known as "mother of civilization", the art of printing is the technology of producing printed images according to the original script or picture. In 1900 a scroll of Diamond Sutra was discovered in Dunhuang grottos, which was printed at the 9th year of Xiantong in the reign of Emperor Yi (868) in the Tang Dynasty. It consists of seven adhered sheets with a total length of 533 centimeters, clearly printed, showing a superb carving skill. It is the earliest printed matter existent now in the world. The earliest carved plate printed matter with a definite date now existent in Europe is the portrait of St. Christopher in the South of Germany, later than the printed scroll found in China by about 600 years.

Before the invention of printing, the circulation of books depended totally on hand-written copies of manuscripts. This was not only a slow process but was liable to mistakes. The first method of printing in China was the seals — in relief or intaglio. Seals were cut in relief to produce a clear effect — black characters on white paper, but their small size prevented them from printing many characters at a time. Then stone tablets were cut in intaglio, inked and impressions taken off, first on silk and later on paper when it was invented, but the impressions were less clear — white characters on the black background. In the Spring and Autumn Period and Warring States Periods, seal-engraving and stone-tablet rubbing were very much in vogue.

This, then, led in the Sui Dynasty to the practice of engraving writing or pictures on a wooden board, smearing ink on it and then printing on pieces of paper page by page. The page was printed when the paper was removed. This was called block printing, combining the two methods used for seals and stone rubbings. In the Tang Dynasty, this technology was already very popular and was introduced successively to countries like Korea, Japan, Vietnam, the Philippines and Iran. Although with this method the speed of printing was much higher than before, the block printing had its drawbacks. That is all the boards became useless after the printing was done and a single mistake in carving would cause a whole board to be wasted. And it was time-consuming, too, for it would take several years to finish making the blocks for a thick book.

By the end of the 11th century during the Song Dynasty, it occurred to a printing carver named Bi Sheng that block-printing was time-consuming, strenuous, and wasteful, and he was resolved to make innovations. He invented movable type printing, which had a far-reaching influence. Bi Sheng first engraved characters on clay dice and put them in fire to turn hard. He arranged these according to sound and tone in a wooden case divided into many sections. At the time of printing, one needed only to pick out the words as required by the manuscript, have them arranged on iron galleys and daub them with ink. When the printing was finished, the pieces of movable type were distributed and put back in the type case for future use. In this way, book printing was made much easier and both the speed and the quality were greatly improved. One county magistrate of the Yuan period had over 30,000 wood characters carved, with which he printed a book he had written. It was a book of more than 60,000 words, and he finished printing 600 copies in less than a month.

Economical and convenient, the use of these types brought about a revolution in printing. This was the beginning of typography. Later, people also made types with tin, copper and other metal.

Before long, typography spread to Japan, Korea and Vietnam, and then gradually to Europe. The technique of typography emancipated education and learning out of Christian abbeys. From then on the learning centers of Europe moved from abbeys to the colleges in various cities. Typography was a powerful weapon for carrying out Religious Reformation and anti-feudalism campaigns in Europe. It promoted the establishment of the capitalist production mode and the exchanges and dissemination of ideologies and culture.

The printing technology today using movable type made of metal is based on Bi Sheng's clay type. Hence we must say that Bi Sheng has indeed made extraordinary contributions to human cultural development and exchanges.

4) Gunpowder

The Chinese invented gunpowder about 1,100 years ago.

China was a home of alchemy. As a by-product of alchemy, the invention of gunpowder was due to the ancient Chinese Taoists' attempt to make "pills of immortality" or elixir and to turn cheap metals into gold. In their pursuit of impossibilities, the chemists and alchemists found that saltpeter, sulphur and charcoal powder mixed together in the right proportion and heated was explosive. The date of this discovery is unknown since the alchemists liked to operate in secret. The first to record the method of making gunpowder was Sun Simiao, a well-known pharmacologist of the Tang Dynasty, who also tried to make "pills of immortality".

Originally, gunpowder was used in China for making fireworks and fire crackers for the sake of amusement. Gunpowder was not used for rock-blasting and military purposes until the end of Tang Dynasty and at the beginning of the Five Dynasties, thus bringing about a revolution to the making of firearms. As far back as 904, besieged cities were attacked with what was then called "shooting fire" or "flying fire", that is, tying a packet of powder to the shaft of an arrow, igniting the fuse and shooting the arrow so as to cause an explosion and set enemy barracks on fire when the target was hit. During the Song period, the making and use of gunpowder reached a new level. Different formulas were already in use for the making of different kinds of powder as a result of constant experiments and weapons involving the use of gunpowder, including the thorn fire ball, the smoky fire ball and the cannon, were invented. Towards the end of the Northern Song Dynasty, weapons with even higher explosive power were made, such as "thunderbolt cannon", "sky shaking cannon", ect. The Song, Jin and Yuan armies all used these weapons in war.

In the 13th century the Yuan troops used various kinds of weapons in the war with the Arab countries in Central Asia, spreading firearms and their manufacture to these countries. Arab military primers of that time recorded the primitive guns and hand-grenades used by the Mongols. In this way, gunpowder was introduced to the Arab world. During the medieval times Europeans translated many Arabic books from which they learned about gunpowder. In 1325 the Arabs attacked a Spanish city using a projector to fire "flaming balls" which sounded like thunder. The Westerners became familiar with gunpowder and started studying and manufacturing it. Some European countries began to make gunpowder weapons with methods they had learned from the Arabians. By the 15th century cannons using gunpowder were being invented by the Europeans.

It was a tremendous impetus to the progress of European history, because the application of gunpowder made feudal separation impossible, thus speedily leading feudalism to its doom in Europe. The invention of gunpowder meant a far-reaching technological revolution that transformed heat energy into mechanic energy, greatly promoting the progress of the global civilization.

3. Other Contributions by China

In addition to these four great inventions and what have been mentioned in the first paragraph, China, in the past chronological dynasties, also invented earthquake detector, porcelain, scull, water-tight ship compartment, stern axial rudder, axial turning rudder, balance rudder, holed rudder, distance-recording chariot, armillary sphere, running horse lantern (embryo of gas turbine), abacus, silk, plough, lunar calendar, acupuncture, oracle, and so on and so forth, all of which have been great contributions to the world civilization and to the development of science and technology of the world as well, which truly proves the fact that "The ancient Chinese were great creators." In the countless inventions lay the wisdom of the Chinese nation.

Today the cultural value of the four great inventions is universally acknowledged.

Decker Hyde, an American scholar, said, "If there were no paper and no typography we would still be living in the medieval times. If there were no gunpowder, the world would probably suffer less, but the medieval European knights in helmet and armor would still act as lords in their moat-surrounded castles, and our society would still be subject to the feudalistic slavery. Finally, without the compass the era of great geographical discoveries would never have arrived. It was these discoveries that stimulated the material and cultural life of the Europeans and brought them knowledge of the world yet unknown to them, including our America."

Compass, paper making, gunpowder and printing were great technological achievements that the Chinese nation dedicated to the world, which altered the historical course of the human being. They reflected and represented the brilliance and prosperity of the ancient Chinese civilization.

Word Bank

navigation 航海
meteorological 气象的
arithmetic 算术，计算
papyrus〔复数 papyri〕(古埃及人等用以造纸的)纸莎草
rudimentary 基本的，初步的
assimilate 吸收(思想、食物、文化等)，同化
ramie 苎麻
exaggerate 夸张，夸大
impetus 动力，促进
parchment 羊皮纸
smelt 冶炼
lodestone 磁石
magnetize 把……磁化
chariot 古代双轮马拉战车
ply (船等)来往于，往返于
in relief 浮雕
in intaglio 凹雕
seal-engraving 印章雕刻
stone-tablet rubbing 石刻
smear 涂，抹，敷
block-printing 木版印刷
movable type printing 活字印刷
typography 排版印刷
emancipate 解放
dissemination 传播，散布
alchemy 炼丹术，炼金术
alchemist 炼丹术士，炼金术士

参考译文

1. 中国——发明与发现的国度

从秦朝到元朝的1 000多年间，中国的科学技术水平一直走在世界的前列，为人类文明的发展进步做出了极大的贡献。英国科学史学家贝尔纳说："许多世纪以来，中国一直是人类文明和科学的伟大中心之一。"另一英国科学史家李约瑟也指出："中国人在许多重要方面有一些科学技

术发明，走在那些创造出著名的'希望奇迹'的传奇式人物的前面，和拥有古代西方世界全部文化财富的阿拉伯人并驾齐驱，并在公元 3 世纪到 13 世纪之间保有西方世界望尘莫及的科学知识水平。"

英国学者罗伯特·坦普尔在《中国——发明与发现的国度》一书中指出，现代世界赖以建立的基本发明创造可能至少有一半以上源自中国，除了指南针、火药、印刷术、造纸术是人们广为知晓的中国四大发明外，现代农业、航运、石油工业、气象观测、音乐、十进位计数制、纸币、多级火箭、水下鱼雷、毒气、枪炮、降落伞、白兰地、威士忌，甚至蒸汽机的核心设计部分，都是中国人在面对自然挑战过程中发现和发明的。这些发明是中国人民智慧的结晶。

中国古代的四大发明是中国人民对世界文明发展的杰出贡献，反映和代表了中国古代文明的辉煌灿烂。

2. 四大发明

1) 造纸术

造纸术的出现是文明发展、交流过程中的一项必然产物。造纸术发明之前，欧洲人在羊皮上书写(据说一本羊皮纸的《圣经》至少需要 300 多张羊皮)；古埃及人在纸莎草茎做成的薄片上书写；古代中国人曾在商朝时把字刻在甲骨、金石和青铜器上，后来又尝试把竹木薄简、丝帛作为书写材料。中国最早的书籍是刻写在竹简或木片上，然后用线穿在一起而成。这种书籍笨重庞大，非常不方便阅读和携带。

西汉时期，人们从缫丝中得到启发，使用丝絮制造出一种薄片叫作絮纸。这是造纸术的开端。由于丝絮昂贵来源又有限，人们开始寻找价格低廉又原料充足的新型书写原料。

人们都认为 105 年东汉时期的蔡伦是第一个造纸的人，这种说法不太准确。应该说蔡伦吸收了前人造纸经验，在这些经验的基础上经过反复试验，改进了造纸方法。最终他成功地利用树皮、苎麻、破布、渔网以及其他原料等制造出一种价钱相对便宜、轻薄耐用的植物纤维纸。这种新的造纸方法大大扩充了造纸原料的来源，大大降低了成本，因而很快地被推广开来。蔡伦就成为后世所传的纸的发明人。

晋朝时，纸张取代了竹简、丝帛，被人们普遍使用。公元 3 世纪初，造纸术传入朝鲜、印度、越南、日本等国。751 年，唐玄宗统治时期，造纸术传到阿拉伯，又从阿拉伯国家传到了欧洲，再逐渐传遍世界，这样才使欧洲人结束了用羊皮书写的历史。1150 年西班牙建造起欧洲第一家造纸厂，此时已比蔡伦的发明晚了 1 000 多年。

无论如何评价造纸术发明的重要性都不会有夸大之嫌，因为它不仅对中国而且对世界的文明发展起到极大推动作用。"纸对后来西方发明整个进程的影响无论怎样估计都不会过分。"(德克·卜德:《中国物品西传考》)中世纪的欧洲，流行以羊皮作为信息的物质载体，文化信息的传播因材料的限制速度极为缓慢。纸的生产为当时欧洲蓬勃发展的教育、政治、商业等方面的活动提供了极为有利的条件。从这一意义上来说，"世界受蔡伦的恩惠要比许多更为知名人士的恩惠大得多。"

2) 指南针

指南针是指示方向的工具。中国人在开采矿石、冶铜、炼铁的过程中，发现了一种能够吸铁和指示南北方向的天然磁石。早在战国时期中国人就已经懂得天然磁石有指示方向的作用。古代人们根据磁石的这种特性，发明了各种指南工具。最先造出的指南工具以天然磁石磨制而成，状如勺形，置于平底的盘中使其转动，转动停止，其勺柄自动指向南方。

后来人们设法使铁人工磁化，制成指南龟和指南鱼，漂在水中，两头分指南和北。

人们又制造了铁针，把这些铁针在磁石上摩擦，使它们具有磁性。然后用根细线把针穿吊起来或者将它们置于可以漂在一碗水上的物体上。无论是漂着还是吊着，针尖都是指向南方。这就是最早的指南针。传说中黄帝乘坐的指南车，大概就是指南工具应用在战车上的结果。后来指南针广泛地应用在古代的航海事业和军事行动中。

指南针的发明，是世界航海业中划时代的事件。北宋时期人们把磁针嵌入一个叫作罗盘的木质圆盘中，发明了航海指南针，广泛用于往返于中国和马来群岛或印度之间的商船上。指南针发明之前人们在大海上航行只能白天依靠太阳、晚上凭借月亮来判断方向。遇到阴雨天，人们就束手无策了。这种靠天辨别方向的状况直到发明了指南针才得以改变。在波涛汹涌的大海上航行，使用罗盘指南针克服了航海中数不清的困难。明代早期的航海家郑和 7 次下西洋，最远曾到达非洲的东海岸。每次出海他的船队都由 100 到 200 只海船组成。指南针在中国古代的远程航海中的重要作用是不言而喻的。中国是第一个在海船上使用指南针的国家。据历史记载，早在 1099 年到 1102 年，中国人就在来往于广州的海船上使用了指南针。

指南针在 12 世纪传入阿拉伯，被尊为“水手之友”。阿拉伯人是在和中国人做生意的接触中学会使用指南针的。随后于 13 世纪由阿拉伯人传入欧洲，从 15 世纪末到 16 世纪初，欧洲航海家们新开辟了多条海路。没有指南针的发明和应用，那些划时代的航海冒险，比如，葡萄牙航海家达·伽马远航印度、哥伦布发现新大陆、麦哲伦环绕地球航行乃至郑和下西洋，都是不可想象的。从某种程度上讲，正是指南针的发明促进了世界各国间的经济和文化交流。

3）印刷术

被称为“文明之母”的印刷术是一项按照文字或图画原稿制成印刷品的技术。1900 年，敦煌千佛洞发现了一卷唐懿宗咸通 9 年（公元 868 年）印刷的《金刚经》，长约 533 厘米，由 7 个印张拼接而成。此卷雕刻精美，刀法纯熟，印刷清晰，是目前世界上最早的印刷物。欧洲现存最早的有确切日期的雕版印刷品，是德国南部的《圣·克利斯托菲尔》画像，大约比中国晚 600 年。

印刷术发明之前，人们必须用手抄来复制书籍，这种方法不仅速度慢，而且很容易出错。最初印刷的方法是效仿印章的浮雕和凹雕。在印章上用浮雕形式刻出清晰的字样，印在白纸上呈现深色字迹。但印章太小，一次刻不了几个字。然后人们就在石板上刻凹雕，刷上油墨，印在丝帛上，后来当纸发明后便在纸上印，但是这些黑底白字不是很清晰易辨。春秋战国时代，刻写图章和拓印碑文等方法是很流行的。

到了隋朝，人们就像刻写图章一样，先将文字或图画刻在一定规格的木板上，涂上油墨，然后再在纸上一页一页地印。把纸揭下来就印好了。这就是木版印刷术，它综合运用了印章和石刻技术。唐朝时期，这种木版印刷术已经非常普及，并相继传到朝鲜、日本、越南、菲律宾、伊朗。这种方法虽然可以提高印刷的速度，但它也有不尽如人意之处：印完以后，大量的刻板就没有用了，而且万一刻错了一个字，整块木板就浪费了。另外，这种印刷方法很费时，如果要印一本厚点儿的书，光制作木版就得花上几年工夫。

到 11 世纪末宋朝年间，有个刻字工人叫毕昇，他感到刻板印刷术费时、费力又费料，决心进行改革。他创造了活字印刷术，具有非常深远的影响。毕昇首先把字刻在一个个用细胶泥制成的大小相同的泥块上，用火慢慢加热烧硬，就制成了一个个活动的字体。再按照字的声、韵的顺序排列在木格子里。印书的时候，只要依照稿本拣出所需要的字，排列在一块块板上，涂上油墨，就可以印刷了。印完后，把活字一个个拆下来放回木格子里，下次还可以用。这样，书籍的印刷工作就更加简便了，印刷的速度和质量也大大提高。元朝的一个地方官刻了 30 000 多个木活字，用来印刷他自己写的书。这本书有 60 000 多字，他一个月内就印了 600 册。

这样，书籍的印刷工作变得既经济又简便，可以说在印刷业引发了一场大的变革。这是排版印刷的开始。后来，人们便用锡、铜等金属制成活字。

活字印刷术产生不久，旋即传入日本、朝鲜和越南，然后再逐步传入欧洲。印刷术在欧洲的出现，把学术、教育从基督教修道院中解放出来。从此，欧洲的学术中心由修道院转移到了各地的大学。印刷术的出现为当时欧洲的宗教改革运动和反封建斗争提供了有力的武器，对资本主义生产方式的确立和思想文化的交流传播起了巨大作用。

今天的活字铅印技术，就是在毕昇的胶泥活字印刷的基础上发展而来的。毕昇对人类文化交流和发展所做的贡献的确是非常了不起的。

4）火药

大约 1 100 年前，中国人就发明了火药。

中国是炼丹术的故乡。火药是炼丹术的副产品，人们在长期炼制"长生不老药"和妄想把普通金属炼成金子的过程中发现了火药，这是它的名称中有"药"的原因。炼丹方士本来是想炼出长生不老的金丹仙丸，不料却发现把硝石、硫黄和木炭按照一定的比例混合然后烧炼就会产生爆炸效果。因为这些炼丹方士炼丹制药都是秘密进行的，所以火药发明的确切时间尚难断定。最早记录火药制作的人是唐朝的药学家孙思邈，他本人也曾力图炼制长生不老药。

火药在中国大多用来制作娱乐用品，如烟火、爆竹等。从唐朝末期、五代初期开始，火药被用于军事目的，遂在武器制造领域引发一场变革。早在公元 904 年，军队曾经使用"火箭"或"飞火"攻城，就是在箭杆上扎一个火药团，点着导火线，用弓箭发射出去，引起爆炸，火烧敌营。经过不断的试验，到宋代火药制造达到了一个新水平，已调配出各种不同配方，制作出多种火药武器，诸如蒺藜火球、烟球和火炮等。北宋末年，已经研制出"霹雷炮""震天窗"等爆炸力较强的武器。宋军、金兵和元军都在战斗中使用这种武器。

13 世纪时，元军在中亚与阿拉伯国家交战时使用了多种不同武器，这样就把武器和火药的制造方法带到了阿拉伯。在阿拉伯国家的军事入门书上记载了蒙古人最早使用的枪械和手雷等武器的情况。这样，火药逐渐传入阿拉伯。在中世纪时期，欧洲人就着手翻译一些阿拉伯文献，从中了解到有关火药的信息。阿拉伯人于 1325 年强攻一座西班牙城市，其间就使用投掷器投射了震耳欲聋的"火球"。14 世纪，欧洲人熟悉了火药，欧洲一些国家开始用从阿拉伯人那里学来的方法制造火药武器。到 15 世纪，欧洲人已经发明制造出使用火药的火炮了。

火药传入西方后，对欧洲历史的发展起到了极大的推动作用，由于火药武器的应用，使得诸侯的封建割据变得不可能，也就大大加速了欧洲封建主义的衰落和灭亡。火药的发明，意味着人类把热能转变成机械能、把热能转变为动力的伟大技术革命，对世界文明进步有着重大影响。

3. 中国的其他贡献

除以上介绍的四大发明和首段提到的其他发明以外，中国在历史上还发明了地震探测仪、瓷器、橹、水密隔仓、船尾轴向舵、轴向转动舵、平衡舵、开孔舵、记里鼓车、浑仪（天文观测仪）、走马灯（燃气轮机雏形）、算盘、丝绸、犁耙、农历、针灸、甲骨文等，所有这些发明对世界文明和科学技术的发展做出了巨大贡献，真正证实了"古代的中国人是伟大的创作者"，中华民族的聪明和智慧也正隐藏在这无数的发明中。

时至今日，四大发明的文化价值仍为世界所公认。美国学者德克·海德说："倘使没有纸和印刷术，我们将仍生活在中世纪。如果没有火药，世界也许会少受点痛苦，但另一方面，中世纪欧洲那些穿戴盔甲的骑士们可能仍然在他们有护城河围绕的城堡里称王称霸、不可一世，而我们的社会可能仍然处在封建制度的奴役之下。最后，如果没有指南针，地理大发现的时代永远不会到来，而正是这个地理大发现的时代刺激了欧洲的物质文化生活，把知识带给了当时人们还不了解的世界,包括我们美国。"

可以说,指南针、造纸术、火药和活字印刷,是中华民族奉献给世界并改变了整个人类历史进程的伟大技术成果,反映和代表了中国古代文明的辉煌灿烂。

Exercises

Section A Thought-provoking questions

1. What do you think contributed to the blooming of the flowers of wisdom among the ancient Chinese?
2. How would you explain the exclamation of "the ancient Chinese were great creators" by the Jesuits who landed on China between the 16th and 17th centuries?
3. What have you obtained from this chapter? What have you been made to think at this very moment?

Section B Decide whether the following statements are true or false

1. "Orientation of pragmatism" and "preponderance of empiricism" contributed to the blooming of the flowers of wisdom among the ancient Chinese, though they limited to a certain extent the development of science and technology.
2. Another great invention of the Chinese people, paper making, is known as "mother of civilization".
3. The *Syllabus of Medical Herbs*, *Encyclopedia of Farming*, and *Technical Wonders* completed in the Ming Dynasty were three works of the highest level in the fields of Chinese medicine and pharmacology and agriculture and technology.
4. It was generally believed that paper was first made by a man called Bi Sheng in 105 during the Eastern Han Dynasty.
5. In 1150 A.D., the first European paper factory was established in America.
6. Rudimentary paper making referred to the fact that people learned to process silk fiber into thin pieces, called silk fiber paper.
7. The invention of gunpowder was due to the ancient Chinese Buddhists' attempt to make "pills of immortality" and to turn cheap metals into gold.
8. The magnetic property of the lodestone was known to the Chinese as early as the Tang Dynasty.
9. Papermaking stemmed from the necessity of cultural development and exchange.
10. The method of powder making was introduced into the Arab world in the 12th century and then into Europe in the 14th century.

Chapter 21

Famous Ancient Towers in China

中国古代名楼

Yueyang Tower, Yellow Crane Tower, Tengwang Pavilion and Penglai Pavilion are the four famous towers in China, whose unique architectural styles are of great significance in understanding the architectural style and characteristics of ancient China.

1. Yueyang Tower

The Yueyang Tower (see picture 21 - 1), standing on the west gate of the Yueyang city wall, looking down at the Dongting Lake, facing the Junshan Island in the distance, and linking the Yangtze River to the north and the Xiangjiang River to the south, is listed as one of the Three Great Towers in the south of Yangtze River, along with the Yellow Crane Tower in Wuhan, and the Tengwang Pavilion in Nanchang. It has long enjoyed the reputation of being the "first tower under heaven", as the Dongting Lake is known as the "first water under heaven".

It is said that Yueyang Tower was originally built for soldiers to rest on and watch out. In the Three Kingdoms Period, Lu Su, General of Wu State, trained his soldiers here and then rebuilt it as a tower for troop inspection.

In the fourth year (716) of Kaiyuan of Tang Dynasty, General Zhangshuo was dispatched to defend at Yuezhou and he rebuilt it into a tower named South Tower, and then Yueyang Tower. After that, many famous poets such as Du Fu, Han Yu, Liu Yuxi, Bai Juyi and Li Shangyin went there and leave many famous poems that made Yueyang Tower well known and a famous tower around China.

In the fourth year (1044) of Qingli of Song Dynasty, Teng Zijing was stationed at Baling Jun, the ancient name of Yueyang city. In the second year, he renovated the Yueyang Tower and invited his good friend Fan Zhongyan, a well-known writer, to compose an essay. In Fan's essay, *Remarks of Yueyang Tower*, he not only described the wonderful scenery, but also wrote the famous lines of one should be the first to bear hardship, and the last to enjoy comforts, indicating his concerns for the country and people. His words were applauded and won the Tower greater fame, and have been deeply rooted in the Chinese people's mind from generation to generation. After numerous renovations, the current structure was rebuilt in 1867 in the Qing Dynasty.

The Yueyang Tower has its special architectural features. Its main building has three stories and is 15 meters in height, with four huge Nanmu pillars supporting the whole building, twelve round log columns supporting the second floor, and another twelve catalpa pillars supporting the roof. Constructed of wood with interlocking brackets that require no nails, the main building is as steady as a monolith. Its roof looks like a general's helmet, grand and unique, which together with the pure wooden construction reflects the unique style and great achievement of ancient Chinese architecture.

The display of the Tower has its own style with the couplets by famous poets or calligrapher through ages hung on the columns of each storey. Fan Zhongyan's *Remarks of Yueyang Tower* is inscribed on the wooden screen on the first and second floor of the Tower. *The Remarks* on the first floor is a copy from the 19th century. Housed on the second floor is a wooden screen written by famous calligrapher Zhang Zhao of the Qing Dynasty, whose handwriting is unique in style, varied in skill, and square in shape. Du Fu's *On Yueyang Tower* is inscribed on the screen of the third floor which is written by Chairman Mao, whose strong handwriting has added glitters to the Tower.

Two pavilions: Thrice Drunken Pavilion and Fairy Plum Blossom Pavilion are located beside the main building, which show up to advantage with the main building. The Thrice Drunken Pavilion, on the right side of the building, was originally built for sacrificing Charles' Wain, and accordingly called Wangxian Pavilion and changed to Doumu Pavilion later. The present name, Thrice Drunken Pavilion was named in 1987 when it was rebuilt after a legend describing Immortal Lü Dongbin who was attracted by the beautiful scenery here and got drunk here three times. The Fairy Plum Blossom Pavilion, on the left side of the main building, was built in the 12th year of Chongzhen of Ming Dynasty (1639). It is said that a flagstone was excavated during the construction of the pavilion and the lines on the stone resembled withered plum blossoms, which were regarded as hand drawings of immortals. After the pavilion was completed, the flagstone was erected in the center of the Pavilion and is still today, which is the reason why the pavilion called Fairy Plum Blossom Pavilion. The pavilion, exquisite and elegant, is 60 meters high, two-storey and is hexagonal with six upturned eaves supporting spire roofs.

2. Yellow Crane Tower

Bordering on the Yangtze River and crouching on the top of the Snake Hill, the Yellow Crane Tower (see picture 21 - 2) enjoys the fame of "the First Scenery under Heaven" and is listed as one of the three most famous towers on the south bank of the Yangtze River. Its cultural significance led to its being made the symbol of Wuhan City.

Up to now, the Tower has a history of over 1,700 years. According to records, it was originally built in 223 during the Three Kingdoms Period by Sun Quan as a watchtower for his army due to the ideal location. As such a famous tower, it is normal that many legends are created as to why it was built. One of the most popular legends goes like that the Tower used to be a wine-shop opened by a Mrs. Xin. One day, a Taoist monk, in order to thank the woman for her favor of free wine, drew a magic crane on the wall and ordered it to dance on hearing claps. Since then, thousands of people came to see the spectacle and the wine shop was always full of guests. 10 years later, when the Taoist monk revisited the wine shop, he played the flute and then rode on the crane to the sky. In order to memorize the supernatural encounter and the monk, Mrs. Xin built a tower here named Yellow Crane Tower.

Legends are legends and are created for entertainment. To build a tower in such a place at the wartime was obviously for military purpose. The military function of the Tower, however, had gradually been forgotten and when in Tang Dynasty, it was enjoyed mainly as a picturesque location for celebrities and poets to get together, treat and meet friends, enjoy the beautiful scenery and make merry and compose poetry. Many great poets in the past dynasties such as Cui Hao, Li Bai, Bai Juyi, Jia Dao, Lu You visited the Tower and wrote hundreds of poems and scores of writings in praise of the magnificent Tower. It was estimated that up to the Tongzhi Reign of the Qing Dynasty, as many as 300 poems about the Tower had been found in the historical literature, in which "Yellow Crane Tower" written by Cui Hao, a famous poet of Tang Dynasty made the Tower well known throughout China. It was these poems that made the Tower so renowned and induced for people to visit. Later, the story about the great poem Li Bai's giving up composing poem after reading "Yellow Crane Tower" by Cui Hao brought the Tower greater fame.

Originally built at a place called Yellow Crane Rock projecting over the water on Snake Hill over 1,700 years ago, the Tower was destroyed many times in successive dynasties, and was rebuilt time and again until 1884 when it was for the last time reduced to ashes. The present tower is the result of four years' construction beginning in 1981. The Tower, 51.4 meters high, five-storied with yellow glazed tiles and red pillars, overlapping ridges and interlocking eaves, is reconstructed on the basis of the one designed during the Tongzhi Reign of Qing Dynasty, but more magnificent than the old one. Modern construction technology was applied to the construction of the Tower and it was built under the framework of reinforced concrete and with imitation wood surface. The ground floor of the new is 30 meters wide in each side and the top floor is 18 meters wide in each side. The appearance of the Tower is the same regardless of the direction it is viewed from.

In the halls of the Tower there are many pictures, portraits and wall-paintings.

On the wall of the first floor, there hangs a wide painted porcelain picture *Cloud and Yellow Crane* which depicts clouds, rivers and cranes to represent a romantic mood in the heaven, with a 7-meter long couplet hung on the column located on each side of the picture. On the second floor, the main wall hangs an inscribed poem written by Yan Bojin which records the historical development of the Tower and anecdotes of celebrities. Two wall paintings on each side of the poems are *Sun Quan Building the City* and *Zhou Yu Hosting Friends* with the former illustrating how the Wuchang City and the Tower were built one after another and the latter reflecting the activities held by celebrities in the Tower during Three Kingdoms Period. The third floor mainly shows poems written to praise the Tower in different dynasties. Poems composed by Cui Hao, Li Bai and Bai Juyi are extracted and displayed here. The hall on the fourth floor is divided into several smaller halls, which hosts paintings drawn by famous artists for visitors to appreciate and purchase. On top of the Tower, a fabulous panoramic view of the Yangtze River is presented and so are some other wall paintings.

Outside the Tower, there are a group of auxiliary buildings such as bronze yellow cranes, memorial, gateways, corridors and pavilions, which adds more charm to the Tower.

The Tower has different architectural features in different dynasties, but all magnificent and individualized. Compared with Yueyang Tower and Tengwang Tower, the horizontal design of Yellow Crane Tower is four-faced and octangular which, according to ancient architecture culture, has complex symbolic and ethic meaning. Seen vertically, each floor with yellow upturned eaves seems to have been designed to resemble a yellow crane spreading its wings to fly, making the Tower vigorous but exquisite, varied and beautiful.

3. Tengwang Pavilion

The Tengwang Pavilion (see picture 21 - 3), located on the east bank of the Ganjiang River, northwest of Nanchang City, Jiangxi Province, is one of the three most notable pavilions south of the Yangtze River together with Yellow Crane Tower and Yueyang Pavilion. It also has the reputation of being "the First Pavilion of Xijiang River" due to its excellent location, height, overall size, and architectural style.

The reputation of Tengwang Pavilion, to a great extent, is due to a well-known prose — *Preface to Tengwang Pavilion* by Wang Bo. It is said that when the author, a reputable poet of the Tang, passed Nanchang on his way to Guangdong, he wrote this prose on the subject of the banquet which was being held to celebrate the reconstruction of the Pavilion. With the spread of this prose, Tengwang Pavilion became proverbial.

The Pavilion was built in 653 A.D., when Tengwang Li Yuanying, a younger brother of Emperor Taizong of the Tang Dynasty, was the military governor of Nanchang. The Pavilion was named after him but it had undergone reconstruction as many as 28 times as a consequence of events during its 1,300 year-long history. In 1926, the Pavilion was destroyed by fire during the conflicts between the Northern Warlords and as a result, the building was burned to ashes and only the bluestone plaque "Tengwang Pavilion" remained. The current building, based on the style of architecture in the Song Dynasty, is the result of rebuilding that was carried out between 1983 and 1989.

The existing pavilion is even more spectacular and magnificent than its predecessors. The main building is 57.5 meters in height and occupies a construction area of 13,000 square meters with a 12-meter-long base symbolic of ancient city walls. Taking the two-storey basement into account, it has nine storeys, that is, three bright, three dark and one top.

The six floors of the Pavilion treasure scores of artistic writings each with a theme relevant to the exhibition there. On the first floor there is a huge white marble relief "*Timely Wind Sending Wangbo to Tengwang Pavilion*" which is drawn based on the story that Wangbo composed *Preface to Tengwang Pavilion*. The second floor is a dark floor on which stands a 2.55-meter high and 20-meter long wall-painting named "*Pictures of Outstanding Figure*" with all the renowned celebrities from Qin Dynasty to Ming Dynasty. The third floor is a bright floor surrounded by cloister. The pictures here are wall-painting "*Linchuan Dream*" and a huge bronze relief which depicts the dancers in the Tang Dynasty, reflecting a prosperous and peaceful look of the Tang Dynasty. The fourth floor, a dark floor, houses a large mural "*The Rich Land*" describing the beautiful mountains and streams in Jiangxi Province from south to north: the Mei Pass of Da Yu Mountain, the magnificent Guifeng Mountain, the Dragon and Tiger Mountain — the birthplace of Taoism, the Chinggang Mountain — the cradle of the Chinese Revolution, the Lu Shan Mountain, the Po Yang Lake — the largest freshwater lake in the country, the Stone Bell Hill — an important military pass in the ancient time, etc. The fifth floor is the ideal place for enjoying the scenery and meeting friends. The paintings such as *Playing Long Flute to Make Phoenix Coming*, *Waiting for Boat at the Foot of Xi Mountain* drawn by Huang Qiuyuan, *Preface to Tengwang Pavilion*, a calligraphic work by Su Dongpo on a bronze stele, and a lacquer painting *One hundred Flowers and One Hundred Butterflies* are placed. The sixth floor is actually the ninth floor if counting the basements, so it is called "the Ninth Level Heaven". On the walls of north, south and east, there is a tri-colored glazed wall painting *Dance Troupe in Tang Dynasty*.

4. Penglai Pavilion

Penglai Pavilion (see picture 21 - 4), seated on the cliff of Danya Mountain close to the sea in the north of Penglai City, is a famous coastal tourist site in eastern China's Shandong Province. It is listed as one of the four famous towers in China together with Yellow Crane Tower, Yueyang Tower, and Tengwang Pavilion. Having long been known as a fairyland and famous place for watching mirages, Penglai Pavilion is regarded as the place where immortals inhabited, and thus it was frequently visited for wonder herbs by emperors since Qin and Han dynasties.

Built in 1061 by Governor Zhu Chuyue in the sixth year of Emperor Jiayou of the Northern Song Dynasty, the Pavilion was intended for people to enjoy the sea view. In the 17th year of Wanli of Ming Dynasty, official Li Dai added more buildings around, which together with the Pavilion was called Pavilion complex. In the 24th year of Emperor Jiaqing of Qing Dynasty, the Pavilion was expanded again on the basis of the existing buildings sponsored by local government secretary Yang Fengchang and garrison commander Liu Qinghe to the present complex occupying a construction area of 18,960 square meters. After 1949, the government has appropriated funds many times for its renovation. In 1965, the Pavilion had resumed its original look, reflecting the traditional architectural characteristics of ancient China.

The Pavilion complex occupies a land of 32,800 square meters, a construction area of 18,960 square meters, composed of six buildings and their attached constructions: main hall of Penglai Pavilion, Longwang Palace, Tianhou Palace, Sanqing Temple, Lüzu Temple and Mituo Temple. Constructed with double-deck wood, the main hall of Penglai Pavilion is seated on the north, facing the south, with symmetrically built side rooms and wing rooms in front of both east and west sides. Wing rooms perform the role of halls, with hallways linking side rooms and stone stairs running up the Pavilion. Its ground floor measures 14.8 meters in length, and 9.65 meters in width, with winding corridors and 16 columns surrounding all sides. Hung on the front door is a huge horizontal tablet inscribed with three Chinese characters: Penglai Pavilion (Penglai Ge), written by famous calligrapher Tie Bao of the Qing Dynasty.

Three huge stone tablets are embedded in the outside of the north wall of the Pavilion's ground floor. One reads Blue Sea, Cool Breeze (Bi Hai Qing Feng), written by Lu Qiguang, a renowned Qing calligrapher. Another reads Placid Seawater (Hai Bu Yang Bo), of which the word Bu was struck by a cannonball during the 1894 to 1895 Sino-Japanese war, leaving a visible scar. The other reads the Clear Sea (Huan Hai Jing Qing).

In front of the wing rooms' north gable wall are three monuments, built during the reigns of Emperors Jiaqing, Daoguang and Guangxu respectively after each renovation or construction of attached buildings. In the west of west-wing room, a 2.3-meter-tall tablet is erected facing the east. Engraved on the tablet is Daoguang's Notes on "Repairing Penglai Pavilion in Dengzhou", written with full power and grandeur. Inside the west-wing room, tablets are embedded into the west wall, with four Chinese characters on each, describing the ten scenes of Penglai: Sunrise on the Sea (Ri Chu Fu Sang), Evening Tide under the New Moon (Wan Chao Xin Yue), Countless Jade Fragments (Qian Hu Sui Yu), Ten Thousand Miles of Clear Water (Wan Li Deng Bo), Pavilion in the Air (Xian Ge Ling Kong), Snow Covered Peak (Shen Shan Xian Shi), Mist and Clouds (Shi Dong Yan Yun), Fishing and Singing on the Yuliang (Yuliang Ge Diao), Shining Waves in Well (Tong Jing Jin Bo) and Rain Drops from Heaven (Lou Tian Di Run). Another ten tablets of past dynasties are in the west side room, all of which have great historiography and calligraphy values.

The second floor of the Penglai Pavilion is 13.5 meters in length and 8.55 meters in width, surrounded by winding corridors, wooden fencing guardrails and 16 columns. The door opens to the south and windows are opened in the north wall for visitors to look over the sea. Wooden folding screens are displayed in the north, east and west. Hung above the outer side of the door is a board carved with Blue Sea, Warm Spring (Bi Hai Chun Rong), and the inner side is a board carved with Scenic Spot on the Divine Land (Shen Zhou Sheng Jing). Tie Bao's powerful handwriting Penglai Pavilion (Penglai Ge) is just hung on the center of north wall, along with Dong Biwu's inscription and Ye Jianying's couplets hung on the west wall. The wooden roof beams are painted with colored drawings like Penglai Ten Scenes, Eight Immortals and Bamboos, etc. With sculptures of eight drunken immortals placed in the center and an old-fashioned square table and chairs placed around, the arrangement of the room is just as what was described in the famous legend of "Eight Immortals Crossing the Sea". It is said that the Eight Immortals (Lu Dongbin, Tie Guaili, Zhang Guolao, Han Zhongli, Cao Guojiu, He Xiangu, Lan Caihe, and Han Xiangzi) got drunk at the Penglai Pavilion and they crossed the sea by different tricks of their own without ships or boats. Their performance hovering over the waves against wind left a popular saying that "like the Eight Immortals crossing the sea, each one showing his or her special feats; each tries to outwit the other".

Beneath the Pavilion is the bridge said to be the place where the Eight Immortals crossed the sea. East section of the pavilion are Palace of Lucidity (Sanqing Temple), Lüzu Temple (Luzu miao), the Tower of Universal Enlightenment (Puzhao lou) and Wave Watching Pavilion (Guanlan ting); west section are Wind sheltering Pavilion (Bifeng ting), the Palace to the Goddess of the Sea (Tianhou gong), and the Palace to the Dragon King (Longwang gong). These buildings, finely arranged and divided, constitute one integrated mass with the Pavilion, which adds glamour to the whole complex.

Word Bank

pavilion	阁	hexagonal	六角的
dispatch	派遣	supernatural	神奇的
renovate	修复	fabulous	神话般的
applaud	高度称赞	panoramic	全景的
pillar	柱子	proverbial	公认的
interlocking	使连接	spectacular	壮观的景色
monolith	整体	garrison	驻军
couplet	对联	appropriate	拨款
flagstone	石板	symmetrical	对称的

参考译文

岳阳楼、黄鹤楼、滕王阁、蓬莱阁并称中国四大名楼，它们独特的建筑风格对了解中国古代的建筑风格和特点具有重要的意义。

1. 岳阳楼

雄踞岳阳市西门城头的岳阳楼（见图 21－1），与武昌黄鹤楼、南昌滕王阁合称为中国江南三大名楼，赢得“洞庭天下水，岳阳天下楼”之美誉。它屹立于岳阳古城之上，背靠岳阳城，俯瞰洞庭湖，遥对君山岛，北依长江，南通湘江，视野开阔，气象万千。

据说，岳阳楼最初是供据守城门的卫兵憩息和瞭望的谯楼。三国时期，东吴大将鲁肃在岳阳操练水兵，将其改建为阅军楼。

唐开元 4 年（716 年），中书令张说谪守岳州（今岳阳），对此楼再次进行了扩建，起名南楼，又叫岳阳楼。从此以后，历代著名诗人如杜甫、韩愈、刘禹锡、白居易、李商隐等均前来登临览胜，留下了不少名篇佳作，使岳阳楼名扬天下。

宋庆历 4 年（1044 年），滕子京谪守巴陵郡（今岳阳），重修岳阳楼，并请自己的好友、著名文学家范仲淹作《岳阳楼记》。文中他不仅凝练地描绘出岳阳楼的景色，而且抒发了他“先天下之忧而忧，后天下之乐而乐”的高洁情操，岳阳楼因此更加声名远扬。岳阳楼久经沧桑，屡毁屡修。现在看到的岳阳楼，是清同治 6 年（1867 年）重修的。

岳阳楼的建筑很有特色。岳阳楼主楼高 3 层，高达 15 米，以 4 根楠木大柱承负全楼重量，再用 12 根圆木柱子支撑 2 楼，外以 12 根梓木檐柱，顶起飞檐，结为整体，整幢建筑物未用一根铁钉及横梁。楼顶的形状酷似一顶将军头盔，雄伟壮丽，风格独特。岳阳楼这种“纯木结构，盔式楼顶”的古老建筑，充分显示了中国古代建筑艺术的独特风格和辉煌成就。

岳阳楼内陈设别具特色。各层内悬挂历代名家撰写的楹联。一、二楼各嵌有一副《岳阳楼记》雕屏。一楼的雕屏是19世纪的复制品；二楼所嵌雕屏为清朝大书法家张照所书，字形方正、笔力雄浑、技法多变、独具匠心，为传世一级珍品。三楼所嵌雕屏是毛泽东书杜甫诗《登岳阳楼》，笔法雄健奔放、形神兼备。雕屏金光耀眼、熠熠生辉。

楼的两侧有三醉亭和仙梅亭，与主楼相互衬托，相得益彰。三醉亭始建于1755年，位于岳阳楼的右侧，原名"望仙阁"，后改为"斗姆阁"，用以专门祭祀北斗星神。传说八仙之一的吕洞宾曾三次到岳阳神游，为这里秀美的山水所迷，每次喝得酩酊大醉。因此，1987年重修时改名为"三醉亭"。仙梅亭建于明崇祯十二年(1639年)，传说在施工中获得一块大青石，青石上刻有花纹，酷似枯梅，当时的人视之为仙迹，等到亭子建成以后，就将此石竖立在亭中，此亭也因此名为"仙梅亭"。亭高60米，六方形，双重檐攒尖顶，檐角高翘，玲珑素雅。

2. 黄鹤楼

黄鹤楼(见图21-2)濒临万里长江，雄踞蛇山之巅，挺拔独秀，辉煌瑰丽，享有"天下绝景"的盛誉，是"江南三大名楼"之一。黄鹤楼在文化方面的重要性使其成为武汉的标志。

黄鹤楼始建于三国时期(223年)，距今有1 700多年的历史，传说是孙权因此地位置极佳，筑城为守，建楼瞭望。名楼多传说，黄鹤楼更是如此。关于黄鹤楼的起源，另一传说为：黄鹤楼原为辛氏开设的酒店，一道士为了感谢她的请酒之恩，临行前在壁上画了一只鹤，告之它一听到拍掌声便下来起舞助兴。从此宾客盈门，生意兴隆。过了10年，道士复来，取笛吹奏，跨上黄鹤直上云天。辛氏为纪念这位帮她致富的仙翁，便在其地盖楼，取名"黄鹤楼"。

以上当然是神话传说。战时在这临江的山巅建楼，首先还是出于军事上的需要，但到了唐朝，其军事性渐弱，逐渐演变为著名的名胜景点，历代文人墨客到此游览，成为文人荟萃、宴客会友、吟诗赏景的游览胜地。历代的名人如崔颢、李白、白居易、贾岛、陆游等都曾先后到这里游览，吟诗作赋，留下不少脍炙人口的诗篇。据估计，到清同治时期，描写黄鹤楼的诗篇已达三百多首。唐代著名诗人崔颢的一首《黄鹤楼》已成为千古绝唱，更使黄鹤楼名声大噪。后来李白也登上黄鹤楼，放眼楚天，胸襟开阔，诗兴大发，正要提笔写诗时，却见崔颢的诗，自愧不如只好说："眼前有景道不得，崔颢题诗在上头。"崔颢题诗，李白搁笔，从此黄鹤楼名气更盛。

黄鹤楼原址在湖北武昌蛇山黄鹤矶头，1 700多年来屡建屡毁，1884年黄鹤楼彻底被毁，此后近百年未曾重修。1981年10月，黄鹤楼重修工程破土开工，历时4年完成，整个建筑具有独特的民族风格。主楼以清同治楼为蓝本，但更高大雄伟。运用现代建筑技术施工，钢筋混凝土框架仿木结构。飞檐5层，攒尖楼顶，金色琉璃瓦屋面，通高51.4米，底层边宽30米，顶层边宽18米，层层飞檐，四望如一。

黄鹤楼内部布置有大型壁画、楹联、文物等。底层大厅正面墙壁上为一幅巨大"白云黄鹤"陶瓷壁画，两旁立柱上悬挂着长达7米的楹联。二楼大厅正面墙上，有用大理石镌刻的唐代阎伯瑾撰写的《黄鹤楼记》，它记述了黄鹤楼的兴废沿革和名人轶事。楼记两侧为两幅壁画，一幅是《孙权筑城》，形象地说明黄鹤楼和武昌城相继诞生的历史；另一幅是《周瑜设宴》，反映三国名人在黄鹤楼的活动。三楼主要展示历朝诗人赞美黄鹤楼的诗句，如崔颢、李白、白居易等，也摘录了他们吟咏黄鹤楼的名句。四楼大厅用屏风分割成几个小厅，内置当代名人字画，供游客欣赏选购。顶层大厅有《长江万里图》等长卷、壁画。

楼外有铜铸黄鹤、神像宝塔、牌坊、轩廊、亭阁等一批辅助建筑，将主楼烘托得更加壮丽。

黄鹤楼的形制自创建以来，各朝皆不相同，但都显得高古雄浑，极富个性。与岳阳楼、滕王阁相比，黄鹤楼的平面设计为四边套八边形，谓之"四面八方"。这些数字透露出古建筑文化中数目的象征和伦理表意功能。从楼的纵向看各层排檐与楼名直接有关，形如黄鹤，展翅欲飞。整座楼雄浑之中又不失精巧，富于变化的韵味和美感。

3. 滕王阁

滕王阁(见图 21－3)位于江西省南昌市西北部沿江路赣江东岸，与湖南岳阳楼、湖北黄鹤楼并称“江南三大名楼”。因其绝佳的位置和高度、整体规模及建筑风格，享有“西江第一楼”之誉。

滕王阁之所以享有巨大名声，很大程度上归功于一篇脍炙人口的诗文《滕王阁序》。传说当时有名的诗人王勃在去广东途中路过南昌，正赶上阎都督重修滕王阁后，在阁上大宴宾客，王勃当场一气呵成，写下这一千古名篇。从此，序以阁而闻名，阁以序而著称。

滕王阁始建于 653 年，为唐太宗李世民之弟李元婴任洪州(今江西)都督时所创建。此后的 1 300多年，滕王阁屡毁屡兴达 28 次。1926 年此阁毁于兵灾，被北洋军阀纵火烧毁，仅存一块“滕王阁”青石匾。后经过南昌市民的 6 年努力，1989 年重阳节，滕王阁终于重新矗立于赣江之滨。

重修后的滕王阁，主体建筑净高 57.5 米，建筑面积为 1.3 万平方米，其下部为象征古城墙的 12 米高台座。全阁共 9 层，高台以下为两层地下室，以上为“明三暗七”，即三层明层(主层)、三层暗层(次层)及最高层(设备层)。

阁中六层的陈设各有特色，层层不同。第一层有一幅表现王勃创作《滕王阁序》的大型汉白玉浮雕《时来风送滕王阁》。第二层是一个暗层，正厅有大型壁画《人杰图》，画高 2.55 米、长 20 多米，生动地描绘了自先秦至明末的江西历代名人。第三层是一个回廊四绕的明层，陈列有壁画《临川梦》和描绘唐朝盛世繁华景象的大型铜浮雕《唐伎乐图》。第四层也是一个暗层，厅中有大型壁画《地灵图》，集中反映了江西名山大川自然景观精华。画面从南往北依次是大庾岭梅关、圭峰、道教发源地龙虎山、中国革命摇篮井冈山、庐山、中国最大淡水湖鄱阳湖、石钟山等。第五层也是一个回廊四绕的明层，是登高览胜、披襟抒怀、以文会友的最佳处，陈列了已故江西当代著名山水画大师黄秋园先生所作的《吹箫引凤图》和《西山待渡图》、苏东坡手书黄铜板制作的王勃的《滕王阁序》碑以及磨漆画《百蝶百花图》。第六层是滕王阁的最高游览层。从台座之下的底层算起，这一层实为第九层，故大厅题匾“九重天”。大厅南北东三面墙上，嵌有大型唐三彩壁画《大唐舞乐》。

4. 蓬莱阁

蓬莱阁(见图 21－4)位于山东省东部，坐落在蓬莱城北面的丹崖山上，与黄鹤楼、岳阳楼、滕王阁并称中国四大名楼。蓬莱，因有海市蜃楼之胜，被视为仙境，历史上曾是秦汉之君巡视的地方。

蓬莱阁始建于北宋嘉祐六年(1061)，由郡守朱处约建一幢单独的阁楼供人游览。到了明万历十七年，地方官李戴在蓬莱阁附近增设了一批建筑物，还是总称蓬莱阁。清朝嘉庆二十四年，知府杨丰昌和总兵刘清和主持在原有基础上扩建，蓬莱阁才形成了现在的规模：一个占地约 1.89 万平方米的古建筑群。新中国成立后，国家多次拨款修缮，至 1965 年，蓬莱阁古建筑群基本恢复原貌，集中体现了中国传统优秀建筑的特点。

蓬莱阁古建筑群占地 32 800 平方米，建筑面积 18 960 平方米，由蓬莱阁主阁、龙王宫、天后宫、三清殿、吕祖殿、弥陀寺等六部分组成。蓬莱阁主阁是一座双层木结构建筑，坐北朝南，东、西两侧前方各筑偏房、耳房，对称分布。耳房亦做门厅，有道路联结偏房及登阁石阶。主阁底层长 14.8 米，进深 9.65 米，四面回廊，明柱 16 根。正门上方悬“蓬莱阁”巨匾，为清代书法家铁保手迹。

蓬莱阁底层北墙外壁嵌有“碧海清风”、“海不扬波”、“寰海镜清”大型石刻 3 方。“碧海清风”石刻为清代著名书法家鲁琪光墨宝，十分珍贵。中日甲午战争期间，日舰炮击蓬莱，击中“海不扬波”石刻,“不”字受损,伤痕至今可见。

阁前两耳房北山墙下均立有清代碑刻,共3方,系嘉庆、道光和光绪年间修葺蓬莱阁及其附属建筑竣工后立下的纪念性碑刻。其中西耳房北面东而立的道光《重修登州蓬莱阁记》碑高2.3米,文以行体大字书就,颇有气势。西耳房内西壁嵌有“日出扶桑”“晚潮新月”“千斛碎玉”“万里澄波”“仙阁凌空”“神山现市”“狮洞烟云”“渔梁歌钓”“铜井金波”“漏天滴润”等蓬莱十大景石刻10方,均为清代之物。西偏房内存有历代碑刻10余块,均具较高的史学价值和书法艺术价值。

蓬莱阁二层长13.5米,进深8.55米,四面回廊,明柱16根,木栅格扶栏,北、东、西侧木屏风,北侧开窗,供游人凭栏观海。二层阁门南向,门外额书“碧海春融”,内额书“神州胜境”。阁内北壁正中高悬清代书法名家铁保所书“蓬莱阁”巨匾,字体雄强浑厚。西壁悬挂董必武题诗、叶剑英题联。室内木质梁柱彩绘“蓬莱十大景”“八仙图”“风竹图”等图案。周遭摆放八仙桌、八仙椅,中央塑有“八仙醉酒”组塑,是根据“八仙过海”传说中八仙在蓬莱阁酒醉后各显神通渡海遨游的情节创作的。谚语“八仙过海,各显其能”就出自这里。

蓬莱阁下方有结构精美、造型奇特的仙人桥,那是神话中八仙过海的地方。东侧有三清宫、吕祖殿、普照楼和观澜亭等;西厢为避风亭、天后宫(俗称娘娘殿)和龙王宫。蓬莱阁楼亭殿阁分布得宜,高低错落有致,与蓬莱阁浑然一体,建筑园林交相辉映,遂成为名扬四海的游览名区。

Exercises

Section A　Thought-provoking questions

1. What are the architectural features of Yueyang Tower?
2. What was the Yellow Crane Tower originally built for?
3. Why is Penglai Pavilion so famous?

Section B　Cloze

The age of the __1__ is disputed. However, it is generally believed that the pavilion was built more than 1,700 years __2__. During the Three Kingdoms Period the rudimentary __3__ of the building was that of a parade (ceremonial) pavilion. During the Western Jin and the Northern and Southern Dynasties, the pavilion was __4__ by the military with the name of “Baling Tower”. It was __5__ until the Tang Dynasty that it was renamed as the Yueyang Pavilion. The Yueyang Pavilion was damaged in the chaos of wars and was __6__ in the Song Dynasty. __7__ then, it has become a tourist __8__ and a place of inspiration for both poets and writers. The pavilion was made very __9__ during the Northern Song Dynasty by the works of Fan Zhongyan __10__ was a great politician and writer.

※ **A sovereign employs a minister with propriety, and a minister serves his sovereign with conscientiousness.**

From *Analects of Confucius*

(君使臣以礼,臣事君以忠。)

——《论语》

Chapter 22

Chinese Ancient Gardens

中国古代园林

1. Ancient Gardens

1) History of Chinese Gardens

Two main garden traditions in China evolved over time: the vast imperial gardens, emblematic of the power and wealth of the empire; and the scholar or literati gardens, built as retreats from the onerous world of officialdom. The earliest references to gardens in China are found in Zhou Dynasty records describing vast tracts of land to be reserved for hunting parks for kings and princes. Success in the hunt was a metaphor for a successful reign. Later, in the *Songs of Chu*, a 4th-century B.C. text, a shaman singer attempts to entice the soul of a dying king back to life with a description of the beauties of a garden with winding streams, lotus lakes, and distant views of the mountains. In the Shanglin park of China's first emperor, Shi Huang Di, were countless animals, birds, and exotic plants gathered as tribute from vassal states, thus creating a living replica of his entire domain. Poets such as the famed Tao Yuanming (365 – 427) recorded in verse the pleasures of strolling though one's garden. Both the Sui and Tang dynasties saw the further development of imperial and individual gardens. Wang Wei (699 – 759) created his Wangchuan villa in Lantian County, Shaanxi, a rustic retreat immortalized in poetry and paintings for centuries as the epitome of the scholar's retreat.

The Song Dynasty gave rise to the proliferation of urban literati gardens, and at Kaifeng, Song Huizong (1082 – 1135) erected the Gen Yue Mountain, an artificial construct approximately seventy-seven meters tall, including many famous garden rocks. Kublai Khan (1214 – 1294) of the Yuan Dynasty built at Beijing an extravagant city complete with lakes and hunting parks. The subsequent Ming Dynasty revised and embellished the Forbidden City with myriad courtyards and gardens and developed the Park of the Sea Palaces, a vast complex of gardens and retreats for the imperial family. The most famous of the gardens of the Qing Dynasty was the imperial Yuanmingyuan, within the precincts of which were countless watercourses, pavilions, libraries, farms, training fields for the emperor's soldiers, and European-style fountains and buildings.

2) Cosmology of Chinese Garden

The unique character of Chinese gardens has its roots in Chinese philosophy, most notably Daoism. A garden was seen as a mirror of the natural world. Everything in the universe was created from a conduct for *qi* (vital energy, or life force). The universe was understood to be a combination of *yin* (female or negative) and *yang* (male or positive) elements in a state of constant fluidity. A balance of opposites in the construction of buildings, natural features, and plantings was a goal of the garden designer. Recreating the natural world in a garden was thought to replicate the benefits of immersing oneself in nature, a belief similar to ideas about the benefits of landscape painting. Scholars whose official duties prevented them from visiting the mountains could enjoy the benefits of nature in their own gardens. The ancient practice of *fengshui* (literally, "wind-water", often translated as geomancy) consisted of situating homes, buildings, graves, and gardens properly in a landscape to receive the optimum benefit.

Traditional Chinese thought places humans as a small part of the infinite universe. Each living creature is a part of nature and the intrinsic link between humans and nature can't be broken. Chinese gardens are an effort to imitate nature in their homes, to conform to nature without breaking this fundamental connection. Each part of the garden is meant to highlight and remind visitors of the harmony between humans and nature, with the goal of breeding harmony between character and emotion.

Imperial gardens symbolized the supreme power of emperors, but were also places of recreation. Private gardens were places of relaxation and contemplation, a sanctuary to satisfy people's longing for nature. Regardless of geographic location or scale, Chinese gardens represent a Chinese tradition of finding harmony within the world by turning to nature.

3) Elements of the Garden

The two main elements of a garden are rocks and water, symbolizing the *yang* and *yin*, respectively. Traditional Chinese gardens are constructed in a series of walled outdoor courtyards, joined by walkways or doorways. Use of garden rocks (*yang*) at strategic locations within a garden brings to mind the mountain ranges and peaks of nature. Incorporation of a watercourse, pool, lake, or cascade adds the water (*yin*) and all its mutable forms. Plants are included for literary and cultural references, for seasonal suitability, and for aesthetic reasons, such as the beauty of their shadows against the light garden walls, or the harmony of the sound of wind and rain in their foliage. Buildings such as *ting* (pavilions with open sides), *xie* (gazebos), tang (formal halls), and covered walkways make accessible the featured sites in the gardens and the effects of the changing hours of the days and seasons.

Such garden structures are named with references to classical literature, and the addition of calligraphy adds another layer of appreciation to the garden. Often potted plants are placed in courtyards at the peak of their blooming seasons, and pools and lakes water lilies, lotus, and fish. Gardens also include rockeries that are constructed of aggregates of bizarrely shaped rocks made into miniature mountains or roofs for artificial caves, both symbolic of the entrance to the realms of immortals and useful as an escape from the heat of summer.

Yuan Zhi (*The Craft of Gardens*, datable to 1631 - 1634), written during the late Ming Dynasty by Ji Cheng, is considered the classic text on garden design. Encompassing both practical and aesthetic advice, the manual advises the garden designer to be sensitive to the proper use of contrasts and juxtapositions of elements and to seek the essence lying behind the forms.

2. Ancient Chinese Garden and Its Culture

Ancient Chinese gardens were created in the same way as a combination of landscape and paintings together with poems — this was the so-called "poetic garden". The design of Chinese gardens was to provide a spiritual utopia for one to connect with nature, to come back to one's inner heart, to come back to ancient idealism. Chinese gardens are a spiritual shelter for men, a place they could be far away from their real social lives, and close to the ancient way of life, their true selves, and nature. This was an escape from the frustration and disappointment of the political problems in China. They used plants as symbols. Bamboo was used in every traditional Chinese garden. This is because bamboo represents a strong but resilient character. Often pine is used to represent longevity, persistence, tenacity and dignity. The lotus is used to symbolize purity. The flowering plum is one of the most important aspects of a Chinese garden, as it represents renewal and strength of will. Flowering peaches are grown for spring color. The chrysanthemum is use to symbolize splendor, luster and "the courage to make sacrifices for a natural life". Peonies symbolize wealth and banana trees are used simply for the sound they make in the breeze.

1) Private Garden in China

In old days private gardens in China were owned by bureaucrats, landlords, rich merchants, and the scholar-gentry. During the Ming and Qing dynasties private gardens were found all over China. In the north most of them were built in Beijing. In the lower Yangtze River Valley the majority of them were found in Suzhou and Hangzhou. In the south private gardens were mostly in the Lingnan region. But among all the private gardens, those in the lower Yangtze River Valley were the most typical of Chinese garden culture — the nation's four best known gardens are all situated in this region: Anlanyuan Garden of Haining, Zhanyuan Garden of Nanjing, Lion Grove of Suzhou, and Qinyuan (Jichangyuan) Garden of Wuxi. Most private gardens are in cities. As extensions of dwellings, they are generally small in size, but look elegant and tasteful, and they perform multiple functions such as lodging, get-together, study, theatrical performance, and sightseeing. With the limited space of a garden, nature is imitated in a fastidious way. The beauty of natural landscape is condensed and reproduced in the form of artificial mountains and tree groves in a garden that could be visited and watched, and in which harmony is achieved between man and nature. In the meantime, no effort is spared to achieve a poetic grace and satisfy the fancy for a lofty and elegant lifestyle.

The Yuyuan Garden in Shanghai: a typical example of the south garden

The Yuyuan Garden is found in the southeast part of the old city of Shanghai. Pan Yunduan, who was Sichuan Provincial Administrative Commissioner of the Ming Dynasty, built this private garden for his parents in 1559. It remains as the only ancient garden in urban Shanghai, and for this reason it is protected as a national cultural legacy. The Yuyuan Garden has had its fill of ups and downs. It has changed hands repeatedly, and undergone major expansions on several occasions. The garden was also associated with many major historical events in Shanghai, but in terms of landscaping culture, it can well be regarded as a crystallization of the Chinese garden culture after the mid-Ming Dynasty. The Yuyuan Garden today is a veritable jungle of architectural structures, where the forms of artificially hills are reflected quiveringly in the ponds, and the entire place is hidden in the rich verdure of trees and plants. No wonder ancients praised it as the "best garden in the southeast".

The Yuyuan Garden abounds in exotic scenes and sights. A total of 48 scenic views-chambers, halls, pavilions, kiosks, corridors, walls, trees, rocks and ponds — are picturesquely laid out in this garden's 20,000-square-metre space. The artificial hills look real, and so do the caves. Five dragon-shaped walls divide the garden into six scenic zones with distinct features. Of all the beauty spots in the Yuyuan Garden, the Giant Artificial Hill is definitely the best. In fact, it is the largest artificial hill built of yellow stone since the Ming Dynasty. Several thousand tons of stones were consumed in constructing this hill, whose main peak stands 12 metres tall. All the stones were quarried from Wukang County in Zhejiang Province. Both the textures of rocks and their shapes were taken into full account when this hill was being piled up to evoke memory of the real thing. The presence of a footpath, cliffs, ravines, and streams has contributed to the realness the builders purported to achieve. A kiosk stands atop the hill to commander the vista beyond the walls of the Yuyuan Garden.

2) Imperial Garden in China

The term "imperial garden" generally refers to those in which emperors lived and entertained themselves. Apart from the general features of classical Chinese gardens, imperial gardens are also marked by the following five salient features.

The guideline for the design of an imperial garden gives expression to feudal autocracy and reflects the idea that the Son of Heaven is the richest man under heaven.

There is a liberal choice of locations, and the construction of an imperial garden is backed up by abundant resources, so that not only mountains and lakes in their original forms could be incorporated, but lakes dug, and mountains constructed, as well, in imitation of natural scenes. All sorts of buildings could be constructed, too.

The general layout of an imperial garden was magnificent, the buildings are beautiful or imposing and perform diverse functions, so that living in his imperial garden the emperor could administer state affairs, take up his lodging, receive tributes, feast his guests, watch theatrical performances, singing and dancing, Wushu contests, pay homage to the Buddha, collect books and treasures, observe crops, and go fishing and hunting.

Materials for the construction of gardens were wide ranging, and vast numbers of artisans could be conscripted for this purpose, so that collective wisdom was pooled and the gardens were richly varied in form.

Most imperial gardens are situated in the north, and thus susceptive to the northern climatic in so far as architectural tradition, coloration and the planting of vegetation are concerned. Despite keen efforts made to imitate famous gardens in the lower Yangtze Valley, these gardens still retain a style unique to the north.

Beijing's imperial gardens are outstanding examples of classical Chinese garden culture; they are also part of the precious world cultural heritage. Among these gardens, the Beihai Park, the Jingshan Park, the Summer Palace, Yuanmingyuan and Xiangshan Park are the most famous ones. The Mountain Summer Resort of Chengde, 250 kilometers northeast of Beijing, is generally regarded as an extension of Beijing's imperial gardens.

The Summer Palace in Beijing: a typical imperial garden

Situated in the western outskirts of Haidian District, the Summer Palace is 15 kilometers (9.3 miles) from central Beijing. Having the largest royal park and being well preserved, it was designated, in 1960 by the State Council, as a Key Cultural Relics Protection Site of China. Containing examples of the ancient arts, it also has graceful landscapes and magnificent constructions. The Summer Palace is the archetypal Chinese garden, and is ranked amongst the most noted and classical gardens of the world. In 1998, it was listed as one of the World Heritage Sites by UNESCO.

Constructed in the Jin Dynasty, during the succeeding reign of feudal emperors; it was extended continuously. By the time of the Qing Dynasty, it had become a luxurious royal garden providing royal families with rest and entertainment. Originally called Qingyi Garden (Garden of Clear Ripples), it was know as one of the famous "three hills and five gardens" (Longevity Hill, Jade Spring Mountain, and Fragrant Hill; Garden of Clear Ripples, Garden of Everlasting Spring, Garden of Perfection and Brightness, Garden of Tranquility and Brightness, and Garden of Tranquility and Pleasure). Like most of the gardens of Beijing, it could not elude the rampages of the Anglo-French Allied Force and was destroyed by fire. In 1886, Empress Dowager Cixi embezzled navy funds to reconstruct it for her own benefit, changing its name to Summer Palace (Yiheyuan). She spent most of her later years there, dealing with state affairs and entertaining. In 1900, it suffered again, being ransacked by the Eight-Power Allied Force.

Composed mainly of Longevity Hill and Kunming Lake, the Summer Palace occupies an area of 294 hectares (726.5 acres), three quarters of which is water. Guided by nature, artists designed the gardens exquisitely so that visitors would see marvelous views and be amazed by perfect examples of refined craftwork using the finest materials.

Centered on the Tower of Buddhist Incense (Foxiangge) the Summer Palace consists of over 3,000 structures including pavilions, towers, bridges, and corridors. The Summer Palace can be divided into four parts: the court area, front-hill area, front-lake area, and rear-hill and back-lake area.

Front-Hill Area: this area is the most magnificent area in the Summer Palace with the most constructions. Its layout is quite distinctive because of the central axis from the yard of Kunming Lake to the hilltop, on which important buildings are positioned including Gate of Dispelling Clouds, Hall of Dispelling Clouds, Hall of Moral Glory, Tower of Buddhist Incense, the Hall of the Sea of Wisdom, etc.

Rear-Hill and Back-Lake Area: although the constructions are fewer here, it has a unique landscape, with dense green trees, and winding paths. Visitors can feel a rare tranquility, and elegance. This area includes scenic spots such as Garden of Harmonious Interest and Suzhou Market Street.

Court Area: this is where Empress Dowager Cixi and Emperor Guangxu met officials, conducted state affairs and rested. Entering the East Palace Gate, visitors may see the main palace buildings: the Hall of Benevolence and Longevity served as the office of the Emperor, the Hall of Jade Ripples where Guangxu lived, the Hall of Joyful Longevity, Cixi's residence, the Hall of Virtue and Harmony where Cixi was entertained.

Front Lake Area: covering a larger part of the Summer Palace, opens up the vista of the lake. A breeze fluttering, waves gleam and willows kiss the ripples of the vast water. In this comfortable area there are the Eastern and Western Banks, the Seventeen-Arch Bridge, Nanhu Island, and so on. On the western bank float six distinct bridges amongst which the Jade-Belt Bridge is the most beautiful.

3. The Influence of Chinese Garden on the World

As early as in the 6th century, Japan had already known of Chinese garden landscaping through Marco Polo, who visited many Song Dynasty gardens in southern China during the Yuan Dynasty. In the 17th century, Chinese garden landscaping was introduced to England where it then spread to France and the rest of Europe. In the late 18th century, Chinese garden landscaping had a huge influence on the European Romantic Movement, and European landscaping moved away from a stiff aristocratic style to a more natural style found in Chinese gardens.

Western and Eastern garden landscaping bear different forms and styles because of different philosophies and sense of aesthetic beauty. In form, Western landscaping embodies artificial beauty with symmetrical, regular and well-knit layouts. Geometry is ever-present as flowers and plants are pruned upright and square. Chinese garden landscaping doesn't require symmetry or fixed regulations as plants, trees and buildings are built to a natural form. Whereas Western landscaping theory aims to remedy the defects of nature, Chinese garden landscaping blends plants and buildings into an organic whole and imitates nature by building mountains (rocky outcroppings) with flowing water to present a quality suggestive of poetry or painting. To fully enjoy the beauty of Chinese gardens, it's important to understand the philosophy implied through the sceneries.

Word Bank

evolve	使逐步形成	fluidity	流动性
emblematic	象征的	optimum	最佳的，最适宜的
literati	文人	cascade	瀑布
onerous	艰巨的，繁重的	mutable	易变的
officialdom	官场	aggregate	集料，骨料
tracts	大块地	juxtaposition	并列，并置
entice	诱惑，怂恿	miniature	微型复制品
tribute	贡品	encompass	包含，包括
replica	复制品	manual	指南，手册
domain	领地，领土	foliage	叶，叶子
cosmology	宇宙学	resilient	有弹性的
intrinsic	固有的，内在的	tenacious	抓牢的，握紧的
epitome	典型的人或事	splendor	华丽
proliferate	快速繁殖、增长	luster	柔和的光泽，荣耀
embellish	美化，装饰	gentry	绅士

fastidious	精心挑选的	elude	躲避,逃避
salient	显著的,主要的	rampage	狂暴地乱冲乱撞
layout	布局	embezzle	挪用
vista	景色	ransack	抢劫,彻底搜索
veritable	名副其实的	exquisite	精美的,雅致的
crystallize	使结晶,使具体化	tranquility	平静,安宁
archetype	原型	dispelling	驱散,使消失
designate	指定,选定		

参考译文

1. 古代园林

1) 中国园林的历史

在中华民族漫长的历史长河中逐步形成了两个园林传统:皇家园林和私家园林。前者是皇室权力和财富的象征;后者是文人学者隐退后,远离尘嚣的居所。中国最早有关园林的记载是在周朝。当时的园林是王侯公子们狩猎的场所。狩猎成功预示统治的成功。后来,在《楚辞》中描述了一位巫师吟歌描述一个美丽的园林以唤醒临死的国王:蜿蜒的小溪、宜人的荷塘、悠悠的远山。在秦始皇的上林苑里,蓄养各种鸟兽,栽培异地引进的植被,还有来自诸侯各国的各种贡品。园林就是一个小王国。晋代诗人陶渊明(365 年—427 年)曾向人们展示了悠然自得的园林生活。隋、唐是中国园林发展时期。山水诗人王维隐退后,建造了蓝田辋川园林(现在陕西省),过着隐居的生活。蓝田辋川园林是传统文人园林的典范。

宋朝的文人园林发展很快。宋徽宗(1082 年—1135 年)大兴土木,他在开封修建的园林,一座假山就高达 77 米。元朝忽必烈(1214 年—1294 年)在京城修建的豪华园林,有山有水,还有狩猎场。明朝修缮、扩建了紫禁城、北海公园以及其他皇家园林。清朝最有名的皇家园林是圆明园,园中水道众多,集楼阁、书院、练武场、西洋建筑于一体。

2) 中国园林宇宙观

中国园林的一个典型特征是它深深扎根中国哲学尤其是道家哲学。园林可以看成是自然界的一面镜子。根据道家的观点,宇宙万物都含“气”。天下万形都是由“气”构成的。一阴一阳的规律普遍存在于天地万物运动变化过程之中,促成万物的生灭变化。因此,中国古代园林的建造、布局、自然环境的取舍、树木植被的配备都十分讲究得体、平衡。中国的园林强调主体意识的参与、强调人与自然合一,强调诗、情、画的统一。文人官员平常事务缠身,不能游山玩水,私家园林就是他们修身养性的好地方。古代中国人讲究“风水”,房屋、墓地、园林等各种建筑选址都必须得当、适宜,以图吉利。

根据中国传统的思想,人是宇宙的一部分,每一个生物都是自然的一部分,人与自然不能分割。中国园林的特点是模仿自然,遵循自然规律。园林中的每一部分都强调人与自然的和谐,可以让人达到内心的平静。

皇家园林象征着皇帝至高无上的权威,但也是他们娱乐休闲的好地方。私家园林是主人退思、享乐、疗养、陶冶性情的地方。总之,无论大小,无论位置的好坏,中国园林都体现着人与自然和谐相处的传统。

3）园林的构成要素

园林构成的两个要素是山和水，它们分别代表着阳和阴。传统的园林由一群庭院组成，庭院之间通过小道和长廊连接。园林里的山布局讲究，是"阳"的象征，有一种使人联想到自然界群山巍峨的雄伟气势（即"阳刚之美"）。而这里的流水、池塘、湖泊、瀑布则是"阴"的象征，增添了园林的柔美秀丽（即"阴柔之美"）。树木植被的选择既要适合季节的变迁更替，又要体现主人的文化修养、审美情趣，要让光与影、动与静和谐统一，风声、雨声和落叶声声声入耳。亭、台、楼、阁、榭、廊等既自成一景，又把整个园林连接成一个整体。

与经典文学和古代书法联系在一起是中国园林的又一特征。庭院里摆放着盆景，池塘、湖泊种满荷花，鱼儿在水里嬉戏。这里还有假山，用各种奇形怪状的石料砌成，形状惟妙惟肖，如同天成。假山里还有些人工洞穴。不管是假山还是山洞，都是通往天国、进入极乐世界的象征。不过，夏天这里是纳凉避暑的好地方。

明朝晚期计成撰写的《园治》是一部有关园林的经典著作。这部著作不仅具有实用价值，而且具有审美价值。他主张将构成园林的诸要素相互比较、相互映衬，寻找各种要素的最佳组合，达到最理想的效果。

2. 中国园林文化

中国古代园林可以称得上是诗、景、画的统一，故中国园林有"诗园"之称。园林是主人的精神家园，在这里，他们回归自然，远离尘嚣，远离人世间的各种悲欢离合，如同一个世外桃源。园林里的陈设、布局都十分讲究。竹或竹林是传统园林的一大特色，因为竹坚固、有弹性，是正直、豁达的象征。园林里松树也是必不可少的，松象征着长寿、矢志不移与人格尊严。荷花喻指清廉、纯洁。梅花喻指意志坚强。桃花代表春天的颜色。菊花象征着华丽、荣耀和敢于自我牺牲的勇气。牡丹象征着财富。而芭蕉树迎风作响为整个庭院带来一丝活力。

1）私家园林

过去，只有官僚、地主、富有商贾、学者、绅士才有私家园林。明、清时期，私家园林遍及全国。北方集中在北京，南方集中在苏、杭。在南方园林中，海宁的安澜园、南京的瞻园、苏州的狮子林和无锡的寄畅园等都享有盛名。大多数私家园林都在城市，面积一般不大，但都很幽雅、美丽。它们既是主人的居所，又是他们学习、聚会、娱乐和玩赏的好地方。私家园林面积虽然有限，但这里的假山假水形象逼真，花草树木五彩缤纷、郁郁葱葱，人与自然浑然一体。有雅兴的人，还可以吟诗作画，意趣横生。

南方园林的典范——上海的豫园

豫园坐落在上海老城的东南部。豫园的原主人是潘允端，明代曾任四川布政使。为了使双亲生活得愉悦，于1559年在上海建造起一座园林。它是上海唯一的一座古代私家园林，系全国重点文物保护单位。它历经兴衰，几易其主，几度扩建，见证了上海的变迁。从文化层面上讲，它是中国古代园林文化的具体表现。今天的豫园融入了多种建筑风格，山石池水，相互映衬，出奇制胜。整个建筑都掩映在茂密的花草树林之中。难怪古人称它是"东南园林一绝"。

豫园有名的景点处处皆是，2万平方米的面积内居室、大厅、亭台、楼阁、长廊、城墙、假山、池塘、花草、树木等，应有尽有。假山生动逼真，城墙形状似龙，把整个园林分成六个风格各异的景区。豫园所有景点中，假山最为夺目耀眼，由几千吨黄石砌成，是明代以后建成的最大假山，最高处达12米。这些石头都是从浙江武康采集而来的，它们纹理清晰、棱角分明。园中小路曲径通幽，悬崖拔地而起，小溪环绕山谷，一个亭子坐落山顶，在这里可以俯瞰豫园全景。

2）皇家园林或皇宫

皇家园林是古代皇帝生活、享乐的地方。除了一般园林的典型特征之外，皇家园林还具备其他5个特征。

皇家园林是封建专制统治的集中体现，表达皇帝是普天下最富有的人这一思想。

皇家园林可以自由选址，园林的建设不受资源的限制。没有自然山水，可以建造假山假水，各类建筑都可以建造。

皇家园林富丽堂皇，既是皇帝生活、施政的地方，又是皇帝宴请宾客、接受贡品、看戏、习武、狩猎、钓鱼、祭祀等的场所。

皇家园林汇集各方优秀的工匠和各种建筑材料，工匠们技艺超群、身手不凡，因此，他们造就的园林建筑千姿百态，栩栩如生。

绝大多数皇家园林都在北方，它们依照北方的建筑传统、气候和植被特征而建，尽管力求模仿长江中下游地区的园林，但还是北方园林的典型代表。

北京皇家园林是中国古典园林文化的代表，也是世界珍贵文化遗产的一部分。在这些皇家园林中，北海公园、景山公园、颐和园、圆明园和香山公园最为有名。位于北京东北面250千米远的承德避暑山庄可以看成北京皇家园林的延伸。

典型的皇家园林——北京颐和园

颐和园位于北京市西北部海淀区，距市中心约15千米。它是中国最大的保存完好的皇家花园，1960年被指定为国家级重点文物保护单位。这里不仅保存着重要文物，而且风景优美，各种建筑富丽堂皇。颐和园是最典型的中国皇家园林，是世界上最负盛名、最经典的花园之一。1998年，颐和园被联合国教科文组织正式列入《世界遗产名录》。

颐和园建于金朝，经历几个朝代的变迁，不断扩大，到清朝已经成为一个豪华奢侈的皇家花园，供皇室成员休闲娱乐。颐和园的前身为“清漪园”，是清代北京著名的“三山五园”中最后落成的一处皇家园林。“三山”是指万寿山、玉泉山和香山。“五园”则是指万寿山的清漪园、畅春园、圆明园和玉泉山的静明园以及香山的静宜园。像北京大多数园林那样，颐和园也遭受了英法联军的烧杀掠夺。1886年，慈禧太后挪用海军军费重新修缮、改造清漪园，并更名为颐和园。慈禧太后基本上就是在这里处理朝政、安度晚年。1900年，八国联军进攻北京，颐和园再遭劫难。

万寿山和昆明湖构成颐和园的主体，它占地294公顷（726.5英亩），其中大部分是水面。这里优美的自然景观和能工巧匠的杰作，交相辉映，浑然天成，令来往游客赞不绝口、惊叹不已！

颐和园以佛香阁为中心，共有3 000多幢建筑，包括亭、阁、塔、桥、廊。全园分勤政殿、万寿前山区、前湖（昆明湖）区、后山和后湖区四部分。

前山是颐和园中最富丽堂皇的区域，大部分建筑都集中在这里。其布局、结构都很分明。从昆明湖至万寿山顶，构成中轴，沿着中轴线是排云门、排云殿、德辉殿、佛香阁，直至山顶的智慧海。

后山、后湖区建筑物较少，但却风景别致。碧水潆回，曲径通幽、古松参天、郁郁葱葱。这里的景点有被称为“园中之园”的谐趣园和苏州街。

勤政殿（后更名为仁寿殿）在颐和园大门东宫门内，是慈禧、光绪坐朝听政的大殿。游客从东宫门进入，便可看到几幢主要的建筑。仁寿殿是皇帝朝政的地方；玉澜堂是光绪皇帝的寝宫；乐寿堂是慈禧居住的地方。德和园是慈禧看戏娱乐的地方。

前湖区占地面积最大。湖面宽阔，微风徐来，波光粼粼，泛起阵阵涟漪。这里有东堤和西堤、17拱桥、南湖岛等景观。其中，用汉白玉雕砌的玉带桥桥拱高耸，远望如一条玉带，造型优美。

3. 中国园林对世界的影响

早在6世纪，日本就通过欧洲人马可·波罗了解了中国的园林（马可·波罗于元朝时来到中国，参观过南方的很多园林）。17世纪，中国的园林被介绍到英国，又从英国传到法国乃至整个欧洲大陆。对18世纪的欧洲浪漫主义运动产生了巨大影响，欧洲园林风格从追求贵族气演变成中国式的自然恬静。

由于哲学观和审美观的不同，中、西园林也有不同的形式和风格。从形式上讲，西方的园林注重人工之美、对称之美、工整之美和结构之美。中国的园林不讲究对称、工整，没有固定的格式，花草、树木、建筑遵循自然规律。西方的园林是弥补自然的不足，中国的园林强调人与自然的和谐，假山、流水、亭台、楼阁如诗如画。要欣赏中国的园林的美，必须熟悉理解隐藏在其中的中国传统哲学。

Exercises

Section A Thought-provoking questions

1. What are the two main garden traditions in China?
2. Why does the author think that the unique character of Chinese gardens has its roots in Chinese philosophy?
3. Why were Chinese gardens called a spiritual utopia?
4. What are the four best-known gardens in the Lingnan region according the passage?
5. What is the "imperial garden"?
6. In 1998, why was the Summer Palace listed as one of the World Heritage Sites by UNESCO?

Section B Decide whether the following statements are true or false

1. Chinese gardens are a spiritual shelter for people because it is a place they could be far away from the sound and fury of social life.
2. Typically, ancient Chinese gardens can be divided into private gardens and national gardens.
3. An imperial garden could be built in any place if the emperor thought it necessary.
4. In old days private gardens in China were owned by bureaucrats, landlords, rich merchants, and the scholar-gentry.
5. The Yuyuan Garden has not undergone ups and downs since it was built.
6. Of all the beauty spots in the Yuyuan Garden, the walls are definitely the best.
7. The Summer Palace is a place where royal families live, rest and entertain themselves.
8. The Summer Palace can be divided into four parts: the court area, front-hill area, front-lake area, and rear-hill and back-lake area.
9. Court Area is where Empress Dowager Cixi and Emperor Guangxu met officials.
10. In the Summer Palace, lake covers more area than hills.

Chapter 23

The Silk Road

丝绸之路

1. What is "the Silk Road"?

The Silk Road was a general name for the ancient strategic transportation channel which started from China and passed through Central Asia, West Asia, Africa and Europe. In the 19th century, when the name of Silk Road was first used by a German geographer, it just included the land road from China's Xinjiang to Central Asia. Later it was expanded gradually and reached West Asia, Europe and Africa. It took in land and water routes. It is not only an important route connecting the ancient world, but also a synonym for economic and cultural exchanges between the western world and the oriental world.

1) Early History of the Silk Road

The Silk Road was an international passage with historical significance. The ancient Silk Road helped to integrate the old Chinese, Indian, Persian, Arabian, ancient Greek and Roman cultures and promote the exchange of the Occidental and Oriental civilizations.

Zhang Qian of the Han Dynasty is the first diplomat who led a diplomatic mission to Xiyu (ancient Xinjiang). He traveled the road and took gold and silk products there between 139 B.C. and 138 B.C. His assistants visited Anxi (now Iran), India and a number of other countries. These countries and regions in turn also sent diplomatic missions to China, which brought a busy trade to Xinjiang. Ancient central China's silk products, iron ware, gold, bronze mirror, bamboo work, medicine, farming techniques were introduced to Xiyu (ancient Xinjiang), India and Europe. And grape, flax, walnut, cucumber, elephant, camel and house and some other plants and animals were taken to central China at that time.

Ban Chao and his assistant Gan Ying are other two diplomats sent to Xiyu by the Han government. They led a diplomatic mission of 36 people and arrived at Xiyu and Daqin (ancient Rome) on the Persian Gulf. India's famous monk also came to central China's Henan through Pakistan and Afghanistan in 147 and 401 respectively, to translate Buddhist Scriptures and enroll thousands of disciples. Chinese high-ranking monk Xuan Zang in the Tang Dynasty visited India and dozens of other countries and districts and did missionary work in these countries along the Silk Road.

Another historic person worth mentioning here is Italy's famous adventurer Marco Polo. He came to Yuan's capital Dadu along the Silk Road in 1275. He gave a detailed description about the local custom and culture in his book *The Travels*.

2) Europe's Fascination with Silk

In only a few decades all the ruling families of Rome were anxious to attire themselves in silk. By A.D. 14, silk had gotten so out of hand that Emperor Tiberius, disgusted by the revelatory bulges of this light and delicate fabric, forbade all men from wearing it. Before long the mystery of silk's manufacture sucked Rome's intellectuals into a blazing fervor. Pliny affirmed that "Silk was obtained by removing the down from the leaves with the help of water". Others countered that it grew like wood in the forest.

Despite the foment of wild curiosity of its customers, the prudent merchants of China made every effort to keep silk's manufacture a secret. It was limited to the far off hinterlands of Sichuan, away from the prying eyes and the "big noses" of venturesome foreigners. Border guards, placed on high alert, double-checked all foreigners' belongings.

A legion of stories of silk smuggling spread far and wide. The most romantic involves a young Chinese princess anxious to please her betrothed, the King of Yutian. When the King's envoy revealed to her his master's passion for silk, the princess resolved to smuggle the secret of silk to him. A few days later the princess set off in a glittering cavalcade on her long journey westwards. Many days later, when they reached China's border at Dunhuang's Yumen Gate, her party was thoroughly inspected. Even the princess' personal belongings were closely scrutinized, much to the displeasure of the king's envoy. After passing through the border gate, he approached the princess to inquire if she had succeeded in satiating his King's love of silk. Removing her crown, the princess revealed silk worms hidden in her hair. Amongst her medicines, she showed him the mulberry seeds she had hidden in plain sight. Pointing at her serving maids, she revealed that, "all women in the Central Plains know how to grow mulberry seeds and rear silk worms." Thus, the secret of silk escaped the confines of China.

3) The Nature of the Route

The description of this route to the west as the "Silk Road" is somewhat misleading. Firstly, although the route started from the capital in Chang'an, there are many branches. The northern route then passed through Yumen Guan (Jade Gate Pass) and crossed the neck of the Gobi desert to Hami. The southern route branched off at Dunhuang, passing through the Yang Guan and skirting the southern edges of the desert, via Miran, Hetian and Shache, finally turning north again to meet the other route at Kashgar.

Secondly, the Silk Road was not a trade route that existed solely for the purpose of trading in silk; many other commodities were also traded, from gold and ivory to exotic animals and plants. Of all the precious goods crossing this area, silk was perhaps the most remarkable for the people of the West. In addition to silk, the route carried many other precious commodities. Caravans heading towards China carried gold and other precious metals, ivory, precious stones, and glass, which were not manufactured in China until the 5th century. In the opposite direction furs, ceramics, jade, bronze objects, lacquer and iron were carried.

4) The Development of the Route

The development of these Central Asian trade routes caused some problems for the Han rulers in China. Bandits soon learnt of the precious goods traveling up the Gansu Corridor and skirting the Taklimakan desert, and took advantage of the terrain to plunder these caravans. Caravans of goods needed their own defense forces, and this was an added cost for the merchants making the trip. This was partially overcome by building forts and defensive walls along part of the route. Sections of the "Great Wall" were built along the northern side of the Gansu Corridor, to try to prevent the Huns from harming the trade. Sections of Han dynasty wall can still be seen as far as Yumen Guan. However, these fortifications were not all as effective as intended, as the Chinese lost control of sections of the route at regular intervals.

After the Western Han dynasty, successive dynasties brought more states under Chinese control. Settlements came and went, as they changed hands or lost importance due to a change in the routes. The Chinese garrison town of Loulan, for example, on the edge of the Lop Por Lake, was important in the 3rd century, but was abandoned when the Chinese lost control of the route for a period. Many settlements were buried during times of abandonment by the sands of the Taklimakan.

The settlements reflected the nature of the trade passing through the region. Silk, on its way to the west, often got no further than this region of Central Asia. The Astana tombs, where the nobles of Gaochang were buried, have turned up examples of silk cloth from China, as well as objects from as far afield as Persia and India. Much can be learned about the customs of the time from the objects found in these graves, and from the artwork of the time, which has been excellently preserved on the tomb walls, due to the extremely dry conditions.

The most significant commodity carried along this route was not silk, but religion. Buddhism came to China from India this way, along the northern branch of the route. The Eastern Han Emperor Mingdi is thought to have sent a representative to India to discover more about this strange faith, and further missions returned bearing scriptures, and bringing with them Indian priests. With this came influences from the Indian sub-continent, including Buddhist artwork. This was considerably influenced by the Himalayan Massif, an effective barrier between China and India, and hence Buddhism in China is effectively derived from the Gandhara culture by the bend in the Indus (a river in Northwestern India), rather than directly from India. Buddhism reached the pastures of Tibet at a rather later period, not developing fully until the 7th century. Along the way it developed under many different influences, before reaching central China. This is displayed clearly in the artwork, where many of the cave paintings show people with clearly different ethnic backgrounds, rather than the expected Central and East Asian peoples.

The greatest flux of Buddhism into China occurred during the Northern Wei Dynasty, in the 4th and 5th centuries. This was at a time when China was divided into several different kingdoms, and the Northern Wei Dynasty had its capital in Datong in present day Shanxi Province. The rulers encouraged the development of Buddhism, and more missions were sent towards India. The new religion spread slowly eastwards, through the oases surrounding the Taklimakan, encouraged by an increasing number of merchants, missionaries and pilgrims. Many of the local peoples adopted Buddhism as their own religion.

Some devotees were sufficiently inspired by the new ideas that they headed off in search of the source, towards India; others started to build monasteries, grottos. The development of the grotto is particularly interesting; the edges of the Taklimakan hide some of the best examples in the world. The hills surrounding the desert are mostly of sandstone, with any streams or rivers carving cliffs that can be relatively easily dug into; there was also no shortage of funds for the work, particularly from wealthy merchants, anxious to invoke protection or give thanks for a safe desert crossing. Gifts and donations of this kind were seen as an act of merit, which might enable the donor to escape rebirth into this world. In many of the murals, the donors themselves are depicted, often in pious attitude. This explains why the Mogao grottos contain some of the best examples of Buddhist artwork.

The best-known grottos are the Mogao grottos at Dunhuang, at the eastern end of the Taklimakan. It is here that the greatest number and some of the best examples are to be found. More is known about the origins of these, too, as large quantities of ancient documents have been found. These are on a wide range of subjects, and include a large number of Buddhist scriptures in Chinese, Sanskrit, Tibetan, Uygur and other languages, some still unknown. There are documents from the other faiths that developed in the area and also some official documents and letters that reveal a lot about the system of government at the time.

The grotto building was not confined to the Taklimakan; there is a large cluster at Bamiyan in the Hindu Kush, in present-day Afghanistan. It is here that the second largest sculpture of Buddha in the world can be found, at 55 metres high.

For the archaeologist these grottos are particularly valuable sources of information about the Silk Road. Along with the images of Buddhas, there are scenes of the everyday life of the people at the time. Scenes of celebration and dancing give an insight into local customs and costume. The influences of the Silk Road traffic are therefore quite clear in the mix of cultures that appears on these murals at different dates. In particular, the development of Buddhism from the Indian style to a more individual faith is evident on studying the murals from different eras in any of the grotto clusters.

The Northern Wei Dynasty, which is perhaps the most responsible for the spread of Buddhism in China, started the construction of the Yungang grottos in northern Shanxi Province. When the capital of the Northern Wei was transfered to Luoyang, the artists and masons started building the Longmen grottos. These two more "Chinese" grottos emphasized carving and statuary rather than the delicate murals of the Taklimakan regions, and the figures are quite impressive in their size; the largest figure at Yungang measures more than 17 metres in height, second only in China to the great Leshan Buddha in Sichuan, which was constructed in the early 8th Century.

5) The Greatest Years

The height of the importance of the Silk Road was during the Tang Dynasty, with relative internal stability in China after the divisions of the earlier dynasties since the Han. The individual states has mostly been assimilated, and the threats from marauding peoples were rather less. Chang'an, as the starting point of the route, as well as the capital of the dynasty, developed into one of the largest and most cosmopolitan cities of the time. By 742, the population had reached almost two million, and the city itself covered almost the same area as present-day Xi'an, considerably more than within the present walls of the city. The 754 census showed that five thousand foreigners lived in the city, like Turks, Iranians, Indians and others from along the Road, as well as Japanese, Koreans and Malays from the east. Many were missionaries, merchants or pilgrims, but every other occupation was also represented. Rare plants, medicines, spices and other goods from the west were to be found in the bazaars of the city. It is quite clear, however, despite the exotic imports, that the Chinese regarded all foreigners as barbarians; the gifts provided for the Emperors by foreign rulers were simply considered as tribute from vassal states.

During this period, in the 7th century, the Chinese traveller Xuan Zang crossed the region on his way to obtain Buddhist scriptures from India. He followed the northern branch on his outward journey, and the southern route on his return; he carefully recorded the cultures and styles of Buddhism along the way and brought back 600 scriptures from India. He is still seen by the Chinese as an important influence in the development of Buddhism in China.

6) The Decline of the Silk Road

Politically, when the Yuan Dynasty was replaced by the Ming Dynasty in 1368, the Ming Dynasty carried on the isolationist policies, these policies did nothing to encourage trade between China and the West. This attitude was maintained throughout the Ming and Qing Dynasties. Therefore, the barriers rose on the land route between East and West.

The decline of the Silk Road also owes much to the development of the silk route by sea. It was becoming rather easier and safer to transport goods by water rather than overland. Ships had become stronger and more reliable, and the route passed promising new markets in Southern Asia. The overland problems of "tribal politics" between the different peoples along the route prompted this move. In the early 15th century, the Chinese seafarer Zheng He commanded seven major maritime expeditions to Southeast Asia and India, and as far as Arabia and the east coast of Africa. Diplomatic relations were built up with several countries along the route, and this increased the volume of trade Chinese merchants brought to the area.

2. *The Travels of Marco Polo* and the Silk Road

Marco Polo (1254 - 1324) was an Italian trader and explorer who gained fame for his worldwide travels. Polo was one of the first Westerners to travel the Silk Road to China (which he called Cathay). The Polo party left Venice in 1271. They spent 17 years in China and left China in late 1290 or early 1291 and were back in Venice in 1292.

After returning to Europe, he wrote *The Travels of Marco Pole*, describing his traveling experiences. The book had been an authoritative book for those who studied the history of China, especially the history of Yuan Dynasty. Marco Polo went east to the capital of Yuan Dynasty from Crimea along the Silk Road. In *The Travel*, Marco Polo recorded in detail what he saw in the Western Region and Persia, from custom and habit, dressing, languages, etiquette, character and script to how they were influenced by the oriental Empire. Marco Polo arrived at Dadu (the Capital of Yuan Dynasty) in 1275, approximately 30 years after the Mongolian army Europe. Despite the attempt of Yuan Taizu to turn the whole world into grassland for tending the animals the Mongolians left nothing but dreadful memory to Europe. It seems that conquest by armed forces is not as effective as civilization. Marco Polo was surprised that even in Yuan Dynasty, the countries of Western Region should retain the ancient oriental civilization of several hundred years ago. Though Tang Dynasty had fallen for nearly 500 to 600 years, its influence and prestige, through the Silk Road, on the West Asia, Mid-Asia and Europe still remained.

Word Bank

integrate	使构成整体,使融合
diplomat	外交家,外交官
missionary	传教士
attire	使穿衣
revelatory	揭示性的
bulge	凸起,膨胀
fervor	热情
affirm	肯定,断定
foment	引起,增长
prudent	精明的
hinterland	内地,腹地
double-check	复查,仔细检查
legion	众多,大批
envoy	使者,外交官
cavalcade	马车队
scrutinize	仔细检查
satiate	使某人充分满足
mulberry	桑树
confine	界限,边界,范围
mislead	误导
skirt	沿着某物的边缘走
caravan	穿越沙漠的旅行队或商队
assimilate	使同化,吸收
cosmopolitan	世界性的
pilgrim	朝圣者,香客
barbarian	野蛮人,粗鲁人
tribute	贡品
vassal	附庸,下属,附属国
isolationist	闭关锁国的,孤立主义的
plunder	掠夺,抢劫
fortification	防御性工程
flux	流量,流出量
oasis (*pl*. oases)	绿洲
devotee	信徒,热情拥护者
monastery	修道院
mason	石匠

参考译文

1. 什么是丝绸之路?

丝绸之路是古代中国联系中亚、西亚、非洲和欧洲的交通要道。19 世纪,德国一个地理学家首次使用"丝绸之路"这一术语,一直沿用到今天。起初,它指从中国新疆到中亚的陆地通道。后来,它延伸到西亚、非洲和欧洲。丝绸之路有水、陆之分。它不仅是中西的交通要道,而且也是中西经济、文化交流的代名词。

1) 丝绸之路的早期历史

丝绸之路是一个国际通道,历史悠久。它促进了古代中国文化与印度文化、波斯文化、阿拉伯文化、希腊文化和罗马文化的交流,在中西文化交流之间建立了一座桥梁。

汉代的张骞是第一个出使西域的人。公元前 139 年至公元前 138 年,他把黄金、丝绸带到西域。他们一行最终到了安息(现在伊朗)、印度等国。这些国家也派外交使团来到中国,双边贸易非常繁荣。那时中原的丝绸、铁器、黄金制品、青铜器、竹器、中药和农耕技术等被介绍到西域、印度和欧洲。葡萄、亚麻、胡桃、黄瓜、大象、骆驼等动植物被带到当时的中原。

班超是另一位汉朝派遣出使西域的使者。他带领的使团 36 人,不仅到达了西域,而且远至波斯湾的大秦(古罗马)。公元 147 年和公元 401 年,印度先后两次派人来华翻译佛经,传播佛教。唐代高僧玄奘也沿丝绸之路西游印度和其他国家,探求佛本法源。

意大利冒险家马可·波罗1275年沿着丝绸之路来到中国。他曾到过元朝首都大都。他把一路上的所见所闻作了详细的描述,完成了著名的《马可·波罗游记》。

2) 欧洲对丝绸的狂热

仅仅几十年,所有罗马统治阶层都渴望穿上丝绸服装。大约公元14年,丝绸极其紧缺,可是人们对丝绸制品的渴望与追求与日俱增,罗马皇帝下令所有人严禁穿丝绸服装。不久,丝绸生产的秘密引起了罗马有识之士的极大兴趣。普利尼断定丝绸是从树叶中提取出来的。有人认为,它像树一样是在森林里长出来的。

尽管人们对丝绸的好奇心日甚一日,但精明的中国商人却严守丝绸生产的秘密。为了避开那些敢于冒险的西方人的耳目,丝绸生产限制在内地(四川一带)。边界有重兵把守,来往外国人必须经过严格的检查,才能放行。

有关丝绸走私方面的故事有很多。最浪漫的是一位中国公主的故事,她爱上了于阗国的国王,而国王对中国的丝绸情有独钟,为了取悦她的未婚夫,她下定决心把丝绸生产的秘密带给国王。几天后,公主及随行车队启程,开始漫长的西行之旅。他们来到玉门关,所有随行人员包括公主都受到了严格的检查,这令国王的使者大为不快。过了玉门关之后,使者便问公主是否带来了心爱的丝绸。公主摘掉帽子,把藏匿在头发里的蚕虫拿出来,又把藏在中药里的桑树种子取出来,并环顾左右,对侍女说:"中原所有的女人都会种桑树,都会养蚕。"自此,丝绸生产的秘密就冲出了国界,传到了西方。

3) 丝绸之路的特征

"丝绸之路"的提法可能导致西方人的误解。首先,丝绸之路虽起于长安,但并非只有一条线路,而是有很多分支。通常有南线、北线之分。北线通过玉门关,沿戈壁沙漠至哈密。南线从敦煌分出,穿越阳关,沿南部沙漠至和田、莎车,最后往北,与其他线路交汇于喀什。其次,丝绸之路作为贸易之路的功能并不仅仅限于丝绸贸易,还包括很多别的商品的交易,如黄金、象牙和各种动植物等。只不过丝绸制品最受西方人青睐罢了。外国商队把珍贵的金属、象牙、宝石、玻璃等带到中国;中国则把皮毛、陶器、玉器、青铜器、中国漆、铁器等传到西方。

4) 丝绸之路的发展

中亚贸易通道的开通,为汉朝统治者们带来了很多问题。运输一些珍贵商品的商人,当他们通过甘肃走廊和塔克拉玛干沙漠时,时常会遭到匪徒们的抢劫。由于商品运输需要防卫,这样运输成本就增加了。朝廷修筑要塞、城墙,起了一定的保护作用。甘肃走廊北部长城的建设就是为了防止匈奴的袭击。汉长城一直修到了玉门关。不过,随着朝廷政权的更替,这些要塞有时是名存实亡。

西汉之后,后续王朝兴衰存亡、不断更替变迁。比如,罗布泊边上的古镇楼兰,3世纪时是丝绸之路上一个重要军事要塞,随着汉人统治地位的丧失,楼兰就被废弃了,无数生命葬身于茫茫的塔克拉玛干沙漠。

丝绸之路沿线生活定居情况反映出了当时的贸易特征。丝绸最远被带到中亚地区。以阿斯塔纳墓为例,这里埋葬的是当时高昌国的贵族阶层。在这个墓里,既发现了来自中国的丝绸,又发现了来自波斯、印度的物品。由于当地气候干燥,坟墓中的物品包括艺术品都保存完好,对了解当时的习俗文化大有帮助。

不过,这条通道上来往最重要的商品不是丝绸,而是宗教。佛教就是通过丝绸之路传到中国的。据说东汉皇帝曾派人出使印度,学习佛教,带回佛教经典。印度文化主要是佛教文化开始影响中国。由于受到印、中之间喜马拉雅山脉的阻隔，佛教及印度文化主要是通过印度河传入中国的。佛教传入西藏地区稍晚一些，直到7世纪才得到全面展开。沿着这条线路，佛教传入中原地区，并受到多种文化的影响。这一点在一些艺术作品尤其是壁画作品上表现得特别清楚：壁画上展示的是多民族的文化背景，绝不仅仅是中东和东亚的文化背景。

佛教传入中国的鼎盛时期是北魏。这时正是中国四分五裂的时期。北魏定都大同（山西省）。统治者信仰、推行佛教，派遣使者出使印度。正是通过这些使者、传教士、香客和商人的共同努力，佛教慢慢向东传播。人们开始把佛教当成他们的宗教信仰。

一些信徒从教义中得到启示，前往印度，虔诚地追根溯源。有人开始修建隐修院，建造大石窟。沿着塔克拉玛干沙漠一线保留着世界上最典型、最完美的石窟。沙漠周围的小山丘，处处是沙石，溪流从山边流过，是石窟建造的理想环境。况且，由于得到商人们的大力支持，资金也不成问题。商人们的捐赠和善举可使他们死后脱离苦海，进入天国。很多壁画的内容实际上描写的就是一些行善者们的德行和善举。他们态度诚恳虔诚。莫高窟为什么保留着最完美的佛教艺术作品，原因就在于此。

最负盛名的石窟是敦煌的莫高窟，位于塔克拉玛干沙漠东端。在这里大量的石窟、珍贵的历史文献（包括佛经）被发现。这些文献用各种语言写成，如汉语、藏语、维吾尔语和一些不知名的语言。它们有的记载了当地形成的其他信仰，有的还是官方文件和信函，有的来自本民族，有的来自其他文化，反映了当时的状况。

石窟不仅局限在中国的塔克拉玛干沙漠地区，在现在的阿富汗也发现了一个大石窟群。在这里发现了世界上第二大的佛像雕像，有55米高。

对于考古学家来说，石窟也许是了解丝绸之路的最有价值的信息来源。沿途除了栩栩如生的佛像，还有当时人民生活的图景。壁画上那些生动的舞蹈和庆典场面反映当时人们的衣食习惯和风俗。在各种文化的交融中，丝绸之路的作用非常明显。尤其是佛教从印度传入中国，又逐步演变成个人的信仰，这在不同时期的壁画上反映得非常清楚。

北魏是佛教在中国传播最盛的时期，云冈石窟便在这一时期开凿。迁都洛阳后，开始建造龙门石窟。这两个石窟更具有中国特色，强调雕刻、雕塑，而不是强调壁画。人物形象高大，云冈石窟最大的人物塑像高达17米，仅次于四川的乐山大佛（建于8世纪）。

5）丝绸之路的鼎盛时期

丝绸之路的鼎盛时期是唐朝。民族统一，政局稳定，经济繁荣。长安作为丝绸之路的起点和唐朝的首都已经发展成为一个国际大都会，到742年，人口已达到两百万。长安城的面积大体相当于今天的西安城。754年，约有5 000外国人居住在长安，如土耳其人、伊朗人、印度人、日本人、朝鲜人和马来人等。他们多数是使者、商人和香客，也有其他行业的人。在长安城里，来自西方的稀有动植物、药材等处处可见。

在此期间，也就是7世纪，大唐高僧玄奘通过丝绸之路前往印度取经。他取道北线到达印度；又从南线返回。他对沿线各地的风俗、文化作了详细的记录，翻译佛教经典，带回600多册印度文献，对佛教在中国的传播做出了不可磨灭的贡献。

6）丝绸之路的衰落

从政治上讲，1368年，明朝取代元朝后，开始实行闭关锁国的政策，这种政策不利于中西方的贸易往来和文化交往。这种形势一直延续到清朝。

陆地丝绸之路衰落的另一个原因是水上丝绸之路的开辟和发展。一方面，水上交通比陆地交通更加容易、更加安全，运输工具也更为结实可靠。另一方面，水上航线经过南亚诸国，这里充满商机,市场潜力很大。再者,陆地部落间的冲突不断,双边贸易并非总是畅通无阻。15 世纪早期,航海家郑和率领的船队 7 次下西洋,到达东南亚、印度,最远抵达阿拉伯、非洲东海岸。中国与这些国家建立了外交关系,增加了中国商人与当地的贸易来往。

2.《马可·波罗游记》与丝绸之路

马可·波罗(1254—1324)是一位意大利商人、探险家。他属于第一批经过丝绸之路来到中国的西方人。马可·波罗一行于 1271 年离开威尼斯,在中国度过了 17 年,1290 年底或 1291 年初离开中国,1292 年回到意大利。

回到意大利后,他完成了著名的《马可·波罗游记》,记录了他的所见所闻。这本书至今还是研究中国历史尤其是元代历史的权威文献之一。马可·波罗从克里米亚出发,经过丝绸之路,来到中国,对沿途各地的风俗、习惯、服装、语言、礼仪,到它们如何受东方帝国的影响等都做了详细的记录。1275 年,大约在蒙古铁骑征服欧洲 30 年之后,马可·波罗一行来到大都。尽管成吉思汗试图通过武力把世界统一纳入草原民族,但是这并没有给欧洲人留下任何有价值的东西,只有可怕的记忆。可见武力的征服远没有文化的影响厉害。令马可·波罗感到惊讶的是,即使是在元朝时期,西方仍然保留着东方几百年前的文明。尽管唐朝灭亡了近五六百年,但是,通过丝绸之路,它对世界的影响、它的良好声誉在中亚、西亚、欧洲仍在延续。

Exercises

Section A Thought-provoking questions

1. What is "the Silk Road"?
2. Besides the silk, what else were introduced to Xiyu (ancient Xinjiang), India and Europe?
3. When was the greatest years in the history of the Silk Road? Why?
4. In the Tang Dynasty, why was Chang'an the most cosmopolitan cities of the time?
5. Why did the Silk Road come to decline in the Ming and Qing dynasties?

Section B Decide whether the following statements are true or false

1. The Silk Road was a general name for the ancient strategic transportation channel which started from China and passed through Central Asia, West Asia, Africa and Europe.
2. The Silk Road took in both land and water routes.
3. The Silk Road was also a route through which the pilgrims did their missionary work.
4. Silk products were the only commodities that were traded to the West.
5. In the Tang Dynasty, Chang'an was the most cosmopolitan cities of the time.
6. The purpose of building forts and defensive walls along part of the route was to prevent the Xiongnu from harming the trade.
7. Buddhism in China is effectively derived from the Gandhara culture by the bend in the Indus River, rather than directly from India.
8. The building of monasteries and grottos got support from the wealthy merchants.
9. The isolationist policies that the Ming and Qing dynasties carried on were one of the causes

that the Silk Road came to decline.

10. The Chinese seafarer Zhang He led his fleet as far as to Europe.

※ **The Master said, "At fifteen I set my heart upon learning. At thirty, I planted my feet firm upon the ground. At forty, I no longer suffered from perplexities. At fifty, I knew what were the biddings of Heaven. At sixty, I heard them with docile ear. At seventy, I could follow the dictates of my own heart; for what I desired no longer overstepped the boundaries of right."**

From *Analects of Confucius*

(子曰:"吾十有五而志于学,三十而立,四十而不惑,五十而知天命,六十而耳顺,七十而从心所欲,不逾矩。")

——《论语》

※ **A journey of a thousand miles begins with a single step.**

From Laozi: *Dao De Jing*

(千里之行始于足下。)

——老子·《道德经》

Appendix Ⅰ

Chinese Culture Words

中国文化词汇

1. **Adelis silk**: the transliteration of the Uygur for Hetian silk, silk produced in Hetian, Xinjiang. It is noted for its vigorous ethnic color, unique rectangular patterns and other geometric figures. It is used for clothing of the Uygur minority and people in Mid Asia. 爱的丽斯绸,维吾尔语对和田绸的音译,富有强烈的民族色彩,大多为矩形或其他几何图案,为维吾尔族及中亚一带民族服装和装饰用丝织物。
2. **Baguwen**: Eight-part essay, a literary composition prescribed for the imperial examinations in Ming and Qing Dynasties, knows for it rigidity of form and poverty of ideas. 八股文是明清科举制度的一种考试文体,段落有严格的规定。形式呆板,内容空泛,束缚思想。
3. **Dao** (or **Tao**): the character *Dao* means "path" or "way", but in Chinese religion and philosophy it has taken on more abstract meanings. Daoist thought focuses on "wuwei" (non-action), spontaneity, humanism, and emptiness. "道"在中国文化中带有浓厚的宗教、哲学意味。道家思想的核心在于无为、本真、人文和虚无。
4. **Eight Banners**: military administrative organizations of the Manchu nationality in the Qing Dynasty. The Eight Banners actually consisted of three ethnic components: the Manchu, the Han, and the Mongols. 清代满族的军队组织和户口编制,以旗为号,分正黄、正白、正红、正蓝、镶黄、镶白、镶红、镶蓝。后又增建蒙古八旗和汉军八旗。
5. **eight characters**: in four pairs, indicating the year, month, day and hour of a person's birth, each pair consisting of one Heavenly Stem and one Earthly Branch, formerly used in fortune-telling. 八字,根据生辰,以年月日时所得的天干、地支,其中每柱干支有两个字,四柱共计八字,用于算命。
6. **Feng Shui**: a kind of geomancy, which guided ancient Chinese people to choose sites to build cities, houses and burial grounds. Feng means wind and Shui means water, both of them are the main components of the geographical surroundings. The core of Feng Shui is earthly breath (Qi). Ancient Chinese believed that Qi would disperse by wind and stop by water. It moves like wind but can eddy and stagnate. So the ideal site for building a city, a house, and a tomb must be able to gather the earthly breath of Qi. Chinese people also believed that Feng Shui can influence the fortune of the family and their descendants. "风水"是一种迷信,专为古代中国人建城、造房、修墓选址提供指导。Feng 即 wind(风),Shui 即 water(水)。两者都是地理环境最重要的组成部分。风水的核心即气。古人相信风和水可以驱散或阻止"气"流。气流可以形成气旋,也可以停滞不动。因此,理想的建城、造房、修墓的地方应该是"气"汇集的地方。中国人相信风水影响家人及后代的财富和幸福。
7. **"Five Elements"**: some things are believed five basic elements consisting of the universe namely as metal, wood water, fire and earth. They produce each other and overcome each

other. “五行”指旧时中国人认为的金、木、水、火、土这五种构成宇宙的元素。它们彼此相生相克。

8. **“Four Books and Five Classics”**: “Four Books” refer to the Great Learning, the Doctrine of the Mean, the Analects of Confucius, and the Mencius. “Five Classics” are Classic of Changes, Classic of Poetry, Classic of History, Classic of Rites, and Spring and Autumn Annals. “四书”指《大学》《中庸》《论语》《孟子》。“五经”指《易》《诗》《书》《礼》《春秋》五种儒家经书。
9. ***kang***: a heatable brick bed in the Chinese North region, especial rural areas. 中国北方特别是农村用砖、坯等砌成的睡觉的台，下面有洞，连通烟囱，可以烧火取暖。
10. ***li***: a Chinese unit of length equal to half a kilometer. 1 里合 500 米。
11. ***lusheng***: a free reed mouth organ with five or six pipes, played by various ethnic groups in southwestern China, especially the Miao. 芦笙，自由簧管气鸣乐器，管数不一，大小各异，传统芦笙以 6 管最为普遍。芦笙流行于中国西南地区少数民族，苗族是最擅长使用芦笙的民族之一。
12. **main schools of Chinese martial arts**: mainly there are the following schools of Chinese martial arts: Long Boxing, Taiji Boxing, South Boxing, Eight-Trigram Boxing, Form Boxing, Monkey Boxing, Wudang Boxing, Shaolin Boxing and E'mei Boxing, etc. 中国武术有如下几种主要的流派：长拳、太极拳、南拳、八卦掌、形意拳、猴拳、武当派、少林派、峨眉派等。
13. ***meipo***: any person (especially female) who functions as a go-between matchmaker or in the old days or whose main job is to connect two strange people together for the purpose of marriage. 媒婆，旧时专门撮合婚事的人。
14. ***Records of the History***: an overview of the history of China written by Sima Qian of Western Han Dynasty, covering more than three thousand years from the Yellow Emperor to Emperor Han Wudi. The work laid the foundation for later Chinese historiography. 《史记》是中国历史上第一部纪传体通史，作者是西汉时期的司马迁。此书记事上起传说中的黄帝，下到汉武帝时期，前后跨越三千多年历史。
15. **Shenyi**: made of linen, a full-length, one-piece robe which links the Yi and Shang together to wrap up the body. It is cut separately, but sewn together. Shenyi was named because when worn the body is deeply wrapped up. 深衣，白色麻布制，其特点为上衣和下裳相连，衣襟右掩，下摆不开衩，将衣襟接长，向后拥掩，垂及踝部。因其前后深长，故称深衣。
16. **“silk road”**(in German, “die Seidenstrasse”): a term was first used by a German geographer named Ferdinand von Richthofen in his book *China* published in 1877. It was widely accepted by Chinese and foreign historians. 丝绸之路(德语：die Seidenstrasse)一词最早出自于德国地理学家费迪南・冯・李希霍芬于 1877 年出版的《中国》，简称为“丝路”。此后中外史学家都赞成此说，沿用至今。
17. **the Four Treasures of the Study**: the writing tools with Chinese characteristics. Also known as “the Scholar's Four Jewels”, namely the writing brush, ink-stick, paper and ink-slab, they got their names in the Northern and Southern dynasties (420 – 589), referring only to the study of the literati. The Four Treasures, varied and colorful, are famous for their *hubi* (writing brush produced in Huzhou, Zhejiang Province), *huimo* (ink-stick produced in Huizhou, Anhui Province), *xuanzhi* (rice paper or *xuan* paper, made in Xuancheng, Anhui Province), and *duanyan* (ink-slab made in Duanxi, Guangdong Province). 文房四宝

是中国独具特色的文书工具。文房之名，始于南北朝时期(420 年—589 年)，专指文人书房而言，以笔、墨、纸、砚为文房中经常使用，故被人们誉为“文房四宝”。四宝品类繁多，丰富多彩，以湖笔、徽墨、宣纸、端砚著称，至今仍享盛名。

18. **the Keju Exam**: an imperial examination system in ancient China, was the most important means of recruiting state officials in the large administration system of the Chinese imperial state. 科举是古代中国一种考试制度，是封建王朝考选文武官吏后备人员的最重要手段。
19. **the silk route by sea**: waterways which provide easy means for distant transport from the shores of the Pacific to Africa and deep into the heart of Europe. 海上丝绸之路，是指中国与世界其他地区之间海上交通的路线，即亚洲、非洲和欧洲之间的水上贸易。
20. **Yangshao culture**: a culture of the Neolithic period dating back to 5000 B.C.- 3000 B.C. Relics of Yangshao culture, characterized by fine painted pottery, were first unearthed in Yangshao Village, Mianchi County, Henan Province, in 1921. 仰韶文化，中国新石器时代以彩色陶器为代表的文化，公元前 5000 年到公元前 3000 年。1921 年首次在河南渑池县仰韶村发现。
21. ***yu***: an ancient Chinese wind instrument. 竽是古代一种管乐器。
22. **Yu Garden**: Yu Garden was finished in 1577 by a government officer of the Ming Dynasty named Pan Yunduan. Yu in Chinese means pleasing and satisfying, and this garden was specially built for Pan's parents as a place for them to enjoy a tranquil and happy time in their old age. 豫园是明朝官员潘允端于 1577 年修建的。豫园是取“愉悦双亲，颐养天年”之意，即“安逸、游乐”之意。
23. **Zen**: a form of Buddhism asserting that enlightenment comes from meditation and intuition, with less dependence upon the scriptures. 禅宗，佛教的一个派别，强调默坐专念。
24. ***zhang***: a Chinese unit of length, approximately equal to 3.33 meters. 中国旧时长度单位，1 丈约合3.33 米。

Appendix Ⅱ

Famous People in Chinese History

中国历史名人

1. **Lu Ban**: a famous architect of ancient China. His real name was Gongshu Ban. Because he lived in the Lu Dukedom during the Spring and Autumn Period, he is referred to as Lu Ban. Chinese carpenters and bricklayers consider him as the first and greatest architect of China. 鲁班，真名公输般，因是鲁国人，且"般"与"班"同音，故后世称他为鲁班。鲁班被视为技艺高超的工匠的化身，更被土木工匠尊为祖师。
2. **Confucius** (551 B.C. - 478 B.C.): educator, great thinker, statesman and founder of Confucianism, was also one of the supremely great cultural giants in world history. He was listed in the first place among the world's ten greatest thinkers by The People's Almanac, which was published in America in 1984. His doctrines, being revered as a symbol of the civilization of the Far East, have had a great and far-reaching influence on China and the rest of the world. In 1988, the Nobel Prize winners made the assertion in Paris that if human beings want to survive the 21st century, they must look back 2,500 years and seek the wisdom of Confucius. 孔子(公元前 551 年—公元前 478 年）是中国古代重要的教育家、思想家、政治家、儒教创始人，同时还是世界历史上最负盛名的文化巨人之一。1984 年美国出版的《人民年鉴手册》把孔子列为世界十大思想家中的第一人。孔子的学说被推崇为东方文明的象征，对中国乃至世界影响深远。1988 年全世界诺贝尔奖获得者在巴黎宣称：人类要在 21 世纪生存下去必须回首 2 500 年，从孔子那里吸取智慧。
3. **Sun Wu** (c.535 B.C - 480 B.C.): courtesy name was Changqing, born at Le'an (now Huimin, Shandong Province). Revered as "Sun Zi (or Sun Tzu)", he was a well-known military strategist in late Spring and Autumn Period. Sun Wu's *The Art of War*, composed of 13 articles, was the first systematic book on military strategies and tactics in ancient China and one of the earliest works on military strategies and tactics in the world. 孙武（约公元前 535 年—公元前 480 年），字长卿，齐国乐安（今山东惠民）人，春秋末年著名军事学家，世称"孙子"。撰有《兵法》13 篇，是中国古代第一部有系统的兵书，也是世界上最早的系统精辟论述战略战术问题的军事学著作。
4. **Mencius** (c.372 B.C.- 289 B.C.): a great thinker of the mid-Warring States Period, was born at Zou (present Zoucheng, Shandong Province). His given name was Ke and courtesy name Ziyu. He was a successor of Confucius and has been called the "Second Sage" after Confucius. Mencius' declaration of "if poor, one attends to his own virtue in solitude; if advanced to dignity, he makes the whole world virtuous as well" has become a standard of social conduct of Chinese scholars for thousands of years. 孟子（约公元前 372 年—公元前 289 年），名轲，字子舆，邹（今山东省邹城市）人，战国中期的思想家。他继承了孔子的学说，被后世尊称为"亚圣"。孟子"穷则独善其身，达则兼济天下"的主张成了后世中国文人立身处世的法则。

5. **Qu Yuan** (340 B.C.- 278 B.C.): the first great patriotic poet in the history of Chinese literature. He composed 25 poems including *Sorrow after Departure*. *Sorrow after Departure* is Qu Yuan's classic work, which is also the earliest long lyric poem in China. The poem resolutely uncloaks the repulsiveness of the ruling class by deploying a series of metaphors, and at the same time portrays some upstanding models who adhere to justice, are unafraid of persecution and very devoted to their country and people. 屈原(公元前 340 年—公元前 278 年)是中国文学史上第一位爱国诗人,他共创作了 25 首诗,包括最著名的《离骚》。《离骚》是屈原的代表作,是最早的一首抒情长诗。诗歌运用大量的比喻,揭露了统治阶级的腐朽罪恶,讴歌了坚持正义、热爱人民、热爱祖国的英雄人物。
6. **Xun Zi** (c. 313 B.C.- 238 B.C.): his given name was Kuang and courtesy name Qing. Born in the State of Zhao, he was a key figure in the Confucius school. Xun Zi, an epitome of his thoughts. A strong critic to Mencius' claim that human beings are good by nature, Xun Zi held that human beings are born evil but they are perfectible through education. 荀子(约公元前 313 年—公元前 238 年),名况,字卿,时人尊称为"荀卿"。赵国人,儒家代表人物之一。《荀子》一书是荀子思想的集中体现。荀子持"性恶论",特别强调人后天的教化和学习,猛烈抨击孟子的"性善论"。
7. **Lao Zi**: a philosopher of ancient China and an important figure in Taoism (also called Daoism). Lao Zi literally means "Old Master" and is generally considered an honorific. According to Chinese tradition, Lao Zi lived in the 6th century B.C. Many historians contend that Lao Zi actually Lived in the 4th century B.C. Lao Zi was credited with writing the central Daoist work *Dao De Jing* (also called *Tao Te Ching*). Its influence on Chinese culture is pervasive, and it reaches beyond China. Next to the Bible, the *Dao De Jing* is the most translated work in world literature. 老子是古代中国哲学家,道家的代表人物。从字面上讲,"老子"即"大师",受到人们的尊敬。一般认为,老子生活在公元前 6 世纪,但有些历史学家认为他实际上生活在公元前 4 世纪。老子的经典著作是《道德经》。《道德经》对中国文化的影响极深,对世界文化也有深远的影响。它是除《圣经》之外,被翻译最多的文学作品。
8. **Lü Buwei**: a big merchant in Spring and Autumn Period. He later became the Prime Minister of Qin. He called together his disciples to compile. The Annals of Lü Buwei, which was composed of 160 essays. 吕不韦,战国商人,曾为秦的相国。吕不韦集门人编写了《吕览》,即《吕氏春秋》,为杂家代表著作,收 160 篇。
9. **Xiao He**: statesman of Western Han. He was a key figure in Liu Bang's rise to power after the fall of the Qin Dynasty. He remained loyal to Liu Bang throughout his life and later became Prime Minister of the Han Dynasty. 萧何,西汉初年政治家。秦末辅佐汉高祖刘邦起义。后刘邦称帝,以萧何为丞相。
10. **Wang Zhaojun**: born to a prominent family, she entered the harem of Emperor Yuan of Han Dynasty. During her time in the Lateral Courts, Wang was never visited by the emperor and remained as a palace lady-in-waiting. In 33 B.C., Huhanxie, the then Chanyu (or Khan) of Hun, visited Chang'an on a homage trip, Emperor Yuan presented him five women from the imperial harem, one of them was Wang Zhaojun. Wang Zhaojun became a favorite of Huhanxie, giving birth to two sons. When her husband died, she was ordered to become the wife of the next Chanyu, the oldest son of her husband's. Her life became the story of

"Zhaojun Departs the Frontier". Peace was maintained for over 60 years between China and Hun. 王昭君出身在一个显赫家庭,汉元帝时入宫。王昭君入宫数年,不得见御。公元前33年,匈奴呼韩邪单于来到长安和亲,元帝以五女赐之,其中一位就是王昭君。王昭君最受呼韩邪单于的宠爱,为他生了两个儿子。单于死后,她又依当地风俗嫁给了下一任单于。这就是"昭君出塞"的故事,从此,汉、匈和平共处长达60余年。

11. **Yue Fei**: the well-known national hero in the war against Jin invaders during the Southern Song Dynasty. He, with his army, had won many great battles, so a minister named Qin Hui was quite jealous of him. Yue Fei was wrongly accused of seriously defying military order during his mission and was subsequently put to death at the age of 39. 岳飞是南宋时期著名的抗金将领。他带领将士与金军顽强战斗,并取得了巨大胜利,但这引起了大臣秦桧的嫉妒。因受到秦桧诬陷,岳飞被害,死时年仅39岁。
12. **Zheng He** (1371 - 1433): a navigator and diplomat of the Ming Dynsaty, was famous for his seven naval expeditions. He led seven expeditions from 1405 to 1433, which traversed the Indian Ocean and the southeast Asian archipelagoes and as far as the Cape of Good Hope. 郑和(1371年—1433年),明代航海家和外交家,因带领船队从1405年到1433年7次下西洋而著名。他的船队经过东南亚群岛,横渡印度洋,到达非洲"好望角"。
13. **Li Shizhen** (1518 - 1593): a renowned doctor and great medicine scientist of the Ming Dynasty, wrote the Guide to Chinese Medical Herbs, an epoch-making encyclopedic work. 李时珍(1518年—1593年),明代医学家和药学家,以三十余年心血写下了划时代的医学巨著《本草纲目》。

Appendix Ⅲ

A Brief Chinese Chronology

中国大事年简表

朝代(Dynasty)	起止时间(Date)	简　介
三皇五帝 Three Sovereigns and Five Emperors	约公元前30世纪—公元前21世纪 c.30th century B.C. - 21st century B.C.	三皇五帝(三皇:伏羲、神农、黄帝;五帝:少昊、颛顼、高辛、尧、舜)大约5 000年前,传说中的黄帝统治着黄河流域的一部分。他与另一位领袖炎帝为中华文明的进步做出了巨大的贡献
夏 Xia Dynasty	约公元前21世纪—公元前16世纪 c.21st century B.C.-16th century B.C.	中国历史上的第一个朝代,系传说中禹的儿子启所建立,奴隶制国家,建都安邑(今山西省夏县北),即夏后氏。共历14代17王 There are three things to know about the Shang: one, they were the most advanced bronze-working civilization in the world; two, Shang remains provide the earliest and most complete record of Chinese writing (there are a few Neolithic pots that have a few characters scratched on them; however, a few characters do not make a complete writing system), scratched out on the shoulder blades of pigs for oracular purposes.
商 Shang Dynasty	约公元前16世纪—公元前11世纪 c.16th century B.C.-11th century B.C.	公元前十六世纪商汤灭夏所建。经几次迁都,盘庚时迁殷(今河南省安阳县小屯),因此亦称殷。传至纣,为周武王所灭。共传17代31王 Most scholars think that the Zhou were much more "Chinese" than the Shang. For one, they used a father-to-son succession system. Also, they weren't too keen on human sacrifice. However, they weren't as good at working bronze as the Shang. Still, it would be centuries before the West was able to cast bronze as well as the Zhou. Some, though not all, scholars believe that the Xia, the Shang, and the Zhou actually were three different cultures that emerged more or less at the same time in different areas of the Yellow River valley. And the historical record supports this view — the Shang were conquered from outside by the Zhou, as the Xia had been conquered from the outside by the Shang.

（续表）

朝代(Dynasty)	起止时间(Date)	简　介
周 Zhou Dynasty	约公元前11世纪—公元前256年 c.11th century B.C.-256 B.C.	公元前11世纪周武王灭商后建立，建都镐京(今陕西西安市南)。历史上称平王东迁以前为西周，以后为东周。东周又分为春秋、战国两个时期。公元前256年为秦所灭，共历34王800多年
秦 Qin Dynasty	公元前221年—公元前206年 221 B.C. - 206 B.C.	中国历史上第一个中央集权的封建王朝。公元前221年，秦王嬴政灭六国，统一中国，自称始皇帝。建都陕西咸阳东。秦始皇曾推行一系列巩固统一、加强中央集权的政策措施。但赋税繁重，刑罚苛暴。秦朝历2代15年。 事件：修筑万里长城；焚书坑儒；统一文字、度量和货币 In 221 B.C., the first Emperor of China, Qin Shihuang, conquered the rest of China after a few hundred years of disunity. There are two major reasons why he won: the first is that he was a devout Legalist, and did things like execute generals for showing up late for maneuvers; the other reason is that the state of Qin had a lot of iron, and consequently, at the dawn of the iron age, had many more iron weapons than the other armies did. Qin Shihuang had a great many accomplishments, not the least of which was the linking together of many of the old packed-earth defensive walls of the old principalities into the Great Wall of China. This is not to say that he built the massive masonry construction that today is called the Great Wall of China.
汉 Han Dynasty	公元前206年— 公元220年 206 B.C.- A.D. 220	公元前206年，刘邦灭秦，称帝，国号汉，建都陕西西安，史称西汉或前汉。公元25年，皇族刘秀重建汉朝，建都洛阳，史称东汉或后汉。汉朝共历24帝406年。 事件：司马迁完成《史记》；发明造纸技术；张衡制成"地动仪" The Han dynasty plays a very important role in Chinese history. For starters, they invented Chinese history as we know it today. Additionally, the overwhelmingly predominant ethnic group in China is called the Han; they are named after the dynasty. But, most importantly, they developed (actually, it was invented by Qin Shihuang, but perfected by the Han) the administrative model which every successive dynasty would copy, lock, stock, and barrel.

（续表）

朝代(Dynasty)	起止时间(Date)	简　介
三国(魏、蜀、吴) Three Kingdoms	公元 220 年一公元 280 年 220 - 280	魏:公元 220 年—265 年,曹丕称帝,国号魏,建都洛阳。共历 5 帝 46 年。蜀:公元 221 年—263 年,刘备在成都称帝,国号汉,史称蜀或蜀汉。共历 2 帝 43 年。吴:公元 222 年—280 年,孙权在江苏南京称帝,也称吴王。史称孙吴或东吴。共历 4 帝 59 年 While there was a great deal of political activity occurring during this period, most of it, consisting as it was of various wars between different kingdoms (one of the great novels of China, *The Romance of the Three Kingdoms*, is about this period), was not terribly important to the later development of China. Perhaps its greatest accomplishment was to reinforce in Chinese thought the importance of having "one Emperor over China, like one sun in the sky."
晋 Jin Dynasty	公元 265 年—公元 420 年 265 - 420	公元 265 年,司马炎称帝,国号晋,建都洛阳,史称西晋。太康元年(公元 280 年)灭吴,统一全国。公元 316 年被匈奴所灭,共历 4 帝 52 年。 西晋之后,公元 317 年,司马睿在南京重建政权,史称东晋,共历 11 帝 104 年
南北朝 Southern and Northern Dynasty	公元 420 年—公元 589 年 420 - 589	自公元 420 年东晋灭亡之后,我国历史上形成南北对峙的局面,称南北朝。南朝从 420 年宋武帝刘裕取代晋朝到 589 年陈朝亡,共经历宋、齐、梁、陈四代。北朝从 439 年北魏统一北方到 534 年分裂为东、西魏,后北齐代东魏,北周代西魏,北周又灭北齐,共历 170 年。 事件:祖冲之创大明历
隋朝 Sui Dynasty	公元 581 年—公元 618 年 581 - 618	公元 581 年,杨坚代北周称帝,国号隋,建都陕西西安,于 590 年灭陈,统一全国。共历 3 帝 38 年。 事件:发明雕版印刷术;修成大运河;创立科举制度 The most important thing to know about this dynasty is that it was very short (by dynastic standards) and that it did a pretty good job of reunifying China. Because it had a northern power base, it was part barbarian, as was the Tang. Despite the fact that the royal houses of Sui and succeeding Tang were not entirely Han Chinese, both of these dynasties are considered to be Chinese.

（续表）

朝代(Dynasty)	起止时间(Date)	简　介
唐朝 Tang Dynasty	公元 618 年—公元 907 年 618 - 907	公元 618 年，李渊在关中称帝，国号唐，建都陕西西安，共历 20 帝 290 年。 事件：玄奘法师西天取经；鉴真和尚东渡日本 The Tang are considered to be one of the great dynasties of Chinese history. Many historians rank them right behind the Han. They extended the boundaries of China through Siberia in the North, Korea in the east, and were in what is now Vietnam in the South. They even extended a corridor of control along the Silk Road well into modern-day Afghanistan. There are two interesting historical things about the Tang. The first is the Empress Wu, the only woman ever to actually bear the title "Emperor". The second was the An and Shi Rebellion, which marked the beginning of the end for the Tang.
宋朝 Song Dynasty	公元 960 年—公元 1279 年 960 - 1279	公元 960 年，赵匡胤代后周称帝，国号宋，建都开封，史称北宋。公元 1126 年，金兵攻入开封，北宋亡。1127 年，赵构在河南商丘称帝，后迁至浙江杭州，史称南宋。共历 18 帝、320 年。 事件：发明指南针，并用于航海；发明火药，用于战争；毕昇发明活字印刷术；司马光撰成《资治通鉴》；沈括撰成《梦溪笔谈》；发明珠算 The Song Dynasty ranks up there with the Tang and the Han as one of the great dynasties. Fifty years after the official end of the Tang, an imperial army re-unified China and established the Song Dynasty. A time of remarkable advances in technology, culture, and economics, the Song, despite its political failures, basically set the stage for the rest of the imperial era.
元朝 Yuan Dynasty	公元 1271 年—公元 1368 年 1271 - 1368	公元 1206 年，蒙古族领袖成吉思汗建立蒙古汗国。公元 1271 年，忽必烈定国号为元，1279 年定都北京。疆域南到南海，西到新疆，西南到西藏、云南，北到西伯利亚，东北到鄂霍次克海。历 18 帝 163 年 The Yuan dynasty also featured the famous Kublai Khan, who, among other things, extended the Grand Canal. While in many ways, the Yuan was a disaster, the reluctance of the Mongols to hire educated Chinese for governmental posts resulted in a remarkable cultural flowering; for example, Beijing Opera was invented during the Yuan.

（续表）

朝代(Dynasty)	起止时间(Date)	简　介
明朝 Ming Dynasty	公元 1368 年—公元 1644 年 1368 - 1644	公元 1368 年，朱元璋称帝，国号明，建都南京，公元 1421 年迁都北京。疆域东北抵日本海，西至河套西喇木伦河，北至新疆哈密，西南至西藏、云南，东南到海。1644 年，李自成攻入北京，明亡。共历 16 帝、277 年 The Ming rulers distinguished themselves by being fatter, lazier, crazier, and nastier than the average Imperial family. After the first Ming Emperor discovered that his prime minister was plotting against him, not only was the prime minister beheaded, but his entire family and anyone even remotely connected with him. Eventually, about 40,000 (no, that is not a misprint) people were executed in connection with this case alone.
清朝 Qing Dynasty	公元 1636 年—公元 1911 年 1636 - 1911	公元 1616 年，女真贵族努尔哈赤建立后金政权。公元 1636 年，皇太极即帝位，改国号为清。公元 1644 年，顺治入关，定都北京。逐步统一中国。公元 1911 年，辛亥革命推翻清王朝，结束了两千多年的封建君主制度。共历 12 帝、296 年 In 1644, the Manchu took over China and founded the Qing Dynasty. The Qing weren't the worst rulers; under them the arts flowered and culture bloomed. Moreover, they attempted to copy Chinese institutions and philosophy to a much greater extent than then the Mongols of the Yuan..
中华民国 The Republic of China	公元 1912 年—公元 1949 年 1912 - 1949	清朝末年，中国的封建统治者实行闭关政策，社会经济发展明显落后于西方国家，而且面临内忧外患。英、法等国在世界范围到处掠夺殖民地，并把眼光盯住了中国。1840 年鸦片战争后，缔结了不平等的《南京条约》，中国逐渐沦为半殖民地半封建社会。人民对清政府腐败无能的不满情绪日益强烈。伟大的资产阶级民主主义革命家孙中山，于 1905 年创立了同盟会，多次在中国领导发动武装起义，失败后流亡国外。1911 年 10 月 10 日，革命军在武昌再次发动起义，各省纷纷响应，史称辛亥革命。同年底，孙中山在各派革命力量的推举下，于 1912 年 1 月 1 日在南京就任临时大总统，宣告中华民国成立，清帝退位，结束了两千年来中国封建王朝的专制统治 At the end of the Qing Dynasty, the feudal rulers faced serious troubles both at home and abroad. Because of their closed-door policy, China was economically backward compared with the West. Major European countries such as Britain and France traveled around

（续表）

朝代(Dynasty)	起止时间(Date)	简　介
中华民国 The Republic of China	公元 1912 年—公元 1949 年 1912 - 1949	the world in search of colonies and, therefore, set China as their target. After the Opium War in 1840, the defeated Qing government signed the humiliating *Treaty of Nanking*, and since then, China was gradually reduced to a semi-colonial and semi-feudal country. The Chinese people became increasingly frustrated with the corrupted and incompetent Qing government. Dr. Sun Yat-sen, a great bourgeois democratic revolutionary, set up *Tongmenghui*, a revolutionary organization, in 1905. He led several uprisings in China but failed and he went into exile overseas. On October 10, 1911, the revolutionary army organized another uprising in Wuchang, known in history as the *1911 Revolution*, and won an unexpected victory. This victory was warmly welcomed by all the provinces throughout the country. At the end of the same year, Dr. Sun Yat-sen returned to China and with the support of various revolutionary forces, he was proclaimed in 1912 the Provisional President of the Republic of China. The Emperor of the Qing Dynasty was forced to abdicate, thus putting an end to the 2,000-year long feudal monarchy.
中华人民共和国 The People's Republic of China	1949 —	1949 年 10 月 1 日，北京 30 万群众齐集天安门广场，举行开国大典。中央人民政府主席毛泽东在天安门城楼上庄严宣告：中华人民共和国正式成立，中国人民从此站起来了。这标志着中国人民一百多年以来的反帝反封建斗争取得了伟大胜利。2009 年是中华人民共和国成立 60 周年 On October 1, 1949, 300, 000 people gathered at Tiananmen Square to celebrate the founding of the People's Republic of China (PRC). Chairman Mao Zedong announced solemnly from Tiananmen Gate: "The People's Republic of China is now officially founded and the Chinese people have since stood up." This marks the great victory of the anti-feudal and anti-imperialist struggle waged by the Chinese people for more than a hundred years. The year 2009 is the 60th anniversary of the founding of the PRC.

Appendix Ⅳ

China's Top Ten

中国之最

1. 世界上最稀有的动物之一是中国的大熊猫。大熊猫生活在中国的四川、陕西、甘肃的偏远高山上，以竹为食，属于第四纪冰川时期的残留物种，有“活化石”之称，被誉为中国的“国宝”。

1. The Giant Panda of China is one of the rarest animals in the world. Giant pandas live in remote high mountains in Sichuan, Shaanxi and Gansu Provinces and eat bamboo. They are a surviving species of the Fourth Ice Age and are known as a “living fossil”. They are regarded as China's “national treasure”.

2. 世界上最古老的树种是中国的银杏树，此树最早出现于 1.6 亿年前的侏罗纪时期。

2. The oldest tree in the world is China's gingko, which first appeared during the Jurassic Age some 160 million years ago.

3. 世界上最大的峡谷是中国的雅鲁藏布大峡谷，长 504.6 千米，最深处达 6 009 米，平均深度在 2 268 米以上。

3. The greatest canyon in the world is China's Brahmaputra Canyon, 504.6 kilometers long and 6,009 meters deep at its deepest.

4. 世界上最高的高原是中国的青藏高原，平均海拔 4 500 米。喜马拉雅山脉位于青藏高原的南部，主峰珠穆朗玛峰，海拔 8 844.43 米，为世界第一高峰。

4. The highest plateau in the world is China's Qinghai — Tibet Plateau with an average height of 4,500 meters above sea level. The Himalayan Mountain is located in southern Qinghai — Tibet Plateau and its highest peak, Mount Qomolangma (or Mount Everest) is 8844.43 meters above sea level. It is the highest peak in the world.

5. 世界上使用人数最多的语言是中国的汉语，有超过 13 亿人以汉语为母语。

5. The Chinese language is the language that has the largest number of speakers, more than 1.3 billion, throughout the world.

6. 世界上最早、最大的百科全书是中国明朝的《永乐大典》，共 22 937 卷，由两千多名学者在 1403 年—1408 年编成。

6. The biggest and earliest encyclopedia in the world is the Yongle Encyclopedia complied between 1403—1408 in the Ming Dynasty by more than 2, 000 scholars. It consists of 22,937 volumes.

7. 世界上最大的广场是中国北京的天安门广场，占地 40 公顷。

7. The largest public square in the world is Tiananmen Square in Beijing. It covers an

area of 40 hectares.

8. 世界上开凿最早、线路最长的人工运河是中国的京杭大运河，始建于公元前 5 世纪，后经隋、元两次大规模扩建，北起北京通县，南至浙江杭州，全长 1 801 千米。

8. The earliest and longest man-made canal in the world is the Beijing — Hangzhou Grand Canal. The canal was first built in the 5th century B.C. and was substantially extended twice during the Sui and Yuan Dynasties. The canal begins at Tong County in Beijing in the north and ends in Hangzhou in Zhejiang Province in the south and is 1,801 kilometers in length.

9. 世界上最大、最完整的古建筑群之一是中国北京的故宫（又称紫禁城），是明清两个朝代的皇宫，建成于 1420 年，占地 72 万多平方米。

9. The biggest and most complete ancient building complex is the former Imperial Palace (also known as the Forbidden City) in Beijing. It was imperial palace of both the Ming and Qing Dynasties. It was first completed in 1420 and covers an area of 720,000 square meters.

10. 世界上最长的人造建筑是中国的长城，它横穿中国北方的崇山峻岭之巅，总长度 6 700 多千米，始建于春秋战国时期。

10. The longest man — made architecture in the world is the Great Wall in China. It climbs and descends on the ridges of mountains in northern China and has a total length of more than 6,700 kilometers. It was first started during the Spring and Autumn and the Warring States periods.

Appendix Ⅴ

Directory of World Cultural and Natural Heritage in China

中国世界自然文化遗产名录

自1987年世界遗产委员会第11届会议批准中国的故宫等6处遗产列入《世界遗产名录》起至2015年7月，中国已有48处文化遗址和自然景观列入《世界遗产名录》，其中文化遗产34项(包括文化景观4处)、自然遗产10项、文化和自然双重遗产4项。

编号	地 域 名 称	批准时间	遗产种类
1	长城 The Great Wall	1987.12	文化遗产
2	北京故宫、沈阳故宫 The Imperial Palace in Beijing & The Imperial Palace in Shenyang	1987.12	文化遗产
3	陕西秦始皇陵及兵马俑 Mausoleum of Qin Shihuang and the Terra Cotta Warriors and Horses	1987.12	文化遗产
4	甘肃敦煌莫高窟 Mogao Grottes in Dunhuang	1987.12	文化遗产
5	北京周口店北京猿人遗址 Peking Man Site at Zhoukoudian	1987.12	文化遗产
6	山东泰山 Mount Taishan	1987.12	文化与自然双重遗产
7	安徽黄山 The Huangshan Mountain	1990.12	文化与自然双重遗产
8	湖南武陵源国家级名胜区 Wulingyuan Scenic and Historic Interest Area	1992.12	自然遗产
9	四川九寨沟国家级名胜区 Jiuzhaigou Valley Scenic and Historic Interest Area	1992.12	自然遗产
10	四川黄龙国家级名胜区 Huanglong Scenic and Historic Interest Area	1992.12	自然遗产
11	西藏拉萨布达拉宫 The Potala Palace at Lhasa	1994.12	文化遗产

（续表）

编号	地域名称	批准时间	遗产种类
12	河北承德避暑山庄及周围寺庙 Chengde Mountain Resort and its Outlying Temples	1994.12	文化遗产
13	山东曲阜的孔庙、孔府及孔林 Temple and Cemetery of Confucius and the Kong Family	1994.12	文化遗产
14	湖北武当山古建筑群 Ancient Building Groups on the Wudang Mountain	1994.12	文化遗产
15	江西庐山风景名胜区 Lushan National Park	1996.12	文化景观
16	四川峨眉山—乐山风景名胜区 Mount Emei and The Leshan Giant Buddha Scenic and Historic Interest Area	1996.12	文化与自然双重遗产
17	云南丽江古城 The Old Town of Lijiang	1997.12	文化遗产
18	山西平遥古城 The Ancient City of Pingyao	1997.12	文化遗产
19	江苏苏州古典园林 The Classical Gardens of Suzhou	1997.12	文化遗产
20	北京颐和园 The Summer Palace	1998.11	文化遗产
21	北京天坛 The Temple of Heaven	1998.11	文化遗产
22	重庆大足石刻 The Dazu Rock Carvings	1999.12	文化遗产
23	福建武夷山 Mount Wuyi	1999.12	文化与自然双重遗产
24	四川青城山和都江堰 Mount Qingchengshan and Dujiang Weirs in Sichuan Province	2000.11	文化遗产
25	河南洛阳龙门石窟 The Luoyang Longmen Grottoes	2000.11	文化遗产
26	明清皇家陵寝 Royal Mausoleums of Ming and Qing Dynasties	2000.11	文化遗产

（续表）

编号	地域名称	批准时间	遗产种类
27	安徽古村落：西递、宏村 Ancient Villages at Xidi and Hongcun in South Part of Anhui Province	2000.11	文化遗产
28	山西大同云冈石窟 Yungang Grottoes in Shanxi	2001.12	文化遗产
29	云南三江并流 Three Parallel Rivers of Yunnan	2003.7	自然遗产
30	高句丽王城、王陵及贵族墓葬 The Capital Cities and Tombs of the Ancient Koguryo Kingdom	2004.7	文化遗产
31	澳门历史城区 The Historic Centre of Macao	2005.7	文化遗产
32	四川大熊猫栖息地 China's Giant Panda Habitat	2006.7	自然遗产
33	安阳殷墟 Anyang Yin Ruins	2006.7	文化遗产
34	中国南方喀斯特 South China Karst	2007.6	自然遗产
35	开平碉楼与村落 Kaiping Diaolou and Village	2007.6	文化遗产
36	福建土楼 Hakka Earth Buildings in Fujian	2008.7	文化遗产
37	江西三清山 Sanqingshan National Park in Jiangxi	2008.7	自然遗产
38	山西五台山 Mount Wutai of Shanxi	2009.6	文化景观
39	河南登封"天地之中"历史建筑群 Historic Monuments of Dengfeng in "The Centre of" Heaven and Earth	2010.8	文化遗产
40	中国丹霞 China Danxia	2011.6	自然遗产

（续表）

编号	地 域 名 称	批准时间	遗产种类
41	杭州西湖 The West Lake of Hangzhou	2011.6	文化景观
42	内蒙古元上都遗址 Xanadu of the Yuan Dynasty in Inner Mongolia	2012.6	文化遗产
43	云南澄江帽天山化石遗址 Fossil sites in Yunnan	2012.7	自然遗产
44	红河哈尼梯田 Hani Terraces	2013.6	文化景观
45	新疆天山 Tianshan of Xinjiang	2013.6	自然遗产
46	京杭大运河 The Beijing—Hangzhou Grand Canal	2014.6	文化遗产
47	丝绸之路 The Silk Road	2014.6	文化遗产
48	中国土司遗产 Tusi Sites in China	2015.7	文化遗产

Keys

参考答案

Chapter 1 A General Outline of China

Section A

1. The topography of China is characterized by high west part and low east part, gradually descending in elevation from the west towards the east to form three steps. The highest step is the Qinghai-Tibet Plateau with the elevation being generally more than 4,000 meters above sea level. The second step is the east of the Qinghai-Tibetan Plateau with much lower elevations, and the third step stretches from the line in the west composed of the Greater Hinggan Mountains, Taihang Mountain, Wu Mountain and the eastern rim of the Yunnan-Guizhou Plateau to the coast in the east, and embraces alternating hills and plains, and there are large areas of low mountains and hills at elevations of less than 500 meters above sea level with only a few peaks being at 2,000 meters, and the elevation of plains is all less than 200 meters.
2. There are generally four climate zones from the south to the north of China: tropical, subtropical, temperate and frigid climate zones.
3. The natural resources of China include the cultivated land, forest, grassland, mineral and water resources.
4. Zhuang, Manchu, Hui, Uygur, Miao, Yi, Tujia, Mongol, Tibetan, Buyi, Dong, Yao, Korean, Bai, Hani, Kazak, Li and Dai nationalities.

Section B

1	ecological	2	provincial	3	conservation	4	lunched	5	dietetic

Chapter 2 A Brief History of China

Section A

1. Because Chinese civilization started with the legendary sage-emperors Huang Di and Yan Di in the area of the Yellow River basin. After centuries, the two tribes gradually merged into one by the time of the Xia Dynasty. The Chinese people, therefore, usually call themselves "the descendants of Yan and Huang", or "Hua Xia People".
2. The Qin Dynasty was the first centralized, unified, multi-ethnic feudal state in Chinese history after a few hundred years of disunity. It marked the beginning of a more than two thousand years long history of a centralized state with an emperor being the head of a state and a comparatively uniformed culture. The Qin made many changes and reforms to unify

China, for example, to standardize the written language, weights, measures and currencies and to consolidate the system of prefectures and counties. The sovereigns of the next 2,000 years actually followed the feudal governmental structure established by the Qin.

3. Open for discussion.
4. Open for discussion.

Section B

1.

(1) 皇位世袭制	(6) 均田制
(2) 诸子百家	(7) 安史之乱
(3) 青铜车马器	(8) 三民主义：民族、民权、民主
(4) 天命思想	(9) 辛亥革命
(5) 三省六部制	(10) 中华民国

2.

(1)《诗经》	(9)《金瓶梅》
(2)《史记》	(10)《牡丹亭》
(3)《梦溪笔谈》	(11)《红楼梦》
(4)《西厢记》	(12)《儒林外史》
(5)《徐霞客游记》	(13)《聊斋志异》
(6)《三国演义》	(14)《长生殿》
(7)《水浒传》	(15)《桃花扇》
(8)《西游记》	

Chapter 3 Ancient Chinese Philosophy and Religion

Section A

1. The two great indigenous philosophical traditions of China, i.e. Confucianism, Daoism and Buddhism have exerted significant impact on Chinese tradition and culture, because they guide Chinese in both governing and people's behaviors, and have formed deep-rooted Chinese traditional values and norms.
2. The core of Confucius' philosophy consists of the main concepts of *ren* (benevolence), *li* (ritual), *xiao* (filial piety), *zhong* (loyalty) and so on. According to Confucius' thought, *li* cannot be separated from *ren* and a man without *ren* is impossible to well exercise *li*. Confucius stated: "A man who is not benevolent, what can he have to do with ritual?"
3. *Dao* means a road, the way or the method, the law, the principle that people must follow. *De* means virtue or quality. The spontaneity of the world derives from *Dao*, and *De* is the intrinsic quality of everything in the universe. Laozi pointed out, "*Dao* produces a thing; *De* maintains it." The relation between *De* and *Dao* is just like something that between the water in river.
4. Buddhism is in conflict with Chinese cultural tradition in many ways. For example, Chinese people usually regard the continuation of the generation line as an importance matter, while

Buddhism advocates bachelorism and celibacy. Confucianism believes that the human body is the sacred inheritance from the parents and so it should be protected from being impaired or injured, but Buddhism adheres to asceticism and self-sacrifice.

5. Open for discussion.

Section B

1. *The Great Learning*, *The Doctrine of the Mean*, *The Analects*, *The Mencius*; *Classic of Changes*, *Classic of Poetry*, *Classic of Rites*, *Classic of History* and *Spring*, *Autumn Annals*
2. Laozi, Zhuang Zi
3. Tibetan, Zen
4. no killing, no stealing, no sexual misconduct, no lying, no alcoholic drink
5. old age, sickness, death, being apart from the loved ones, being together with the despised ones

Chapter 4 Ancient Chinese Education

Section A

1. Yes, it has.
2. The imperial examinations include three parts: the local district exams known as the *tongshi*, the provincial exams called *xiangshi*, and the "joint" exams called *huishi*.
3. He made many wise phrases and theories about law, life, and government. It's these thoughts and theories that teach other people lessons about moral principles and rules of life.
4. "Six Arts" are rites, music, archery, chariot-riding, calligraphy and computation.
5. He regards morality as the most important subject.

Section B

1	2	3	4	5	6	7	8	9	10
F	T	F	T	F	T	T	T	F	F

Chapter 5 Chinese Names

Section A

1. Open for discussion.
2. These respectively refer to surnames of the noble families: Liu of Pengcheng (now Xuzhou, Jiangsu), Chen of Yinchuan (now Xuchang, Henan), Wang of Taiyuan (now Taiyuan, Shanxi), Zhou of Runan (now Shangcai, Henan), Du of Jingzhao (Xi'an, Shaanxi), Zhang of Nanyang (now Nanyang, Henan), Lu of Fanyang (now around Beijing), Cui of Boling(now around Li County, Hebei), Li of Longxi (now Tianshui, Gansu), Zheng of (Xingyang, Henan).
3. People got their hao (literary name) either from themselves or from other people. When people chose hao for themselves, they usually chose those that suggested their aspiration or ambition; when a person gave hao to another person, the hao was usually complimentary or

respectful. A person's hao normally suggested one of the following things: the person's aspiration or ambition; the person's living place or surroundings; the person's personal characteristics; the person's official rank, or bestowed title; the person's famous literary creation — a famous sentence or a famous article title.

4. The matriarchal society, because every surname contains the same Chinese character "女" meaning woman.

Section B

1	Confucius	Zhong Ni(仲尼)
2	Liu Yuxi	Meng De(梦得)
3	Sun Wu	Chang Qing (长卿)
4	Li Bai	Li Taibai(李太白)
5	Bai Juyi	Le Tian (乐天)
6	Su Shi	Zi Zhan (子瞻)
7	Zhuge Liang	Kong Ming (孔明)
8	Cao Xueqin	Meng Ruan(梦阮)
9	Cao Cao	Meng De(孟德)
10	Li Shangyin (李商隐)	Yi Shan(义山)

Chapter 6 Chinese Language and Characters

Section A

1. The six categories of Chinese characters refer to the pictographic, indicative, associative, pictographic-phonetic, referential, and synonymic (象形、指事、会意、形声、转注、假借).
2. Their discovery was by accident. In 1899, Wang Yirong, an official under the Qing Dynasty, fell ill. One of the medicaments prescribed by the physician was called "longgu" (dragon bones). They turned out to be fragments of tortoise shells which were found to bear strange carved-on patterns. He kept the "dragon bones" and showed them to scholars who, after careful study, came to the conclusion that the carvings were written records from 3,000 years before and were of great historical significance. Further inquiries revealed that the "dragon bones" had been unearthed at Xiaotun Village, Anyang County, Henan Province, site of the remains of the Shang Dynasty capital. Further digs made at the site in later years brought to light a total of more than 100,000 pieces of bones and shells all carved with words. About 4,500 different characters have been counted, and 1,700 of them deciphered. Three thousand five hundred years ago, Anyang was a marshy area teeming with tortoises, a favorite food of the local inhabitants. And the Shangs were a very superstitious people. Their rulers would resort to divination and ask the gods for revelation whenever there was a gale, downpour,

thunderstorm, famine or epidemic. Before going on a war or a big hunt, they would still more want to divine the outcome. The method of divination then was to drill a hole on the interior side of the tortoise shell and put the shell on a fire to see what cracks would appear on the obverse side. By interpreting the cracks the soothsayer predicted the outcome of an event. After each divination, the dates, the events and the results would be written down and carved on tortoise shells or bones. And the collection of these became the earliest recorded historical material in China, from which modern scholars have divined "how things were in the Shang society". Later on, the area around Anyang became dry, and tortoises grew scarce, so people began to use bamboo strips instead for divination. From this grew the practice of asking the gods about the future by drawing bamboo sticks, as one may see today at certain temples — a practice that has its remote root in the superstition of the Shang people.

Section B

1	2	3	4	5	6	7	8	9	10
I	H	A	J	B	G	C	F	E	D

Chapter 7 Chinese Idioms and Fables

Section A

1. A fable is a short story devised to convey some useful lesson or an apologue. A distinctive feature of the fable is that it contains a moral truth.
2. It means to make the finishing point or to add the finishing touch to something.
3. It is usually used to analogize with those who take advantage of one's or somebody else's power to bully people.
4. It means "Misfortune may be an actual blessing".

Section B

1. An illusory snake in a goblet
2. "bringing the painted dragons to life by putting pupils in their eyes"
3. "no more tricks, Mr. Nan Guo! "
4. "marking the boat for a dropped sword"
5. "plucking up a crop to help it grow"
6. "blessing or blame"
7. "the donkey of Guizhou"
8. "a walk learner in Handan"
9. "playing the tune to a cow"
10. "mending the fold after a sheep is lost"

Chapter 8 Chinese Food Culture

Section A

1. Open for discussion. But it is highly necessary for the teacher to point out the fact that the

eating of any kind of animal meat is not a matter of cruelty, but of culture difference.

2. According to some Japanese scholars, to properly handle chopsticks requires the coordination of over 80 joints and 50 muscles; what's more, certain cranial nerves are also involved. Therefore, using chopsticks can help make people more dexterous and intelligent. The correct way to use chopsticks is to hold the pair in the hollow between the thumb and forefinger of your fork hand. The one closest to your body should rest on the first joint of the ring finger and stay relatively immobile. Hold the other one with the forefinger and middle finger, which manipulate it like pinchers to pick up the food. The strength applied by the fingers should vary with the things to be taken hold of. The skill to pick up, with speed and dexterity, small things like beans and peanuts and slippery things like slices of preserved eggs can only come from practice and coordinated action of the fingers. Westerners are often impressed with the cleverness of the Chinese hand that makes embroideries and clay sculptures with such consummate skill. Couldn't this skill be attributed to the constant use of chopsticks?

Section B

1	油炸	2	快炒	3	清炒	4	烩	5	煎
6	卤	7	烤	8	焖	9	炸	10	爆炒
11	扒	12	回锅	13	软炸	14	酥炸	15	烫、白灼

Chapter 9 China's Tea Culture

Section A

1. It is not simply a type of drink, but a transmitter of culture, representing the philosophy, aesthetic views and way of life of the Chinese people, from which the spiritual world of the Chinese people can be discerned.
2. By treating/cultivating a teapot and matching it with the right type of tea. The purple clay teapots that have been treated before use and been nurtured/cultivated/lubricated for some time can upgrade the quality of tea, add luster to the surface of the teapot, and soar the value of the teapot in a shorter time.
3. Tea is a mysterious but harmonious combination. It is spiritual as well as material, and invigorating as well as pacifying. Its character is flexible in different environments. For example, for the Chinese, tea drinking and tea tasting are not the same. Tea drinking is for refreshment and tonic effect while tea tasting has cultural meaning. Tea and tea wares should match surrounding elements such as breeze, bright moon, pines, bamboo, plums and snow. All these show the ultimate goal of Chinese culture: the harmonious unity of human beings with nature.

Section B

1	best	2	revolves	3	rain	4	cheer	5	forget
6	sentiment	7	company	8	favorite	9	imaginary	10	daily

Chapter 10 Chinese Plants and Their Cultural Connotation

Section A

1. Bamboo culture is deeply rooted in the daily life of the Chinese. Bamboo chopsticks are the most common tableware in China. *Dizi* (Chinese flute) is made of bamboo. Today people are still using paintbrush made from bamboo. There are usually exhibitions of bamboo carvings, poems and paintings. Bamboo painting is an important part of Chinese traditional painting. You can also see all kinds of bamboos, listen to them as well as feel their spirit with your heart to bring you peace and harmony.
2. Peony. Because it received the most votes in a survey conducted in 1994 in every district in China asking people to select a National Flower — a high honor for the peony in a country that loves flowers.
3. Out of the muddy swamp blossoms the pure lotus. The lotus grows in mud, yet itself is not soiled. Interestingly, science has recognized this self-cleaning attribute and aptly named it the "lotus effect", applying the principle to various technologies — even a self-cleaning house paint is called Lotusan.

Section B

1. as pretty and bright as a peach blossom
2. have a well-thought-out plan; do something with calm assurance
3. red peach blossoms and green willows — beautiful spring scene
4. (said of a beautiful woman) peach-like cheeks and almond-shaped eyes
5. walk in a gliding and graceful manner
6. (of a master or teacher) have pupils/disciples everywhere
7. peaches and plums do not speak, yet a path is worn beneath them — men of true worth need not speak, yet they will win admiration
8. (of water lilies) rise unsullied from mud; emerge unstained from the filth; come out the dirty mud unsoiled — remain undefiled/unaffected in spite of general corruption

Chapter 11 Wedding Traditions in China

Section A

1. It is the color of "Love and Joy" in China. At one time it was the bride's favorite color of choice for the wedding garment, candles, gift boxes, money envelopes that were presented to the bride and bridegroom, and everything that went along with the wedding. In China today, many girls still choose to go by the old traditions of their forefathers, but the country is becoming westernized and more and more brides are opting for the exquisite white gowns worn throughout the world.

2. Wedding traditions have long-held great significance to the bride and the groom in China. Many recognize the need for tradition, value and strong beliefs. Many couples include the basic traditional customs into their ceremonies, while others choose to go by the old wedding customs and practise the full extent. Even nowadays, many traditions are a normal part of the ceremony and the celebration, which have specific origins and historical value.
3. Open for discussion.

Section B

1	back	2	privilege	3	waiting	4	wish	5	loyalty

Chapter 12 Chinese Traditional Folk Entertainments

Section A

1. Coin, cloth and cock feathers.
2. These games help children strengthen their legs and enhance their coordination of limbs and their concentration as well. Some children's games, such as shuttle-cock-kicking and rubber band skipping, are employed in school physical education. These items are very effective in improving the physical quality of the students.
3. "Qin, qi, shu, hua" are regarded as literary pursuits by old scholars. Qin, qi, shu and hua not only act as entertainments for traditional scholars, but also exert immeasurable influence on the character of traditional scholars and creation of the Chinese cultural heritage.
4. Jia Shidao, the Cricket Prime Minister of Southern Song Dynasty, was so fond of cricket fighting that he often failed to attend to military and national affairs.

Section B

1	date	2	specializing	3	business	4	held	5	climax
6	of	7	to	8	kicking	9	which	10	forth
11	advance	12	level	13	among	14	strengthen	15	decline
16	regained	17	make	18	bunch	19	attached	20	rising

Chapter 13 Ancient Chinese Martial Arts

Section A

1. Not until after the Spring and Autumn Period did martial arts begin to incorporate sophisticated aspects of ancient Chinese culture.
2. Martial arts practitioners begin with the irregularity and infinity of Dao and seek to reach a stage in which he or she blends harmoniously with nature. The arts teach practitioners to train the inner spirit and mind as well as the external muscles, bones and skin. Martial arts stress the combination of the physical being with the mental being and emphasize a close relationship between physical exercises and the surrounding environment.

3. Ancient Chinese aesthetics advocated a balance between hardness and softness, voidness and solidness, notion and stillness, and negative and positive, as well as the expression of the spirit of an object through its form. Under this influence, Chinese martial arts have formed their own aesthetic standards that incorporate a stage of conceptual contentment, harmony, and nature, as well as beauty and elegance.
4. The most outstanding characteristic of Shaolin Boxing is that the practitioner works on one straight line. It means that his movements of advancing, retreating, turning around, sideways, or jumping are restrained on one line. His arms are kept slightly bent so that he can stretch out to attack or withdraw for self defense freely.
5. The Eight-Trigram Boxing is characterized by changing positions of the palms and changing paces. Its fighting principle is the "combination of attack and defense".
6. Taiji Boxing is characterized by the unification of mind, breath and motions (body), requiring concentration of mind and calmness of motions.

Section B

1	2	3	4	5	6	7	8	9	10
F	T	F	T	T	T	F	T	T	F

Chapter 14 Chinese Calligraphy and Painting

Section A

1. They are paper, ink, brush, and ink stone, considered as the Four Treasures of the Study by the Chinese people.
2. The Tang Dynasty witnessed the prosperity of figure paintings. Figure painting of this period depicted the life of noble women and court ladies and exerted an eternal influence on the development of *shi nü hua*, which comprise an important branch of traditional Chinese painting.
3. The main themes of traditional Chinese paintings include figures, landscape, flowers and birds, etc.

Section B

1	2	3	4	5	6	7	8	9	10
F	T	F	T	T	F	F	F	T	T

Chapter 15 Chinese Carving

Section A

1. The special properties of jade has been endowed contributed to the development of jade carving. The permanence and practicality of stone contributed to the development of stone carving.

2. People metaphorically equate jade with human virtue due to its solidity, durability and (moral) beauty.
3. In terms of application and decoration, there are three types of wood carving: architecture carving, furniture carving and display art ware carving, which will be explained in detail in this part; in terms of representation, there are carving such as piercing carving, basso-relievo, solid tondo, piercing decal, etc; in terms of different wood texture, there are two types: hard (often called rosewood carving) and soft wood carving (ash wood carving).

Section B

1	valuable	2	lies	3	over	4	especially	5	treasure
6	by	7	hold	8	scarce	9	hardness	10	hard

Chapter 16 Chinese Farmers' Painting

Section A

1. In China, farmers constitute a large portion of the Chinese population, so it is natural that they have their own form of art due to the differences in customs, living background and educational background. The paintings reflect both styles and scenes of their life in the vast countryside of China.
2. The characteristics possessed by Chinese farmers' paintings in subjects, color and techniques make it rather a unique form of art. The subjects of Chinese Farmers' paintings are taken from the experience of the daily life in rural communities. With subjects focusing on simple and small things in the countryside, these paintings reveal farmers' understanding of life and their expectation for a better life. Regarding color, the typical Chinese farmers' painting is hand-painted with gouache watercolors on paper. Farmers use color to show what they feel rather than what they see and they draw the pictures following their feelings. Therefore, the color of the grounding is mainly deep and colors like red, purple, blue are usually applied. These colors are rather brilliant and vibrant, which makes the whole compositions look naive. In terms of technique, some of the farmers' paintings use the keyline technique which is adopted from ukiyoe, Japanese woodblock prints. The whole design is drawn with strong black outlines, and then the areas are filled with colors. Many of the Chinese poster designs use the same technique.
3. They are common in the subjects farmers choose and the color they use.
4. The three types are Taohuawu New Year Painting, Yangliuqing New Year Painting, and Weifang Yangjiabu New Year Painting. Their characteristics are clearly explained in the chapter.

Section B

1	known	2	like	3	created	4	abroad	5	appreciate
6	rare	7	originated	8	rural	9	primitive	10	bright

Chapter 17 Chinese Folk Musical Instruments

Section A

1. Based on the method by which they are played Chinese musical instruments can be divided into 4 basic categories: "blown", "bowed", "plucked", and "struck" (i.e. percussion) instruments.
2. Silk instruments are mostly string instruments including the plucked, bowed, and struck. Since the very beginning, the Chinese have used silk for strings, though today metal or nylon are more frequently used.
3. Chinese wind instruments include the *dizi*, *lusheng* and *suona*.
4. The history of Chinese percussion instruments is longer than any other section of traditional Chinese instruments. As many different percussion instruments produce different sound effects, it is frequently used in depicting joyful and exciting occasions such as harvests, marriages, as well as other traditional Chinese festivals.
5. Among the diverse musical instruments in China, those from the ethnic minorities also hold an important position in Chinese folk musical instruments.

Section B

1	*yangqin*	2	*liuqin*	3	*guzheng*	4	*konghou*	5	*suona*
6	Percussion	7	*luo*	8	*muyu*	9	*hulusi*	10	*Lusheng*

Chapter 18 Appreciation of Chinese Folk Music

Section A

1. It is based on *Spring River*, *Flowers*, *Moonlit Night* written by Zhang Ruoxu, a famous Tang poet. It is considered as the most famous and certainly the most antimetabolic early Tang ballad.
2. The composer of this well-known *erhu* piece was Hua Yanjun (1893 – 1950). Hua was a blind street musician with Blind Ahbing as his nick name. Shortly before his death in 1950 two Chinese musicologists recorded him playing a few *erhu* and *pipa* solo pieces, the best known being *Erquan Yingyue* (*The Moon Reflected in the Erquan Spring*).
3. The expression is often used by the Chinese people to describe the fluency of a musical piece.

Section B

1	2	3	4	5	6	7	8	9	10
C	D	I	A	F	E	B	D	D	F

Chapter 19 Chinese Folk Art and Handicraft

Section A

1. Paper-cuttings refer to handicrafts made by cutting paper with scissors or an engraving knife

to form different patterns for practical use or decoration.

2. The main characteristics of Chinese knot are that every knot is made of a single rope and named by its specific form and meaning.
3. Chinese folk art boasts long history, fine handicraft and wide popularity.
4. There are quite a lot of other Chinese handcrafts: jade carving, wood carving, sandal wood fan, dough figure, clay figure and leather silhouette, to name just a few.

Section B

1	2	3	4	5	6	7	8
T	F	T	T	F	F	T	F

Chapter 20 China Wisdom

Section A

1. "Orientation of pragmatism" and "preponderance of empiricism" contributed to the blooming of the flowers of wisdom, though they limited to a certain extent the development of science and technology.
2. When the Jesuits landed on China between the sixteenth and seventeenth centuries, they were amazed at the brilliant inventions of ancient Chinese science and technology, so as to exclaim earnestly that "The ancient Chinese were great creators." In the countless inventions lay the wisdom of the Chinese nation.
3. Open for class discussion.

Section B

1	2	3	4	5	6	7	8	9	10
T	F	T	F	F	T	F	F	T	T

Chapter 21 Famous Ancient Towers in China

Section A

1. Its main building has three stories and is 15 meters in height, with four huge Nanmu pillars supporting the whole building, twelve round log columns supporting the second floor, and another twelve catalpa pillars supporting the roof. Constructed of wood with interlocking brackets that require no nails, the main building is as steady as a monolith. Its roof looks like a general's helmet, grand and unique, which together with the pure wooden construction reflects the unique style and great achievement of ancient Chinese architecture.
2. According to records, Yellow Crane Tower was originally built as a watchtower for Sun Quan's army due to the ideal location in 223 during the Three Kingdoms period (220 – 280).
3. Having long been known as a fairyland and famous place for watching mirages, Penglai Pavilion is regarded as the place where immortals inhabited, and thus it was frequently visited

for wonder herbs by emperors since Qin and Han dynasties.

Section B

1	pavilion	2	ago	3	form	4	used	5	not
6	rebuilt	7	Since	8	attraction	9	famous	10	who

Chapter 22 Chinese Ancient Gardens

Section A

1. Imperial gardens and private gardens.
2. A garden was seen as a mirror of the natural world. Everything in the universe was created from a conduct for *qi* (vital energy, or life force). The universe was understood to be a combination of *yin* (female or negative) and *yang* (male or positive) elements in a state of constant fluidity.
3. The design of Chinese gardens was to provide a spiritual utopia for one to connect with nature, to come back to one's inner heart, to come back to ancient idealism. Chinese gardens are a spiritual shelter for men, a place they could be far away from their real social lives, and close to the ancient way of life, their true selves, and nature.
4. Anlanyuan Garden of Haining, Zhanyuan Garden of Nanjing, Lion Grove of Suzhou, and Qinyuan (Jichangyuan) Garden of Wuxi.
5. "Imperial garden" generally refers to those in which emperors lived and entertained themselves.
6. Containing examples of the ancient arts, it also has graceful landscapes and magnificent constructions. The Summer Palace is the archetypal Chinese garden, and is ranked amongst the most noted and classical gardens of the world.

Section B

1	2	3	4	5	6	7	8	9	10
T	F	T	T	F	F	T	T	F	T

Chapter 23 The Silk Road

Section A

1. The Silk Road was a general name for the ancient strategic transportation channel which started from China and passed through Central Asia, West Asia, Africa and Europe.
2. Besides the silk products, ironware, gold, bronze mirror, bamboo work, medicine, farming techniques were introduced to Xiyu (ancient Xinjiang), India and Europe.
3. The height of the importance of the Silk Road was during the Tang dynasty, with relative internal stability in China after the divisions of the earlier dynasties since the Han. The individual states has mostly been assimilated, and the threats from marauding peoples was

rather less.

4. By A.D. 742, the population of Chang'an had reached almost two million, and the city itself covered almost the same area as present-day Xi'an, considerably more than within the present walls of the city. The 754 census showed that five thousand foreigners lived in the city, like Turks, Iranians, Indians and others from along the Road, as well as Japanese, Koreans and Malays from the east.
5. First, politically, when the Yuan dynasty was replaced by the Ming dynasty in 1368, the Ming dynasty carried on the isolationist policies, these policies did nothing to encourage trade between China and the West. This attitude was maintained throughout the Ming and Qing dynasties. Second, the decline of the Silk Road also owes much to the development of the silk route by sea. It was becoming rather easier and safer to transport goods by water rather than overland.

Section B

1	2	3	4	5	6	7	8	9	10
T	T	T	F	T	T	T	T	T	F

Bibliography

参考文献

[1] 白寿彝. 中国通史纲要[M]. 北京:外文出版社,2002.

[2] 本书编委会. 新编中国古代建筑典型图集汇编[G]. 北京:中国建筑科技文化出版社,2007.

[3] 曹林娣. 中国园林文化[M]. 北京:中国建筑工业出版社,2005.

[4] 常任侠. 丝绸之路与西域文化艺术[M]. 上海:上海文艺出版社,1981.

[5] 长泽和俊. 丝绸之路史研究[M]. 钟美珠,译. 天津:天津古籍出版社,1990.

[6] 常宗林,李旭奎. 中国文化导读[M]. 北京:清华大学出版社,2006.

[7] 陈定安. 英汉比较语翻译[M]. 北京:中国对外翻译出版公司,1995.

[8] 陈忠诚. 汉英词语翻译漫话[M]. 北京:汉语大词典出版社,2002.

[9] 程裕祯. 中国文化要略[M]. 北京:外语教学与研究出版社,1998.

[10] 丁往道.孔子语录一百则(译)[M]. 北京:中国对外翻译出版公司,1999.

[11] 丁往道. 中国文化掠影[M]. 北京:外语教学与研究出版社,2001.

[12] 杜顺宝. 中国园林[M]. 北京:人民出版社,1997.

[13] 方立天. 中国佛教简史[M]. 北京:宗教文化出版社,2001.

[14] 高厚永. 民族器乐概论[M]. 南京:江苏人民出版社,1981.

[15] 顾雪梁. 花语浅涉[J]. 现代外语, 1994,3.

[16] 郭榕. 花文化[M]. 北京:中国经济出版社,1995.

[17] 郭尚兴,盛兴庆. 中国文化史[M].郑州:河南大学出版社,1993.

[18] 国务院侨务办公室,国家汉语国际推广领导小组办公室. 中国文化常识[M]. 北京:高等教育出版社,2007.

[19] 河北省曲阳县人民政府. 中国曲阳雕刻[M]. 北京:中国建材工业出版社,2005.

[20] 何小颜. 花与中国文化[M]. 北京:人民出版社 1999.

[21] 何道宽. 中华文明撷要[M]. 北京:外语教学与研究出版社,2004.

[22] 华德韩. 中国东阳木雕[M]. 杭州:浙江摄影出版社,2007.

[23] 黄仁宇. 中国大历史[M]. 北京:三联书店,2007.

[24] 金惠康. 汉英文化旅游实用手册[M]. 广州:广东旅游出版社,2004.

[25] 金学智. 中国园林美学[M]. (第二版)北京:中国建筑工业出版社,2005.

[26] 李建中. 中国文化概论[M]. 武汉:武汉大学出版社,2005.

[27] 李民雄. 民族器乐概论[M]. 上海:上海音乐出版社,1987.

[28] 李霞. 畅谈中国文化 50 主题[M]. 北京:外文出版社,2007.

[29] 李小山. 中国现代美术全集·农民画[M]. 长沙:湖南美术出版社,1998.

[30] 李志林,潘丽丽. 孔孟老庄名言精粹[M]. 北京:汉语大词典出版社,2001.

[31] 梁志刚. 中国历史文化简介[M]. 青岛:青岛出版社,2001.

[32] 林梅村. 西域文明[M]. 北京:东方出版社,1995.

[33] 林梅村. 汉唐西域与中国文明[M]. 北京:文物出版社,1998.

[34] 林之光. 中国的气候及其价值[M]. 北京:商务印书馆,1995.

[35] 刘敦桢. 中国古代建筑史[M]. 北京:中国建筑工业出版社,1984.

[36] 刘托. 园林艺术欣赏[M]. 太原:山西教育出版社,1997.
[37] 罗哲文,刘文渊,刘春英. 中国名楼[M]. 天津:百花文艺出版社,2007.
[38] 吕思勉. 中国简史（上、下卷)[M]. 北京:工人出版社,2007.
[39] 马克斯·韦伯. 儒教与道教[M]. 洪天富,译. 南京:江苏人民出版社,2008.
[40] 马贤达,等. 中国武术大辞典[M]. 北京:人民体育出版社,1990.
[41] 牟钟鉴,张践. 中国宗教通史[M]. 北京:中国社会科学出版社,2007.
[42] 邱丕相. 中国武术教程[M]. 北京:人民体育出版社,2004.
[43] 沈从文. 中国古代服饰研究[M]. 上海:上海世纪出版社,2005.
[44] 申士安. 中国地形[M]. 北京:中国地图出版社,1999.
[45] 沈寿. 太极拳谱[M]. 北京:人民体育出版社,1991.
[46] 斯文·赫定. 丝绸之路[M]. 江红,李佩娟,译. 乌鲁木齐:新疆人民出版社,1996.
[47] 孙维新,朱旭,等. 经典中国[M]. 上海:上海译文出版社,2004.
[48] 孙振发. 中国农民画[M]. 北京:中国世界语出版社,1996.
[49] 王福林. 论语详注及英译(注译)[M]. 上海:世界图书出版公司,1997.
[50] 王建荣. 中国茶艺[M]. 济南:山东科学技术出版社,2005.
[51] 王毅. 中国园林文化史[M]. 上海:上海人民出版社, 2004.
[52] 王宜峨. 中国道教(英文)[M]. 曾传辉,译. 北京:五洲传播出版社,2004.
[53] 夏法起. 中国东阳木雕[M]. 福州:福建美术出版社,2007.
[54] 徐永成. 名山出名茶[M]. 北京:中国农业出版社,2003.
[55] 亚瑟·威利.论语(译)[M]. 北京:外语教学与研究出版社,1998.
[56] 杨伯峻. 论语译注[M]. 北京:中华书局,1980.
[57] 杨建新. 丝绸之路[M]. 兰州:甘肃人民出版社,1988.
[58] 杨敏,王克奇,王恒展. 中国传统文化通览[M]. 青岛:中国海洋大学出版社,2003.
[59] 杨敏,王克奇,王恒展. 中国文化通览[M]. 北京:高等教育出版社,2006.
[60] 余太山. 西域通史[M]. 郑州:中州古籍出版社,1996.
[61] 袁静芳. 民族器乐[M]. 北京:人民音乐出版社,1987.
[62] 张践. 中国佛教[M]. 广州:广东人民出版社,2001.
[63] 张箭. 论美洲花生、葵花的传播和对中国饮食、文化的影响[J]. 中国经济史论坛,2004,5.
[64] 张应杭. 中国传统文化概论[M]. 杭州:浙江大学出版社,2005.
[65] 赵永魁,张加勉,潘丽丽. 中国玉石雕刻工艺技术[M]. 北京:北京工艺美术出版社,2000.
[66] 郑平. 中国地理:自然·经济·人文[M]. 北京:五洲传播出版社,1999.
[67] 中国大百科全书编委会. 中国大百科全书(哲学卷)[M]. 北京:中国大百科全书出版社,1987.
[68] 中国国家地理杂志社. Chinese National Geography[M].北京:外文出版社,2006.
[69] 中央教科所教育史研究室. 孔子教育思想论文选[M]. 北京:教育科学出版社,1981.
[70] 周连宽. 大唐西域记史地研究丛稿[M]. 北京:中华书局,1984.
[71] 周伟良. 中国武术史[M]. 北京:高等教育出版社,2003.
[72] 周武忠. 中国园林艺术[M]. 北京:中华书局,1991.
[73] 周仪. 中国文化概论[M]. 重庆:重庆大学出版社,2003.
[74] 周汛,高春明. 中国古代服饰风俗[M]. 西安:陕西人民出版社,1988.
[75] 祝鸿杰,等. 论语(注译) [M]. 西安:太白文艺出版社,1997.
[76] 祝鸿杰,等. 孟子(注译) [M]. 西安:太白文艺出版社,1997.
[77] AMES R,HALL D. Thinking through Confucius [M]. Albany: Suny Press. 1987.
[78] BROWNELL S. Training the Body for China: Sports in the Moral Order of the People's Republic [M]. Chicago: University of Chicago Press, 1995.

[79] Cheng Ji. The Craft of Gardens [M]. HARDIE A. translator. New Haven: Yale University Press, 1988.
[80] FINGARETTE H. Confucius: the secular as sacred [M]. New York: Harper and Row Publishers, 1972.
[81] HOOK, B. The Cambridge Encyclopedia of China [G]. 2nd ed. Cambridge and New York: Cambridge University Press, 1991.
[82] HOPKIRK P. Foreign devils on the Silk Road [M]. Oxford: Oxford University Press, 1980.
[83] KESWICK M. The Chinese Garden [M]. New York: St. Martin's Press, 1986.
[84] KNOBLOCK J. Xunzi: A Translation and Study of the Complete Works [M]. 3 Volumes. Stanford: Stanford University Press, 1988, 1990, 1994.
[85] POLO M. The travels [M]. LATHAM R. translator. London: Penguin Books Limited London, 1958.
[86] PRANCE G, NESBITT M. Cultural history of plants [M]. London: Routledge, 2005.
[87] SCHWARTZ B. The World of Thought in Ancient China [M]. Cambridge: Harvard University Press, 1985.
[88] SHAHAR M. The Shaolin Monastery: History, Religion and the Chinese Martial Arts [M]. Honolulu: University of Hawaii Press, 2008.
[89] WILSON T A. On Sacred Grounds: Culture, Society and the Formation of the Cult of Confucius [M]. Cambridge: Harvard University Asia Center, 2002.
[90] Wu Dingbo MURPHY P. D. Handbook of Chinese Popular Culture [M]. Westport, Conn: Greenwood Press, 1994.